920.009
CON   Contemporary Black
         biography

DUE DATE

ISSN 1058-1316

CONTEMPORARY

$\mathcal{B}$lack

$\mathcal{B}$iography

Profiles from the International Black Community

Volume 11

L. Mpho Mabunda
and
Shirelle Phelps, Editors

GALE

⊚™ This book is printed on acid-free paper that meets the minimum requirements of American National Standard for Information Sciences— Permanence Paper for Printed Library Materials, ANSI Z39.48-1984.

Contemporary Black Biography
Advisory Board

Contents

Introduction ix

Photo Credits xi

Cumulative Nationality Index 265

Cumulative Occupation Index 271

Cumulative Subject Index 281

Cumulative Name Index 310

Introduction

Contemporary Black Biography provides informative biographical profiles of the important and influential persons of African heritage who form the international black community: men and women who have changed today's world and are shaping tomorrow's.

Contemporary Black Biography covers persons of various nationalities in a wide variety of fields, including architecture, art, business, dance, education, fashion, film, industry, journalism, law, literature, medicine, music, politics and government, publishing, religion, science and technology, social issues, sports, television, theater, and others.

In addition to in-depth coverage of names found in today's headlines, *Contemporary Black Biography* provides coverage of selected individuals from earlier in this century whose influence continues to impact on contemporary life. *Contemporary Black Biography* also provides coverage of important and influential persons who are not yet household names and are therefore likely to be ignored by other biographical reference series.

Designed for Quick Research *and* Interesting Reading

- **Attractive page design** incorporates textual subheads, making it easy to find the information you're looking for.

- **Easy-to-locate data sections** provide quick access to vital personal statistics, career information, major awards, and mailing addresses, when available.

- **Informative biographical essays** trace the subject's personal and professional life with the kind of in-depth analysis you need.

- **To further enhance your appreciation** of the subject, most entries include photographic portraits.

- **Sources for additional information** direct the user to selected books, magazines, and newspapers where more information on the individuals can be obtained.

Helpful Indexes Make It Easy to Find the Information You Need

Contemporary Black Biography includes cumulative Nationality, Occupation, Subject, and Name indexes that make it easy to locate entries in a variety of useful ways.

Available in Electronic Formats

Diskette/Magnetic Tape. *Contemporary Black Biography* is available for licensing on magnetic tape or diskette in a fielded format. Either the complete database or a custom selection of entries may be ordered.

The database is available for internal data processing and nonpublishing purposes only. For more information, call (800) 877-GALE.

Online. *Contemporary Black Biography* is available online through Mead Data Central's NEXIS Service in the NEXIS, PEOPLE and SPORTS Libraries in the GALBIO file.

We Welcome Your Suggestions

The editors welcome your comments and suggestions for enhancing and improving *Contemporary Black Biography.* If you would like to suggest persons for inclusion in the series, please submit these names to the editors. Mail comments or suggestions to:

The Editor
Contemporary Black Biography
Gale Research, Inc.
835 Penobscot Bldg.
Detroit, MI 48226-4094
Phone: (800) 347-GALE
FAX: (313) 961-6741

Photo Credits

PHOTOGRAPHS AND ILLUSTRATIONS APPEARING IN *CONTEMPORARY BLACK BIOGRAPHY,* VOLUME 11, WERE RECEIVED FROM THE FOLLOWING SOURCES:

AP/Wide World Photos: pp. 1, 21, 58, 64, 77, 85, 94, 100, 135, 145, 168, 189, 194, 202, 219, 232, 259; **Photograph courtesy of Jason Weinberg & Associates:** p. 9; **Photograph by Arnold Anaya-Lucca, courtesy of Ralph Lauren Publicity:** p. 15; **Photograph by Thomas Fleisher Photography, courtesy of KTCA-TV, St. Paul, Minnesota:** p. 26; **Photograph courtesy of Mandy Carter:** p. 30; **Photographs courtesy of NetNoir Inc.:** p. 36; **Photograph by Carol Halebian, courtesy of the Gamma Liaison Network, reproduced by permission:** p. 39; **Photograph by A. Horvathova, courtesy of Archive Photos, reproduced by permission:** p. 42; **Photograph courtesy of Johnnie Coleman Institute:** p. 46; **Photograph courtesy of Pro-Line Corporation:** p. 49; **Photograph by Martine Bisagni, Pantheon Books, reproduced by permission:** p. 54; **Photograph courtesy of USA Gymnastics:** p. 62; **Photograph by Andrew E. Williamson, courtesy of David Driver:** p. 66; **Photograph courtesy of Michael Eric Dyson:** p. 69; **Photograph courtesy of Tom Feelings:** p. 80; **Photograph courtesy of The Gamma Liaison Network, reproduced by permission:** p. 90; **Photograph courtesy of MasterMedia Limited Speakers Bureau:** p. 104; **Photograph courtesy of National Basketball Players Association:** p. 108; **Photograph courtesy of Atlanta Police Department:** p. 121; **Photograph courtesy of CNN, Inc.:** p. 124; **Photograph by Lee Holden, courtesy of Lee Holden/Ben & Jerry's:** p. 127; **Photograph courtesy of Holland House Publishing Co.:** p. 131; **Photograph courtesy of Ron Kirk:** p. 148; **Photograph courtesy of James Meredith:** p. 164; **Photograph by Ron Ceasar, reproduced by permission:** p. 176; **Photograph by A. Berlinger, courtesy of The Gamma Liasion Network, reproduced by permission:** p. 181; **Photograph courtesy of Time-Warner Inc.:** p. 185; **Photograph courtesy of William Loren Katz:** p. 198; **Photograph courtesey of PBS:** p. 210; **Photograph courtesy of Joseph Sanders:** p. 215; **Photograph courtesy of Barbara Smith's:** p. 223 **Photograph by Marvin T. Jones & Associates, (c) 1994, courtesy of Roderick von Lipsey:** p. 227; **Photograph by Jo McColty, courtesy of Gregory Williams:** p. 236; **Photography by Gabriel Amadeus Cooney, courtesy of Gabriel Amadeus Cooney, reproduced by permission:** p. 240; **Photograph courtesy of The Bettmann Archive, reproduced by permission:** p. 244; **Photograph courtesy of William T. Williams:** p. 250; **Photography courtesy of Motown Records:** p. 254; **Photograph courtesy of The Bettman Archive, reproduced by permission:** p. 256.

Sani Abacha

1943—

Nigerian military ruler

General Sani Abacha, long hovering close to the central power base of successive military governments in the coastal West African nation of Nigeria, finally assumed that country's center seat with a coup in November of 1993. Trained in Nigeria, Great Britain, and the United States, Abacha began his career as second-lieutenant in the Nigerian Army in 1963, rose through the ranks to the Armed Forces Ruling Council (AFRC) and eventually assumed the head of state. Although back-up plans, including tanks and soldiers were in place, the transition occurred quickly and without bloodshed. An Associated Press (AP) report in the *Boston Globe* credited Abacha with having forced the former military ruler, General Ibrahim Babangida, to resign in August of 1993--two months after Babangida annulled the results of the national presidential elections of June 12, an election that the wealthy industrialist Moshood Abiola was widely believed to have won.

While continuing to assert his intention to bring democratic civilian rule to Nigeria, Abacha has received criticism from prominent Nigerian democracy campaigners, human rights advocates, civil rights lawyers, and world-renowned authors. These critics doubt his sincerity and commitment after 11 straight years of virtually uninterrupted military rule, all accompanied by promises made by other dictators for a return to democracy. Except for the four-year period of the Second Republic in 1979, Abacha's command of the state represents a final ascendence for him in successive military governments dating back to 1966, six years after Nigerian independence in 1960.

Rose in Rank During Civil War

Abacha was born on September 20, 1943, in Kano, Kano State, Nigeria. Kano had been a part of the British colony of Nigeria until the nation won independence in 1960. From 1957 to 1962 Abacha was a student, first in the City Senior Primary School of Kano and then in the Provincial Secondary School (now Government College). During the years immediately following independence, from 1960 to 1966, Nigeria was governed by a civilian regime, the First Republic. In these years Abacha trained for the military and received his first appoint-

At a Glance . . .

Born September 20, 1943, in Kano, Kano State, Nigeria; married Mariam Jidah, 1965; children: six sons, three daughters. *Education:* City Senior Primary School, Kano, Nigeria; Provincial Secondary School (now Government College), Kano, Nigeria, 1957-62; Nigerian Military Training College, Kaduna, 1962-63, 1964; MONS Defence Officers' Cadet Training College, Aldershot, United Kingdom, 1963; School of Infantry, Warminster, United Kingdom, 1966, 1971; Command and Staff College, Jaji, Nigeria, 1976; National Institute for Policy and Strategic Studies, Kuru, Jos, Nigeria, 1981; Senior International Defence Course, Montery, CA, USA, 1982.

Nigerian Army, Commissioned Second Lieutenant, 1963, promoted lieutenant, 1966, captain, 1967, platoon and battalion commander, training department, commander, 2nd Infantry Division, major, 1969, lieutenant colonel, 1972; commanding officer, 2nd Infantry Brigade, colonel, 1975, brigadier, 1980, announced coup, December 31, 1983, appointed general officer commanding, 2nd Mechanized Division, 1984-85, major-general, 1984, announced coup, August 27, 1985. Appointed army chief of staff and member, Armed Forces Ruling Council (AFRC), 1985, Lieutenant-General, 1987, Chairman, Joint Chiefs of Staff, 1989, ministry of defense, 1990, secretary of defense, August 26, 1993; seized head of state in coup, November 17, 1993.

Member: National Institute (mni), 1981.

Addresses: *Office–* c/o Ambassador Zubair Mahmud Zazaure, 1333 16th St., NW, Washington, D.C. 20036.

ment in the Nigerian Army. He attended the Nigerian Military Training College in the Northern Nigerian city of Kaduna from 1962 to 1963 and received his appointment as Second Lieutenant in 1963. Following was a series of promotions within the Nigerian military.

When the nominally democratic First Republic fell to a military coup in 1966, Abacha received his first significant promotion from second lieutenant to lieutenant. The military hoped to stem the tide of strikes, work-to-rule actions, demonstrations, and.riots by workers and peasants that had erupted across the country in protest

against the civilian regime which had unleashed an unchecked police force against Nigerian citizens and had failed to maintain public services. Meanwhile individual politicians displayed their enormous wealth arrogantly in the face of abject poverty, massive illiteracy, unemployment, and hunger. The military proved unable to impose order on the nation, however.

During colonial times, Nigeria had been divided into three regions, roughly corresponding to the areas of the largest ethnic groups, specifically the predominantly Muslim Hausa and Fulani peoples of the North, the largely Christian Yoruba people of the West, and the largely Christian Igbo people of the East. In 1967 the East seceded and formed the Biafran Republic; the ensuing civil war, lasting until 1970, caused the death of approximately one million people, according to journalist Peter da Costa in *Africa Report.* At the beginning of that war in 1967, Abacha assumed the position of captain; over the next three years, he rose in the Nigerian Army from platoon and battalion commander to commander of the training department, 2nd Infantry Division, and to major in 1969. In 1972, soon after the war ended and the boundaries of the nation were restored, Abacha gained the post of lieutenant colonel. During the next few years, Abacha received subsequent promotions to colonel in 1975 and to brigadier in 1980.

Commensurate with his military positions, Abacha received further training and education in Nigeria, the United Kingdom, and the United States. In the United Kingdom, he studied at the MONS Defense Officers' Cadet Training College in Aldershot in 1963, and at the School of Infantry in Warminster in 1966 and 1971. In Nigeria he attended the Command and Staff College in Jaji in 1976, and the National Institute for Policy and Strategic Studies in Kuru, Jos, in 1981. In 1982 Abacha studied finally at the Senior International Defence Course in Monterey, California.

Entered National Limelight

Abacha first entered the national limelight at 7 a.m. on December 31, 1983, in a broadcast over Radio Nigeria announcing the overthrow of the civilian regime. Citing the "Text of Coup Broadcast to the Nation, 31 December 1983" in their book, *The Rise and Fall of Nigeria's Second Republic, 1979-84,* Nigerian historians Toyin Falola and Julius Ihonvbere quoted Abacha as having stated, "I am referring to the harsh intolerable conditions under which we are now living. Our economy has been hopelessly mismanaged. We have become a debtor and beggar-nation." For these reasons, Abacha said, the armed forces "in discharge of [their] national role as the promoters and protectors of our national interest decided to effect a change in the leadership of the government of the Federal Republic of Nigeria...."

Falola and Ihonvbere criticized Abacha's ambitions for the new administration in the light of previous military governments in Nigeria. "Experience has shown however that ... the military can hardly be seen as a solution," the authors wrote. "The populist approach often adopted as soon as power is seized--hard statements, imprisonment or dismissals, even execution of corrupt businessmen and politicians and a few popular actions, soon die down...." Immediate and more popular actions were often passed whenever new military governments faced the limited position of the country internationally and the enormous difficulty of enacting substantial reforms across the whole of society. Military administrations frequently backed off from early reforms and generally just imposed the basic institutional status quo--once again raising the ire of the people.

After announcing the coup to initiate what became 11 years of military rule, Abacha participated centrally in succeeding coups and continued to move ever closer to holding ultimate power himself. With the first coup on December 31, 1983, General Muhammadu Buhari became head of state and Abacha became both a member of the ruling Supreme Military Council (SMC) and a general officer commanding, Second Mechanised Division, Ibadan, Nigeria. Next, on August 27, 1985, Abacha appeared in camouflage on Nigerian television to announce another coup. Having been promoted to major-general before the coup, afterward he moved up to chief of army staff and member of the AFRC. General Babangida took the absolute lead as Nigeria's first military president.

Throughout Babangida's subsequent eight-year rule, Abacha survived high-level reorganizations and steadily gained power, concluding finally with the lead of the entire military upon Babangida's departure in August of 1993. Promoted to lieutenant-general in 1987, Abacha survived Babangida's cut in the AFRC from 28 to 19 members in 1989, and in the same year received another promotion to chairman of the joint chiefs of staff. When Major Gideon Orkar, attempted a coup on April 22, 1990, Abacha defended Babangida and announced the crushing of the coup on Radio Nigeria. In September of 1990, Babangida shuffled Abacha out of the chief of army staff position and into the head of the ministry of defense.

In 1993 Abacha survived even the exit of Babangida himself. When Babangida handed over the reins of government on August 26, 1993 to Ernest Shonekan,

a civilian appointee, Abacha assumed the lead of the military as defense secretary. Babangida resigned amid a series of strikes and protests for annulling the results of the presidential election held June 12 and "apparently" won by Abiola, according to the *New York Times.* Babangida reportedly voided the elections for fear that Abiola, a wealthy Yoruba-speaker from the Southwest, would upset the hold on power formerly wielded by military generals from the North.

Usurped State Reigns

In an attempt to gain legitimacy for his term as president of the Interim National Government (ING), Shonekan freed political prisoners, lifted press restrictions, and dismantled the oil bureaucracy, the target for accusations of squandering the nation's substantial oil revenues. However, Shonekan also imposed a fuel price increase of 600 percent at the urging of the World Bank and the International Monetary Fund (IMF), world financial development institutions, according to the *New York Times.* That increase precipitated a national general strike. Police fell into clashes with pro-democracy demonstrators across the Southwest while banks, major shops, and factories remained closed for one week. Finally a Lagos High Court declared the ING an illegal government. In the midst of this civic unrest, on November 17, 1993, Abacha requested Shonekan's resignation and seized control of the state himself.

> Abacha's command of the state represents a final ascendence for him in successive military governments.

Abacha initially offered a few concessions to pro-democracy forces, Abiola supporters, and Yoruba contenders for power, but over the course of the first year those actions lost their substance. He also immediately dissolved all remnants of democratic structures inherited from Babangida's transition to democracy. Existing political parties, gatherings, the National Electoral Commission, and federal, state, and local governments were all banned and slated for replacement by military commanders. With no political parties allowed and no campaigning admitted, Abacha's calls for a constitutional conference met with abysmally low voter turnout and boycotts from every region except the North, from where Abacha hails. Next Abacha bypassed civil rights lawyer Olu Onagoruwa, who was his appointment from the pro-democracy movement, in drafting and implementing a decree to dissolve a militant union. When Onagoruwa complained, Abacha fired him.

Directed Uneasy Ship of State

In 1994, his first year of governance, Abacha's attempts to chart a new economic course for Nigeria according to a three-year plan were not successful, *West Africa* reported. He had turned away from the suggestions of the International Monetary Fund (IMF), headed by Babangida since 1986, and reimposed controls on the economy. Specifically, he stabilized the exchange rate between the Nigerian naira and the U.S. dollar, imposed interest rate ceilings on deposits and savings at between 12 and 15 percent and on loans at 21 percent, and banned the free repatriation of export revenue. The Nigerian economy lacked the infrastructure to achieve those rates, however, and production costs skyrocketed. In addition, the petroleum workers went on strike to protest the annullment of election results that projected Moshood Abiola to be head of state and to press for economic demands. "The unions also contributed to the failure of the budget by grinding the economy to a halt," the general manager of Belhope Plastics, Chief Alapuye Isokariari, said in *West Africa*. "How could we perform with basic industrial materials locked at Lagos seaports?"

In addition to economic concerns, Abacha has been wrangling with the pro-democracy movement. Much of that movement opposed his military rule from the beginning. Wole Soyinka, a Nigerian human rights advocate and winner of the 1986 Nobel Prize for Literature, was one such dissenter. "It is a regime of infamy and it should be isolated," Soyinka said in the *New York Times*. "This is going to be the worst and most brutal regime that Nigeria ever had. This regime is prepared to kill, torture, and make opponents disappear." A number of organizations pressed for democratic government including the National Democratic Coalition (Nadeco), the Campaign for Democracy, and the Movement for the Survival of the Ogoni People (MOSOP).

In his own defense, Abacha continued to maintain that he still intended to bring democracy to the country. In *West Africa* for instance, Abacha appealed for noninterference from Western governments and for sympathy from Western media. "Africa is faced with strident calls for democratisation," he was quoted as saying.

"Nigeria is an integral part of this global quest for democracy, contrary to what our detractors feel. The international media and the West must admit that their nations had gone through similar or even worse problems than what we are currently experiencing." In late 1994, as head of state Abacha was concerned primarily with refining his direction for Nigeria and resolving the deep political crises gripping the West African nation of approximately 90 million people.

In 1995, international pressure on Nigeria increased. Nigeria's military rulers were criticized by Western and African leaders after the execution of playwright Ken Saro-Wiwa and eight other anti-government activists, the *Detroit News* reported. Sanctions included the suspensions of Nigeria's membership in the Commonwealth of Britain, a halt of U.S. military sales to Nigeria by President Clinton, and the recalling of ambassadors from the United States, Britain, France, the Netherlands, Austria, Germany, and South Africa. *Time* magazine even voted him "Thug of the Year." Abacha promised, however, to hand over power to a democratically elected government on October 1, 1998, according to a report in *USA Today,* and to cede power to civilians.

Sources

Books

Falola, Toyin, and Julius Ihonvbere, *The Rise and Fall of Nigeria's Second Republic, 1979-84,* Zed Books, 1985, pp. 229-30, 254-57.

Osso, Nyaknno, editor, *Who's Who in Nigeria,* Newswatch Communications, 1990, p. 9.

Periodicals

Africa Report, January/February 1994, pp. 47-49; July/August 1994, pp. 62-64; September/October 1994, pp. 38-41.

Boston Globe, November 19, 1993, p. 2.

Detroit News, November 12, 1995, p. 5A.

Newswatch (Lagos, Nigeria), November 22, 1993, pp. 12-16; November 29, 1993, pp. 15-17.

New York Times, November 18, 1993, p. A15; November 20, 1993, p. A5; November 25, 1993, p. A10.

Time, December 25, 1995, p. 40.

USA Today, October 2, 1995, p. 3A.

West Africa, September 12-18, 1994, p. 1594; September 19-25, 1994, p. 1627; October 3-9, 1994, p. 1705.

—*Nicholas Patti*

Xenobia Bailey

1955(?)—

Designer, artist

Xenobia Bailey is trying to entrench an African American aesthetic in American culture. All of her artistic endeavors are geared toward this goal, from the handmade crocheted hats that established her reputation, to her installations, short stories, cookbooks, and critical writing. Bailey also believes that the highly individual and inherently resourceful stylistic impulse she calls "funk," and its role in African American culture, must be more fully acknowledged.

Born in Seattle, Washington, Bailey learned about hard work early. At times her father, Joseph M. Bailey, held several jobs, including one with the railroad; he also maintained a janitorial business. In addition to helping with that concern, Bailey's mother, Alice Olivia Bailey, briefly maintained a day-care center and drove a bus. When she was in junior high and high school, Bailey would join her mother, father, and brother cleaning three restaurants before school. After school she would work for a couple of hours at her job with the parks department. "I think my ideas about aesthetics were largely formed by the time I spent out of doors," she told *Contemporary Black Biography (CBB)*.

When *Essence* contributor Joy Duckett Cain asked Bailey why she feels compelled to create, she responded, "I'm actually creating myself. I've always felt like a misfit. Even in my own home, where I was raised, I felt like a misfit because it wasn't an environment that complemented my insides. The walls, the colors, the furniture, the clothes—they weren't a reflection of what was inside of me, of the state that I was living in."

Clearly, long before she learned the meaning of the word aesthetics, Bailey felt the energy of her surroundings and understood instinctively how they affected her. To *CBB* she recalled, "I noticed that even the restaurants we were cleaning, they were always interesting environments. And I noticed how it was easier to clean the really nice ones and a chore to clean the dumps because they never sparkled when you were finished; you couldn't get that gratification."

Learned Value of Visual Arts

Bailey discovered in elementary school that she could communicate through the visual arts. When one of her teachers noticed that she liked to draw, she set her up with simple art supplies to play with after school. Once, Bailey spent nearly a week drawing a life-size bicycle. "I didn't really know that I wanted one, I was just drawing this bike," she told *CBB*. "At the end of the week my teacher invited my mother up to see this picture, and when she saw it she said, 'That's nice.' But later on—I got a bike! I thought 'Wow, this stuff works.' It was like magic to me."

At a Glance . . .

B orn c. 1955, in Seattle, WA; daughter of Joseph M. (worked for the railroad; proprietor of a janitorial service, dry cleaners, and pool hall), and Alice Olivia (a bus driver, day-care center operator, and janitorial service assistant) Bailey. *Education:* Attended University of Washington; Pratt Institute, bachelor's degree in industrial design, c. 1978.

Assistant to costume designer, early 1970s; taught art at community centers, late 1970s; worked for department of social services, late 1970s; began designing and selling hats, early 1980s. Designs have appeared in films, including *Do the Right Thing,* 1989; television series, including *The Cosby Show* and *A Different World;* and numerous advertisements. Writer of folktales and cultural criticism.

Addresses: *Office*—P.O. Box 1114, New York, NY 10156.

Though her parents encouraged her interests, there were few avenues available to Bailey for further study in art. "I wasn't particularly intrigued by libraries or books," she told *CBB.* "When everybody else was into Nancy Drew [mystery novels], I wasn't, because I didn't like where Nancy Drew was going. There didn't seem to be books with the kinds of characters that I wanted to read about." Bailey did not even know that an "art world" existed, but, she says, "I knew there was this thing happening in me. There were these ideas and there were these visions."

The closest Bailey came to grasping this as a child was through her love of Disneyland and television's *Mickey Mouse Club.* Bailey knew that people crafted animated films and the fanciful lands found in amusement parks, but it didn't occur to her that she played a role in that world as the observer of such magic, and that she could be a more active participant in its creation. She nonetheless learned to sew by watching cartoon birds and mice miraculously assemble a ball gown in Disney's classic *Cinderella.*

With no outlet open to Bailey in the visual arts, she turned to music. When her friends in the neighborhood took piano lessons, she insisted that they teach her what they had learned. One of their parents finally told Bailey's parents about this, and they started her on

lessons too. She did not learn to read music, however, because the songs used for instruction in this discipline bored her. Instead, she memorized each song.

Delved into Ethnomusicology

Bailey attended the University of Washington in Seattle. She discovered ethnomusicology (the study of music that is outside the European art tradition) when she visited a graduate course in music. "I still hadn't made the connection to visual arts yet because I thought everybody could draw," she recalled to *CBB.* "So when I went to that class, that was it, boy. It was like a whole world opened up. I just got caught up in the instruments, the songs, and the cultures we were studying."

Instructors from around the world introduced Bailey to sights and sounds she never new existed. She became fascinated by the way entire cultures could be glimpsed in their music, dance, and costumes. And though transfixed by the beauty of what she uncovered, her always evident practical side knew this was not something with which she could make a living. She didn't want to become an instructor, nor was she interested in research. With that decision she left the university.

Bailey then started working for a costume designer in a local community theater. She had no real experience in sewing or design, only her innate abilities. After she mounted an exhibit of her creations in the theater's gallery, a stage manager told her about Pratt Institute in New York City. Her subsequent application to Pratt was accepted, and Bailey moved to New York in 1974. It wasn't until she began classes with her fellow students— young, trained artists from all over the world—that she realized what an honor it had been to be accepted on raw talent alone.

Freshman year at Pratt was not easy for Bailey; she had never even used a paintbrush, let alone the myriad tools now at her disposal. "I was fascinated and overwhelmed at the same time," she told *CBB,* "because I couldn't conceive of so many people with so much talent all in one place." When it came time to declare a major, Bailey assumed she'd choose sculpting. Of the two art forms with which she had become most familiar—sculpting and painting—she preferred the three dimensions and enhanced tactile awareness that sculpting offered. But when a counselor introduced her to her other options, Bailey began to reconsider.

The counselor told Bailey about industrial designers, for example, who design telephones, cars, furniture, and many other consumer goods. Bailey told *CBB,* "While she was talking I was already thinking, 'Well, people design telephones. I can design a better telephone. I can design a better TV.' And all the packages designed for these products to make them sell better—I could do that." The idea of pursuing commercial art, as opposed to fine art, also satisfied her practical nature.

Crocheting Spurred Career

Bailey spent the remainder of her education developing her character and style as an artist. But when she graduated from Pratt she found that she was unable to get a job in her field because her designs were generally too complex, perhaps too personal as she was still in the early stages of her artistic development. Still, she needed to find work. For a while she taught art classes at community centers. At one she met a woman who would be extremely influential: the crochet teacher. This woman, who had learned the art of fine hand work from children at an Italian Catholic orphanage when she was a child, taught Bailey everything she knows about crocheting. Because she had never been exposed to patterns, Bailey learned without them. "This way," Bailey recalled her teacher saying, "you can create whatever you want."

Bailey later accepted a position in social services, but after a year she realized that this work was not her true calling. She had spent so much time and money on her education; it was time she earned her living through her artistic gifts. She began designing wooden toys, then puppets, then dolls, and finally wearable art. "I've always worn hats, but they didn't do what I wanted them to," she explained in the *New York Times.* "The knit hats became unraveled and the floppy hats just had no style." She told *Essence,* "I started doing the wearable art because I could make a living selling hats and also the garments—the coats, the jumper dresses."

Bailey sold her designs at fairs and bazaars in New York City, sometimes even working as a street vendor. She had a stamp made with her business information and stamped slips of paper, passing them out as business cards. She allowed pure imagination to dictate her work, incorporating her design training throughout. Her hat designs evolved to continually pique her customers' interest. She used contrasting colors to create a sense of motion. Her prints related to one another, demonstrating a cohesive overall use of color.

In the beginning, the shapes of Bailey's pieces were inspired by African hairdos and African architecture. Later, decorative and ceremonial headdresses from

Africa and other cultures served as inspiration. Hindu mythology, too, particularly the depiction of religious figures, also figured in her work. An all-girl Chinese drill team she saw perform in Seattle introduced her to Chinese opera head pieces. She would make each of these aesthetic ideas her own through original stylistic modifications.

Bailey wore her hats wherever she went; photographers she met regularly asked to shoot her work for their portfolios. After making a deal with one, she photocopied the resulting pictures and sent them to every fashion magazine she could think of. *Elle* was the only one to respond, but the magazine's fashion editors' overwhelmingly enthusiastic response was enough to get the ball rolling. *Elle* frequently featured Bailey's designs; after a full-page article on her appeared in the magazine, other publications that had previously ignored Bailey's requests for exposure in their pages suddenly came calling. Advertising agencies started ringing her phone as well, and her hats were soon gracing print ads and billboards as part of a high-profile Benetton clothing campaign.

> "Peanut butter is an African American food, but people don't recognize it as such. I want people to say 'as American as peanut butter,' not just 'apple pie.'"

Then Bailey was contacted by the costume designer at 40 Acres and a Mule, hip director Spike Lee's film production company. 40 Acres wanted to use her headgear in Lee's *Do the Right Thing,* which caused a sensation in 1989. It wasn't long before a friend connected Bailey with actor/comedian Bill Cosby, who began featuring her pieces on his wildly popular TV series, *The Cosby Show,* as well as on its spin-off program, *A Different World.* She even sold hats to Cosby for personal wear. After that, museums around New York and eventually the nation began requesting her work for exhibits.

Championed the "Funk" in Style

Late 1995 found Bailey stretching her creative wings, conceiving of a "coronation" that would include a performance piece and a short film showcasing her always changing hats. She planned to crown 12 people from all walks of life who, as she told *CBB,* "have upheld the basic principles of funk. I have to give my work an identity. People see it, but they don't know what it is or what it does or how you use it. With the coronation they can put what I do in a larger context." The multimedia crowning would travel to museums throughout the country.

In a broader sense, Bailey has always concerned herself with spreading the gospel of "funk," the particular quirks or idiosyncrasies and spirit of improvisation we bring to our creative endeavors. As she told *CBB,* "The basis of any culture is a funkiness—everything starts with funk. Funkiness comes from a passion, a personal taste, and not necessarily from training. It comes from not having the materials you need to make what you want to make. There are no rules—whatever works works. Often, what starts as raw individuality gets polished, and then funk is forgotten. What I'm doing with this coronation is acknowledging the high brow of funk."

Ultimately, everything Bailey does comes back to the creation of a specifically African American art that has its roots in the make-do tradition of funkiness. This principle extends to her work with architects to create interior designs, from textiles to furniture. It encompasses a cookbook of contemporary funk cuisine gathered from friends who have traveled the world and who have combined their exotic new discoveries with down-home memories.

To make up for the books she never had as a child, Bailey is writing folktales about African American heroes who use their funky talents to overcome adversity. In telling the story of one such character she devised an art installation comprised of a crocheted residential compound—teepee-like structures that are in some ways huge versions of her hats. Bailey has also taken to writing cultural criticism on the work of artists "with a sophisticated funky aesthetic."

Bailey hopes that one day American design will feature not only Swedish-inspired products, or objects created with an Asian orientation, but distinctively African American pieces as well. To do this she is taking the spirit of Africa and, using the technology and influences of her American upbringing, education, and training, fashioning artworks in that strictly African American style. "Peanut butter is an African American food," she reminded *CBB,* "but people don't recognize it as such. I want people to say `as American as peanut butter,' not just `apple pie.'"

Sources

Essence, May 1995, p. 70.
New York Times, August 19, 1990, sec. 1, p. 38.
Philadelphia Tribune, August 20, 1993, p. 1C.

Additional information for this profile was provided through a *CBB* interview with Bailey on December 26 and 27, 1995.

—Joanna Rubiner

Tyra Banks

1973—

Fashion model and actress

A film career, the dream of many of international fashion model Tyra Banks's colleagues, came quickly for the Los-Angeles-born woman--yet it had been part of her plan all along. A hit on the runways of top designers since the early 1990s, Banks's career segued first into television and later into film, when she was cast in a leading role in the 1995 film *Higher Learning,* written and directed by John Singleton. She and Singleton eventually became one of Hollywood's most talked-about couples. With the help of a supportive family, Banks has successfully managed her newfound fame in positive ways, and has chosen roles and collaborations with other up-and-coming African American arts professionals who seek to portray their community in a diverse, multifaceted way.

Dreamed of a Public Career

Banks was born in Los Angeles December 4, 1973, to Carolyn and Don Banks. Her mother was a medical photographer at NASA's Jet Propulsion Lab, while her father is a computer consultant. They divorced when Tyra was six, although the relationship between parents

and children--including Tyra's older brother Devin--remained amicable. Growing up, she would often parade around the family's Inglewood duplex in her mother's high heels and long robes, play-acting at being a model. Her view of the profession came largely from watching the weekly CNN program *Style with Elsa Klensch,* and later the MTV feature *House of Style* starring Cindy Crawford. In more serious moments, Banks entertained the idea of going to veterinary school. Yet her unusual looks sometimes made life difficult, as she told GQ writer James Ryan. "People called me Olive Oyl, Lightbulb Head, and Fivehead, because my forehead was so big," Banks recalled.

Banks attended Immaculate Heart High School, a rigorous Catholic girls' school in the Los Feliz section of Los Angeles, where classmates also teased her because of her increasing height (5'11") and weight (around 125 lbs). She told the *Chicago Tribune* that her most humbling experience in life was losing the prom queen crown to a girl she described as the smartest in her class. After graduating, she decided to try modeling on a lark, thinking it might be a good way to do some traveling. Since her mother was a photographer, putting a port-

At a Glance . . .

Born December 4, 1973, in Los Angeles, CA; daughter of Don Banks (a computer consultant) and Carolyn London-Johnson (a business manager).

Model and actor. Began modeling in Paris, France, 1991. Cast in recurring role on the NBC-TV sitcom *The Fresh Prince of Bel-Air,* 1993; first film appearance in the 1995 drama *Higher Learning.* Tygirl, Inc., founder and CEO, c. 1995.

Addresses: *Home*—Los Angeles, CA.

folio together was not a problem. Banks took her book to agencies, but, as mother Carolyn London-Johnson recalled for *People* magazine writers Tom Gliatto and Bryan Alexander, "The market for black models was not very good. They would say, 'We have this many black girls already.'"

After encountering one too many dead ends, Banks decided to go ahead with her backup plan to start college and study film. Accepted at Loyola Marymount University in Los Angeles, Banks was walking down the street two weeks before classes started when a model scout from France spotted her. The scout offered her immediate work for the upcoming fall haute couture shows in Paris, and Banks accepted. "Her sensual lope and sleek, space-age frame gave her instant catwalk charisma,"*People*described the model in its "Fifty Most Beautiful Women" issue. Designer Todd Oldham likened Banks to "an antelope. She was just born with grace."

Within Banks's first week in Paris, other designers were so entranced by her presence on the runway that she was booked for an unprecedented 25 shows--a record in the business for a newcomer. Next, Banks was offered lucrative contract deals, where the real money in the modeling industry lies. She was the first African American woman on the cover of *Sports Illustrated's* high-profile swimsuit issue; American designer Ralph Lauren wanted her for another one of his lush, multipage ad campaigns; and cosmetics giant Cover Girl made her the second African American to be offered a longterm deal with them.

Encountered Racism

Yet Banks's early days in the modeling business were difficult for her, despite a naturally exuberant and flexible demeanor. Subtle racism within the industry was partly responsible; from the start, Banks was called the "new Naomi Campbell," in comparison to the more experienced supermodel who had been the star woman of color on the runways for some years. Campbell, known for her diva-like behavior, was incensed, and managed to get Banks barred from appearing in a Chanel show after refusing to speak to her on several other occasions. "No model should have to endure what I went through at 17," Banks told *Essence* writer Deborah Gregory. "It's very sad that the fashion business and press can't accept that there can be more than one reigning black supermodel at a time."

Banks discussed the racism in the modeling industry with *Cosmopolitan*writer Jamie Diamond in 1993. "I've had bookers tell me, 'You've got light skin and green eyes. You're easy to sell.'" She admitted to relaxing her hair and having hair extensions done "because that's what 'beautiful' is supposed to look like--and that's how I make my living." Nevertheless, success does not insulate Banks from random acts of racism in everyday life. When she and a friend went to a New York City newsstand to purchase a magazine whose cover the model graced, the proprietor yelled at the two women and ordered them out of the store. When her friend pointed out the issue and Banks's image, he responded by saying "I don't care. You all look alike."

> "No model should have to endure what I went through at ....17 It's very sad that the fashion business and press can't accept that there can be more than one reigning Black supermodel at a time."

Shored up Her Resources

The difficulties engendered by her daughter's new profession helped convince Carolyn London-Johnson to heed Banks's urgings and get involved. She quit her job and moved to Paris for a time to become her full-time manager, an arrangement that has suited them well. Banks's father handles her finances, and the supermodel daughter did not move out of her mother's house until she was 21. A magazine cover for *Essence* in June of 1993 sparked the next big move in Banks's career. John Singleton, director of the Academy-Award-nominated *Boyz 'N the Hood,* spotted the magazine and thought she would be perfect for an as-yet-uncast role in his next film. After mutual friends introduced them, Singleton attended one of Banks's appearances on the runway. He was entranced. They struck up a friendship that blossomed into romance.

Meanwhile, Banks had been cast in an occasional recurring role on the NBC-TV sitcom *The Fresh Prince of Bel-Air,* starring former hip-hop star and feature-film actor Will Smith. Banks portrayed Jackie Ames, a love interest of Smith's title character. The acting experience made it easier when Singleton and the producers of his upcoming film *Higher Learning* asked her to read for the role of Deja, a star athlete at the film's fictional university. Some assumed that she had gotten the role because of her relationship with Singleton, the film's director, but Banks told *Entertainment Weekly* reporter Tim Appelo that "John said, 'Read for it, but if you're bad, you don't get it. I'd look like I'm thinkin' with my you-know-what.'" Her performance at the audition made an impact, however, and she won the role.

Higher Learning won kudos from critics for its performances, and Banks's acting career now seems quite certain. Her relationship with Singleton is also on steady ground, although she was initially hesitant to become involved. When he told her early on that he would like them to only date one another, she was reluctant. "I didn't want to rush things," she recalled for *People* writers Carol Schatz and Vicki Sheff-Cahan. Yet later, during a walk through Manhattan, she had a change of heart. "I told him I wanted to be his girl," Banks recalled, and Singleton chimed in, "It sounds so corny. But it's real." Banks, however, refuses to take the relationship one step further by cohabitating. "Not until I get married," she told Schatz and Sheff-Cahan for *People.* "I am old-fashioned."

Planned Future Achievements

After the success of *Higher Learning,* Banks bought herself a five-bedroom abode in Los Angeles. She has also endowed her alma mater, Immaculate Heart, with a scholarship for African American girls. "I was very privileged that my mother and father sent me to private school," Banks told Gregory in *Essence.* "I want other African-American girls who can't afford it to experience that kind of education." Although still modeling, she planned to pursue her career on the screen, starting by reading up on the history of the film industry. Banks told *Essence's* Gregory that she had planned on a career in film prior to even thinking about modeling, but realized that the yoke of Supermodel would be a hard one to shed. "Even when I'm 50 and no longer modeling, everyone will still refer to me as 'Tyra the model.' Once a model, always a model."

Yet being an African American model in an industry dominated by Caucasians has been difficult. "It's long overdue that black models receive the same benefits as white models," she told *Essence's* Gregory. "But I still don't make as much as the white supermodels do." Plans for a college degree, a family, and more film roles were in the works for Banks, yet she planned on guiding her career herself, and quite firmly.

Banks formed a corporation--Tygirl, Inc.--to better handle her multifaceted career, and declined further involvement in *The Fresh Prince of Bel Air,* in part because "everybody started coming up to me on the street and calling me Jackie Ames," she told Ryan in *GQ.* "I felt like I didn't want to get stereotyped into that character." The actor declined a role as a one-night stand with Tom Cruise's character in the 1993 film *The Firm,* primarily because of the one-dimensional, decorative nature of the character. "I don't want roles that scream, *I AM SO PRETTY!,*" Banks told *People* magazine's Gliatto. Another rule? She freely admitted an important one to Appelo in the *Entertainment Weekly* article: "I'm not takin' off my clothes."

Sources

Chicago Tribune, August 6, 1995, p. C14.
Cosmopolitan, September 1993.
Detroit News, June 1, 1995, p. C3.
Entertainment Weekly, January 13, 1995, p. 33.
Essence, February 1995, p. 60.
GQ, June 1995, p. 176.
Jet, February 13, 1995, p. 30.
People, April 11, 1994, p. 57; May 9, 1994, p. 118; January 23, 1995, p. 33.

—Carol Brennan

William Banks

1903–1985

Broadcasting executive, attorney, minister

William Banks was a man committed to improving his community as evidenced by numerous career accomplishments that successfully managed to do just that. An attorney, Baptist minister, business owner, founder of a fraternal organization, and television and radio station owner, Banks's list of achievements spanned the twentieth century and with it the range of possibilities for African Americans in the United States. As a community supporter, investor, and activist, Banks lived most of his adult life in the Detroit area and contributed greatly to the city's rise to prominence as the one of the first places in North America where an African American community wielded political and economic power.

The son of a tenant farmer, Banks was born May 6, 1903, in Geneva, Kentucky. He attended the Lincoln Institute there before relocating to Michigan. In Detroit he found work in the automotive factories while attending college, graduating first from Detroit City College, now Wayne State University, and later graduating with a law degree from the Detroit College of Law. He began practicing as a private attorney in 1930, and with his wife Ivy Bird raised two daughters, Tenicia and Harumi, and a son, Alterio. Banks also became active in numerous civic organizations, including the local branch of the Masonic lodge. However, he had also been attending Detroit Baptist College, working toward a doctorate in divinity, and was growing dissatisfied with the fraternal group's fundraising practices that involved liquor sales and gambling.

After being ordained a Baptist minister in 1949, Banks founded the International Free and Accepted Masons and Eastern Star the following year. The organization began in Canton, Ohio, with less than two dozen members, but grew to 1,500 one year later. With Banks at its helm as Supreme Director, the Black Masons--as the group came to be known--raised money for numerous projects in the African American community. To do this the Masons sold endowments in blocks of $100 to members, who were then obligated to pay 35 cents each month toward every $100 endowment in their name. The Masons invested this money wisely, especially in real estate, and founded vocational schools in the Detroit area like the Universal Barber College and the International School of Cosmetology.

In 1964, Banks and the Masons bought an FM radio station at the end of the dial in the Detroit market. They encouraged local ministers to buy broadcast time for religious programming and added to that a funky, R&B-based musical format, eventually making a financial success of the station. The station's call letters were WGPR, which soon came to be know as "Where God's Presence Radiates." By this time Banks had become a prominent local business leader, active in area Republican organizations and the National Association for the Advancement of Colored People (NAACP). When then-U.S. president Richard Nixon invited him to the White House for dinner in the early 1970s, the two discussed the lack of African Americans among media owners in the country. The chief executive promised to help Banks secure a Federal Communications Commission (FCC) license to assist in his bid to become the first African American owner of a television station.

Banks's dream became a reality in September of 1975, when WGPR-TV went on the air in Detroit. Several of the Masons' savvy real estate investments, including property in northern Michigan and Florida, had been sold to finance the purchase of the first African American-owned television outlet in the United States. Important Michigan corporations pledged advertising dollars to help WGPR get underway that first year, and Banks and the Masons received national media attention for

their achievement. His daughter Tenicia Gregory took leave from her English professorship to work for the fledgling television station. Hopes were high from the start--WGPR promised 90 percent locally produced programming and a format geared toward Detroit's increasing African American community.

Yet Banks and his staff ran into numerous roadblocks during the first few years of WGPR's operation. "The plans were too big. Too unrealistic. The town's top TV stations couldn't afford to produce 90 percent of their programming," wrote *Detroit Free Press* reporter Larry Gabriel in a 1994 article on WGPR. Banks's daughter Gregory recalled, "The first thing we learned was we didn't know a heck of a lot about what you needed for a TV station. We did not realize how expensive television was." Technical problems with commercials made advertisers wary, and when they began cancelling their advertisements, WGPR began losing much-needed revenue. The staff was reduced, and those that stayed on worked for negligible or no compensation.

> Bank's list of achievements spanned the twentieth century and with it the range of possibilities for African Americans.

Success for WGPR came from unusual sources during its first decade. One was an in-house local dance show called "The Scene" that regularly attracted hundreds of area teenagers who came down to the studio looking for a chance to dance. Years after its cancellation, reruns of old episodes were still popular on Detroit cable television. The station was also the first to broadcast 24 hours a day, beginning in August of 1978 with cult movies running until 6 a.m. spliced in between advertisements for local businesses sold at discount rates. Additionally, Banks used his extensive contacts to help keep the station afloat during these lean years, selling air time to local churches for religious programming. The station was also one of the first to feature national televangelists like Jim Bakker. More significantly, during its first few years on the air WGPR provided a valuable training ground for African American broadcasters and behind-the-scenes personnel.

The shaky financial status of the television station made it an easy target for acquisition-hungry media players during the 1970s and 1980s. Banks was continually offered bids to buy WGPR, but turned them down despite the often large sums mentioned. During its eighth year in operation the station finally started earning money. Meanwhile WGPR had indirectly benefitted the community by providing a launching pad for African Americans in the media. Many who began at the station eventually left for better-paying positions elsewhere. The station "made peace with the fact that its impact on broadcasting would be to funnel African Americans into the business," wrote Gabriel in the *Detroit Free Press*. "Dr. Banks never wanted to hold anybody back," his widow, Ivy Banks, told the newspaper. "He was happy for them. He knew that they could get a better salary somewhere else."

Banks died in August of 1985 at the age of 82. At the funeral service, then-mayor of Detroit, Coleman Young, spoke of Banks's lifelong commitment to Detroit, its citizens, and its future. "He did more than talk about this," the *Detroit News* quoted Young as saying. "He acted on it, he invested in it, and he had the kind of faith that kept this city moving." Sadly, subsequent court battles between Banks's widow and the Black Masons severed the connection between his survivors and the organizations he founded. After her husband's passing Ivy Banks planned to take over the helm of the Masonic group, but was legally thwarted by a group of 46 members. Both she and daughter Tenicia Gregory resigned from WGPR and the Masons; less than a decade later the Masons sold the station to CBS, who was looking to replace an affiliate in the Detroit market. Several African American business people challenged the reported $24 million sale of the station and the transfer of the FCC license on grounds of the station's historical significance to the African American community.

Sources

Black Enterprise, March 1995, p. 19.
Detroit Free Press, August 27, 1985, p. 4C; November 27, 1994, p. 1G.
Detroit News, August 30, 1985, p. A3.

—Carol Brennan

Tyson Beckford

1970—

Fashion model

In a world of fashion that has been dominated by women--from the British Twiggy of the 1960s to the multi-ethnic Naomi Campbell of today--Tyson Beckford was not only the first black male "supermodel," he was the first *male* supermodel. As Scott Poulson-Bryant wrote in *Vibe,* "Fabulous females like Christy [Turlington], Linda [Evangelista] and Naomi [Campbell] used to epitomize the world of high fashion. That was until a brother bumrushed the menswear show." In fact Beckford has become big enough that he is now primarily known as Tyson. Ralph Lauren, one of the biggest fashion designers and clothing manufacturers of the 1980s and 1990s, attributes Tyson's success to his "all-American look with a dramatic edge. He conveys power, style and intelligence in a very exciting way."

Tyson's current wealth and high visibility are not the result of a privileged background. He was born in the Bronx to parents of Jamaican descent. He points out that the exotic cast to his features comes from a Chinese grandparent. Soon after he was born, his mother took the family back to Jamaica where they stayed until he was seven. Coming back to New York City, they first lived upstate before returning to Harlem, where Tyson still maintains a residence.

Bethann Hardison, Tyson's agent, credits his mother with a large part of Tyson's success, saying that she raised him to be unusually sensitive. His mother worked for a time as a fashion model. Realizing her son's extraordinary charisma from a young age, she dragged him with her from one runway show to another. Despite his mother's influence, he was not immune to the usual tensions of growing up poor in the ghetto. Never disowning his past, he admits that he lived a wild life, sometimes running with a dangerous crowd and often courting trouble. He even spent a night in jail for stealing a car, though the charges were reduced.

Rather than hanging out all the time with the chic crowd of the international fashion world, Tyson still spends most of his increasingly rare free time with the same friends he had in the summer of 1993. It was at this time that a reporter for an influential New York City journal, *The Source,* asked Tyson if he would be willing to pose. Tyson was at first reluctant, not sure of what was being offered. When he was satisfied that the offer was legitimate, he made what proved to be an excellent

At a Glance . . .

Born Tyson Beckford, December 19, 1970, in New York City, NY; son of Lloyd Beckford and Hillary Dixon Hall.

Fashion model. Posed for the *Source* magazine, 1993; has appeared in various publications, including *Arena*, *British GQ*, *Details*, *EM*, *Essence*, *GQ*, *Mondo Uomo*, *New York Times*–fashion section, *Paper*, *Vibe*, and *Vogue Hommes*; signed with Bethann Management Company, 1993; first black to sign exclusive contract with Ralph Lauren, 1995. Fashion shows include Tommy Hilfiger; Nautica; Hugo Boss, Calvin Klein, and Donna Karan.

Awards: Named one of *People*'s "50 Most Beautiful People," 1995; Male Model of the Year, VH1 Fashion and Video Awards, 1995.

Addresses: *Agent*–c/o Bethann Management Company, Inc., 36 North Moore, New York, NY 10013.

career decision by accepting the opportunity.

Beckford's next big break was coming to the attention of Bethann Hardison, an important agent in the world of fashion. Not only does she handle talented models through her own successful agency, but she also has taken the lead in demanding the use of a more fair proportion of African Americans among models. Although in the 1990s, it is not uncommon to see black faces in catalogs and in commercials, they are still extremely under-represented when compared to the number of black readers and buyers. To help fight this, Hardison formed the Black Girls' Coalition, an organization of successful models who use their clout to demand that all black models receive a fair shake.

Hardison admits that she did not see right away what made Tyson a supermodel. She realized quickly, though, that he was a unique combination of strength, intelligence, power, and sensitivity. The best fashion photographers loved to photograph Tyson and felt his shots were great from the start. With Hardison and her agency behind him, his rise was dramatic. He appeared in the fashion section of the *New York Times*, in *Gentleman's Quarterly*--both the American and English versions--and in the *Mark & Spencer Catalog*, perhaps the most prestigious catalog for a male fashion model in the world.

In 1994, *People* named him one of the 50 most beautiful people in the world. Popular magazines do not dominate the fashion world, however; the designers do. Thus, Tyson's most prestigious accomplishment was modeling for Ralph Lauren. He was the first black man to wear Ralph Lauren clothing in the company's advertising. Beyond that, Ralph Lauren signed him to an exclusive contract worth hundreds of thousands of dollars, an unprecedented sum for a male model. The rising model had become a supermodel. He told the *Source*, "I haven't let anything go to my head. New York [City] keeps you grounded. If you're acting funny in the city, someone will let you know in a minute."

> "I haven't let anything go to my head. New York keeps you grounded. If you're acting funny in the city, someone will let you know in a minute."

Even with his phenomenal success, Tyson has not forgotten his roots or the other black models still fighting for some success; any job he does not get he wants to go to another black model. He turned down a chance to work the annual Milan fashion shows one year, because he was the only black man invited from the United States. As he told *Vibe*, "There are so many African-American and African men who are trying to get jobs, and they weren't giving the jobs to them.... I'm not the only brother out here trying to make it. So I didn't go." This stance put him in some conflict with Hardison who felt his appearance in Milan would open doors of opportunity for himself and others. Both can see that Tyson's success will be important to aspiring black models of the future.

Tyson's discomfort with affluence and celebrity implies that he is ready for the challenges of sudden wealth and fame, even at his young age. He knows that some will be looking at him and to him as a role model. He is wise enough, though, to know that this is an unfair burden, but one he should not shoulder aside. As he told the *Weekly Journal*, "I just want to be looked at as a brother who's doing something positive."

Sources

Ebony, September 1995, p. 48.
People, May 8, 1995.
Source, January 1995; June 1995, p. 24.

Vibe, September 1995, pp. 100-02.
Weekly Journal, April 13, 1995, p. 4ff.

—*Jim McDermott*

Ben Ami Ben-Israel

1940-

Religious leader

A former Chicago bus driver, Ben Ami Ben-Israel is the founder and head of the World African Hebrew Israelite Community, a religious sect that believes blacks in the Western Hemisphere are the descendants of the original Hebrews and, therefore, are the rightful heirs and stewards of the Holy Land, Israel. From his home in the Negev Desert in Israel--and from centers in major U.S. cities--Ben-Israel delivers the message that blacks should "repatriate" Israel and Africa; that meat, alcohol, and drugs are poison; and that truly righteous people should follow the laws of the Torah, the first five books of the Christian Bible's Old Testament. Since 1969 Ben-Israel and several thousand of his followers have eked out a tenuous living in Israel, often at odds with government authorities over the sect members' status and citizenship. Nothing has deterred the controversial leader from his crusade, however. Convinced that the United States does not offer a healthy and nurturing environment for black people, Ben-Israel encourages them to return to the homeland of their ancient forebears--and to religious practices that place emphasis on family, self-determination, and a personal relationship with God.

The African Hebrew Israelite Community is one of several African American Hebraic sects that work and worship according to ancient Jewish laws. While not terribly numerous, these groups exist in most major American cities and in the Caribbean and Africa as well. What sets Ben-Israel's Hebrew Israelites apart is that some of them have realized their core objective: to live in Israel and raise their children there. It is estimated that almost ten percent of the worldwide membership of the African Hebrew Israelite Community lives in Israel. Of the rest, many would like to relocate in the future. "America for us is a land of chastisement," Ben-Israel told the Knight Ridder wire service. "After that time of suffering, naturally we would desire to return to our land."

Message from an Angel

Knight-Ridder correspondent William R. Macklin noted: "To a world accustomed to flavor-of-the-month prophets, Ben-Israel may seem like the latest in a long line of poseurs, charlatans, and con artists. But viewed purely as a religious quest, his story has the ring of a Biblical epic." Born Ben Carter and raised in a Baptist home in the Chicago projects, Ben-Israel gravitated to the African American Hebraic movement after hearing his grandparents say the family's true roots were in Israel. While supporting himself and his family as a bus driver and foundry worker, he studied Old Testament scriptures and spent much of his spare time at the Abeta Israel Hebrew Cultural Center in Chicago. His associations there, as well as with the Black Nationalist movement, convinced him that the United States would never be a comfortable homeland for blacks.

Ben-Israel spent many hours each evening in prayer,

At a Glance . . .

Born Ben Carter, 1940 in Chicago, IL; married to four wives; 15 children.

Bus driver and foundry worker in Chicago, IL, 1960-66; World African Hebrew Israelite Community, spiritual leader, 1967-.

Address: *Home*—Dimona, Israel.

mulling over his concerns and his hopes for a brighter future for black Americans. His devotion, he told the Knight Ridder wire service, was answered in February of 1966 with a vision of an angel. The angel prophesied that the humble bus driver would lead blacks "back to the promised land" by 1977. Ben-Israel was stunned by the prophecy. "When the vision came, I thought that the angel did not have the right address," he admitted. "I felt there were others more qualified. It was very trying for me." Nevertheless, he spread the message to his friends and family and eventually persuaded about 350 people to sell their possessions, quit their jobs, and journey with him to Liberia. The move to Africa was seen as the first step in the fulfillment of the prophecy.

Through two difficult years Ben-Israel and his small band of followers lived in a village of makeshift huts and tents in the Liberian interior. Nearly two-thirds of the members gave up and returned to the United States. The rest went with Ben-Israel to Israel, where after being detained at the airport they were granted temporary visas and allowed to settle in an abandoned absorption center in the southern Negev desert town of Dimona. Many of these newcomers--from such cities as Detroit, Chicago, Philadelphia, and Los Angeles--renounced their U.S. citizenship and allowed their temporary visas to expire. Then, as they began to find jobs and bear children in the Israeli community, they encouraged other sect members to join them. Their numbers grew, causing consternation within the Israeli government.

A Controversy over Citizenship Status

Many Black Hebrews arrived in Israel on tourist visas and then stayed in the country illegally. Problems arose because the Jewish government did not consider the American blacks Jews. Although the sect practices Jewish rituals and honors Jewish holidays, it also allows polygamy; Black Hebrew males are allowed to marry as

many as seven women. Trouble with the Israeli authorities began in 1979, when an official investigation labeled the sect a "cult" and described Ben-Israel as having total control over his followers. Beginning in the 1980s, some members of the sect were detained and deported to the United States. The sect's case for full Israeli citizenship reached the U.S. Supreme Court, which ruled that as non-Jews the American blacks were not entitled to automatic Israeli citizenship under that country's Law of Return. That meant that sect members were denied such automatic benefits as work permits and social services and were thereby denied all but clandestine laboring jobs.

> "I'm the messenger of God. My position is similar to that which is written in the Latter Days, to sit on the throne of David."

Efforts to deport the sect intensified when ultra-Orthodox Rabbi Yitzhak Peretz became interior minister of Israel. One compromise solution--the members' conversion to standard Judaism--was rejected because the members already considered themselves Jews. As more Black Hebrews arrived and remained in Israel illegally, the government began refusing entry to some black American tourists on suspicion that they were members of the sect.

Ben-Israel was hurt by the allegations that his sect was a "cult" and that he was some sort of manipulative zealot and by the deportation of more than 50 of his followers, some of whom had borne children in Israel. Finally he asked the U.S. government for help in stopping the expulsions. In 1990, members of the Illinois Black Caucus, working with the Israeli Midwest Consulate General in Chicago, Jewish legislators, and U.S. federal officials, drew up an agreement with the Israeli government on behalf of the Black Hebrews. New, longer visas were issued to sect members who agreed to restore their U.S. citizenship, with the promise that future Israeli citizenship would be decided on a case-by-case basis.

"Time to Change or Die"

As the 1980s progressed and the Black Hebrews normalized relations with their Israeli neighbors, attitudes toward the sect changed. By 1994 Ben-Israel and his followers were granted permanent-resident status in Israel, allowing them to qualify for full civil and social rights under Israeli law, including eligibility for old-age pensions, work permits, cash allowances for large families, disability payments, educational opportunities, and childbirth subsidies. Ben-Israel told the Knight Ridder wire service that the early problems the sect had with the Israeli government were simply a case of failure to communicate. "You have to picture how it looked having these African Americans coming and saying they want to establish the kingdom of God in Israel," he said.

An estimated 1,500 Black Hebrews live in several Negev Desert communities some 80 miles from Tel Aviv. Another 25,000 members of the World African Hebrew Israelite Community are scattered throughout the major American cities. The sect members are vegetarians and are not permitted to smoke, use drugs, or consume alcohol. Women are encouraged to stay home and raise children, but at least one sect member told the *St. Paul Pioneer Press* that because her husband has more than one wife to help with the household chores, she has more time for self-fulfillment than she would ordinarily have.

Traditional Jewish rites are performed, and members fast one day each week. The children are encouraged to speak Hebrew instead of English, although the sect profits from a small cottage industry in American-style pop music. Men and women wear African-styled clothing, sometimes including turbans. Ben-Israel's followers see their strict religious practices as a way to save them from the evil influences of American culture. Echoing their founder, they often proclaim that the time has come to "change or die."

From his home in Dimona, Israel, and during occasional visits to the United States, Ben-Israel exhorts his followers to seek the kingdom of God that is their birthright. Husband of four and a father of 15 children who range in age from preschoolers to more than 30, Ben-Israel wants other black Americans to be aware of the alternative the Black Hebrews offer. "We're not a cult, we're a nationalistic community," he explained to the Knight Ridder wire service. "But cults are not the problem.... The mainstream way of life accepted by most Americans is the problem." In the *Chicago Tribune* the energetic religious leader concluded: "I'm the messenger of God. My position is similar to that which is written in the Latter Days, to sit on the throne of David."

Sources

Chicago Tribune, August 14, 1986, p. 12; September 11, 1986, p. 23; September 14, 1990, p. 1.
St. Paul Pioneer Press, December 29, 1991.

Additional information for this profile was obtained from the Knight Ridder wire service, January 6, 1995.

—*Anne Janette Johnson*

Jim Brown

1936—

Former professional football player, actor, social activist

Some 30 years after his retirement from professional football, Hall-of-Famer Jim Brown still ranks among the very best running backs in the game's history. As a member of the Cleveland Browns from 1957 until 1966, Brown made a mockery of his opponents, scoring a record-setting 126 touchdowns and leading the league in yards gained for eight of his nine seasons. A combination of speed, intelligence, and sheer strength, enabled Brown to set 15 National Football League (NFL) records. *Sports Illustrated* attested that Brown "dominated pro football like no player ever had…. It is possible that had he continued to play, he would have put all the league's rushing records so far out of reach that they would have been only a distant dream—like [New York Yankees baseball player] Joe DiMaggio's hitting streak—to the runners who followed him."

Brown is one of the first professional football players to parlay his gridiron fame into notable off-the-field accomplishments. Since retiring from sports he has devoted his energies to other projects, becoming an actor and a social activist. Brown has founded and run several well-known community programs aimed specifically at im-

proving economic opportunities for American minorities. His latest enterprise is Amer-I-Can—its name emphasizing the "I Can"—a project aimed at fostering self-esteem and diffusing tensions among urban gang members. Brown has created a 15-step course in personal responsibility that he has introduced everywhere from maximum-security prisons to encounter sessions in his own Hollywood living room.

Part of Brown's success in these ventures has rested on his image as a hard-working football player who never forgot the pressing issues of the black community despite his fame and fortune. Brown's own life is an illustration of his philosophy that economic development is the best strategy for success in the United States. Said *Los Angeles Times* columnist Mike Downey, "Brown doesn't offer gang members dispassionate advice to be better citizens, to be cool, to go out and get decent jobs. He gives them a way. Brown doesn't counsel prison inmates to get themselves straightened out, to lead more productive lives. He shows them how. He does something."

At a Glance . . .

Born James Nathaniel Brown, February 17, 1936, on St. Simons Island, GA; son of Swinton and Theresa Brown; married Sue James, 1958 (divorced); children: Kim, Kevin, Jim, Jr. *Education:* Syracuse University, B.A., 1957.

Athlete, actor, activist. Cleveland Browns, full back, 1957-66. Actor, 1964–; film appearances include *Rio Conchos,* 1964, *The Dirty Dozen,* 1966, *Ice Station Zebra,* 1968, *100 Rifles,* 1969, and *I'm Gonna Git You, Sucka,* 1989. Minority enterprises activist, 1965–; founder, Negro Industrial and Economic Union (name later changed to Black Economic Union, 1965, Vital Issues, 1986, Amer-I-can, c. 1989. Spokesperson for Pepsi Cola Company, Coors Gold Door program, and Jobs Plus.

Selected awards 25th Silver Anniversary Award, National Collegiate Athletic Association; Rookie of the Year, National Football League (NFL), 1958; Player of the Year, NFL, 1959; Jim Thorpe Trophy, 1959, 1965; named football back of the decade for 1950-60; named to NFL Pro Bowl, 1958-65; Player of the Year, NFL 1964; Bert Bell Memorial Award, 1964; Hickoc Belt Athlete of the Year, 1964; elected to Pro Football Hall of Fame, 1971.

Addresses: *Office*—Amer-I-can, 6290 Sunset Blvd, Ste. 925, Hollywood, CA 90028.

Experienced Culture Shock on Long Island

In 1936, James Nathaniel Brown was born on St. Simons Island, off the coast of Georgia. His father, who had been a professional boxer, left the family when Jim was still an infant. For the first seven years of his life, Brown was raised by his great-grandmother on the island. His mother, Theresa, had moved north to Long Island, New York, where she found work as a housekeeper. Eventually Brown joined her there, undergoing a sort of culture shock in his new surroundings. He told *Newsday* that on his first morning at Manhasset Valley grade school he got into a fight. "My mother had dressed me in new clothes," he remembered. "That morning

when they gave us recess, a black boy made a wisecrack, said I looked 'pretty,' and he shoved me. I reacted Georgia-style. I tackled him, pinned him with my knees, punched him. The closed circle of kids watching then started chanting, 'Dirty fighter, dirty fighter.' I stopped fighting. I was mystified. How did these boys fight up here?"

Circumstances improved for Brown when he found his way onto sports teams. He was a natural athlete who excelled at virtually every game, from baseball and football to lacrosse and track events. A policeman named Jack Peploe encouraged Brown to join the Manhasset Police Boys' Club and even gave Brown the keys to the high school gym so he could open it for Boys' Club games.

As early as his freshman year of high school, Brown was grabbing the attention of local coaches. Ed Walsh, who ran the Manhasset High School football program, recruited Brown and pushed him to work on his already formidable skills. Walsh told *Newsday* that Brown "probably had more drive to succeed of anybody I have ever coached. Whatever he did, he wanted to do better than anybody else."

With Brown's talent and leadership, Manhasset High became a powerhouse in football, baseball, and lacrosse. The students at the school were so impressed with their star athlete that they elected him chief justice of the high school court. Even so, Brown admits that he did indulge in a bit of minor gang activity as a teenager—chiefly breaking in on rival parties and fighting occasionally. This mischief, however, did not impinge on his athletic career or his academic potential. During most of his high school years he was a member of the honor society for scholastic achievement. "I was a poor kid from a broken home," he told *Newsday,* "but I was not insecure, because where there is love there cannot be insecurity."

Brown was recruited by 45 colleges and universities. He chose New York's Syracuse University at the prompting of a friend, attorney Ken Molloy. Unbeknownst to Brown, Molloy had canvassed Manhasset businessmen for funds to pay Brown's tuition until the young man could earn a full athletic scholarship. That proved more difficult than anyone had anticipated when, as a freshman at Syracuse, Brown was passed over for less talented white players in basketball and football. As a sophomore, he was benched in football until a timely injury to another player opened a place for him on the offense. Once he found his way into a game, he plowed down the opposition so forcefully that the fans began to chant his name. He became a starter after that, ultimately earning ten varsity letters as a Syracuse Orangeman—three each in football and lacrosse and two each in basketball and track. With only a slight knowledge of the various events, he placed fifth nationally in the 1956 decathlon competition and qualified to attend the Olympic Games.

Brown did not go to the 1956 Olympics, however, choosing instead to concentrate on football. During his senior year at Syracuse, his team qualified for the prestigious Cotton Bowl, where they lost 28-27 to Texas Christian University. Brown, who scored 21 points in that game, was later named to the 1957 College All-Stars. When he graduated in the spring of 1957, he had gained 2,091 yards and scored 187 points—including 25 touchdowns—for the Orangemen.

Best of the Browns

Brown was the first-round draft choice of the Cleveland Browns in 1957. With little fanfare, he joined the team's training camp for summer workouts. While most professional football players need several years to adjust to the level of play in the NFL, Brown starting at fullback made his presence known immediately. By his fifth game, he had surpassed the team record for most touchdowns scored in a single season. He played a key role in Cleveland's Eastern Division championship of 1957, and with the first of his seven season-rushing records in hand, was the unanimous choice for rookie of the year. In 1958, he again won the rushing title with 1,527 yards, tying the single-season touchdown record with 18.

Year after year Brown continued his onslaught. If teams could contain his rushing on the ground—and few could—he would catch "hail Mary," or long "bomb" passes and streak into the end zone. He was voted onto every All-Pro team between 1958 and 1965, and he was named football back of the decade for 1950 to 1960. In Cleveland especially, he was hailed as a conquering hero, a superstar for a sports-obsessed city.

Still, by 1962 Brown was dissatisfied with his role with Cleveland. His response, more or less, was to lead a player revolt against the coaching of Paul Brown, who was fairly conservative in his play selection. In 1963, Jim Brown prospered again, this time under replacement coach Blanton Collier. Brown rewrote the record books by gaining 1,863 yards, catching 24 passes, and scoring 15 touchdowns in a single season. In December of that year he visited then-President Lyndon Johnson at the White House.

The era of product endorsements and athlete-actors was just dawning, and Brown was a pioneer in both respects. He signed a contract with Pepsi Cola and traveled in the off-season as an executive and spokesperson for the soft drink company. He also took a role in a feature film, *Rio Conchos,* about U.S. Cavalry troopers in the 19th century. The movie work opened up a whole new realm of possibilities for Brown. Although he was still at the top of his form as an athlete and the highest-paid football player of his day, he actively sought film roles as a means to move away from sports.

In 1966 Brown starred in the box office hit *The Dirty Dozen,* earning praise for his portrayal of a black man victimized but unbroken by the white world. Shooting for *The Dirty Dozen* was repeatedly delayed, and ultimately conflicted with football training camp in 1966. It was then that Brown abruptly announced his retirement from football. He was 30 years old and at the height of his game. Regarding his decision to leave football, Brown told *Sports Illustrated,* "I quit with regret but no sorrow. I've been able to do all the things I wanted to do, and now I want to devote my time to other things. And I wanted more mental stimulation than I would have had playing football."

Film Star, Social Pioneer

For some years after Brown retired from football he continued to win major film roles in works such as *Dark of the Sun, Ice Station Zebra,* and *100 Rifles.* The latter featured an American cinematic first, when Brown did a love scene with costar Raquel Welch, a white actress. Brown told *People* that he thinks the interracial love scene and his tendency to play strong, confident characters, proved his undoing in the industry. "I think Hollywood just got tired of a big ol' black Negro kissin' all their women," he said.

Others, such as *Gentleman's Quarterly* contributor John Lombardi, claimed that highly publicized charges of battery by several women—none of them resulting in a conviction—undermined Brown's image. Lombardi wrote, "Brown's movie career was only a memory by the early eighties, his ten-year publicity contract with Pepsi-Cola went unrenewed, ... and he found himself hustling Celebrity Bowling tournaments on TV for $20,000 paydays."

Brown admitted in *People* that his numerous relationships with women led him astray for a time. "I've done things I'm not particularly proud of," he said in *Esquire,* "but at least I'm honest enough to talk about them." When the film and television offers dried up, he founded his own production company, Ocean Productions, to encourage minority participation in movie-making. Though that venture has not seen great success, other Jim Brown projects have not only enhanced the athlete's image, but have also brought him substantial financial reward.

Brown has been no stranger to the field of public service. As early as his playing days in Cleveland, he founded the Black Economic Union (BEU), which used professional athletes as facilitators in the establishment of black-run enterprises, urban athletic clubs, and youth motivation programs. The BEU eventually folded, but Brown took his ideas to the Coors Golden Door program and Jobs Plus. In 1986, he founded a new endeavor, Vital Issues, aimed at teaching life management skills and personal growth techniques to inner-city gang members and prison inmates. By 1989, Vital Issues had evolved into Amer-I-Can.

The image most often associated with Amer-I-Can is that of Brown—aging but still powerful—surrounded by teenage gang members in various stages of the self-improvement program. Brown conducts sessions of Amer-I-Can from his home in the hills above Los Angeles. In 1992, Amer-I-Can won more than a million dollars in grant money to expand its programs into cities such as San Francisco and Cleveland. *Los Angeles Times* correspondent Jesse Katz explained that Amer-I-Can, as set forth by Brown, "draws on the self-determination of [1960s social activist] Malcolm X, the capitalism of [conservative U.S. president] Ronald Reagan and the recovery plan of Alcoholics Anonymous," adding, "At a time when police and politicians are at a loss to stem the rising tide of gang violence, Amer-I-Can is one of the hottest tickets in town."

While he may not be the only athlete to reach out to others less fortunate than himself, Brown urges his peers to do more than "make gestures" when facing society's ills. As he told Stephan Garnett of *Dollars & Sense,* "If they [black athletes] ever united and created a capitol base and put up a pool of resources to oversee that money, they would really be doing something great." Regardless of whether or not his vision is manifested, Brown's example serves to bolster his community. He suggested to Garnett that "for too long black Americans have been chasing the shadow of the rabbit. It's time for us to start chasing the rabbit, not his shadow." Amer-I-Can provides one way to do so.

Ultimately, Brown does not want to be seen as yet another wealthy athlete who made his way in the world through his physical ability. "I was a highly paid, over-glamorized gladiator," he told the *Washington Post.* "The decision-makers are the men who own, not the ones who play. I was never under an illusion as to who was the boss." Brown's aim is to give a new generation the courage to succeed. "The young black male is the most powerful source of energy and change we have," he told the *Washington Post.* "My hope is to start a direction where these young men will be given respect and taught how to utilize it."

In the years since hanging up his cleats, Brown has continued to win accolades from being inducted into the Pro Football Hall of Fame in 1971 to being named one of the most important sports figures of the preceeding 40 years by *Sports Illustrated* in 1994. The 12,312 yards he gained rushing stood as a record for nearly 20 years, until Walter Payton of the Chicago Bears broke it on October 7, 1984. Even more impressive, Brown's 126 career touchdowns record stood for nearly 30 years, until San Francisco 49ers wide receiver Jerry Rice broke it on September 5, 1994. Still, no fullback or running back has maintained Brown's average of more than 5.22 yards per carry.

> "When I lay down, I think of all the experiences I've had and the respect that I've gotten. That's my glory."

Despite having cemented a phenomenal page in sports history, Brown told *Jet* magazine, "I have no trophies in my home. When I lay down, I think of all the experiences I've had and the respect that I've gotten. That's my glory." In *Esquire* he added, "My performance is still there. They can try to make the numbers do tricks now, make them say something they really don't, but the other runners know who the man was…. I have always carried myself in a way that made people afraid to take liberties."

Selected writings

Off My Chest (autobiography), 1964.
Out of Bounds (autobiography), 1989.

Sources

Dollars & Sense, May 1994, p. 34.
Ebony, October 1987, p. 134.
Esquire, January 1990, pp. 35-36.
Gentleman's Quarterly, November 1992, pp. 232-39, 315-16.

Jet, October 30, 1989, pp. 46-51.

Life, October 25, 1963.

Los Angeles Times, September 24, 1991; May 3, 1992.

Modern Maturity, June 1994, p. 18

Newsday, December 19, 1962; October 3, 1991.

People, November 25, 1991.

Sports Illustrated, September 19, 1994, p. 57.

USA Today, September 6, 1994, p. C1.

Washington Post, December 5, 1959; February 15, 1991; May 25, 1992.

—Mark Kram

Robert Byrd

1952—

Documentary film producer and director

The pressing societal ills of cultural misunderstanding and intolerance have been the subject of numerous documentaries, but producer and director Robert Byrd examines these issues in a manner that is both revealing and thought-provoking. Since the early-1980s, Byrd has made close to one dozen films, and has won nearly as many awards. The recognition has given Byrd many unique opportunities, including that of working with a British broadcasting company.

Byrd was born on March 30, 1952, in Pensacola, Florida, where his father was stationed in the U.S. Air Force. The Byrd family soon relocated to Air Force bases in Germany and later England. As a teenager, Byrd returned with his family to the United States. However, his parents divorced shortly thereafter, and Byrd was raised by his mother in the Crenshaw District of Los Angeles.

In an interview with *Contemporary Black Biography (CBB),* Byrd recalled that early on he dreamed of becoming a filmmaker and relished any opportunity he had to attend the movies. He did not consider it a realistic goal, however, imagining it "far too glamorous a career

to be possible." Instead, he set his sights on becoming a lawyer and took the advice of a counselor friend who recommended the University of Chicago over the Ivy League schools that also accepted him. Byrd thrived at the school, which is renowned for its culture of academic rigor and critical thought, and he found his study of sociology, to be a good preparation for the documentary films that he would later produce and direct.

After graduating from college in 1975, Byrd held a number of jobs unrelated to his college experience or his later career. A sister living in Omaha, Nebraska, convinced him of job opportunities there, and he worked for one year as a life insurance underwriter at Mutual of Omaha. The offer of a training manager's position at International Harvester in St. Paul, Minnesota, occasioned another move, and Byrd spent one year there before going to work for a social service agency in Minneapolis, Minnesota. Seeking a break from two years of emotionally straining work, Byrd decided that instead of waiting for another opportunity to come his way, he would find one and pursue it. "Ever since then every job I've gotten has involved heavy lobbying on my part--convincing someone I can learn to do something I

At a Glance . . .

Born Robert Oliver Daniel Byrd, III, March 30, 1952, in Pensacola, FL; son of Robert Oliver Daniel Byrd, II (a U.S. Air Force pilot) and Louella (a secretary; maiden name, Richardson) Byrd; *Education:* University of Chicago, B.A., 1975.

Mutual of Omaha Insurance, life insurance underwriter, 1975-76; International Harvester, training manager, 1976-77; Pilot City Regional Center, intake director, 1978-79; Minnesota Civil Liberties Union, assistant director, 1979-80, associate director, 1980-82; Continental Cable, Minneapolis, MN, producer, 1982-85; KTCA, Twin Cities Public Television, Minneapolis/St. Paul, producer, 1985-89, senior producer, community affairs, 1989--.

Selected awards Recipient of numerous production and directorial awards, including three Cable ACE Awards for *Legacy of Tears, A Red Star in Minnesota,* and *Questions of Racism;* American Film and Video Festival Red Ribbon for *A Red Star in Minnesota;* Chicago International Film Festival Certificate of Merit, Page One Journalism Award, both for *Questions of Racism;* Chicago International Film Festival Gold Hugo, New York International Film and Television Festival Bronze Medal, and Houston Worldfest Gold Award, all for *Diary Series;* Houston Worldfest Certificate of Merit for *Can We All Get Along?;* Chicago International Film Festival Gold Plaque for *Understanding Hate;* Chicago International Film Festival Silver Plaque for *Apart and Together;* Corporation for Public Broadcasting Gold Award, Chicago International Film Festival Certificate of Merit, both for *Get Over It.*

Addresses: *Office*–Twin Cities Public Television, 172 E. Fourth St., St. Paul, MN 55101

don't necessary have the experience in yet," he told *CBB.*

In 1979, Byrd secured an assistant director position at the Minnesota Civil Liberties Union, a branch of the national organization that defends the freedoms guaranteed in the U.S. Constitution's Bill of Rights. His responsibilities included managing the fundraising, member recruitment, and literature distribution efforts, as well as

coordinating press activity for guest speakers. Though he had been promoted to associate director, Byrd soon began to feel the pull of creative endeavor and decided it was time to take a shot at his dream of becoming a filmmaker.

Embarked on Filmmaking Career

In 1982, Byrd convinced a local cable company executive to give him a position as a producer. He put in 16-hour days at Continental Cable, learning the craft of filmmaking. He completed his first documentary, *Legacy of Tears,* the same year. The film recounts the experience of the Hmong, an ethnic minority in the Southeast Asian country of Laos who were caught in the crossfire of the Vietnam War. Byrd summarized their story in an interview with *CBB:* "The Hmong were primarily recruited by the [Central Intelligence Agency] CIA, to rescue downed American pilots flying secret, and basically illegal, missions against the communists in Cambodia and Laos. Eventually they were involved in direct combat against Vietnamese communists who made their way into the mountainous regions of Laos." The film won a Cable ACE Award--virtually unheard of for a local cable company production--and helped establish Byrd's name as a producer and director.

This success led Minneapolis/St. Paul's PBS station to recruit Byrd in 1985 to produce community projects such as talk shows, town meetings, and documentaries. In 1987, Byrd produced and directed a documentary for KTCA entitled *Torture: The Shadow of a Beast,* which premiered on the Discovery channel and was broadcast on 16 major market PBS stations. The film portrayed the personal and social effects of politically-motivated torture and was selected for an exhibit called *Beyond Interrogation* at the Maryland Institute of Arts. A number of other award-winning documentaries followed--at least one a year through 1993--including *A Red Star in Minnesota,* chronicling then-Soviet leader Mikhail Gorbachev's 1988 visit to Minnesota.

Produced Award-winning Documentaries

Byrd's work pace increased in 1990, when KTCA selected him to produce in a single year a three-part series on the everyday lives of black, Asian, and Native American Minnesotans. *Diary: Black Minnesotans* featured people from various walks of life with differing social perspectives. John Lyght, Minnesota's only black sheriff--and one of only a handful nationwide--talks of his acceptance within his rural town and his view that disadvantaged blacks need to earn respect through honest work instead of complaining that society is holding them back. In contrast, Philip True, a Minneapolis computer engineer who gives gang-oriented and at-risk youth training in computer skills and workplace expectations, believes that American society is failing these kids. He agrees, however, that young people have to take charge of their own future, in spite of the obstacles. The series won awards at international film festivals in New York City, Chicago, and Houston, as well as Regional Emmy awards for editing and camera work.

The following year Byrd produced and cohosted *Can We All Get Along?,* an hour-long program featuring 27 ethnically and socially diverse people with varied educational backgrounds engaged in a dialogue about racially charged matters. Ranging in age from 16 to 70-something, the participants tackled such potent topics as institutional racism, affirmative action, slavery, and the Holocaust--the Nazi Germany-led genocide of millions of Jews during World War II. A moving experience, *Asian Pages* reported that "this enlightening conversation delves into deep emotions, and smiles become winces as the truth is peeled back in layers and reality strikes painful chords."

Interpreting the passionate sentiments unearthed by the debate, Byrd commented in *Asian Pages,* "It seems that what we're going through in this country is a severe identity crisis because everybody wants to know who they are. We've come up with all these terms to define ourselves. But the question is: `Are those terms dividing us?'" Though *Can We All Get Along?* does not provide a definitive answer, it does, as Byrd further noted, initiate "an exchange of views and experiences to find out more about how people feel about a problem [racial tension] that's tearing at the American fabric."

Byrd continued his look at the United States' ethnic identity with *Apart and Together,* an examination of race relations that received a Silver Plaque award at the Chicago International Film Festival in 1993. The piece began with two separate discussions on race in the United States, one among whites only and the other among blacks. Byrd then brought the two groups together for a discussion he described as, "at times explosive and at other times revealing." He told *CBB* that this format was the only way to get people--especially whites--to be completely honest about their views on race.

Probed Gay and Lesbian Life

After producing and directing *Get Over It,* an award-winning two-hour documentary on the 1993 Gay and Lesbian March on Washington, Byrd followed with

Generation Q, the "youth" segment of a four-part series on the gay and lesbian civil rights movement entitled *A Question of Equality.* Financed by Britain's Channel Four and the Independent Television Service, 1995's *Generation Q* portrayed in poignant detail the lives of gay and lesbian teenagers, a number of whom attended an alternative Los Angeles high school for gay and lesbian students. Named after Harvey Milk, the San Francisco gay activist who was murdered by a city councilman, the Harvey Milk School was founded to provide an accepting environment for a teen population that drops out of school at an alarmingly high rate.

In a departure from Byrd's earlier documentaries, *Generation Q* lacked a narrator, instead focusing almost exclusively on kids telling their stories and expressing their frustrations, with an occasional comment by a teacher or parent. Byrd described this technique as part of a new, less intrusive approach to documentary filmmaking that lets the subject matter speak for itself. Nevertheless, Byrd expected much of the inevitable negative reaction to the *Question of Equality* series to be directed at his segment because it deals with young people. "Young people speaking their minds forcefully--I think some will be threatened by that. It's different in Britain where, sexually repressed and proper as they are, you can discuss issues like this more easily, as long as you do it intelligently," he told *CBB.*

> "We've come up with all these terms to define ourselves. But the question is: `Are those terms dividing us?'"

In fact, the British backers of *Generation Q* were so impressed with Byrd's work that in mid-1995 they were exploring the possibility of financing a feature film directed by Byrd that would be a departure from his previous documentary work. Other projects Byrd had in progress in the mid-1990s included a documentary on a 12-year-old boy badly disfigured in a fire at the age of three. "Basically the piece looks at how he navigates his way through a world that rejects and fears him, due to his appearance," Byrd said in an interview with *CBB.* He was also completing a half-hour talk show follow-up to the fall of 1995 national broadcast of *Hoop Dreams*--the popular documentary about the professional basketball aspirations of two Chicago boys--in which the filmmakers talk with the young men and their families about their lives since the film was made.

Selected documentaries

Legacy of Tears, Continental Cable, 1982.
Torture: The Shadow of a Beast, 1987.
A Red Star in Minnesota, 1988.
Questions of Racism, KTCA, 1989.
Diary Series, KTCA, 1990.
Can We All Get Along? KTCA, 1991.
Understanding Hate, KTCA, 1992.
Apart and Together, KTCA, 1993.
Get Over It, KTCA, 1993.
Generation Q, Independent Television Service and
    Channel Four (Britain), 1995.

Sources

Asian Pages, October 14, 1992, p. 8.
Minneapolis Star Tribune, November 5, 1991, p. 6E;
    November 26, 1991, p. 6E; January 7, 1993, p.
    12E; September 20, 1993, p. 10E.

Additional information for this profile was obtained from
a *CBB* interview with Byrd in June of 1995.

—*John F. Packel, II*

Mandy Carter

1946—

Civil rights activist

"Prejudice is prejudice!," proclaimed Mandy Carter in an interview with *Contemporary Black Biography (CBB),* "whether it is based on skin color or sexual orientation. And maybe the best folks to be making this point are gays and lesbians of color who embody both." Carter has been, in the words of *BLK* writer Frankie Lennon, "one of the few highly placed African American lesbians." As such she has waged a ceaseless battle against homophobia, organizing against efforts of the religious right to infiltrate black churches and attempting to unseat ultraconservative politicians like North Carolina senator Jesse Helms. Carter described her mission to Lennon as "trying to make change for the better of all. I am committed to standing up for rights, fighting oppression and taking risks."

Carter was born in Albany, New York, in 1948. Raised in two orphanages and the Schenectady Children's Home—a foster home--she had "no opportunity to identify myself as unique or have that idea conveyed to me from a parental figure," she told Lennon. "With so many of us in the home, it was about being competitive to stand out from the crowd and be noticed." Despite the disadvantages of this environment, Carter excelled in school and was able to enroll at Hudson Valley Community College in Troy, New York.

Carter pursued "basic pre-med courses" in hopes of becoming a doctor or physical education instructor; at Hudson Valley she planned to gather the necessary credits to gain acceptance into a four-year institution. Her high school grade point average had been lowered dramatically by a failing grade in Spanish, which necessitated the detour to a two-year college. In retrospect, Carter mused to *CBB,* "that F in Spanish is partly responsible for my being an activist. It turned out to be a good thing!"

Involved With 1960s Activism

After one year at Hudson Valley, Carter reported, "[school] became unappealing to me. I was living at the YWCA in downtown Troy, and it felt like I was back at the home again." She dropped out in 1967, and, with less than $100 to her name, made her way to New York City. It was there—broke and reduced to sleeping in

At a Glance . . .

Born November 2, 1948, in Albany, NY; raised in orphanages and foster care. *Education:* Attended Hudson Valley Community College.

Worked with War Resister's League, beginning c. 1969; served on planning committees for North Carolina Lesbian and Gay Pride marches, 1986-91; served on national steering committee for March on Washington for Lesbians and Gays, 1987 and 1993; coproducer of Rhythm Fest musical festival for southern women; director of North Carolina Senate Vote '90 and North Carolina Mobilization '96 (initiatives to defeat N.C. senator Jesse Helms); founding member, Our Own Place (a lesbian center) and black gay and lesbian organization UMOJA. Member of Stonewall 25 executive committee; member of board of governors of Black Gay and Lesbian Leadership Forum; former member of board of directors of Human Rights Campaign Fund.

Awards: North Carolina Lesbian and Gay Pride Community Service Award, 1990; Peace Award, War Resister's League, 1993; Distinguished National Service Award, Gay and Lesbian Attorneys of Washington, D.C., 1993; Mab Segrest Award, North Carolinians Against Religious and Racist Violence (NCARRV); humanitarian award, *North Carolina Independent.*

Addresses: *Office*—North Carolina Mobilization '96, P.O. Box 28718, Raleigh, NC 27611.

Central Park—that she happened on the headquarters of the League for Spiritual Discovery, an organization founded by radical philosopher and psychedelic drug champion Timothy Leary. "I went in and asked if I could answer phones in exchange for food and a couch to sleep on," Carter told *BLK's* Lennon. "They agreed, and I stayed there the whole summer. It was the height of the hippie flower-child movement—a fascinating time to be in New York. Near the end of the summer, I met some people who were migrating to San Francisco. I went with them."

In San Francisco Carter became involved in the struggle against the war in Vietnam; taking shelter with draft resistance advocate Vince O'Connor, she quickly became versed in the tactics of the movement. Still, the

principles of civil disobedience—non-violent resistance to perceived injustice—were not exactly new to her. "I was first exposed to the idea by some Quakers who came to my high school," she noted in *BLK*. "Something about those ideas—working for change, activism, non-violence—intrigued me." And though Carter has kept mum about specific relationships in interviews, she allowed to *CBB* that she first came out about her sexuality to her War Resister's League (WRL) comrades in 1969; she said, "I wanted them to know that I was a lesbian."

Several people Carter cites as inspirations gained prominence during those tumultuous days of the 1960s, among them singer Joan Baez, civil rights activist Bayard Rustin—whose homosexuality marginalized him even within the movement—and two women she met in the WRL, Irma Zigas and Norma Becker, who she said "showed that women can be dynamic leaders." During the course of the following decades Carter herself learned a lot about becoming a dynamic leader. Staying on at the WRL office in San Francisco and then moving to its Los Angeles headquarters, she learned much about not only activism but fundraising. 1977 saw Carter return to San Francisco, at which time she became involved in the gay and lesbian political movement, which was flowering in the city's bars.

Immersed in Gay and Lesbian Causes

A central figure in the city's lesbian political movement was Rikki Streicher, who owned two popular bars. "Rikki felt a bar was more than a place to drink," Carter told *BLK*. "It was a place where women gathered and it was the center of activity. She would encourage me to sit in on these meetings to plan things like the Lesbian and Gay Pride Parade. I was able to use my organizing skills, and I became more and more drawn to doing things in the community." In 1982 she returned to her native North Carolina, where she worked at WRL's southeast office and served on the planning committee for the annual Lesbian and Gay Pride march; she later worked as a national steering coordinator for the 1987 lesbian and gay march on Washington. She also became actively involved in Rhythm Fest, an annual festival of music, art, and politics for southern women.

Despite the stereotype of the South as a bastion of bigotry, Carter praised its mellow pace and "balmy weather." Besides, she pointed out, "it is home to the most important movement ever to come down the pike in this country—the civil rights movement." She added that southerners are at least honest about their views, while people in the North tend to be "polite but still biased and prejudiced."

Still, Carter has long disdained any idea of separatism. "Mainstream electoral politics do matter," she insisted to *CBB*. "While we are waiting for something better to come along to replace our two-party system, what we now have keeps rolling along whether we--blacks, gays, and lesbians--are there or not. If we want to impact change electorally then we must be at the table no matter how uncomfortable it is." Understanding that blacks and gays have long been set against one another in mainstream politics, Carter has set about making her mark.

One important battle was the effort to unseat North Carolina senator Jesse Helms, an ultraconservative Republican who championed segregationism in his early days and battled affirmative action and other anti-discrimination remedies in his later ones. Carter served as campaign director of North Carolina Senate Vote '90, the project to defeat Helms. To her dismay, she found that James Meredith—the first black student to attend the University of Mississippi and an important symbol in the history of desegregation—was working for Helms, who narrowly won re-election.

Equally unsettling, Carter learned of a white gay man who despised Helms but couldn't bear to vote for his black opponent, Harvey Gantt. "I was just blown away," she reflected in *Uncommon Heroes: A Celebration of Heros and Role Models for Gay and Lesbian Americans*. "Maybe that's why the vote was so close." Yet this loss was instructive for Carter. To beat Helms, she declared to *CBB*, "We are going to have to get all of our respective voters out—the arts, environment, choice, lgbt [lesbians, gays, bisexuals, and "transgender" people], people of color, youth, [and] senior citizens."

Resisting the Right

Carter's other large-scale battle of the 1990s has involved fighting the attempts of right-wing Christian groups to foment and exploit anti-gay feeling in the black church. Appointed by the gay rights organization the Human Rights Campaign Fund (HRCF) as its liaison to the National Black Gay and Lesbian Leadership Forum, she has waged a tireless battle against well-funded conservatives who tell blacks that white gay men are usurping the civil rights struggle to gain "special rights." Discussing the matter with the *Philadelphia Tribune*, Carter reflected on the right's "classic divide

and conquer [strategy]," explaining, "When they start going into the community, besides going into the church, they start talking about 'gays have this and gays have that.'" Among the arguments harbored by conservatives, according to Carter: "It [homosexuality] is immoral; they are taking jobs away from you; they are trying to hijack the civil rights movement of the '60s."

Unfortunately, even the most dedicated campaign can be hamstrung by a lack of funds. "In 1993 the HRCF sent me to Cincinnati to help fight an anti-gay ballot initiative in Ohio," Carter recalled in *Uncommon Heroes*. "Colorado for Family Values [a conservative organization] poured $400,000 into their campaign. They outspent us at Equality in Cincinnati nearly ten to one. They got one minister to be the 'official' black voice of faith. He spoke out against 'the wealthy, white gay men who want special rights.' Well, guess what. We lost."

Carter told *CBB* that she was disheartened to find that one of her early idols, civil rights leader Rev. James Bevel, was among those black clerics friendly with the religious right. But her most persistent opponent has been the Rev. Lou Sheldon of the Traditional Values Coalition. Sheldon has recruited numerous black religious figures into his movement, circulating anti-gay videos and utilizing the slogan "There Is No Comparison"—insisting that the black struggle for civil rights and the gay struggle for equal protection under the law share no commonalities. "That, in a snapshot, showed why this movement must be more multiracial," Carter opined to *HRCF Quarterly*. She claimed that in general, "the black community opposes all discrimination, but there are some who side with the right. Sheldon has created a small but very vocal group."

> "People were hung from trees for being black. Today, people are beaten up and murdered for being gay and lesbian. Any black person who can't equate being gay with being black is essentially denying that gay and lesbian black people exist."

In *Uncommon Heroes,* Carter attempted to dispense with the "no comparison" argument by appealing to history. "People were hung from trees for being black," she noted. "Today, people are beaten up and murdered for being gay and lesbian. Any black person who can't equate being gay with being black is essentially denying that gay and lesbian black people exist." In her interview with the *Philadelphia Tribune,* she went on to indict the entire conservative movement. "It is not just the anti-gay agenda that they are after," Carter emphasized. "They are up there now talking about welfare reform, they are talking about affirmative action, they are talking about crime. And most times they are coming after us in the black community; yet they want to use us in the anti-gay stuff, then turn around and come after us in terms of their other agendas."

For that reason, she ventured in *BLK,* black gays and lesbians are ideally suited to fight against such encroachments. "This struggle is going to give us the opportunity to do some actual coalition work," she ventured. "But we've absolutely got to come out standing strong to serve them notice. We're the ones that have to make this happen. Sometimes you have to be bold and take a risk." At the same time, Carter wondered why "the African American gay community doesn't, in the mid-90s, have a national organization on the level of HRCF or the National Gay and Lesbian Task Force [NGLTF] with the capacity to pay staff for their work as professionals? We need to be doing something about that."

Even in the midst of her intense schedule, Carter acknowledged to *CBB* that she has no intention of doing such feverish work forever. "I have led a very exciting and fulfilling activist life over these past 28 years," she noted, "but I definitely can feel myself slowing down and wanting to settle down here in North Carolina now." She added that many of her peers, approaching age 50, feel the same way: "Many of us are thinking about how we want to live out our senior years. Many in the lgbt community don't see retirement homes as an option compared to coming up with our own ideas of where and when we live out our golden years." It seems likely that Mandy Carter's talents for organization and mobilization will come to bear on this issue as well—when the time comes.

Sources

Books

Uncommon Heroes: A Celebration of Heroes and Role Models for Gay and Lesbian Americans, edited by Samuel Bernstein, Fletcher Press, 1994.

Periodicals

BLK, February 1994, pp. 7-19.
HRCF Quarterly, Summer 1995, p. 4.
Philadelphia Tribune, April 28, 1995, p. 3A.

Additional information for this profile was obtained by *CBB* via e-mail with Mandy Carter in December of 1995 and from biographical materials provided by the National Black Gay and Lesbian Leadership Forum, 1995.

—Simon Glickman

Malcolm CasSelle and E. David Ellington

Computer entrepreneurs

Best known as the founders of NetNoir Online, a service that bills itself as "The Cybergateway to Afrocentric Culture," E. David Ellington and Malcolm CasSelle have created perhaps the highest-profile minority new media enterprise. By establishing a black-oriented site on the net, the two entrepreneurs have provided a versatile new forum for the discovery and discussion of African American culture. Yet the online service is only the beginning of what they hope will be a plethora of new media endeavors. "There will be plenty of other Afrocentric sites or black sites" on the internet, Ellington insisted in an interview with *Contemporary Black Biography*. "And I have no problem with that. The issue is, there has to be a leading site, and we think we're in a position to create that brand name. And we're determined to do that."

Ellington was born in the Harlem section of New York City. His parents divorced when he was seven, and he was raised primarily by his mother, who worked in social services at an affiliate of the Urban League and elsewhere. His father died when he was 15. It was around this time that Ellington began to see his career path. While living in Connecticut he took sailing lessons from a black man whom he described as "a guy on a boat who had an M.B.A. and a J.D., and I thought that was the killer combination. I needed to get that. And sure enough, that was my motivation for deciding to go for it."

Ellington's Circuitous Education

Ellington's education would not be a straight line to law, however. He earned his undergraduate degree at Adelphi University, then acquired a master's at the historically black college Howard, studying African politics. He also interned in the government, working for the House Subcommittee on Africa and in the office of a congressional representative. "It was great and exciting," he noted of those experiences, adding that he realized, "the only way to be involved in politics is on the financing side. I decided the best way to be effective in politics was to go to the private sector, make a chunk of money, and come back." With this knowledge in hand, he took a job with the telemarketing arm of Public Interest Communications, an organization championing progressive political, social, and environmental causes.

Ellington had intended to move to Africa during these years, but this plan never came to fruition. Instead, after applying to law school, he took the $1,500 his stepfather had willed him and used it to travel to Europe. While there he found out he'd been accepted to Georgetown University's law school; he chose to have his enrollment deferred so that he could earn some money before enrolling. Several months after his return from Europe, he decided to travel to Japan. Ellington spent four months there, teaching English and studying Karate. Instead of going straight back to the States, however, he returned by way of Asia.

At a Glance . . .

Malcolm CasSelle, born March 22, 1970, in Allentown, PA; parents were in the food business. *Education:* Bachelor's degree in computer science, Massachusetts Institute of Technology (MIT); attended MIT Japan Program; master's degree in computer science, Stanford University.

Worked for Schroders Securities and NTT Software Labs, Tokyo, Japan; worked for Apple computer, Inc. as market researcher and programmer; served as director of digital publishing and marketing for Blast Publishing and *Morph's Outpost on the Digital Frontier*; launched NetNoir Inc. with E. David Ellington, 1995, and served as chief technology officer.

E. David Ellington, born July 10, 1960, in New York, NY; mother was a social worker. *Education:* Bachelor's degree, Adelphi University, c. 1981; master's degree, Howard University, c. 1983; law degree, Georgetown University.

Served on House Subcommittee on Africa and worked in the office of a U.S. congressman, early 1980s; traveled in Europe, Japan, China, and India, among other locales, 1980s; worked for telemarketing department of Public Interest Communications; worked as law clerk for McKenna & Cuneo, Los Angeles; practiced at law firms specializing in entertainment law; established the Law Offices of E. David Ellington, Los Angeles, early 1990s; chaired international law section of Beverly Hills Bar Association; launched new media company NetNoir Inc. with Malcolm CasSelle, 1995, and served as chief executive officer.

Addresses: *Office*—NetNoir Inc., 564 Mission St., Unit 4, San Francisco, CA 94105.

After graduating from law school Ellington began studying Japanese in a concentrated language program at Cornell, then moved to California. He intended to focus on Pacific Rim trade issues in his law practice, but he soon took another detour. He worked at two firms specializing in entertainment law—with an emphasis on music—and then opened his own Los Angeles offices.

There he focused on international entertainment law, but he also handled a fair share of cases relating to multimedia and new technology.

CasSelle: Legos, TinkerToys, and Computers

Through a mutual friend, Ellington met Malcolm CasSelle, a brilliant computer science graduate student at Stanford who had worked in Japan. Raised on a Pennsylvania farm, CasSelle—whose family sold fresh foods around the state—developed a passion in childhood for building with Legos and TinkerToys; he discovered the joy of computers in high school. "I wrote programs and played with the computer constantly," he told *CBB*, adding that he'd helped do the layout for his school's yearbook. "Eventually I got my own Apple II computer and got much deeper into programming." Though CasSelle "hated to study," he earned good grades as an undergrad at the Massachusetts Institute of Technology (MIT) and entered its Japan Program. "I left for Japan three days after graduating," he recalled.

In Tokyo CasSelle worked at Schroders Securities and NTT Software Labs; on his return to the U.S. he took a job with Apple Computer. After earning his master's at Stanford he occupied the position of director of digital publishing and marketing for Blast Publishing, among other new media posts. It was he who introduced Ellington to the wonders of cyberspace. "I'd always been interested in technology," the latter noted, "but only things I thought were cool, and passing fads and fancies." CasSelle remembers finding Ellington "intelligent, well-travelled, and serious," with "a deep personal history and strong points of view." He stated to *CBB*, "David and I immediately bonded and became like brothers."

"When Malcolm and I went to new-media seminars and conferences," Ellington related in *Essence,* "I saw the business and cultural opportunity and convinced Malcolm that was the best next thing to do." Together, they decided to undertake a black-oriented online site. Ellington wrote an overview in 1994, and they began plotting their business strategy. They gathered funding from various sources, notably the Greenhouse Program of America Online (AOL), one of the nation's most popular providers of online content.

The Greenhouse fund was specifically designed to assist trepreneurs in cyberspace. Ellington told *Essence* that two days after executive Ted Leonsis announced the creation of the fund, Ellington made an appointment with him. Leonsis and his associates "thought NetNoir was a brilliant idea. They provided us with seed capital, in-kind support, and distribution." With the assistance of business planner Marcelino Ford-Livene and finance expert Gregory Mays, the intrepid pair set about assembling what Ellington described to *CBB* as "a full-blown, top-shelf service."

Launched NetNoir Online

In 1995 the San Francisco-based NetNoir Online became available on AOL; users could enter the keyword "NetNoir" and explore a wide range of news, information, and message areas, or electronic bulletin boards. Divided into music, sports, education, and business departments, the service channeled content from *VIBE* magazine, Motown Records, and the clothing company Blue Marlin, among other concerns. A "fact sheet" released by NetNoir claimed, "The core customer will be college-educated, urban or suburban, hip, between 18-40, and male and female." Other materials noted

that purchasers of Afrocentric merchandise were predominantly white males.

With the enthusiastic participation of well-known figures like journalist Charlayne Hunter-Gault and athlete Carl Lewis, NetNoir rapidly demonstrated that it would not be following anyone else's lead. In July, Hunter-Gault managed to set up an online interview with Haitian president Jean-Bertrand Aristide. "It was a blackculture that was the first to do this," Ellington hastened to remind *The Progressive.* "If that's not forward-looking, I don't know what is."

Ellington—much of whose time during the service's first year was spent raising money, while CasSelle served as "chief technology officer," as the company's press materials put it—posted a letter to users each month. Surveying the electronic mail he'd received, he noted in his July letter that "65 percent of the mail was purely congratulatory" and that the 30 percent that "pointed out some of our shortcomings" was still upbeat and

Malcolm CasSelle

E. David Ellington

encouraging. "The final 5 percent (approx.) sought our destruction," he remarked wryly, deeming this "a surprisingly low percentage."

Some of the approving words were more public; *Los Angeles Times* writer David Colker enthused in his "Cyburbia" column about the quality of the prose he'd seen on NetNoir, adding that if the service "continues on this path and explores topics in more depth, it will surely be a model for how cyberspace can wrest itself out of adolescence, grow up and get a far richer life." *Fortune* magazine named NetNoir, Inc. one of its "25 Cool Companies" of the year.

A Philosophy of Inclusion

"You don't have to be black to participate," Ellington told *USA Today;* he observed in *The Progressive* that although some non-blacks using the discussion boards have been disruptive, he's made an effort to discourage insular thinking among regular users of the service. "From time to time I have to go on-line and say, 'Hey, ya'll cool out for a while," he explained. "If your interests are genuine, and you want to support and celebrate Afrocentric culture, then come on in here. If you want to debate affirmative action, I want you to be here." CasSelle, in an interview with *CityBeat,* elaborated: "Our goal is to be *in*clusive, not exclusive. We are creating a place for anyone of any race to come in and enjoy Afrocentric culture."

> "The internet, as a low-cost, multimedia channel for communication, provides an opportunity for many people to rapidly experience our culture. This opportunity can cause a shift in our thinking and perspective on humanity. We are in the middle of a re-evolution."

Even so, Ellington declared to *CBB,* the message bulletin boards and other services are merely "another tool and another option for users to take advantage of. If they don't choose to, then I don't worry about it. I get upset if there's an opportunity for us to do something and we

don't provide the mechanism or the tool to do it." He added that he wanted NetNoir Online to remain politically neutral rather than advance his agenda; his primary goal is that it collect information and reflect the insights of users. "I want our service to grow organically and not just be my vision exclusively. How could it be? There's no one voice for all of black America or the entire Afrocentric community."

NetNoir Online, however innovative, is only the first public venture for NetNoir New Media. While the story of NetNoir in 1995 was the funding of its "mission" by minority investors and AOL, Ellington announced in his first 1996 President's Letter that its story in the new year would be "the execution of its mission on the World Wide Web—the ultimate distribution platform." He promised more participation in chat rooms by NetNoir staff, including a weekly "Founder's Chat," and more news, as per users' requests. But Ellington hastened to remind *CBB* that the company had other fish to fry. "Our whole service is called NetNoir New Media Services, and through it we consult and do other projects," which may include CD-ROMs and designing and hosting web sites. "I think there's a great deal of opportunity for us, being a minority vendor, with many companies out here in Silicon Valley."

Asked by *CityBeat* what advice he had for black youth, CasSelle replied, "Education, education, education. Be inquisitive and focus your ambition. I didn't know exactly where I was going even a year ago, but I did have a sense of how to put my skills to work. And somehow the opportunity found me." The opportunities have been such, in fact, that they've left him thus far without much of a social life. "I live by myself in a warehouse," he informed *CBB.* "I don't have time for a girlfriend, but I love meeting new people." Ellington's personal saga is similar; he noted that he had "a very serious girlfriend," and while his intense work schedule "is straining on my relationship, she's also in new media, so that helps."

CasSelle waxed prophetic in describing the impact of new media on African American culture, and on American society in general: "Afrocentric culture is deeply profound and affects everyone who comes in contact with it," he proclaimed. "The internet, as a low-cast, multimedia channel for communication, provides an opportunity for many people to rapidly experience our culture. This opportunity can cause a shift in our thinking and perspective on humanity. We are in the middle of a re-evolution." In *Essence* he expressed satisfaction with the dialogue he'd seen online, reporting, "When I go into the service I'm excited to see the quality of discussion in our chat rooms and on our message boards, and to see how people have embraced our service. Response to NetNoir has been very positive."

Ellington, too, keeps his eye on the horizon—and on the bottom line. "I had no idea it would cost this much money to run a company on a regular basis," he divulged to *CBB*. "You run out of money very quickly, so you have to keep figuring out ways to either raise money or increase revenues. My job is to maintain standards, providing a full-blown, top-shelf service. That's all I really want to focus on; I think that's the best I can do."

Sources

CityBeat, August 3, 1995.
Essence, November 1995, p. 42.
Los Angeles Times, June 30, 1995, pp. E2-E3.
Progressive, September 1995, p. 13.
USA Today, May 18, 1995, p. 7D.

Additional information for this profile was obtained through a *CBB* interview with Malcolm CasSelle and E. David Ellington in January of 1996 and by materials provided by NetNoir Inc. and obtained from NetNoir Online.

—Simon Glickman

Manno Charlemagne

1948—

Haitian folk singer, politician

People in the United States chuckled when former entertainer Sonny Bono was elected mayor of a California town. In Haiti, political events are rarely a source of amusement. Prior to 1995, Manno Charlemagne was one of Haiti's most popular singer-songwriters. However, his career took an ironic twist in July of that year when he was elected mayor of Haiti's largest city, Port-au-Prince. Charlemagne had spent his entire musical career writing and singing songs of protest against the oppressive regimes that had governed his country. Often, he paid for this agitation with beatings and imprisonment. His election victory raised a poignant question for politically oriented artists all over the world: Is it easier to affect political change from within a system or as an outsider?

Charlemagne was born in 1948, in one of the many impoverished sections of Port-au-Prince. Like many children in Haiti, he grew up largely on the streets, and it was there that he received his early political education. Rebellion, though brutally supressed, was constantly in the air. In a 1995 interview with *The Progressive*, Charlemagne recalled the 1956 overthrow of President Paul Magloire. He told of witnessing bloody battles and

the construction of homemade bombs by local agitators. This atmosphere of political unrest helped to shape the revolutionary outlook that Charlemagne articulated so clearly in his songs.

Battled Papa Doc's Regime

At the age of 15, Charlemagne was arrested and tortured after fighting with a member of the Tonton Macoutes, the notoriously brutal police force of Haitian dictator Francois (Papa Doc) Duvalier. Over the next several years, Charlemagne occupied himself with political activism. This period lasted until the end of the 1960s when, as he told Fernando Gonzalez of the *Boston Globe* in a 1992 interview, "there was a major political repression against intellectuals and everything that was cultural or political."

In the 1970s, Charlemagne began to hone his singing and songwriting skills as part of the *kilti libete,* or "freedom culture" groups that were emerging around Haiti. Rather than playing formal concerts, Charlemagne and other performers followed the troubadour

At a Glance . . .

Born Emmanuel Charlemagne, in 1948, in Port-au-Prince, Haiti. *Education:* Studied with Catholic priests. *Politics:* "Left-wing."

Singer and songwriter, c. 1970—; recorded first album, 1978; exiled from Haiti, 1980-1986; Mayor of Port-au-Prince, Haiti, 1995—.

Addresses: *Office*–Office of the Mayor, Port-au-Prince, Haiti.

tradition. They performed mainly on street corners and in other public places free of charge. In addition to original material, many of the songs Charlemagne and his comrades sang were reworkings of traditional songs with new words to fit the political conditions.

By 1977, government intimidation of Haitian artists had eased somewhat and Charlemagne was able to launch his performing career. He released his first album in 1978. The album, which combined the language of protest with beautiful music, was extremely popular among Haiti's poor and disenfranchised. Although Charlemagne's music was officially banned by the Haitian government, bootleg cassette tapes of his music were often available.

Spent Early '80s in Exile

In June of 1980, Charlemagne was in the middle of a performance when he was dragged off the stage by Haitian dictator Jean Claude Duvalier's henchmen. He was arrested and eventually deported. During the next several years, he spent most of his time in New York City, where he recorded three more albums. The albums, although popular among Haitians living in the United States, did not gain much of an audience among mainstream American listeners.

Charlemagne remained in exile until 1986, the year Jean Claude Duvalier's regime was ousted from power. He returned to Haiti and became one of the staunchest supporters of his close friend Jean-Bertrand Aristide's bid for the Haitian presidency. With the support of a gigantic populist movement, Aristide was elected president of Haiti in 1990. The following year, however, Aristide was overthrown in a military coup. Because of his close ties to Aristide, Charlemagne found himself in

a precarious position. Two weeks after the coup, police officers came to his home, beat him in front of his family, and threw him in prison. He was released after one week. However, as he left the prison, he was arrested again by another group of men in plain cloth es. Charlemagne was released again, and, fearing further abuse and imprisonment, sought refuge at the Argentine embassy.

Escaped With Celebrity Help

Charlemagne's plight caught the attention of many international human rights activists. Filmmaker Jonathan Demme assembled "Americans for Manno," an organization composed of concerned show business friends. The group, which included actors Robert DeNiro, Michelle Pfeiffer, and Paul Newman; directors Spike Lee and Woody Allen; and singer-songwriter Bob Dylan petitioned Haitian prime minister Jean-Jacques Honorat on Charlemagne's behalf. Former U.S. Attorney General Ramsay Clark also came to Charlemagne's aid. Charlemagne was finally allowed to leave Haiti on December 29, 1991. He later credited Demme's celebrity crusaders with saving his life.

> "As president, you are the guy that people are always focusing on, and I prefer to be the guy down below, pointing his finger."

During his second exile, Charlemagne continued to perform regularly while waiting for the opportunity to return to Haiti. He spent most of his time in cities with large Haitian populations such as Miami and New York City in the United States and Montreal, Canada. He also attempted to broaden his appeal to English-speaking audiences by singing songs in English, rather than his native Creole. American listeners tended to refer to him as the "Haitian Bob Dylan," or the "Haitian Bob Marley" the latter in reference to the Jamaican singer-songwriter. Although neither of those comparisons held water musically, they did accurately reflect the element of protest in his songs.

Charlemagne's appearance and musical style generally gave no hint of the passionate message behind his music. On stage, he usually looked like a peasant. Fernando Gonzalez of the *Boston Globe* described Charlemagne's singing voice as "dark, robust, but small." Charlemagne frequently described himself and his art as "anti-imperialist." In several of his songs, he criticized French and American interference in Haiti's affairs. His musical style also draws from the African storytelling tradition, which is an essential mode of communication in a country like Haiti, where much of the population is illiterate.

Traded Concert Stage for Political Office

With the support of the U.S. government and armed forces, Aristide was returned to power in 1994. Aristide's reinstallation as president allowed Charlemagne to return again to Haiti. In 1995, Charlemagne decided to take his political activism in a new direction by running for mayor of Port-au-Prince, an office considered by many to be the country's second most powerful. According to the Reuters news service, Charlemagne spent most of the campaign at home in New York City and on tour in Europe. He generated support by distributing flyers containing his picture and guitar logo throughout Port-au-Prince. Although Aristide did not officially endorse either Charlemagne or the incumbent Evans Paul, Charlemagne was widely perceived as having Aristide's backing because of their long association. He won the election with 45 percent of the vote, to Paul's 18 percent. Charlemagne's landslide victory caught the U.S. government by surprise, since Paul was generally considered to be the logical successor to Aristide as president in 1996. Paul claimed that the election was tainted by widespread fraud.

As mayor of Port-au-Prince, Charlemagne found the transition from rebel to political insider a difficult one. He was accustomed to simply speaking out against whatever he thought was wrong, rather than seeking solutions to these injustices. Diplomacy, a trait that did not come naturally to Charlemagne, was often necessary in order to get things accomplished. He also found that the funds required to meet his objectives, which included improving schools and health care in poor neighborhoods, simply did not exist. Although he remained close to Aristide, Charle-

magne was frequently critical of his old friend and many of his associates. He accused Aristide of withholding funds—under instruction from the U.S. government—to which the mayor's office was entitled. He believed that the U.S. State Department wanted to make trouble for him because of his left-wing views. Charlemagne also felt that Aristide was incapable of ridding his own Lavalas party of corruption.

Even with Aristide back in power, the political situation in Haiti remained volatile. In November of 1995, Port-au Prince's city hall was strafed with gunfire in an attempt to intimidate Charlemagne as national elections approached. However, Charlemagne refused to be cowed. Frustrated with administrative solutions to problems, Charlemagne began planning fund-raising concerts to raise money for his programs. While Evans Paul had seen the mayor's office as a springboard to bigger things, Charlemagne emphatically denied any interest in holding a higher office. In a *New York Times* interview, he told Larry Rohter that, "As president, you are the guy that people are always focusing on, and I prefer to be the guy down here, pointing his finger." If Haiti's struggle for democracy is to ultimately succeed, Manno Charlemagne's eloquent fingerpointing will have had something to do with it.

Selected discography

La Fimen
(With others)*Konbit: Burning Rhythms of Haiti,* 1987.

Sources

Boston Globe, May 1, 1992, p. 59; July 14, 1995, p. 2.
Los Angeles Times, July 14, 1995, p. A13.
New York Times, March 8, 1992, sec. 2, p. 31; October 17, 1995, p. A4.
Progressive, January 1995, p. 16.
Vibe, November 1994, p. 33.
Village Voice, November 19, 1991, p. 90.
Wisconsin State Journal, November 19, 1995, p. 9A.

—Robert R. Jacobson

Johnnie Cochran

1937—

Attorney

Johnnie L. Cochran, Jr. led the winning team of lawyers in the "trial of the century," and in the process became arguably the most famous lawyer in the world. Cochran's successful defense of former football great O. J. Simpson against charges of murder in the televised trial was followed by millions of Americans. Although his trial tactics are still sparking debate, his legal acumen and ability to sway a jury have characterized his legal career. In fact, the *People v. O. J. Simpson* is only the most recent and most visible of a string of Cochran's courtroom victories, some involving superstars such as Michael Jackson and others involving ordinary people thrust into extraordinary circumstances. *Ebony* magazine once described Cochran as "a litigator who'd taken the cases people said he might win when hell freezes over, then laughed all the way to the bank when the multimillion-dollar verdicts came rolling in."

Handsome and well-spoken, Cochran was established in the West-Coast power elite well prior to his defense of O. J. Simpson. Today he is more sought-after than ever as both an attorney and a celebrity. If he is detested in some circles as an opportunist, he is just as widely admired as a black American success story. Cochran told *Essence* that he has never been bothered by his detractors. "I have learned not to be thin-skinned, especially when I think I'm doing the right thing," he said. "It's not about money, it's about using the law as a device for change."

Johnnie Cochran, Jr. was born in 1937 in Shreveport, Louisiana, and is the great-grandson of a slave. He grew up in a stable and prosperous family, with a father and mother who stressed education, independence, and a color-blind attitude. While Cochran was still young the family moved to Los Angeles, and he attended public schools there, earning excellent grades. Although his father had a good job with the Golden State Mutual Life Insurance Company, Cochran always managed to find friends who had more money and more luxuries than he did. "If you were a person who integrated well, as I was, you got to go to people's houses and envision another life," he recalled in *The American Lawyer*. "I knew kids who had things I could only dream of. I remember going to someone's house and seeing a swimming pool. I was like, `That's great!' Another guy had an archery range in his loft. An archery range! I could not believe it. I had

At a Glance . . .

Born Johnnie L. Cochran, Jr. on October 2, 1937, in Shreveport, LA; son of Johnnie L. (an insurance company executive) and Hattie Cochran; married, second wife's name, Dale; children: (first marriage) Tiffany, Melodie; (with Patricia Cochran) Jonathan. *Education:* University of California, Los Angeles, B.A., 1959; Loyola Marymount University School of Law, J.D., 1962. *Politics:* Democrat. *Religion:* Baptist.

Attorney, 1963–. Deputy city attorney for the City of Los Angeles, 1963-65; private attorney, 1965-78; assistant district attorney, Los Angeles County, 1978-82; private attorney and head of law firm, 1982–. Former adjunct professor of law at University of California, Los Angeles School of Law and Loyola University School of Law. Chairman of rules committee, Democratic National Convention, 1984. Served on special congressional committee for ethics and official conduct.

Member: American Bar Association, American College of Trial Lawyers, YMCA, American Civil Liberties Union.

Selected awards Trumpet Award, Turner Broadcasting System, 1995.

Addresses: *Office*–4929 Wilshire Blvd., Suite 1010, Los Angeles, CA 90010.

never thought about archery! But it made me get off my butt and say, `Hey, I can do this!'"

Law Career Beckoned

Cochran earned a bachelor's degree from the University of California, Los Angeles, in 1959, supporting himself by selling insurance policies for his father's company. He was accepted by the Loyola Marymount University School of Law and began his studies there in the autumn of 1959. "I was the kind of student that didn't want to look like a jerk, always raising my hand," Cochran recalled in *The American Lawyer*. "But I would sit there and pray that I would be called on. That was my competitive spirit lying in wait."

Having finished his law studies and passed the California bar by 1963, Cochran took a job with the city of Los Angeles, serving as a deputy city attorney in the criminal division. There he worked as a prosecutor. In 1965 he entered private practice with the late Gerald Lenoir, a well-known local criminal lawyer. After a short period with Lenoir, he formed his own firm, Cochran, Atkins & Evans. "That was the closest to a storefront I ever had," Cochran remembered in *The American Lawyer*. Johnnie Cochran's career was launched from this office with a highly-publicized and inflammatory case.

In May of 1966, a young black man named Leonard Deadwyler was shot dead by police as he tried to rush his pregnant wife to the hospital. Cochran represented Deadwyler's family, who accused the police of needless brutality in their son's murder. The Los Angeles Police Department insisted that the officers had acted in self-defense. "To me, this was clearly a bad shooting," Cochran maintained in *The American Lawyer*. "But the [district attorney] did not file charges, and when our firm filed a civil suit we lost. Those were extremely difficult cases to win in those days. But what Deadwyler confirmed for me was that this issue of police abuse really galvanized the minority community. It taught me that these cases could really get attention."

Another memorable case further steered Cochran toward working on behalf of his race. In the early 1970s he went to court in defense of Geronimo Pratt, a former Black Panther who stood accused of murder. Cochran lost that case too, but he insists to this day that Pratt was railroaded by the F.B.I. and local police. "White America just can't come to grips with this," Cochran explained in *Essence*. "To them the police are as they should be: saving children, acting like heroes in the community. They aren't setting up people, they're not lying, they aren't using their racist beliefs as an excuse to go after certain people." Cochran has continued to press for a re-trial in the Pratt case.

"Best in the West"

Such headline-grabbing cases quickly made Cochran's name among the black community in Los Angeles, and by the late 1970s he was handling a number of police brutality and other criminal cases. In an abrupt about-face in 1978, however, he joined the Los Angeles County district attorney's office where one of his subordinates was a young lawyer named Gil Garcetti. Cochran has said that he took the job because he wanted to broaden his political contacts and refashion his image. "In those days, if you were a criminal defense lawyer, even though you might be very good, you were not considered one of the good guys, one of the very top rung," he explained in *The American Lawyer.*

Cochran's position at the district attorney's office did not spare him a brush with racist police. One afternoon as he drove his two young daughters across town in his Rolls Royce, he was pulled over. The police yelled at him to get out of the car with his hands up, and when he did he could see that they had drawn their guns. "Well, talk about an illegal search and seizure!" Cochran exclaimed in *The American Lawyer,* recalling the event. "These guys just go through ripping through my bag. Suddenly this cop goes gray. He sees my number three badge from the D.A.'s office! He's like, `Ahh! Ahh!' They all go apoplectic. I never got stopped again, but I'm careful not to make any weird moves. I might get shot!"

Cochran never publicized the incident, but he was deeply disturbed about its effect on his two daughters. "I didn't want to tell them it was because of racism," he added. "I didn't want to tell them it happened because their daddy was a black guy in a Rolls, so they thought he was a pimp. So I tried to smooth things over.... As an African American, you hope and pray that things will be better for your children. And you don't want them to feel hatred."

Returning to private practice in 1983, Cochran established himself as "the best in the West," to quote *Ebony* magazine. One of his first major victories occurred in the case of Ron Settles, a college football player who police said had hanged himself in a jail cell after having been picked up for speeding. On the behalf of Settles's family, Cochran demanded that the athlete's body be exhumed and examined. A coroner determined that Settles had been strangled by a police choke hold. A pre-trial settlement brought the grieving family $760,000.

The Settles case settlement was the first in a series of damage awards that Cochran has won for clients--some observers estimate he has won between $40 and $43 million from various California municipalities and police districts in judgments for his clients. *Essence* reporter Diane Weathers wrote: "Cochran is not just another rich celebrity lawyer. His specialty is suing City Hall on behalf of many fameless people who don't sing, dance or score touchdowns and who have been framed, beaten up, shot at, humiliated and sometimes killed at the hands of the notorious LAPD."

Success begot success for Cochran. The Settles case was followed by another emotional case in which an off-duty police officer molested a teenager and threatened her with bodily harm if she told anyone. In that case Cochran

spurned an out-of-court settlement in six figures and took the issue to the courtroom--where a jury awarded his client $9.4 million. A post-verdict settlement paid the young woman $4.6 million.

As Cochran's fame grew, his client list began to include more celebrities, of which pop singer Michael Jackson is the best known. On Jackson's behalf, Cochran arranged an out-of-court settlement with a boy who had accused the singer of molestation. Cochran had the case retired in such a way that the charges against Jackson were withdrawn, and Jackson could publicly proclaim his complete innocence. Cochran also engineered an acquittal for *Diff'rent Strokes* star Todd Bridges, who stood accused of attempted murder.

The "Trial of the Century"

No celebrity trial was more followed than O. J. Simpson's trial, however. In the summer of 1994, Simpson was arrested and charged with the murders of his ex-wife, Nicole Brown Simpson, and her friend Ron Goldman. Simpson declared that he was innocent, and he engaged Cochran as part of an expensive "dream team" of lawyers dedicated to his defense. Before long, Cochran had replaced Robert Shapiro as leader of the "dream team" as the matter was brought to trial. Calling the O. J. Simpson trial a "classic rush-to-judgment case," Cochran vowed to win an acquittal for the football star-turned-television celebrity. Responding to questions about the nickname for his legal team, Cochran told *Time:* "We certainly don't refer to ourselves as the Dream Team. We're just a collection of lawyers just trying to do the best we can."

> "I have learned not to be thin-skinned, especially when I think I'm doing the right thing...It's not about money, it's about using the law as a device for change."

One week into the Simpson trial in February of 1995, *Time* reported that Cochran had "unveiled an unexpectedly strong defense." With his engaging manner and sincerity, Cochran sought to poke holes in the case against Simpson as presented by district attorneys Marcia Clark and Christopher Darden. Piece by piece he challenged the evidence, paying special attention to the racist attitudes of one of the investigating officers, Mark Fuhrman.

Cochran was effective--and controversial--in his closing arguments on Simpson's behalf. He claimed his client had been framed by a racist police officer, and that if such injustice were allowed to persist, it could lead to genocide as practiced by Nazi dictator Adolf Hitler. Speaking to the jury, Cochran concluded: "If you don't speak out, if you don't stand up, if you don't do what's right, this kind of conduct will continue on forever." After deliberating only four hours, the mostly black jury found Simpson not guilty on all counts.

Observers called Cochran's remarks the "race card," and some castigated the attorney for proceeding in this manner. Cochran offered no apologies for his strategy, claiming that his scenario represented the truth as he saw it. "I think race plays a part of everything in America, let alone this trial," he maintained in a *Newsweek* interview. "That's one of the problems in America. People don't want to face up to the fact that we do have some racial divisions."

After handling the post-trial publicity, Cochran returned to other cases, including pending civil litigation against Simpson. The trial has had its impact on Cochran's life. Once a celebrity lawyer only in Los Angeles, he is now a celebrity lawyer across America, receiving a million-dollar advance to write his memoirs and a hefty fee for any personal appearances he makes. Cochran has had his share of negative publicity, however. His first wife, Barbara Cochran Berry, wrote a memoir during the Simpson trial in which she accused Cochran of abuse and infidelity. Cochran's longtime mistress, Patricia Cochran, also claims to be writing her own memoir. "I did a lot of stupid things," Cochran admitted in *Essence*

when asked about his private life. "I paid a price with my eldest daughter and with my [first] marriage. I would like young lawyers not to make the mistakes I made."

Married for a second time, Cochran lives in a luxurious home with a commanding view of the Los Angeles basin. His father, whom he calls "the Chief," lives with him. Having won an acquittal for O. J. Simpson--and having made himself famous in the process--Cochran concluded in *Newsweek* that he wants to initiate a "healing" between the races in America. If that is to happen, he believes, white America will have to become more sympathetic to the hardships facing African Americans. "It doesn't make sense for us to go back into our individual camps after this is over," he noted. "African Americans ... respond to what I have to say. I spoke what they feel is happening, and I spoke it as an African American lawyer. This case cried out for that.... I don't want to exacerbate racial problems. But you have to be true to who you are....This is not for the timid."

Sources

American Lawyer, May 1994, p. 56.
Ebony, April 1994, pp. 112-16.
Essence, November 1995, p. 86.
Newsweek, January 16, 1995, p. 60; October 9, 1995, pp. 31, 34; October 16, 1995, pp. 37-39, 42.
People, April 10, 1995, pp. 55-56.
The Source, January 1996, p. 34.
Time, January 30, 1995, pp. 43-44; February 6, 1995, pp. 58-63; January 1, 1996, pp. 102-03.
U.S. News and World Report, January 23, 1995, pp. 32-35.

—Mark Kram

Johnnie Colemon

1921(?)—

Religious leader

Not everyone agrees with the Reverend Dr. Johnnie Colemon's interpretation of the message of Jesus Christ, but it is hard to argue with her independent spirit or the success she has achieved through the practice of her principles. Her conviction, as stated in "What We Believe" published by the Universal Foundation for Better Living (UFBL), which she founded, is that "it is God's will that every individual on the face of this earth should live a healthy, happy, and prosperous life." She has promised that every person has access to the power of God in him or her for living a loving and successful life. Given this, her own prosperity can be seen as a confirmation of that promise.

Colemon classifies her teaching as part of the worldwide "New Thought" religious movement. *Dollars and Sense* calls it the "message of practical Christianity." Despite her charisma and success, she is not without her detractors. Critics claim that she is too enamored of wealth, saying she ignores Bible passages in which Jesus warns against trusting in earthly treasure. She responds by pointing out that money can be the instrument through which God's message is heard on earth. Addressing this issue, Colemon said in the *Chicago Tribune*, "money is

God in action. God is my source of supply ...." So on the other hand, in a culture in which money and religion are growing more inextricably linked, her candor might even be viewed as a breath of fresh air.

Early Ambition

As a child, Colemon was not particularly religious. While growing up in Columbus, Mississippi, her early ambitions were tied to music and show business. At one time she hoped to play the saxophone professionally, at another she worked towards becoming a Broadway dancer. In the 1940s, she left Mississippi to attend Wiley College in Marshall, Texas. During that time the college was known, at least partially, for the beauty of its women. Attending Wiley was not always an easy experience for this self-proclaimed "ugly duckling," but Colemon excelled and was even elected by her classmates to the honorary position of "most versatile student on campus."

After graduation from Wiley, Colemon moved to Chicago, where her exceptional talent helped her to succeed in a wide variety of occupations, including a position as

At a Glance . . .

Born in Centerville, AL; daughter of John and Lula (Parker) Haley; married Don Nedd (deceased). *Education:* Wiley College, Marshall, TX, B.A., 1943.

Chicago Market Center, price analyst; Chicago Public Schools, teacher; Chicago Port Authority, director; Chicago Transit Authority Oversight Committee, member; Association of Unity Churches, president; Christ Unity Temple, founder and pastor, 1956-74; Universal Foundation For Better Living, founder, 1974—; Christ Universal Temple and Complex, founder and pastor, 1974—; Johnnie Colemon Institute, founder and president, 1974—; International New Thought Association, chairperson of 60th Anniversary Congress, 1975; operator, Heavenly Hamburger House.

Awards: Citations, Association of Unity Churches, 1966, 1969, 1970; Golden Anniversary Award, Alpha Kappa Alpha Sorority, 1972; Service to Youth Award, Young Men's Christian Association (YMCA), 1973; Outstanding Christian Service, Civic Liberty League of Chicago, 1974; Women's Day Annual Black Excellence Award, Operation People United to Serve Humanity (PUSH), 1974; Year of the Woman Award, PUSH Foundation, 1975; Certificate of Appreciation, Chicago City Council, 1975; Humanitarian Award, *Blackbook Business and Reference Guide,* 1976; Excellence in Religion, PUSH Foundation, 1977; Top 100 Black Business and Professional Women citation, Delta Sigma Theta Sorority, 1985; Par Excellence Award, *Blackbook Business and Reference Guide,* 1986; Candace Award, National Coalition of 100 Black Women, 1987; numerous citations and commendations from various city governments; awarded several honary degrees including, Honorary Doctorate in Divinity, Wiley College, 1977; Doctor of Human Letters and Doctor of Divinity, Monrovia College and Industrial Institute of the African Methodist Episcopal Church of Monrovia, Liberia, West Africa.

Addresses: *Office–* Pastor, Christ Universal Temple, 11901 S. Ashland, Chicago, IL 60643.

public school teacher and also price analyst for the Chicago Market Center. Other noteworthy public service positions she has held include director of the

Chicago Port Authority, a very important position in a major city with a large shipping trade, and commissioner on the Chicago Transit Authority Oversight Committee. Her commitment to Chicago was not overlooked. August 18, 1985, was declared "Reverend Dr. Johnnie Colemon Day" in Chicago by then-mayor Harold Washington. Colemon has been most noted for accomplishments in her religious career, however, a career that received a jump-start when she was diagnosed with a fatal illness in her early 30s.

Experienced Religious Conversion

In an interview with *Dollars & Sense,* Colemon referred to her illness as the "greatest thing that ever happened in my life." At the time, of course, it hit her with a devastating impact. Having learned that she was expected to live only six months more, she came upon some pamphlets of the Unity School of Christianity. The cover of one pamphlet in bold letters proclaimed, "God is your health; you can't be sick." Having just learned of her condition, these words provoked a great deal of disbelief and resentment in Colemon. "I began to question and examine the nature of God," Colemon told *Dollars & Sense.* Her mother encouraged her to travel to the Unity School of Practical Christianity in Missouri and see for herself whether there was anything to the Unity School's doctrine.

Colemon felt a conversion take place within her the minute she walked in the door, and a representative of the school promised that what they taught could cure her. Not only did she find a cure there, but she started taking classes and decided to become an ordained minister. One of the first miracles to take place in her life was a rise in self-esteem that pertained to her physical beauty. She warned, however, that one should not think of miracles as being produced like "a cake from a recipe" but should realize that miracles are already "produced inside of you, waiting for you to bring [them] forth in the form that you need ...," she emphasized in *Dollars & Sense.* She excelled at the seminary as she had done in her early career in Chicago, and even became the first African American to attain the office of president of the Association of Unity Churches while still in the seminary.

Having finally been ordained a minister, Colemon set up her first ministry in Chicago, the Christ Unity Center, in a local Young Men's Christian Association (YMCA). The center, a member of the Association of Unity Churches, had a congregation of only a few dozen members at its inception in 1956. Church growth was steady, and by

1963 she was able to incorporate and build the Christ Unity Temple, a building large enough to serve 200 worshippers. It was then that word of her unique approach to the message of Christ began to spread and church attendance soared. An expansion program was begun that included a 1,155 seat wing that was already too small by the time it opened in 1973.

Founded Universal Brotherhood of Better Living

During this period of growth, Colemon began to re-examine her ideas about God. She realized that she no longer fit comfortably within the Unity School of Christianity, partly because of a latent racism she still found within its structure. Never one to be timid when bold action is required, Colemon disassociated herself and her congregation from the Association of Unity Churches to become an independent church in 1975. She renamed her church Christ Universal Temple and also founded the UFBL, a nondenominational organization of "New Thought" movement churches dedicated to putting the tools for abundant living within the reach of each individual.

With church facilities still too small and faced with the challenge of founding a new religious organization, Colemon knew that she had to build. She wanted her facility to be much more than a conventional church that simply offered religious services. She saw the potential to create a center of education, prayer, and outreach all across the nation and indeed the world. She had the idea but no tangible resources with which to bring it into being. This may have stopped a less hardy soul, but the Reverend Colemon trusted in God; she also fel confident about her own ability to understand and unlock the potential of Christ's power.

Colemon announced plans to build a large center with an auditorium to hold up to 4,000 worshippers comfortably. At first she was only able to raise $1.5 million, well short of the money necessary to realize her dream, but an anonymous donor came forward and offered her about 50 acres of prime land on the south side of Chicago. Based on the strength of her faith, she knew that God was bringing about the completion of the goal she had set for herself. She proved in action what she had always believed through faith. "God supplies my every need ... anything I need when I need it, and all I need do is name it," she told *Dollars & Sense.* It did not take long for UFBL to find the remaining money, a whopping $3.5 million, to complete the new Christ Universal Complex--the largest religious facility in Chicago--which opened in August of 1985.

It was none other than the Reverend Jesse Jackson, a minister from the comparatively conservative Baptist tradition, who was on hand to help Colemon launch the new Complex when she held her first service that August day. Then-governor of Illinois Jim Edgar even set aside the day on which her church opened as "Christ Universal Complex Day." Colemon did not grow complacent in the face of her success, however. She called her complex, "God's city in the making," *Dollars & Sense* reported, a description that implicitly looks forward to sustained achievement. Beyond just offering religious services in the complex, she has also set up the Johnnie Colemon Institute to train other ministers to go out and spread the word of "practical Christianity" and abundant living.

The Nature of Her Beliefs

Coleman's late husband, the Reverend Don Nedd, wrote a small creed for the organization entitled, "What We Believe." Beyond stating that it is God's will that everyone should be happy and prosperous, a statement which Colemon and her followers use very inclusively, the creed announces that the power to be happy and prosperous lies within each individual. Nedd added that Jesus Christ is the soul who has most perfectly shown the way to unleash these forces in our lives. UFBL's adherents also believe that love is the basis of all "right thinking" and that the individual seeking personal "self-unfoldment" must learn to be guided by "the still small voice within" of which the prophet Isaiah spoke.

> ## "Money is God in action. God is my source of supply."

Colemon's most controversial stances probably have to do with her position on the issues of heaven and hell and Christ's crucifixion. She does not view heaven and hell as "places" you go or "experiences" the soul goes through after death. Instead, as she related in *Dollars & Sense,* "you are in heaven when you have the things that make you happy.... When you do not ... you are in hell. They're both ... where you are now, and you can be in either place; it's up to you." As disturbing as some people find her inversion of the usual ideas of heaven and hell, others find her emphasis on religion in this life and not the next extremely liberating.

Also upseting to many people is Colemon's rejection of

the Christian belief in Christ's presence on the cross. She has explained that she is not denying that a crucifixion took place, but believes it was Jesus who was crucified. She elaborated in *Dollars & Sense,* "You can't crucify Christ because Christ is God's idea of himself." She added, "Christ has always been, so they couldn't crucify Christ, they crucified the human Jesus." Again for all those who are disturbed by her new theology, there are others who feel liberated from guilt and bad feeling, from a belief that God wants them to remain poor and unhappy.

Often referred to as the "First Lady of Religion in America," it is hard to put a limit on what Colemon will achieve as she continues to proclaim her gospel of success and prosperity. So far, her accomplishments, as well as the large crowds that have responded so positively to her preaching and teaching, have served as strong witnesses to the power of her message. Many are looking with great interest to see what the future holds for this talented and charismatic religious leader.

Sources

Chicago Tribune, July 28, 1985, Sec. 2, p.3.
Dollars & Sense, December 1985-January 1986, pp. 12-25.
Essence, May 1995, p. 146.

Additional information for this profile was provided by the Universal Foundation for Better Living, Inc., December 1995.

—*Jim McDermott*

Comer Cottrell

1931—

Entrepreneur

Starting a cosmetics company alone and with almost no funds in 1970, Comer Cottrell built up his firm into a major player in the industry by focusing exclusively on the beauty needs of black customers. Eventually his lineup included such popular lines as *Curly Kit, Kiddie Kit,* and *Perm Repair,* to name a few. By 1988 his Dallas-based Pro-Line Corporation was the largest black-owned firm in the Southwest and one of the most profitable black companies in the United States.

Cottrell had various sales jobs. His highest position before starting his cosmetics concern was as a sales manager for Sears Roebuck, a position he held for five years. A contributing factor to his future choice of business was his management of a military base's post exchange. "I managed an Air Force base exchange and noticed that there were no hair products for blacks," he said in *Nation's Business.* "Twenty percent of the people on the base were black. I talked to the authorities, and they told me there was no need for such products."

Cottrell's interest in business was spawned at an early age while he was growing up in Mobile, Alabama. By the age of eight he often accompanied his father, an insurance salesman, on visits to clients. "It gave me a lot of pride to see him walk into those people's homes, sit down in the living room and talk to them about when they die and how he would give them money to bury them," he told *The Black Collegian.* "At that age I didn't think people ever died. He gives them a receipt, a little piece of paper, and he comes back every week and gets money from them until they die. My God, I thought, this is business? I love it!"

After graduating from the University of Detroit in 1952,

Started Company on Shoestring

Years later Cottrell approached some chemical companies to see if they could create products for the "Afro" hairstyle that was popular at the time. With only $600, a borrowed typewriter, and a rundown 700-square-foot warehouse, Cottrell began Pro-Line Corporation in Los Angeles. He had to agree to make improvements in the warehouse to get a six-month reprieve from paying rent. Lacking the funds for advance payment to a manufacturer, he convinced a small firm to take a

At a Glance . . .

Born December 7, 1931, in Mobile, AL; married Isabell Paulding; children: Renee, Comer III, Aaron. *Education:* University of Detroit, 1952.

Was sales manager at Sears Roebuck, 1964–1969; founded Pro-Line Corporation in Los Angeles, CA, 1970; moved company to Dallas, 1980; became sponsor of Miss Collegiate African-American Pageant, 1989; became part owner of Texas Rangers, 1989; bought property of bankrupt Bishop College in Dallas, TX, 1990; persuaded Paul Quinn College to relocate to former grounds of Bishop College, 1990; donated $25,000 to Spelman College in Atlanta, GA, 1994; served as part of an entourage of black businessmen visiting the Republic of South Africa, 1994. Military service: served in U.S. Air Force.

Memberships: Board of Directors of Republic Bank, Southwest Dallas Hospital Corporation, Western Pacific Industries, Dallas Financial Corporation, Pro-Ball Inc.

Addresses: *Business*–Pro-Line Corporation, 2121 Panoramic Circle, Dallas, TX 75212.

chance on him. He entered the cosmetics market with a strawberry-fragranced, oil-based hair spray, which he promoted to black beauticians and barbers. The product proved popular and enabled him to pay off his manufacturer in less than a month.

Profitability did not immediately come to Pro-Line, and Cottrell was forced to work hard to cut into markets around the country. As he told *The Black Collegian*, "I came to New Orleans driving the truck, loaded down with boxes of grease. I was raggedy and broke and had to sell a case of hair spray to be able to eat and buy gas." After several months, Cottrell added a few more products to his inventory and was on his way to building his company into a major business.

Within five years Pro-line had its own distribution center in Birmingham, Alabama. Despite such gains, Cottrell was having difficulty getting his products into stores because Johnson Products Company, the top black cosmetics company, dominated the market. In an attempt to get marketing ideas from his competitor, he contacted Johnson. As a result of this meeting, Cottrell met Isabell Paulding, a former Miss Black Alabama who was one of Johnson's managers. Cottrell married Paulding and brought her into his own company.

By 1980 Cottrell's company had grown too large for the available facilities in Los Angeles, so he moved Pro-Line to Dallas. Just as he was ceasing production in California, he introduced his Curly Kit Home Permanent. When the product caused sales to soar by $11 million in the next ten months, it turned out to be a mixed blessing: production lines were closed due to the upcoming move. "Here we were moving our equipment from California to Texas, and we couldn't keep up with the orders," Cottrell noted in *Nation's Business*. "Competitors jumped in with similar products."

Overseas Expansion Triggered Growth

Critical to Pro-Line's growth was Cottrell's tapping of overseas markets. Remembering his experience as a PX manager, he helped to bring African American cosmetics to military bases both in the United States and abroad. Eventually his products were reaping big domestic sales as well as succeeding in the Caribbean, Europe, Africa, Saudi Arabia, and the Asia. In addition he had set up licensing and royalty arrangements with firms in Nigeria, Kenya, Trinidad, and Taiwan. In the years that followed, he developed more sophisticated marketing that targeted specific segments such as salons, individuals, and children. Working hard to increase his share of the market, Cottrell turned Pro-Line into the fourth-largest ethnic beauty enterprise in the United States. In 1987, his company was ranked 39th on *Black Enterprise's* list of the top 100 black businesses. By 1989, Cottrell's corporation had risen to number 19 on the list with yearly sales of $36 million worldwide.

Cottrell sees his success in business as an avenue open to all blacks, if they are willing to pay their dues. "I firmly believe that if young persons, beginning even during childhood, spent as much time as possible learning to verbalize their thoughts, reading business publications, practicing the business techniques of successful people, and learning the vocabulary of the business world they could, by the time they are adults, be `pros' equipped with all the necessary tools for success," he wrote in an article in *Ebony* in 1980. By following his own advice, Cottrell has continued to increase his business knowledge and thereby expand his areas of expertise.

Broke New Ground in Baseball

In 1989 Cottrell became a part owner of the Texas Rangers, becoming the first black to hold such a stake in a Major League Baseball team. Cottrell was part of a 14-member purchasing group led by George Bush, Jr., son of the former U.S. president George, Sr. Cottrell's share of the estimated $25 million purchase was around $1 million. He felt that he could use his new position to induce affirmative action in the realm of professional sports and was highly vocal about the lack of minority involvement in the Rangers organization. At the time he also claimed that he would make efforts to get the local black community more involved in the team.

Demonstrating his concern for youths, Cottrell kicked off the "Say No to Drugs and Yes to Education" Back to School Promotion in 1990. The program encouraged all Pro-Line customers to pledge 25 cents each, which would be donated in their behalf to support anti-drug efforts and grant scholarships. Cottrell has considered such programs to be an essential responsibility of all black business professionals. In *Ebony* he explained: "As we support black businesses those businesses have a responsibility to support the black community by reinvesting in that community for the improvement of its physical environment and for the inspiring of its youth."

Saved Bankrupt College

Cottrell became a hero to higher education for blacks in 1990, when he came to the rescue of Bishop College, which had become bankrupt after years of scandal and financial problems. Founded by freed slaves and Baptist missionaries, the Dallas-based institution was thought to be the first educational campus to be auctioned off due to bankruptcy. Cottrell held an honorary degree from Bishop, was a trustee of the college, and had previously tried in vain to prevent the school's collapse. In 1981, when an audit revealed that the institution was in debt to the federal government for $3.5 million, Cottrell was appointed acting chairman of the school. During his five-year stint in this position, he arranged for significant layoffs and aggressive fund-raising, but the school went bankrupt in addition to losing its accreditation in 1986.

Bidding took only ten minutes, with Cottrell being awarded the property for $1.5 million. He was in tears at the result, expecting to have to pay around $5 million for the school. "I waited until the last minute for someone or some group to come through and buy it," he said in *Jet* in 1990. "But no one floated to the surface. It would have been a real blow to the developing black community here if the school was dissolved."

As the new owner, Cottrell was faced with having to raise an estimated $40 million to restore the destitute campus. He planned to turn it back into a predominantly black college, and open it as soon as a board of trustees was established and construction crews had cleaned up the campus. "It won't be precisely what it was before," he told the *New York Times*. "It will be a college that is operated as a business."

Cottrell considered it his moral duty to do what he could to save Bishop College, in order to help blacks better themselves. "As long as it serves the black community, that's all that matters," he said in *The Chronicle of Higher Education.* Cottrell told *The Black Collegian,* "It was not just a purchase but an investment. I think that a company that calls itself black, and asks for black support, is really asking the black community to grant it license to call itself that. And it has an obligation to give back." Cottrell's plan was to establish schools of nursing and life sciences and one in education that would train teachers to work in urban areas and provide them with inner-city teaching skills.

> "I think that a company that calls itself Black, and asks for Black support is really asking the Black community to grant it license to call itself that. And it has an obligation to give back."

Eventually Cottrell persuaded Paul Quinn College, an African Methodist Episcopal church-supported institution, to relocate its operations from Waco to the former grounds of Bishop College in 1990. He contributed another $1.7 million to pay for renovations. "I've always been an advocate of higher education," he said in an October 1991 issue of *Jet.* "Also, to get the local business community to invest in higher education is a perfect tie-in. The economic impact for this community will be felt for years."

Continued Support of Education

In the late 1980s, Cottrell made Pro-Line a sponsor of the newly founded Miss Collegiate African American Pageant. He later offered a $25,000 gift to Spelman College after DaShawnda Gooden, a student there, won the pageant in 1992. "Pro-Line will continue its support and dedication to historically black colleges and universities through the Miss Collegiate African American Pageant," Cottrell said while presenting a check to

Spelman College President Johnnetta Cole, according to *Jet*.

Cottrell took his business savvy abroad in 1994 as part of an entourage of black businessmen sent to the Republic of South Africa. Organized by Langston University and its National Institute for the Study of Minority Enterprise (NISME), the group explored options for helping with research and training of black South African entrepreneurs. It also sought to make professional connections with the country's established black entrepreneurs.

Pro-Line has continued its great success into the 1990s, and has become a family affair for Cottrell. His wife has served as an executive, his brother James has been a vice president, and his daughter, Renee Brown, has worked for the firm as a vice president of marketing and advertising. Throughout his business career, Cottrell has stressed the importance of good relations with others as the cornerstone of a successful business. "When you get in business you have to treat people as you would have them treat you," he remarked in *The Black Collegian*. As for his success in the cosmetics industry, he told *Nation's Business* that he made his mark by "selling hope-- that's all the beauty business is."

Sources

The Black Collegian, September/October 1990, pp. 115, 204.

Black Enterprise, September 1989, p. 18; May 1990, p. 18.

Call and Post (Cleveland), April 14, 1994, p. 2A.

Chronicle of Higher Education, March 7, 1990, p. A2.

Ebony, August 1980, pp. 128, 130.

Jet, March 2, 1990, p. 5; October 28, 1991, pp. 34–35; January 31, 1994, p. 17.

Nation's Business, January 1988, p. 24R.

New York Times, February 24, 1990, p. A9.

—*Ed Decker*

Stanley Crouch

1945—

Writer, social critic

"I usually write something I think is true," Stanley Crouch insisted to *New York Times* contributor Lynda Richardson, "and if in the process it's provocative, it's too bad." Crouch's capacity to provoke his readers is virtually unparalleled in modern American letters. Yet despite his having pilloried many cherished ideas and figures of black culture—in a manner frequently described as vindictive—Crouch is no neoconservative black writer cosying up to a right-wing audience. Rather, he has followed his own idiosyncratic muse; to say that he operates with disregard for sacred cows of any kind is to understate the case. Contempt for unquestioned orthodoxies, in fact, is one of the few consistent aspects of his work.

In countless essays, a novel, and numerous other forums, Crouch has applied a jazz fanatic's exacting standards to popular culture and politics and found them largely wanting. At the core of his work is a desire to break down cultural barriers and make good on the promise of America's diversity. *Nation* critic Gene Seymour, reviewing Crouch's 1990 essay collection *Notes of a Hanging Judge,* found in its pages "a search for common ground and a reaffirmation of the social con-

tract," adding that "like any good jazz player, Crouch never repeats himself or does the predictable."

Made Enemies

For Crouch—and this view has earned him some formidable enemies—the civil rights movement of the 1960s gathered its moral impetus from a far-seeing humanism that was betrayed by the black nationalism that replaced it. The goal of the earlier movement was to sweep away racist institutions so that American blacks could contribute their multifaceted talents to their country unhindered, he has noted; black nationalism, meanwhile, "helped send not only black America but this nation itself into an intellectual tailspin on the subjects of race, of culture, of heritage," reads an essay quoted by Richardson in the *New York Times.* "Where there was not outright foolishness, there was a mongering of the maudlin and a base opportunism."

It is this repudiation of black militant politics—which he briefly endorsed during the late 1960s—and its cultural offspring in music and literature that has made Crouch the target of the most vociferous attacks he has weathered. To esteemed critic bell hooks, who has herself felt the sting of Crouch's poisoned pen, he "apes a peculiar hybrid of jungle-bunny masculinity and new-right Fascism. He has seen that it pays off when you kiss the ass of white supremacy." Crouch's pugilistic nature extends to his personal comportment, though whether his physical blows smart more than his scathing prose is perhaps worthy of an essay in itself. "I have a wild side to my personality," he averred to Richardson. "I'm not always the Cub Scout leader I'd like most adults to be, sometimes in ways that are surprising to [me]."

Crouch was born in 1945 in Los Angeles; his father, James, was in jail on a drug charge when Stanley entered the world, according to several sources. Stanley's mother, Emma Bea, worked an exhausting schedule as a maid to support him and his siblings; when she wasn't working, she was exposing her children to culture as best she could. Crouch described her to Robert C. Boynton of the *New Yorker* as "Little Miss Perfect Lower Class," explaining, "She was an aristocrat in that strange American way that has nothing to do with money."

Stanley suffered from asthma and was often forced to stay indoors as a result; he turned his confinement to his advantage by reading constantly. Apart from literature—he had familiarized himself with some of the greatest American writers before he finished high school—his other grand passion was jazz. Soon, like any good critic-to-be, he had amassed an almost encyclopedic knowledge of that subject as well.

Crouch spent his first few years after graduating from high school in an unfocused course of study at two junior colleges. His interest in literature broadened to include drama and poetry, and the riots that devastated the Watts area of South Central Los Angeles in 1965 inspired him to raise funds for the Student Nonviolent Coordinating Committee (SNCC), one of the civil rights movement's staunchest organizations. By the late 1960s, however, impatience with the slow pace of progress had contributed to the growth of black militancy.

Crouch, too, was briefly swept up in the fervor. "I was very impressed by the nationalist business for a while," he reflected to the *Wall Street Journal's* Helen Dudar. "It had a certain appeal that stuff always has—it simplified the world. And all the ambiguities of human conduct don't have to be addressed. If you have two people in a store and one is selling superiority while the other is selling equality, the person selling superiority is going to have a line around the block. That is the appeal of Black Nationalism: it is saying that black people are superior and white people are inferior."

Gravitated Toward Theater, Academia

Around that time Crouch met and became involved with Jayne Cortez, a prominent poet who ran Studio Watts, a theater group that had captured his imagination. Joining the group was pivotal for Crouch, but Cortez's example was even more so: "I'd never met anyone with that kind of aesthetic commitment," he noted to *New Yorker* writer Boynton, "who'd drawn a line in the dirt and said, 'I am an artist.'"

Crouch's poetry began to gain some notice, fusing urgent political messages, jazz rhapsodies, and literary allusions. Yet during a poetry workshop he'd helped organize in 1967, he told Boynton, he had an experience that could be called "critical" in more ways than one. Watching a white workshop leader soft-pedal his critique of a black participant's poem—one that Crouch thought simply abominable—was "one of the pivotal moments of my life, because I saw how even a guy with the best intentions could be incredibly paternalistic and encourage third-rate work." The incident inspired the tactless honesty that has been the hallmark of Crouch's critical writing ever since.

1968 saw Crouch join the faculty of Pitzer College, part of California's Claremont College group, as poet-in-residence. He later moved to the faculty of the Black Studies Center, then gained a position in Pomona College's English department. Though he had not earned a degree himself, Crouch's prodigious background in all varieties of literature allowed him to campaign among the faculty and impress each one. "I always knew something about the subject at hand that they hadn't ever heard before," he related to Boynton. During the 1970s, after making a substantial mark as an instructor and dramatist at Claremont, Crouch decided to move to New York. Thanks to a jazz critic friend, he began working for the *Village Voice,* one of nation's premiere counter-cultural publications and a bible of the East Coast arts scene.

Crouch's tenure at the *Voice* hardly transformed him into a doctrinaire leftist, however. Indeed, he became, if anything, more unpredictable in his work and often seemed dedicated to puncturing the most revered black figures on the cultural landscape. Though originally focused on jazz—and during the 1980s his stylistic allegiances shifted from avant-garde to traditional practitioners of this music—Crouch was soon firing broadsides at literature, film, and virtually everything else. He seemed to reserve a special venom for black nationalism and its ideological cousins; complaining, in a piece cited by *Wall Street Journal* contributor Dudar, about "a weak-kneed, crybaby bitching vision of the world in which, if everything is not working perfectly for you all the time, you have been betrayed by society."

Crouch created a unique body of resentment by trashing or severely criticizing work by novelist Toni Morrison, filmmaker Spike Lee, and others who had received virtually unanimous praise elsewhere. *New Yorker* contributor Boynton's article cites a hair-raising litany of Crouchian opinion—the writer took a swipe at martyred activist Malcolm X, called bell hooks a "terrier with attitude," dubbed Afrocentrism a "hustle," and called "gangsta" rappers Uncle Toms.

Prone to Fisticuffs

But Crouch's bellicosity wasn't restricted to the page; many of his colleagues complained that he baited them and clearly desired confrontation. Most notably, an argument with *Voice* music critic Harry Allen—a partisan of rap, which Crouch has long publicly disdained—turned into an all-out fistfight. Crouch was subsequently

fired from the publication, though he was later re-hired in a free-lance capacity. A former colleague told Boynton that the magazine underwent "a lot of ridiculous hand-wringing, but the fact is that Stanley is just a bully—a mean guy with a violent streak and a dumb schoolyard attitude."

Others at the *Voice* felt that the firing was an overreaction and that Crouch's temper was largely manifested in posturing. What's more, editor Doug Simmons recalled to Boynton, Crouch often wanted people to stand up to him. "His most endearing moment," Simmons related, "was when he gave me an awful piece—which was unusual—and I told him it sucked. He started to get angry and said 'What do you mean, it sucks?' And I said, 'Look, it's just no good and we won't print it.' He thought for a minute and said, 'You know, you're right, it does suck.' And he rewrote it. He was just happy to have someone engage him."

Crouch took a swipe at martyred activist Malcolm X, called bell hooks a "terrier with attitude," dubbed Afrocentrism a "hustle" and called "gangsta" rappers Uncle Toms.

Crouch was allegedly devastated and remorseful after his firing, but he later claimed to have been liberated by it. He certainly didn't fall into inactivity. 1990 saw the publication of a collection of his pieces, *Notes of a Hanging Judge;* the following year he was given a $30,000 Whiting Foundation Writers' Award. Among several ongoing projects that have engaged him since are a lengthy and agonizingly well-researched biography of jazz giant Charlie Parker and a novel called *First Snow in Kokomo* that he has been threatening to publish for several years. At the National Book Awards in 1990 he was able to rub elbows with two of his literary idols, novelists Ralph Ellison and Saul Bellow. In 1993 Crouch won a MacArthur Foundation "genius grant" of $296,000.

As a founder of Jazz at Lincoln Center, Crouch has helped authorize the new jazz orthodoxy. To the dismay of avant-garde fans, he lent his approval to the neo-traditionalism of trumpeter Wynton Marsalis and other young classicists; to Boynton he remarked, "The real problem with the avant-garde is that many of them simply can't play." Nonetheless, it was Crouch who had taken the young Marsalis under his wing and taught him an appreciation not only for jazz pioneers like Duke Ellington but also for maverick figures like saxophonist Ornette Coleman.

As a social critic, Crouch has reserved much of his ammunition for those elements of popular culture that engage in what he called "the panting exploitation of our worst inclinations" in a brief essay included in a *Time* roundtable. Among these he numbered the "slut chic" of singer/actress Madonna, the anti-Semitism and misogyny of much rap music and black nationalist rhetoric, the "shock of gore" of modern action films, and the "calculated" rebellion of rock stars. "I do not believe censorship is the answer," he concluded. "But I have no doubt good taste and responsibility will not limit the entertainment industry's ability to provide mature work that attacks our corruption, challenges our paranoia and pulls the covers off the shortcomings that Balkanize [segregate] us." And it is Crouch's unceasing assault on this "Balkanization" that redeems much of his work for even leftist critics. Though many of Crouch's keenest observations are offset by "bilious sneering," Seymour noted in his *Nation* review of *Hanging Judge* that Crouch is "nobody's kneejerker," nor is he "a Dedicated Follower of Fashion."

Still, it is Crouch's most inflammatory writing that has gained him the most attention, and this seems unlikely to change. "When I see black people going through this shit today about the importance of being *African-*Americans, I know they're still lost," he asserted to Boynton. "They're constantly talking about what some mysterious 'they' are trying to do to some unified 'us.'" Heedless of the rancor he inspires among many intellectuals—the famed poet Amiri Baraka deemed him "a backward, asinine person" in a very brief phone conversation with Boynton—Crouch claims that ordinary people support him. "I've been applauded by black bus drivers, subway drivers, mechanics, various people who have come up to me and said 'I'm sure glad somebody is saying it,'" he told Richardson. "That's enough for me. I don't care what some trickle-down Negro Marxist says. That means nothing to me. And I don't care what some confused group of what a friend calls 'lumpen bourgeoisie middle-class black folks who want to be street' say." Though he's unlikely to endear himself to the black or leftist establishments anytime soon, Crouch remains one of the most stubbornly independent critics of our culture working in any medium.

Sources

Nation, May 21, 1990, pp. 710-11.
New Yorker, November 6, 1995, pp. 95-115.
New York Times, August 29, 1993, section 4, p. 7.
Time, June 12, 1995, p. 35.
Wall Street Journal, November 29, 1991, p. A5.

—Simon Glickman

Anthony Davis

1951—

Composer, pianist, educator

In the 1980s and early 1990s Anthony Davis, an award-winning composer and jazz pianist, became known for his unique, challenging, and ingenious operas. In addition, he has written three film scores, one of which was awarded an Oscar in 1980. He is also an educator, having taught music and Afro American studies at several universities, including Yale and Harvard. As a composer and pianist, Davis has been labeled too intellectual by conventional jazz musicians and too jazz-oriented by classical musicians. His compositions are notated, yet improvisational in tone and are often built around complicated, constantly changing atonal lines.

Davis studied classical music in college, but his music has been heavily influenced by the African American tradition of swing and bebop. As a composer and pianist, Davis has been labeled too intellectual by conventional jazz musicians and too jazz-oriented by classical musicians. His compositions are notated, yet improvisational in tone and are often built around complicated, constantly changing atonal lines. Davis often struggled to conform his musical style to well-established norms. Eventually, he created his own niche. "I always tried so

hard to fit in, and then I figured out I didn't want to fit," Davis said in the *New York Times.* "I knew I could never be accepted as a straight-ahead jazz musician, nor would I accept myself as that. I would never be accepted as a minimalist. I wouldn't be a "downtown" composer. Because I find all orthodoxies, all doctrines, to be ultimately banal."

Anthony Davis was born on February 20, 1951, in Paterson, New Jersey, and grew up in a family with a long history of academic achievement. His father was the first black English professor at Princeton University and later became the first chairman of Afro American studies at Yale University. Several of his ancestors founded the Hampton Institute, one of the oldest black colleges in the United States. Although he was a gifted child, Davis often felt lonely growing up as a black youngster in predominantly-white college towns. This was particularly true when his father taught at Penn State University in 1961. "I was in a community where everyone was listening to the Beatles and the Rolling Stones," Davis recalled in the *New York Times.* "I was the only one who listened to Temptation records. But the isolation gave me a freedom to explore things for myself."

An Early Interest in Jazz and Classical Music

Davis was exposed to jazz at an early age because his father loved music and was acquainted with several jazz musicians, some of whom performed at the Davis home. Davis taught himself to play jazz tunes and composed his first piano piece, *A Pirate's Song*, before the age of six. He took piano lessons and temporarily gave up studying jazz in favor of classical works by Beethoven, Mozart, and Chopin. By the age of 15, Davis's interest in jazz had returned and he began listening to the music of jazz artist Thelonious Monk, who became his role model.

Davis attended college at Yale University. While he was a student, he and several other musicians formed the group "Advent," which played free jazz concerts at the university. Davis met jazz trumpeter and composer Leo Smith in 1974 and became a member of Smith's band,

New Dalta Ahkri. He also collaborated with Smith on two recordings. In 1975, Davis graduated from Yale with a B.A. in music.

After completing college, Davis continued to perform with Leo Smith and other musicians such as Leroy Jenkins, Anthony Braxton, and Marion Brown. He also formed his own quartet with musical artists Jay Hoggard, Mark Helias, and Ed Blackwell. In 1977, Davis moved to New York and played concerts at jazz lofts, nightclubs, and colleges. He gigged with violinist Leroy Jenkins's trio from 1977 to 1979 and with flutist James Newton. Davis often played his own adaptations of compositions by jazz artists such as Thelonious Monk, Duke Ellington, and Cecil Taylor. He released his first albums *Past Lives*, *Of Blues and Dreams*, and *Crystal Texts* in 1978. In 1979 his album, *Hidden Voices*, was released for the first time on an American record label. Davis also composed musical scores for movies.

Created His Own Jazz Ensemble

In 1981, Davis formed "Episteme" ("knowledge" in Greek), an ensemble of flute, piano, bass, clarinet, trombone, violin, cello, and three percussion instruments. Members of the ensemble included trombonist George Lewis and cellist Abdul Wadud. The group's first album, *Episteme,* contained compositions that blended jazz with African and Southeast Asian musical rhythms. Two of these compositions, "Wayang 2" and "Wayang 4," were named for a word or phrase connected with music played by percussion orchestras in Bali and Java. Members of Episteme initially wanted to experiment with different musical styles. However, they eventually devoted themselves to playing Davis's compositions exclusively, which made use of improvisation and notated forms, blended jazz, non-Western music, and classical avant-garde music.

Although some conservative jazz critics chastised Davis's work, his reputation as a composer and performer continued to grow. He was commissioned to create pieces for dancer and choreographer Molissa Fenley, the Laura Dean Dance Company, and the Brooklyn Philharmonic. Several of Davis's works received critical acclaim and "Wayang 5," which he created for the San Francisco Symphony in 1984, was nominated for a Pulitzer Prize.

Created Opera About Malcolm X

In 1983 Davis, his brother Christopher, and their cousin, poet Thulani Davis, decided to compose an opera entitled *X, The Life and Times of Malcolm X,* about the life of black activist Malcolm X. The opera, which dealt with Malcolm's life from his childhood in Omaha, Nebraska to his conversion to Islam and assassination in 1965, took three years to complete. The musical score was written for a full orchestra and incorporated elements of jazz, African American, and popular music to dramatize the controversial leader's life and times. In the fall of 1986, *X, The Life and Times of Malcolm X* was performed before four sold-out audiences at the New York State Theater. It was only the second opera by a living black composer to debut in a leading American opera house.

Critical reviews of *X, The Life and Times of Malcolm X* were generally favorable. *Time* magazine described it as a "powerful, chilling opera.... Like its incendiary subject, *X* is notable not only for its accomplishment but also for what it represents.... With a fierce, angry and brilliant libretto by Thulani Davis, the composer's cousin, *X* is at once a musical entertainment, a folk epic, a cautionary tale and a cri de coeur [cry from the heart]." Robert Schwartz observed in the New York Times, "Most remarkable is that Mr. Davis seamlessly integrates the diverse languages of Ellington, John Coltrane, non-Western music, and Alban Berg. By anyone's standards, this is an astonishing first opera." Although *X, The Life and Times of Malcolm X* was successful, it has not been performed since 1986 partly because of its controversial subject matter and prohibitive production costs.

In 1987, Davis began working on another opera, *Under the Double Moon.* He was compelled to compose the opera after reading science fiction stories written by his wife, Deborah Atherton. The libretto, which was written by Atherton, tells the story of telepathic twins who live on a planet that is nearly underwater. The twins must decide whether they want to remain above water or opt for a more spiritual existence below the ocean. The music in *Under the Double Moon* was written for full orchestra and incorporated elements of gamelan, Indonesian orchestral music heavily influenced by gongs, xylophones, and drums. *Under the Double Moon* premiered at the Opera Theater of St. Louis in 1989 and received mixed reviews.

Davis's third opera, *Tania,* told the story of the Symbionese Liberation Army's kidnapping of newspaper heiress Patty Hearst in 1974. This opera raised several controversial issues concerning race, gender, and identity in the United States. *Tania* received some negative criticism following its premier at the American Music Theater Festival in 1992. A reviewer in *Commonweal* remarked, "The opera is serious about the problem of

identity, not only for Tania/Patty, but within the society at large; but it is never as funny or as frightening as it ought to be to make so complex a point. . . . Nonetheless, it is theatrically fascinating because Davis's eclectic score (his conscious use of jazz and popular music), Paul Steinberg's sets, and Robert Wierzel's lighting suggest a cohesiveness that the work as a whole never quite achieves."

> "I always tried so hard to fit in, and then I figured out I didn't want to fit. I knew I could never be accepted as a straight-ahead jazz musician, nor would I accept myself as that."

In addition to his operas, Davis composed the music for the Broadway production of *Angels in America, Part I: Millenium Approaches,* which premiered in 1993. He created a work for the String Trio of New York entitled *Sounds Without Nouns,* performed at Pennsylvania State University in November of 1995. He has also been commissioned to work on another opera entitled *Amistead,* about a slave rebellion and mutiny in 1839. It is scheduled to premier at the Lyric Opera of Chicago in 1997. Davis is also working on *The Circus of Dr. Lao,* a music theater production for the Public Theater.

Selected works

Operas

X, The Life and Times of Malcolm X, premiered at New York City Opera, 1986.
Under the Double Moon, premiered at the Opera Theater of St. Louis, 1989.
Tania, premiered at the American Music Theater Festival, 1992.

Other works have included the musical composition for the Broadway production of Tony Kushner's *Angels in America, Part I: Millenium Approaches, Angels in America, Part II: Perestroika, Sounds Without Nouns,* commissioned for New York's String Trio; *Amistad,* an opera in collaboration with director George C. Wolfe; *The Circus of Dr. Lao,* a music theater work commissioned by the Public Theater in New York City; and recordings including *Of Blues and Dreams, Hidden Voices, Lady of the Mirrors, Variations in Dreamtime,*

Episteme, I've Known Rivers, Hemispheres, Middle Passage, Undine, and *Under the Double Moon.*

Sources

Periodicals

Commonweal, August 14, 1992, pp. 27-28.
Down Beat, August 1981, p. 54; January 1982, pp. 21-23, 68;
May 1984, pp. 6, 65; January 1986, p. 10.
Fanfare, January-February 1993.
Horizon, June 1986, pp. 34, 36.
High Fidelity, April 1984, p. 13; July 1985, p. 24.
Jazziz, February/March 1993, pp. 14, 16, 26.
Nation, December 6, 1986, pp. 651-652.

New Republic, December 8, 1986, pp. 30-32.
Newsweek, December 14, 1981, pp. 119; November 28, 1983, pp. 98-99.
New York, October 13, 1986, p. 98.
New York Times, January 15, 1994, Sec. A, p. 11; October 28, 1994, B9.
New Yorker, October 27, 1986, p. 118, 120; July 31, 1989, pp. 67-69.
Opera News, June 1989, pp. 24, 26-29.
People Weekly, October 6, 1986, pp. 129-130.
Time, May 16, 1988, p. 88.
U.S. News & World Report, November 3, 1986, pp. 73-74.

—*Alison Carb Sussman*

Dominique Dawes

1976—

Gymnast

Dominique Dawes has a lifetime of accomplishments to her credit, and she is just entering her twenties. A top-ranked athlete in the demanding sport of gymnastics, Dawes was one of the first black American woman ever to make the United States Olympic gymnastics team. She also holds the honor of being the first black woman to win a national gymnastics championship. Still competing at an age when most gymnasts are compelled to retire, she plans to be a force to be reckoned with at the 1996 Summer Olympic Games as well.

Dawes was the 1994 American national champion in gymnastics, the first woman in 25 years to earn first place in every category of competition at the championship event. Her petite stature and slender figure disguise the fact that she is one of the most muscular, agile, and daring participants in gymnastics today. Olympic gold medalist Mary Lou Retton extolled Dawes in *USA Weekend* magazine as a "real '90s gymnast, explosive and athletic. Nobody does it like her."

Dawes was born in 1976 in Silver Spring, Maryland, a suburb of Washington, DC. Far from being pushed into

sports by overzealous parents, she had to do some pushing of her own. As an active six-year-old, she jumped on the family furniture and tumbled down the stairs until her mother--fearful for the child's safety--enrolled her in gymnastics classes at a nearby club in Wheaton, Maryland. The club was run by a former University of Maryland gymnast named Kelli Hill, herself just out of college. Despite her own youth, Hill recognized Dawes's natural talent immediately and encouraged her parents to give her all the lessons they could afford. "I knew [Dawes] was good," Hill explained in the *Washington Post*. "The question was if she was focused enough. You never know about that. Could she do it mentally?"

Eyed the Olympics

Women's gymnastics is a sport with very young competitors, principally because women's centers of gravity change as they mature. The lean lines of a young girl's body are more suited to work requiring balance and pinpoint precision. Thus many gymnasts peak at an alarmingly young age--some succumb to the pressure and develop eating disorders or other pathological behavior. Others become frustrated and quit. Dawes proved quickly that she had the stamina and determination to reach the top in her sport. "At first I thought [gymnastics] was another play activity," she admitted in the *Washington Post.* "I didn't start taking it all seriously until I was about 11. Now gymnastics is my life."

In the late 1980s coach Hill moved her operation to the Hill's Gymnastic Training Center in Gaithersburg, Maryland. Gaithersburg is a 40-minute drive from Silver Spring on one of the busiest arteries leading into the nation's capital. Nevertheless, Dawes rose each morning at five o'clock to make the trip to Gaithersburg in time for a two-hour morning workout before school. After school ended, she would spend an additional five hours in the gym practicing, almost always under the watchful eye of Kelli Hill.

Gymnastics competitors must be able to perform a number of different specialties: uneven parallel bars, floor exercises, vault, and balance beam. Dawes showed promise in each area. By 1991 she was ranked 13th nationally in compulsories, third in optionals and ninth

overall. Her achievement was considered particularly impressive because she was not working with a well-known Olympic coach or at one of the more prestigious Olympic training centers.

Asked her goals by the *Washington Post* in 1991, the 14-year-old Dawes said she wanted to make the 1992 Olympic Team. And if she failed? "I'll try for 1996," she declared. "If I don't make it then, I'll switch sports." Dawes did not have to wait until 1996 to make an Olympic team. She first announced her superiority at a dual 1992 U.S.-Japan meet by scoring a perfect 10 in floor exercise. At the nationals that same year she placed first in the uneven bars and fourth in the all-around, easily qualifying to travel to Barcelona. Her number four ranking in the all-around was doubly impressive in that she finished within one-tenth of a point of winner Kim Zmeskal, the 1991 world champion and a favorite to win a medal at the 1992 Summer Games.

As for Dawes, her performance at the Barcelona Olympics was a slight disappointment. She won a team bronze medal but finished 26th overall. Her inability to win any individual events did not faze the young athlete, however. She looked at Barcelona as a learning experience, a rare opportunity for a high school student to travel, receive worldwide attention, and come home with honors. "Competing at the high level I do has helped me to develop my skills and confidence," she maintained in the *Washington Post.* "I try not to get frustrated. Sometimes it's a little difficult to balance school, gymnastics, and my schedule, but most of the time, it's easy."

Won National Championship

Dawes's schedule-balancing became easier when she moved in with her Gaithersburg-based coach so that she would have more time to train. The decision paid off when she finished second in the individual all-around competition at the 1993 national championships. Her accomplishments at that meet also included first place finishes in both the vault and the balance beam--longtime nemesis Shannon Miller won the uneven bars and the floor exercise. In an interview with the *Washington Post* after the event, Dawes admitted that she felt somewhat inferior to Miller, who had beaten her in the 1993 world championships in Birmingham, England. "I think Shannon works harder than I do," Dawes said. "When I see her work out, it seems like she's trying harder than anyone else. If I want to beat her, I have to train harder and longer."

Dawes returned to her Gaithersburg gym and set herself

to the task of surpassing Miller--and any other up-and-coming competitor who might be waiting in the wings. Her hard work paid off in August of 1994 at the national championships held in Nashville, Tennessee. There she took the national all-around championship and first place in all four women's events: the vault, uneven bars, balance beam, and floor exercises. No one had accomplished such a feat in 25 years, and the last gymnast to do it had been competing at a time when the field of opponents was much weaker. Dawes became an instant celebrity, sought after for television interviews, magazine profiles, and autographs. "It's kind of overwhelming," she said of her sudden success in the *Washington Post*. "It seems kind of neat for me, that it's only been done one time before. It's neat for my own self-esteem. It means I've accomplished something very unusual. I just went out there to hit my sets. I never imagined I'd win all the events."

When talk turned to the 1996 Olympics, however, Dawes demurred. "I don't want to say anything about the next few years because I want to make sure that if I stay around for Atlanta, my body will be able to hold up-

-both physically and mentally," she explained. "You're concentrating all the time in this sport. I'm really excited right now, but I don't like to get overexcited about competitions. You know there will be good days and bad days. And I know I still will have some bad days."

Actually, bad days have been few for the engaging Dawes. Having graduated from Gaithersburg High School in 1994, she accepted an athletic scholarship to Stanford University but deferred enrollment until after the summer of 1996. In the meantime she began taking courses at the University of Maryland. Medicine is one possible field of study she says she would like to pursue. Her training continued at Hill's Gymnastic Training Center, and her round of appearances included the nationals, the world championships, and exhibitions in Europe, Japan, and America. In the 1995 nationals, she turned in a creditable performance with first-place finishes in the uneven bars and the floor exercise. Her gold medal floor exercise presentation included a dar-

Dawes over high bar in Birmingham, England, 1993.

ingback-and-forth tumbling pattern that included 11 aerial moves and a nonstop criss-cross of the 40-foot by 40-foot mat.

> "I've been going through exactly what a lot of teenagers are going through— just at a gym instead of an office."

Dawes has not yet won a world championship, but her performances in world competition have been impressive nonetheless. She is particularly strong in the floor exercise and is the only gymnast who executes the two complete criss-cross tumbling passes as a part of her routine. In two world championships, Dawes was in strong medal contention until she tried--and failed--some extremely difficult vaults in order to enhance her scores. These near-misses and her consistently excellent work in national competition earned her a ranking of fourth in the world as of 1995.

More Olympic Hopes?

Dominique Dawes stands on the threshold of 20 as the 1996 Summer Games loom. As Christine Brennan notes in the *Washington Post,* that age "is about 100 in gymnastic years." Even without sustaining any injuries--and Dawes has had her share--she must face competition with younger athletes such as defending national champion Dominique Moceanu, who is 13. Despite new rules about the age of Olympic competitors, Dawes is still a senior statesman at any world-class event. Her body alone tells the tale: in Barcelona in 1992, she stood four-foot-nine and weighed 81 pounds. In 1995 she had grown to five-foot-one and 106. Dawes is not one to accent the negatives, however. Considering her height and weight gains, she told the *Washington Post:* "It hasn't been bad. You've got to change some things, like your steps on floor exercise. But it really hasn't been a problem."

Most observers agree that Dawes will make the 1996 Olympic team, if not necessarily as its star then at least as a "steadying force for the girls who are coming behind her," noted Brennan. She has managed to navigate the tricky business of world-caliber gymnastics without falling victim to the troubles that prey upon younger athletes, such as eating disorders and strain-induced injuries. Not that Dawes is a hearty eater--she absolutely avoids desserts, claiming she doesn't like them.

As for a personal life, Dawes has attempted to keep hers as normal as possible, given the constraints of her practice schedule. She was popular enough at high school to have been named queen of the senior prom, and she has a close relationship with her older sister. When asked by the *Washington Post* if she felt she had missed anything growing up, Dawes said: "Kids ... don't just go home and watch TV. They usually have a sport to do or a job and they stay at their job pretty late. So I've been going through exactly what a lot of teenagers are going through--just at a gym instead of an office." In *USA Weekend* she declared that she would much rather work hard than "jut sit in a house and be rich and famous."

If any aspect of her career puzzles Dawes, it would have to be her level of fame. Shy and retiring by nature, she finds it "weird" that strangers stop her in the street and ask for her autograph. Fellow superstar Mary Lou Retton told *USA Weekend* of Dawes: "She's not in it for the exposure. She's true." In the same *USA Weekend* profile, Marguerite Del Giudice notes a similar preoccupation in Dawes not for the glory of the applause but for the sheer thrill of the moves themselves: "When she works out, there's nothing in her head, nothing she can put into words. And perhaps that is the secret: to linger mindlessly in the powerful place between the thoughts where actions and intentions form."

Dawes credits her parents, who are now separated, for their patience and generosity in allowing her to pursue her goal. "They just let me do it, and if I didn't want to, I didn't have to," she told *USA Weekend.* "But whenever I wanted to go to the gym, they would take me." As for her own advice to other Olympic hopefuls, Dawes told *Ebony:* "Don't set your goals to be a star; set your goals to be the best that you can be and go from there."

Sources

Ebony, February 1995, p. 134; May 1995, p. 84.
Los Angeles Times, March 4, 1995, p. 1C.
People, December 26, 1994-January 2, 1995.
San Francisco Chronicle, July 17, 1993, p. 3D.
USA Weekend, April 7-9, 1995, pp. 4-7.
Washington Post, June 30, 1991, p. 3B; June 10, 1992, p. 1C; August 31, 1993, p. 1G; April 12, 1994, p. 8D; August 30, 1994, p. 1E; August 21, 1995, p. 1D.
Washington Post Magazine, November 20, 1994, p. 9.

—Mark Kram

David E. Driver

1955—

Book publisher, social activist, investor

Thriving in spite of childhood poverty, David Driver's career successes have ranged from institutional investing in the booming 1980s to book publishing in the 1990s. In all these ventures, he has committed himself to giving something back to his community by engaging in various forms of social activism. These activities include working with the Boys and Girls Clubs of America and various speaking engagements.

porary Black Biography (CBB).

This confidence, along with excellent grades, garnered Driver admission to Lindblom High School, an elite public trade school. It was there that Driver first became aware of his family's poverty. "At Lindblom you had a lot of kids from middle-class black families. My clothes were not as nice looking [as those of the other kids], and so I became very fashion conscious for awhile,!" he stated fondly in an interview with *CBB*. Though Driver and his siblings were raised by their single mother and were the first generation to attend college, it has always been an unstated assumption that they would seek a higher education despite the family's shaky financial situation. Determined to earn degrees, Driver and his siblings managed to find grants and loans that enabled them to attend college.

As a child, David Driver's small stature did not lend itself to athletic activities, therefore, he was "a real bookworm type," he told the *Chicago Tribune.* This did not preclude such high ambitions, however, as becoming a race car driver. With his grandfather's admonition that he instead become a professional, such as a doctor or an attorney, Driver set his sights on the latter--not in the least because he could not stand the sight of blood. But, growing up on public assistance in an inner-city neighborhood on Chicago's West Side did not pave an easy path to a legal career. "I always had high aspirations, though I never really doubted that I was going to make it at something," he stated in an interview with *Contem-*

At Bradley University in Peoria, Illinois, Driver confronted his immersion in an almost all-white student body by running successfully for sophomore class president, becoming the first black to do so. He also joined groups, such as the Black Student Union and a black fraternity, Phi Beta Sigma, both of which involved him in volunteer

At a Glance . . .

Born David E. Driver, October 17, 1955, in Chicago, IL; son of Edward (a postman) and Esther (a homemaker; maiden name, Williams) Driver. *Education:* Bradley University, B.A., 1976; University of Chicago Business School, M.B.A., 1984.

Arthur Young & Company, staff accountant, 1976-78; International Hospital Supply Corporation, finance manager, 1978-80; Merrill Lynch Capital Markets, account executive, 1980-82, vice president, 1982-88. The Noble Press, Inc., founder and president, 1988--. Author, 1989--.

Member: Black Literary Society (founder); Society of Illinois Book Publishers (secretary); National Association of Black Book Publishers (founding member).

Addresses: *Office*--The Noble Press, Inc., 213 W. Institute Place, Suite 508, Chicago, IL 60610; phone: (312) 642-1168.

work that was to play a significant role in his life and career. Among the projects Driver was associated with--or initiated--were an inner-city literacy tutoring program and numerous food drives. Having decided to become a business attorney, Driver followed the advice of a counselor who suggested that he change his major from political science to accounting.

Entered Corporate World

In 1976, upon receiving his BA from Bradley, and a CPA license from the State of Illinois, Driver accepted a position as a staff accountant at Arthur Young & Company. He worked there for two years, until a client contact led him to a job at the International Hospital Supply Corporation.

As a finance manager from 1978 to 1980, Driver dealt with foreign currency markets, where companies buy and sell money from other countries in order to protect their foreign investments from exchange rate fluctuations.

With this experience in foreign currencies, Driver landed a job at Merrill Lynch Capital Markets in 1980, where he served as an account executive until becoming vice president in 1982. He became a pioneer in the emerging field of stock and bond futures, wherein an investor speculates on what the price of these securities will be at a specified date in the future. Because it was such a new field, Driver spent nearly two years trying to convince clients of the value of such investments--difficult in an industry that worked primarily on commission, but Driver's supervisors had faith in his judgment. When it turned out that these new kinds of investments were extremely lucrative, he was, for some time, Chicago's only institutional futures broker, or "the only one in town playing the game," as he put it in an interview with *CBB.* Driver parlayed this advantage into huge profits for Merrill Lynch--and himself--as well--while the competition scurried to catch up. Meanwhile he received his MBA in economics from the prestigious University of Chicago Business School in 1984.

By 1988, Driver told *Publisher's Weekly,* "It was time to take the money and run." In fact, he had been plotting his departure from the world of corporate finance since about 1985. As Driver told *CBB,* he found the brokering to be "self-serving and lacking in social significance," a drawback he was finding increasingly unacceptable as corporate demands on his time and energy left less room for his varied volunteer efforts. These activities included working with the Boys and Girls Clubs of America, coaching a basketball team of homeless children, and speaking to black MBAs as the head of a United Way recruitment committee.

> "We were always well-thought-of in our little literary circle as a progressive, high-quality publishing company, but this book has risen us to new levels."

A longstanding interest in writing prompted Driver to take a number of creative writing classes at the University of Chicago, and this, coupled with his community activism, gave him the idea to start his own publishing company, one that would focus on books with social or environmental significance. Driver hoped that certain business tools he had acquired, including the use of demographic surveys and databases, would help overcome the marketing obstacles such titles traditionally face.

Founded a Publishing Company

In 1988, Driver founded The Noble Press and its first title was his own, *The Good Heart Book: A Guild to Volunteering.* This book detailed the issues surrounding a number of social ills, ranging from illiteracy to inner-city poverty, and it provided a step-by-step approach to becoming an effective volunteer. He started the company with an initial outlay of $250,000. Able to live off the interest on investments he had made during his previous career, Driver received no salary, but hired a small staff and initially ran the operation out of his apartment.

By 1991, Noble Press had a full-time staff of five working in the refurbished loft of a former bicycle factory, and a number of its titles had received critical notice. *The Parents' Guide to Innovative Education,* by Ann W. Dodd, for example, received a *Child* magazine award in 1992. However, the company struggled financially as it released titles true to its social mission but lacking sufficient sales, including *Eco-Warriors, A Just And Lasting Peace,* and books tackling the issues of homelessness and child abuse. Driver concluded that such titles were perhaps better suited to college presses and decided to take a more market-driven approach by shifting Noble's focus to general interest titles for the black community-at-large, including fiction and even romance novels.

Secured a Successful Niche for Noble Press

The Noble Press' breakthrough book, *Volunteer Slavery: My Authentic Negro Experience,* had significant popular appeal and a social message, as well. The book gave an irreverent and unforgiving account of black author Janet Nelson's four years as a liberal activist struggling to make her voice heard as a writer for the *Washington Post Magazine.* It also explored the meaning of black identity in the United States. Released in the spring of 1993, *Volunteer Slavery* sold more than 40,000 hardcover copies before Noble sold it to Penguin for a paperback release that became a national best-seller. It also won an American Book Award in 1994. "It's changed our lives around here a lot," Driver told the *Chicago Tribune.* "We were always well-thought-of in our little literary circle as a progressive, high-quality publishing company, but this book has risen

us to new levels." Other publications, such as *Black and Single* by Larry E. Davis, sold equally as well for Noble.

These and other successes proved the wisdom of diversifying the company's catalog and targeting a black audience. Noble turned its first profit in 1993, as annual sales reached nearly one million dollars, and its distribution outlets increased to 6,000. Unwilling to let the opportunities of new technology pass by Noble Press, Driver began exploring avenues for Internet applications, which included placing the firm's catalog on-line. He also founded the Black Literary Society, a book club that places its reading list of Noble Press and other black-oriented books on the Internet. In 1995, Driver explored the possibility of a CD-ROM that would document a traveling museum exhibit featuring black architects.

Unsatisfied with simply publishing significant and entertaining books and helping to manifest the potential of a once underestimated and under-served black reading public, Driver continues the volunteer work that has always been his marker of personal success. He founded and runs a program called Young Chicago Authors that provides Saturday morning workshops for aspiring high school-age writers. Driver invites accomplished writers and others well-versed in the trade to speak to the students and help them hone their skills.

Selected writings

The Good Heart Book: A Guide to Volunteering, The Noble Press, 1989.
Defending the Left: An Individual's Guide to Fighting for Social Justice, Individual Rights and the Environment, The Noble Press, 1992.

Sources

American Banker, December 6, 19990, p. 10.
Booklist, December 1, 1992, p. 637.
Chicago Tribune, July 25, 1993, section 7, p. 3; April 11, 1990, section 2C, p. 1.
Essence, November, 1993, p. 44.
Los Angeles Sentinel, April 19, 1990, p. A8.
Publishers Weekly, March 15, 1991, p. 28; March 15, 1993, p. 22; May 2, 1994, p. 57.
Time, October 10, 1994, p. 70.

Additional information for this profile was obtained from a *CBB* interview with Driver, April 20, 1995.

—John F. Packel, II

Michael Eric Dyson

1958—

Educator, writer

Hailed as one of a group of "new intellectuals," Michael Eric Dyson is a scholar based at the University of North Carolina in Chapel Hill. Dyson, who heads the university's Institute of African American Research, is an author who addresses issues of race and culture in such diverse publications as *Christian Century* and *Rolling Stone.* He has published three full-length books, including the well-received *Making Malcolm: The Myth and Meaning of Malcolm X.* He has also lectured from the college podium, appeared on popular talk shows, and even testified before congressional subcommittees on various issues of concern to black Americans. *Washington Post* correspondent David Nicholson noted that Dyson "belongs to a group of young intellectuals who may yet define our view of black American culture as did their predecessors Ralph Ellison and Albert Murray."

"Young" is an important operating word when describing Dyson. Most professors do not become nationally known while still in their thirties, nor do they often head whole departments at that age. Dyson has done both while still in his mid-thirties, due in part to the success of his books and the strength of his journalism. *Philadel-* *phia Inquirer* book critic Carlo Romano called Dyson "crown prince ... to the two most established black male intellectuals: [Cornel] West and ... scholar Henry Louis Gates, Jr."

Born in 1958 in Detroit, Michigan, Dyson grew up in a comfortable middle-class family. His father was an auto worker, his mother a paraprofessional in the city schools. In a piece published in *Details* magazine, Dyson suggested that, due in large part to his age, he was somewhat isolated from the bitter civil rights struggles that occurred in the 1960s. "I was nine years old when Martin Luther King, Jr. died," he said. "I had never heard of him before then. I remember a newscaster interrupted the regular programming and broke the news. My father, sitting in his chair, went `Hmph.' A *hmph* that said both `I can't believe it' and `How predictable.' That was my initiation into the world of white and black."

When Dyson was a teenager, a well-meaning neighbor gave him a full set of the Harvard Classics. This standard literature of mostly white European authors may not

At a Glance . . .

Born October 23, 1958, in Detroit, MI; son of Everett (an auto worker) and Addie (an aide in the public schools) Dyson; married second wife, Marcia Louise, June 24, 1992; children: Michael II, Maisha. *Education:* Carson-Newman College, B.A. (magna cum laude), 1982; Princeton University, M.A., 1991, Ph.D., 1993.

Former instructor at Mathy College, Princeton University, Hartford Seminary, and Chicago Theological Seminary; Brown University, Providence, RI, assistant professor, 1993-94; University of North Carolina, Chapel Hill, NC, director of Institute of African American Research, 1994–. Ordained Baptist minister.

Member: Democratic Socialist Society of America.

Selected awards National magazine award from National Association of Black Journalists, 1992.

Addresses: *Office*–Institute of African American Research, University of North Carolina, Chapel Hill, NC 27599.

1993.

Although scholars traditionally distance themselves from popular culture, Dyson chose to focus on topics of interest to mainstream readers. He became a regular contributor of record reviews to *Rolling Stone*, a popular columnist for *Christian Century* and *The Nation*, and reviewed books and films for newspapers. His first book-length collection of essays, *Reflecting Black: African-American Cultural Criticism*, contains pieces on racism in the seminary, filmmaker Spike Lee, entertainer Michael Jackson, sports star Michael Jordan, and black religious leaders as diverse as Martin Luther King, Jr. and Malcolm X. By addressing himself to some of pop culture's icons, Dyson noted that he was attempting to resist "the labored seductions of all narrow views of black life, whether they be racist, essentialist, or otherwise uncritically disposed toward African American culture."

> "Gangsta rap's in-your-face style may do more to force America to confront crucial social problems than a million sermons or political speeches."

Dyson embarked upon his book Making Malcolm after a confrontation with some of his black male students at Brown University. The students objected to the presence of whites in Dyson's class on the radical Muslim leader, claiming that the whites "discuss things they don't know about," especially Malcolm X's life and philosophy. In response Dyson decided to write a "comprehensive and critical examination of what [Malcolm X] said and did so that his life and thought will be useful to future generations of peoples in struggle around the globe," as quoted from the book's introduction.

sound like preferred reading for a black teenager, but Dyson devoured the whole set. "I was reading *Two Years before the Mast* and also getting my [link to black culture through black musicians like] Smokey Robinson," he joked in the *Philadelphia Inquirer.* Dyson graduated from high school in 1976 and at the same time became a teenaged father. His responsibilities led him to accept a series of jobs in maintenance and auto sales, but he lost all of his employment just weeks before his son was born. For a time he was on welfare.

Studied in Tennessee, New Jersey

With the assistance of his church pastor, Dyson became a Baptist minister and traveled south to Tennessee's Knoxville College to attend divinity school. He later transferred to Carson-Newman College in Jefferson City, Tennessee, earning his bachelor's degree with high honors in 1982. Three years later he began his ascent into academia by accepting a graduate fellowship at Princeton University. During the years in which he was completing his master's and doctorate degrees he also taught at Princeton and at Hartford Seminary and Chicago Theological Seminary. He earned his Ph.D. in

Making Malcolm Reached Wide Audience

Making Malcolm was published late in 1994 by Oxford University Press. The target audience was hardly just a group of ivory tower academicians, however: The book's dust jacket included praiseworthy blurbs from figures such as Angela Davis, the Reverend Jesse Jackson, Senator Carol Moseley-Braun, and rapper Chuck D of Public Enemy. Oxford University Press marketed the work through mainstream booksellers such as B. Dalton and Waldenbooks, recognizing that the audience for *Making Malcolm* would extend far beyond the scholarly community.

Los Angeles Times Book Review critic Natasha Tarpley declared that in *Making Malcolm* Dyson exhibits "great respect, sensitivity and love--a balance Malcolm himself mastered." The critic added: "Dyson assesses Malcolm's role in the resurgent black nationalism(s) of this generation's young black artists and students ... [and] criticizes this generation for failing to learn Malcolm's greatest lesson, that of self-criticism; for seeing only the parts of Malcolm, of ourselves, of our struggle that *we want to see.*" In the *Washington Post Book World,* Salim Muwakkil praised Dyson for his "willingness to embrace [Malcolm X's] complexity," a quality that "lifts this volume above those so far that have sought simply to shape Malcolm's message to serve their particular passion." *New Yorker* correspondent Michael Berube concluded: "Dyson gives us Malcolm as 'public moralist'--and a study that is as substantive and comprehensive as 'public' cultural criticism of such a figure can hope to be."

In the wake of the reception for *Making Malcolm,* Dyson has addressed another issue in the black community: the cultural significance of gangsta rap. Dyson is a sought-after authority on rap music, having been asked to testify about it before a congressional subcommittee and, according to the *New Yorker,* being lauded by Chuck D as a "bad brother." Typically, Dyson's approach to the genre is thoughtful and thorough, neither completely condemning the music nor embracing it.

In Dyson's third book, *Between God and Gangsta Rap,* as well as in essays and editorials, including one in the *Wichita Eagle,* he has sought to put gangsta rap in its cultural and social perspective. "Gangsta rap often reaches higher than its ugliest, lowest common denominator," he noted. "Misogyny, violence, materialism and sexual transgression are not its exclusive domain. At its best, this music draws attention to complex dimensions of ghetto life ignored by most Americans.... Indeed, gangsta rap's in-your-face style may do more to force America to confront crucial social problems than a million sermons or political speeches."

Among the "New Intellectuals"

The success of his books in particular has led to increased visibility for Dyson, who has appeared on talk shows and at book signings in the largest American cities. Berube included Dyson when he spoke in the *New Yorker* of a "generation of African American intellectuals [whose] work has become a fixture of mall bookstores, talk shows, elite universities, and black popular culture." Berube added: "Plainly, they have consolidated the gains of the civil-rights and Black Power move-

ments in at least this regard: they have the ability and the resources to represent themselves in public on their own terms." Robert S. Boynton, in an *Atlantic Monthly* essay, also identified Dyson as residing among "an impressive group of African American writers and thinkers [who] have emerged to revive and revitalize [the role of the public intellectual]. They are bringing moral imagination and critical intelligence to bear on the definingly American matter of race--and reaching beyond race to voice what one calls 'the commonality of American concern.'"

Reflecting on his current position as a man of letters and sought-after commentator, Dyson told the *Philadelphia Inquirer:* "I have to constantly negotiate the tension between past neighborhood and present neighborhood." He added that his success "is affirming, of course, but it also feels awkward. I think of myself as a Trojan Horse. I don't have an earring in my nose or ear. I don't have my hair combed back in a ponytail, or rough-hewn. I look like an insider. But there's a whole lot of Negroes inside of me. There's a whole lot of black men inside of me. And when I get in somewhere, I let them out."

Selected writings

Reflecting Black: African-American Cultural Criticism, University of Minnesota Press, 1993.
Making Malcolm: The Myth and Meaning of Malcolm X, Oxford University Press, 1994.
Between God and Gangsta Rap, Oxford University Press, 1995.

Sources

Books

Dyson, Michael Eric, introduction to *Making Malcolm: The Myth and Meaning of Malcolm X*, Oxford University Press, 1994.
Dyson, Michael Eric, introduction to *Reflecting Black: African-American Cultural Criticism,* University of Minnesota Press, 1993.

Periodicals

Atlantic Monthly, March 1995, pp. 53-70.
Details, October 1995, pp. 162-67, 189.
Los Angeles Times Book Review, March 26, 1995, p. 4.
New Yorker, January 9, 1995, pp. 73-80.
Philadelphia Inquirer, April 12, 1995, pp. 1F, 5F.
Washington Post, October 12, 1993, p. 3C.
Washington Post Book World, December 18, 1994,

p. 11.
Wichita Eagle, July 2, 1995, p. 19A.

—Mark Kram

Chaka Fattah

1956—

Politician

The Republican party may have won a majority in the U.S. House of Representatives in 1994, but a seat was still found for a liberal named Chaka Fattah. The freshman Democratic congressman from Philadelphia is a lawmaker who has advanced through the rocky terrain of Philadelphia politics without help from party or celebrity endorsements. In a year of unprecedented Republican gains in Congress, Fattah won 85 percent of the bote in his district on a platform that is brimming with liberal ideology. Nevertheless, he is viewed as an independent thinker who is willing to listen to any serious discussion of the issues. *Philadelphia Inquirer* columnist Acel Moore described Fattah as "a seasoned legislator and a skillful politician who has earned the respect and support of a diverse group of constituents from his Second Congressional District." Moore concluded that Fattah has "an impressive record ... and has established expertise in housing and education issues and has a reputation of being bright, thoughtful, and innovative about urban issues." Fattah wants to be a shaper of urban public policy.

Even prior to his election to Congress, Fattah has demonstrated his commitment to the issue by organizing national conferences on cities and making proposals to the Bush and Clinton presidential administrations. Aware that he is asking for more federal and state aid to urban areas--at a time when government belt-tightening has become fashionable, the new Philadelphia congressman offers passionate arguments for his position. "The majority of Americans live in metropolitan areas, and therefore, are impacted to the degree that as the core decays--crime, poverty, drug abuse--it moves out, it spreads to the suburbs surrounding that core," he commented in the *Philadelphia Inquirer Magazine.* "So, the suburbs are inextricably tied to the cities, and this beating up on cities is a false political argument.... The country would be much more productive if we had everyone in the game, if we focused our resources on lifting those boats stuck at the bottom."

Social Activism Brings a Name Change

Chaka Fattah was born Arthur Davenport, the fourth of six sons of a U.S. Army sergeant named Russell Davenport and a journalist named Frances "Frankee" Brown.

At a Glance . . .

Born Arthur Davenport, November 21, 1956, in Philadelphia, PA; son of Russell (a U.S. Army sergeant) and Frances (a social activist; now named Falaka Fattah) Davenport; married, second wife's name Patricia Renfroe (an attorney); children: (first marriage) Frances, Chaka Jr.; (second marriage) Christian (stepson). *Education:* Attended Community College of Philadelphia and University of Pennsylvania, Wharton Community Education Program; University of Pennsylvania, Fels School for State and Local Government, M.A., 1985. *Religion:* Baptist.

Office of Housing and Community Development, Philadelphia, PA, special assistant to managing director, 1980-82; Pennsylvania General Assembly, Harrisburg, PA, state representative, 1982-88, state senator, 1988-94; U.S. House of Representatives, Washington, DC, congressman, 1995–. Former assistant director of House of Umoja, Philadelphia, PA.

Selected awards Pennsylvania House of Representatives "outstanding contribution award"; Simpson Fletcher Award for religion and race.

Addresses: *Home*–Philadelphia, PA.*Office*–1205 Longworth House Office Building, Washington, DC 20515-3802.

His mother worked for the *Philadelphia Tribune* and as an occasional publicist for musicians such as Sam Cooke and Otis Redding. The Davenport marriage failed while Arthur was still young, and his mother became deeply involved in the Civil Rights movement. At a 1968 national conference on black power, she met a fellow activist named David and married him two months later. Together they founded the magazine *Umoja*, a Swahili word for unity. The couple also decided to take new names that would emphasize their African roots. Frankee Brown became Falaka Fattah; her fourth son became Chaka Fattah, named after the Zulu warrior Chaka.

"I think my name is an advantage," Fattah noted in the *Philadelphia Inquirer Magazine.* "It makes people pay attention. All ethnic groups in this country have ethnic names.... Had it not been for slavery, my name

would have been more African anyway." In another era, a name like "Chaka Fattah" may have been a political liability, but in the days of such political figures as Kweisi Mfume of Maryland, Julius Caesar Watts of Oklahoma, and Newt Gingrich of Georgia, a unique name is becoming a handy political tool. For Fattah, the African-inspired name is not only a source of racial pride, it is also a means by which to establish his individuality.

As a young teen, Fattah moved with his family to the 1400 block of Frazier Street in West Philadelphia. There his mother began a study of Philadelphia's gang wars for her magazine. When she discovered that another of her sons was member of a gang, she took a drastic step to keep him off the streets--she invited his whole gang to live in the Frazier Street rowhouse. Fattah's home was suddenly a makeshift hostel for as many as 25 youths at a time. "I thought it was great," the congressman remembered in *Philadelphia Inquirer Magazine.* "All my older brothers and their friends, they were my idols.... Having more than a dozen people with all kinds of perspectives and experiences--good and bad--was helpful in getting a more dynamic view of life."

Falaka Fattah's personal war on gangs became the House of Umoja, an urban "Boy's Town" that has developed into a nationally-known youth program. Chaka Fattah himself played a part in the project's success. As the need for space quickly outpaced his parents' modest home, he began to eye the 20-odd abandoned houses in his block that were simply rotting away. It seemed to him that the House of Umoja might expand into some of these empty dwellings if they could be donated to the project. After consulting with his parents--who admired his initiative, but doubted that anyone would listen to him--Chaka produced a slide presentation and written report on his idea and asked to see the president of the First Pennsylvania Bank, which held the mortgages to some of the houses. Fattah was 14 at the time, but Jim Bodine, the bank president, agreed to see him. The bank president was impressed by the earnest young man and his proposal. A few months later, the bank turned several of the properties over to Falaka Fattah.

Politics Was "Fun"

Fattah became interested in politics while he was a student at Shoemaker Junior High School in Philadelphia. He signed on as a campaign volunteer for mayoral candidate, Hardy Williams, and learned grass-roots politicking by handing out leaflets, tacking up posters, and cheering at rallies. Later, when his parents founded the House of Umoja, Fattah met influential congressman

Bill Gray, who helped them to secure a federal grant to fix-up the abandoned houses they needed for their project. Fattah supported Gray through some of his early campaigns, and the two have remained friends ever since. As a student at Overbrook High School, Fattah helped to organize the Youth Movement to Clean Up Politics, a junior wing of the black political movement aimed at ousting the old-style, white-run Democratic machine in Philadelphia. Fattah and his friend, Curtis Jones, participated in voter registration drives and helped black constituents to get to the polls on election day in an effort to give citizens in their community more power over the political process.

Fattah decided to run for elected office himself. He persuaded Jones to join him as a candidate for city commissioners. The commissioners race is a citywide contest in which the top two vote-getters from each party face-off for three open slots. Tens of thousands of votes would be required for either Fattah or Jones to win a position. Undaunted, the two young men found a benefactor who bought each of them a business suit and dress shoes. A local printing company, called the Resistance Press, printed their campaign flyers at cost. With the Youth Movement behind them, the pair raised about $7,000 and posed together for a poster in which they appeared pushing brooms--as if to imply they would sweep the established candidates out of office. So persistent were the two young men that they won endorsements from the *Philadelphia Inquirer* and its rival the *Philadelphia Bulletin*. On election day, Fattah placed fourth in a field of 24 Democrats. Only after the election did anyone bother to find out his age--at 22, he was three years too young even to qualify for the commissioner's job.

Reflecting on those day, Fattah observed in the *Philadelphia Inquirer Magazine*: "We had a lot of fun, we got to see the city and meet a lot of people. It was the foundation for the beginning of a political organization that has a great deal of credibility in Philadelphia today." Fattah learned from his experience in the commissioners campaign. For his next try at public office, he assembled an effective grass-roots team from block captains to wards and district leaders. These volunteers helped him spread his message in door-to-door fashion and provided him with enthusiastic teams of helpers at special events in the city. According to Vanessa Williams in the *Philadelphia Inquirer Magazine,* Fattah has since established "one of the city's most effective independent political operations." Williams added that Fattah has the services of "an almost unlimited supply of talent, time, and tenacity" among his many volunteers. Indeed, high-ranking workers in any Fattah campaign are asked to sign "mission statements" in which they

pledge to work diligently and display "intelligence," "initiative," and "caring."

In 1982, Fattah--who was then working for Philadelphia's Housing and Community Development office-- announced his plans to run for the Pennsylvania General Assembly. It was the first of many occasions when the maverick Fattah would challenge the veteran politicians in the Democratic party. Fattah won a seat in the state House of Representatives by 58 votes over Nicholas Pucciarelli, an established politician with a widespread power base. At 25, Chaka Fattah became the youngest person ever elected to the Pennsylvania General Assembly. As he learned the process of shaping state government, Fattah also completed his education, earning a master's degree in government administration from the Fels School for State and Local Government at the University of Pennsylvania.

State Senator with National Vision

Fattah served as a state representative until 1988, when he won an election for state senator in the Seventh District, comprising parts of West and North Philadelphia, East Falls, Germantown, and Manayunk. By the time he assumed his senate seat, Fattah was a seasoned lawmaker with the education and experience to handle politics in Harrisburg. In an arena where hundreds of pieced of legislation are proposed in any given term, Fattah saw seven bills he had sponsored become law, including a job-training bill, an act that toughened regulation of for-profit trade schools, and an act intended to protect the rights of people without credit cards.

> "All of my older brothers and their friends, they were my idols....Having more than a dozen people with all kinds of perspectives and experiences—good and bad—was helpful in getting a more dynamic view of life."

With Fattah's new responsibilities also came increased publicity for his ideas--and he had plenty of them. It was Fattah, who in 1990 persuaded more than 20 corporations, colleges, and foundations to make advance payments on their city wage taxes in order to help Philadelphia meet its payroll when funds ran short. Fattah crusaded against high-rise public housing projects, launching a campaign to relocate families from the grim public apartment complexes in the city to rehabilitated single-family neighborhood homes. The audacious state senator also proposed a Big City Initiative, challenging the federal government to invest $100 billion per year for ten years to rebuild 100 of the nation's largest cities. The proposal won Fattah an invitation to the White House to discuss the issue with an aide to then-president George Bush. Fattah also organized a 1992 national conference during which urban officials from all over the country described their ideas about fixing America's crumbling cities.

State Senator Chaka Fattah's interests were obviously leaping beyond the bounds of his Philadelphia senatorial district. No one was particularly surprised in 1991, when he announced himself as a candidate to fill the congressional seat vacated suddenly by his old mentor, Bill Gray. Fattah was one of three candidates in a special congressional election held that year. In the race he finished a distant second to Lucien Blackwell. a "long-time party warhorse," to quote Williams. Blackwell finished the rest of Gray's term and won a subsequent term as well. In 1994, Fattah challenged him again. Williams described the primary election, held on May 10, 1994: "Fattah and his machine emerged like a stealth bomber. He annihilated Blackwell, beating him by 16 percentage points. And in November, when a [Republican] GOP [Grand Old Party] juggernaut crushed Democrats from coast to coast, Chaka Fattah defied the trend: He won his seat with 85 percent of the vote, the largest margin of victory for any incoming freshman in [the 1995] Congress."

Ambition Is an Asset

Those who have criticized Fattah claim that he has put his personal ambitions ahead of Democratic party protocol. His challenge to the popular Lucien Blackwell was deemed premature, and he is still viewed by some Philadelphia Democrats as being too independent-minded. "Ambition can be a cross or a crown--and more often than not it's both," Fattah explained in the *Philadelphia Inquirer Magazine.* "Yeah , I'm ambitious. I think there's nobody in politics who is not ambitious.... The question is, What has my ambition and other positive and negative attributes been able to produce in terms of results?" He added: "It's funny how people admire ambition in most professional circumstances. People who are ambitious in business create companies, in journalism they win Pulitzer Prizes. In politics we win elections."

As a Democrat passionately involved in urban revitalization, Fattah joins a Congress expected to propose a veritable landslide of conservative, cost-cutting legislation. The congressman from Philadelphia's Second District has revealed that he plans to work hard for his agenda, whether it be from a majority or minority position. "I'm not at all in awe of the Republican majority," he confided to the *Philadelphia Inquirer.* "I believe that the only majority that counts is the majority of American people who want change." Elsewhere in the *Philadelphia Inquirer* he concluded: "I would like to be in the majority, but I don't feel handcuffed in terms of my ability to do anything because I'm in the minority.... Hey, I've been a minority all my life. Let's get it on."

Sources

Philadelphia Inquirer, October 25, 1991, p. 1B; October 29, 1991, p.8A;
January 16, 1993, p.1B; May 12, 1994, p. 1B; January 5, 1995, pp. 9A, 15A.
Philadelphia Inquirer Magazine, January 15, 1995, pp. 23-28.
Philadelphia Magazine, February 1992, pp. 49-53.

—Anne Janette Johnson

Walter E. Fauntroy

1933—

Minister, politician

Walter E. Fauntroy's career of community service in the District of Columbia spans four decades. A longtime pastor of the New Bethel Baptist Church in Washington, DC, Fauntroy was also the first elected delegate to represent the people of Washington in the U.S. Congress. Throughout his 19 years on Capitol Hill, Fauntroy fought for home rule and even statehood for the District of Columbia, retiring from Congress before he had reached all his goals. He continues to serve as a social advocate and congressional lobbyist on behalf of black American citizens in Washington, DC and elsewhere.

Fauntroy told the *Washington Post* that his message has remained the same through 35 years of preaching and more than 20 in public service--he wants to preach "good news to the poor ... which must be preached every day." Besides his professional duties, Fauntroy is researching and writing a book about Martin Luther King, Jr. Fauntroy, who headed a congressional committee that investigated Dr. King's assassination in 1978, would like to see the case reopened by an official delegation.

Fauntroy served almost ten terms in the U.S. Congress, but his was not a typical congressman's career. As a delegate to the Congress, he could never vote on the House floor, even on legislation he introduced himself. Thus Fauntroy found himself a restricted representative of a city with a population greater than several Western states. As his prestige on Capitol Hill grew, he successfully attempted to assure some measure of home rule for the District of Columbia. His efforts to achieve statehood for the area met with failure, however, and he retired from the House of Representatives in 1990. Reflecting on his career in the *Washington Post,* Fauntroy said he was proud to have been part of the core of change "in my neighborhood, in our city and our nation."

The fourth of seven children, Walter Fauntroy was born and raised in Washington, DC His father was a clerk in the U.S. Patent Office, and the government salary was stretched thin by the size of the Fauntroy family. Walter grew up in the Shaw community in northwest Washington, then as now a poverty-stricken area plagued by crime, drugs, and unemployment. He found a safe haven in the New Bethel Baptist Church just a few blocks

At a Glance . . .

Born Walter Edward Fauntroy, February 6, 1933, in Washington, DC; son of William T. and Ethel (Vine) Fauntroy; married Dorothy Simms, August 3, 1957; children: Marvin, Melissa. *Education:* Virginia Union University, B.A. (cum laude), 1955; Yale University Divinity School, B.D., 1958. *Religion:* Baptist.

New Bethel Baptist Church, Washington, DC, pastor, 1959–; City Council of Washington, DC, vice-chairperson, 1967-69; House of Representatives, Washington, DC, delegate, 1971-90, chairman of Congressional Black Caucus, 1981-83; Walter E. Fauntroy & Associates, president, 1990–.

Member: Southern Christian Leadership Conference (chairman of the board), Poor People's Campaign (national director, 1969), National Black Leadership Roundtable.

Selected awards Hubert H. Humphrey Humanitarian Award from National Urban Coalition, 1984; honorary degrees from Georgetown University Law School, Yale University, and Virginia Union University.

Addresses: *Home*–Washington, DC. *Office*–Walter E. Fauntroy & Associates, 1025 Connecticut Ave. N.W., Washington, DC 20036.

from his home. "I didn't understand then that we were living on a plantation," he told the *Washington Post,* "but I sensed it--the dope, the bootleg liquor, the payoffs to the cops, the general fear of the white man."

As a high school student Fauntroy felt a call to the ministry. He was an excellent student who graduated second in his class at Washington's all-black Dunbar High School, and the members of his church held fundraising dinners to provide him with a college scholarship. When he graduated from Dunbar in 1952, his church gave him enough money to pay for his entire first year at Virginia Union University in Richmond. He graduated from that institution in 1955, with honors and then earned a degree in divinity from Yale.

Fraternized With M. L. King, Jr.

During his stay at Virginia Union University, Fauntroy met the 22-year-old Martin Luther King, Jr., himself an

ordained Baptist minister. With so much in common, the two men formed a fast friendship that began with a single all-night discussion of theology. Fauntroy joined King's Southern Christian Leadership Conference (SCLC), and upon his return to Washington, DC, became an influential lobbyist for civil rights in Congress. Fauntroy also helped to coordinate the seminal 1963 March on Washington at which King gave his famous "I Have a Dream" speech.

After completing his education, Fauntroy became pastor of the New Bethel Baptist Church. He returned home with a rather unorthodox view of Christian service that his parishioners immediately embraced. Believing that religion was something more than a Sunday-morning pastime, forgotten by half past noon, Fauntroy took part in civil rights demonstrations, sit-ins, and marches--both in Washington, DC, and elsewhere.

> "I believe that all things work together for the good of those who love the Lord."

As a high-ranking official in the SCLC, Fauntroy coordinated national civil rights activities; as a pastor he worked to improve social conditions in his church's neighborhood. One of the programs he helped to initiate was the Model Inner City Community Organization (MICCO). This organization, which Fauntroy headed until 1971, used federal grants to improve inner city neighborhoods using black architects, city planners, and construction engineers to design and build homes, schools, stores, and other projects in urban Washington. At one time the budget for MICCO was well over $30 million.

Stepped Into Politics

Because his religious beliefs placed a premium on community service, Fauntroy naturally gravitated toward the political arena. In 1967, he was named vice-chairperson of the Washington City Council, a nine-member body appointed directly by the president of the United States. Fauntroy sat on the city council for two years, resigning when his commitments as director of MICCO began to take all of his time. He was not out of politics for long, however.

The District of Columbia had no formal representation in Congress before 1970. That year, President Nixon signed a bill giving the District one non-voting delegate to Congress. Fauntroy wanted the job. With the support of his fellow pastors in the city--and with appearances by his friend Coretta Scott King--he defeated two primary opponents who had both spent twice as much money as he did. Because Washington, DC is a heavily Democratic city with a black majority, the Democratic primary election was the important race for the seat. Having won the primary by a substantial margin, Fauntroy easily beat a Republican candidate and was sworn in March 23, 1971, as the first congressional delegate from Washington, DC.

Although Fauntroy's status in the Congress did not allow him to vote on the House floor, he was allowed a vote in committee and could introduce legislation on any issue. Fauntroy therefore became influential with the Congressional Black Caucus (CBC) as a liberal with an agenda that included all the concerns of inner city residents, the poor, and minorities. Fauntroy's special quest was for home rule--and eventually statehood--for the District of Columbia. Using his considerable political clout, he oversaw legislation that provided for direct election of a mayor and a city council in Washington by 1973. Fauntroy briefly considered running for mayor of Washington himself but instead decided to stay in Congress. He was returned to his office five times over the ensuing years, sometimes with as much as 85 percent of the vote.

"The Nation's Last Colony"

By the early 1980s Fauntroy was an important mainstay in the halls of Congress, an early chair of the CBC, and holder of a seat on the Committee on Banking, Finance and Urban Affairs. Still he chafed at the restrictions of his office, feeling that the citizens of the District of Columbia were not properly represented in Congress. As early as 1975 Fauntroy began his quest for statehood for Washington, DC. His ongoing efforts in this regard brought him national publicity, but he still did not achieve his goal. At one point--following many years of struggle--Fauntroy's frustration became so great that he urged Washington residents not to pay their federal taxes, because they lived in a "colony" just as their American ancestors had.

Fauntroy stepped down from his seat in Congress in

1990 to run for mayor of Washington, DC. He was defeated by Sharon Pratt Kelly. The loss was far from devastating for the energetic Fauntroy. He told the *Washington Post:* "I put together a very careful and thorough plan, but unfortunately that never got over. But I believe that all things work together for the good of those who love the Lord." Indeed, Fauntroy merely returned to his first and constant home, the New Bethel Baptist Church, where he resumed a full-time ministry and rededicated himself to community service.

Fauntroy also founded Walter E. Fauntroy & Associates, a consulting firm that provides lobbying services for a variety of clients. The first and biggest client to sign on with Fauntroy was Nelson Mandela's African National Congress (ANC). Since 1992, Fauntroy has been busy lobbying Congress to pass legislation to create an "enterprise fund" for South Africa. He has been actively encouraging new private U.S. investment in South Africa as well. "I'm having a great time," Fauntroy told the *Washington Post* from his new offices on Connecticut Avenue. "The chances are very slim that I would run for local office in the District."

Robust and athletic through most of his life, Fauntroy was diagnosed with tuberculosis in 1993, treated, and cured. He took his condition public to demystify the illness and to assure those who might be afflicted by it that they could be cured. He and his wife, Dorothy, also adopted an abandoned crack baby whom they named Melissa Alice. "We have loved the crack out of her," Fauntroy told the *Washington Post.* "With a profusion of love and affection, you can reclaim those infants both physically and, ultimately, emotionally and mentally." The Fauntroy family, including a grown son, are a focal point in Walter's life. Fauntroy is one man who practices what he preaches.

Sources

Ebony, January 1989, pp. 44-7.

Jet, March 23, 1987, p. 5; October 15, 1990, pp. 4-5.

Time, March 5, 1990, p. 21.

Washington Post, April 6, 1969, p. C1; March 10, 1971, p. A1; January 25, 1992, p. D19; August 31, 1992, p. D3; February 4, 1993, p. B3.

—Anne Janette Johnson

Tom Feelings

1933—

Illustrator

If any man should be regarded as the personification of the "black is beautiful" philosophy, that man is Tom Feelings. Feelings has spent a lifetime as a painter, sculptor, and book illustrator underscoring this message. Ever since the dawn of the U.S. civil rights era, when he came of age as an artist, Feelings has been passionately committed to the mission of encouraging black children to understand their own spiritual and physical beauty. Feelings has remained faithful to that mission for more than 40 years.

While the "black is beautiful" creed admits that support is needed for life's downside, Feelings believes that having great joy is possible in the lives of African Americans. He acknowledges that the sorrow arising from slavery and racism--as it resonates against the joy of surviving such ordeals--expresses the uniqueness of being black in the United States. He summed up this belief in the foreword to his picture book about slavery, *The Middle Passage:* "As the blues, jazz, and the spirituals teach, one must embrace all of life, both its pain and joy, creatively. Knowing this, I, *we,* may be disappointed, but never destroyed."

Devoted to developing the theme of black equality in a

society that does not always practice what it preaches, Feelings has left no doubt about how he wishes his work to be understood. In every book he has illustrated, whether written by him or not, he has been faithful to the statement he made in a 1985 interview with *Horn Book Magazine.* "I bring to my work a quality which is rooted in the culture of Africa and expanded by the experience of being black in America."

Drawing the Story of a Neighborhood

Thomas Feelings was born in 1933, in the ultra-urban, Bedford-Stuyvesant section of Brooklyn, New York. He began to draw at age four, copying pictures from newspaper comic strips into a book of blank pages sewn together by his mother. He was just a little older when he heard about Thipadeaux, a black artist who was teaching at the Police Athletic Academy in his neighborhood. Feelings showed some of his drawings to Thipadeaux. The teacher suggested that, rather than copying from other people's work, he try to draw some of the real people in his neighborhood. Feelings began at home with oil paintings of his mother and his aunt and

At a Glance . . .

Born Thomas Feelings, May 19, 1933, in Brooklyn, NY; son of Samuel (a cab driver) and Anna Nash (Morris) Feelings; married Muriel Grey (a school teacher and author), 1968, divorced, 1974; children: two sons, Zamani and Kamili. *Education:* Cartoonists and Illustrators' School, New York, NY, 1951-53; School of Visual Art, New York, NY, 1957-60.

New York Age, creator and writer of *Tommy Traveler in the World of Black History* comic strip, 1958-59; freelance illustrator and contributor to various magazines, 1961-64; Ghanian government, illustrator for *African Review,* illustration instructor, art consultant, Tema, Ghana, 1964-66; Ministry of Education, teacher and consultant, Guyana, 1971-74; University of South Carolina, artist in residence, 1990-95. *Military:* U.S. Air Force, illustrator in Graphics Division, London, England, 1953-57.

Selected awards Caldecott Honor Book, 1972, for *Moja Means One;* Coretta Scott King Award runner up for *Black Pilgrimage,* Outstanding Achievement Award, School of Visual Arts, 1974; Coretta Scott King Award, for *Something on My Mind,* 1979, and for *Soul Looks Back in Wonder,* 1994; Visual Artists Fellowship Grant, National Endowment of the Arts, 1982; National Book Award nomination for *Jambo Means Hello,* 1982; Distinguished Service to Children Through Art award, University of South Carolina, 1991.

Member: Schomburg Center for Research (commissioner, 1986–).

Addresses: *Home*–180 Wateree Avenue, Columbia, SC 29205-3041.

world of the adult library. Faced with a school assignment involving black educator Booker T. Washington and George Washington Carver, a famed black inventor and scientist, Feelings was dazzled to discover that the achievements of African Americans had merited respect from Americans outside of his realm of experience. He was too young to understand the artistic importance of this discovery--that he was beginning to see his neighborhood with the eyes of the objective observer.

A Mission Born

Feelings's surroundings broadened after he left high school. First, courtesy of a three-year scholarship, came a period of study at the Cartoonists and Illustrators' School in New York City. Next came a four-year hitch in England for the U.S. Air Force. After his return to the United States in 1957, Feelings pursued further study at the School of Visual Arts. While there, Feelings's personal style received an unexpected boost. During a discussion of art history that ranged through the works of many artists, Feelings asked the professor why none of the artists being studied were African. He was told that African art was regarded as "primitive" rather than innovative art. Clearly, the teacher felt that a painter's method was far more important than what was being expressed. Feelings refused to accept that as a lesson worth studying, so he walked out of the room.

Feelings returned to the world of the comic strip to bring the achievements of black Americans to the world's attention. His creation, *Tommy Traveler in the World of Negro History,* began to appear in *New York Age,* a Harlem newspaper with a black readership. Reproduced in a 1991, *Tommy Traveler* told the story of a black boy who read his way through all the library's books on African American history. Referred by the librarian to a book collector named Dr. Gray, an awed Feelings was able to imagine himself back into the lifetimes of Frederick Douglass, Phoebe Fraunces, and other celebrated African Americans. The strip ran for about one year, but Feelings eventually discontinued it because the story form was too restrictive to display his reactions to the world around him.

went on to draw the adults and the wary, diffident children he saw around him.

At first, learning to draw was difficult. Thipadeaux pushed Feelings to improve, often making him draw things over and over. Nevertheless, Feelings was anxious to improve and enjoyed being treated like a serious student. When he was about nine years old, his eagerness to learn was heightened even further by the magic

By 1961 Feelings finished art school with an extensive portfolio. He tried to obtain freelance assignments but was often told by editors that he was limiting his chances by concentrating solely on black subjects. Encouraged by the magazines *Freedomways* and *The Liberator,* both with wide black readerships, he continued to concentrate on African Americans and their lives. In 1962 his determination was rewarded by an assignment that would appear in *Look* magazine.

While on assignment for *Look,* Feelings traveled to New Orleans, Louisiana. Despite the fact that he had to stay in a segregated hotel, he found the children happier and more relaxed as a result of the sunlight and the abundant food. This difference showed in his pictures of the children, who looked far less vigilant and tense than their New York City counterparts. Feelings did not forget to convey the sad truth that went along with these pleasures--blacks in the South seemed to have no more control over their lives than they did in the North.

African Is Beautiful

The awakening spirit of African self-worth in the United States--symbolized by Rosa Parks's 1955 refusal to give up her bus seat--appeared even more strongly in Africa, where many former European colonies overthrew their oppressors. In 1957 Ghana gained independence. The new head of state, Kwame Nkrumah, made known his desire for an international cadre of black educators who could take his people by the hand and point them toward a future of profitable self-determination.

In 1964 Tom Feelings went to the Ghanian city of Tema to join other African Americans recruited by the Nkrumah government. He worked both for the government's magazine, *African Review,* and as a children's book illustrator. Feelings exulted in being among the majority and in achieving his most important goal--to aid in the production of positive images for black children.

As Feelings told *Horn Book* magazine in 1985, "Africa helped make my drawings more fluid and flowing; rhythmic lines started to appear in my work." Some of this new movement appears in illustrations of robed Ghanian women that he painted for his 1972 autobiography *Black Pilgrimage.* Proud and graceful, they often seem to be on the point of swirling off the page. Another picture in the book shows the same state of mind. Against a forest background of gentle greens and beiges, women in Western dress with baskets on their heads actually seem to sway in unison along a path.

Ghana proved an idyllic setting for the developing artist. The entire experience was a spiritual odyssey for Feelings. He knew that Africa was the homeland of his people as well as the cradle of civilization before the European slave-traders had docked there. His closeness to such history strengthened the bond he had always felt. It brought home to him the most enduring lesson about himself that he was ever to share. Feelings explained in *Black Pilgrimage:* "I am an *African,* and I know now that black people, no matter in what part of the world they may live, are one African people."

New Worlds to Conquer

In 1966 Nkrumah was ousted by a coup d'état. Feelings returned to the United States to find that the publishing industry had changed significantly. The blossoming civil rights movement had produced an insatiable hunger for African American history, literature, and especially children's books suitable for both recreational reading and teaching purposes. Educators' research had revealed a shameful scarcity of material with accurate representations of black dialogue and black people--stereotypes still dominated the written word. As a result, new emphasis was placed on literature of only the highest quality to be produced with black children in mind. New children's bookshops worked to supply the burgeoning market. Their demand in turn brought a wider scope to publishers, who eagerly produced a growing number of books for and about different cultures. It was a fertile environment for a culturally-oriented artist able to offer authentic visions of Africa.

Buttressed by an overflowing portfolio, Feelings started to illustrate children's picture books immediately. First came *Bola and the Oba's Drummers* from McGraw-Hill; then in 1971 he illustrated *Moja Means One: A Swahili Counting Book. Moja* proved to be a turning point. The text, written by his wife Muriel, explained the numbers in Swahili, a language spoken by millions of people in East Africa. Feelings's drawings gave African American children an authentic feel for a different culture by introducing them to Kenyan landmarks and cultural features in particular. Many reviewers agreed that the drawings were beautiful and instructive, so much so that they expanded the book's original marketability.

Praise for the book was not universal, however. Sidney Long, writing in *Horn Book Magazine,* noted that the drawing technique sometimes seemed too sophisticated for its intended readers--between six to eight years of age. The sophistication, he claimed, made it difficult to find the objects to be counted. A second reviewer criticized the appropriateness of the muted grey and ocher colorings of most of the pictures. Feelings explained that he simply wanted to make his work stand out in quiet comparison to all the bright reds, blues, and greens other picture-book illustrators used.

Applauded for Cultural Achievement

The following year *Moja Means One* was chosen as a Caldecott Honor selection, marking it as a runner-up for the Caldecott Medal. Named in honor of Randolph Caldecott, an English picture book illustrator who died in 1886, the award has been a mark of excellence in children's literature since it was established in 1938. The accolade to *Moja Means One* ensured that Feelings was on his way to professional success.

Feelings was also on his way to Guyana, a former British colony in South America that had once done a brisk business in slaves from Ghana. The Guyanese government in 1971 intended to instill its own educators and people with pride and patriotism while providing them with the modern education accessible to more industrialized nations. Feelings joined in the effort partly to complete the spiritual quest he had begun with his journey to Ghana.

Feelings headed the Guyanese Ministry of Education's newly-created children's book project while also training young government illustrators. Since the country possessed printing presses capable of reproducing only two-color work, he found the work challenging. He did not quit, however. Instead, he "rediscovered the lesson of improvising within a restrictive form," as he noted in *The Horn Book Magazine.* Feelings did leave Guyana and the government project there in 1974 in order to return to the United States.

By the mid-1970s Feelings had illustrated six books, including a volume of diary extracts collected by Julius Lester, called *To Be A Slave.* Shortly thereafter, he was asked to do ten color illustrations for a new edition of Booker T. Washington's autobiography, *Up from Slavery.* Despite the tragic subject, Feelings found himself continually painting pictures in warm and radiant colors that were quite inappropriate to such a project. Knowing these pictures would convey a falsely positive image of slavery, he cancelled the contract.

Multi-generational Picturebooks

If the 1970s had been a time of new experiences, the 1980s found Feelings firmly grasping the themes that had been germinating within his work since his youth in Bedford-Stuyvesant. His autobiography, *Black Pilgrimage,* records a conversation with an eight-year-old girl that proved unforgettable for the artist. Feelings tried to explain to her that his drawings were of "pretty little black children, like you." The young girl expressed her refusal to see anything beautiful about the black children, replying, "Ain't nothin' black pretty." Feelings's lifelong dedication to the beauty of African people and their descendants graphically illustrates his inability to accept such a hateful attitude.

In 1981 Feelings's urge to show readers the potential

and the intelligence of black children blossomed into *Daydreamers,* a book filled with the drawings of 20 years accompanying a poem by Eloise Greenfield. *Daydreamers* marked the beginning of a conscious effort by Feelings to appeal to adults as well as to the elementary-school-age children for whom the book was intended. This appeal to adult/junior readership came across even more strongly in *Now Sheba Sings the Song,* published in 1987, in which Feelings collaborated with poet laureate of the United States, Maya Angelou.

> "I bring to my work a quality which is rooted in the culture of Africa and expanded by the experience of being black in America."

Warming to the idea of a multi-generational readership, Feelings used short poems about children by several black authors for his 1993 publication, *Soul Looks Back in Wonder.* In addition to another Maya Angelou poem, there was a never-before published poem by Langston Hughes, who had died in 1967. Margaret Walker, whose 1966 novel *Jubilee* had become a classical description of American life under slavery, also contributed text. Though publishers and reviewers considered *Soul Looks Back in Wonder* most appropriate for children in grades three through six, one reviewer noted that several of the poems in the collection probably would appeal more to adults than to children. This divided readership is purely intentional, reflecting Feelings's profound belief that adults must help smooth the way for children. "Young black kids really are having a hard time nowadays," he said in *Sandlapper* magazine. "That's why I made this book [*Soul Looks Back in Wonder*]."

The Middle Passage

Feelings's 1995 masterpiece, *The Middle Passage,* is not a children's book to be enjoyed by adults; it is an adult picture book that children can enjoy. Illustrated in his trademark style of understated color tones ranging from cream to storm-cloud charcoal to black, the book depicts the journey on slave ships from Africa through the middle passage to the Caribbean and North America. With realistic details and no text to explicate his drawings, Feelings shows the terror and horror of slavery. The slaves were shackled together between decks, many were killed by sharks while trying to escape, and torture and starvation were used to force submission to the ships' overseers. *The Middle Passage* is Feelings's way of telling the whole truth about slavery that adults do not want exposed.

Though the Guyanese Ministry of Education was emphatic about the need for children to know the truth in their history books, Feelings found it impossible to work on *The Middle Passage* while he worked for them. His return to the United States allowed him to fathom the reason. "I had to be in a place that constantly reminded me of what I was working on and why I was working on it," he wrote in the introduction to *The Middle Passage.* "For me that was New York City. That's where the pain was."

Despite the grim visions of inhumanity that are illuminated in *The Middle Passage,* in the book's introduction, Feelings encourages African Americans not to feel depressed by them. "They should be uplifted and say to themselves: `You mean we survived this? We made it through all this and we are still here today?'" Recently retired from the University of South Carolina, where he taught book illustration, Feelings still cautions black children never to waste their own potential.

Selected writings

(Illustrator) *Bola and the Oba's Drummers,* McGraw, 1967.
(Illustrator) *To Be A Slave,* Dial, 1968.
(Illustrator) *Zamani Goes to Market,* Seabury, 1970.
(Illustrator) *Jambo Means Hello,* Dial, 1971.
Black Pilgrimage, Lothrop, 1972.

(Illustrator) *Moja Means One: A Swahili Counting Book,* Dial, 1974.
(Illustrator) *Something on My Mind,* Dial, 1978.
(Illustrator) *Daydreamers,* Dial, 1981.
(Illustrator) *Now Sheba Sings the Song,* Dial, 1987.
Tommy Traveler in the World of Negro History, Black Butterfly Books, 1991.
Soul Looks Back in Wonder, Dial, 1993.
The Middle Passage: White Ships/Black Cargo, Dial, 1995.

Sources

Books

Hearne, Betsy and Roger Sutton, eds., *Evaluating Children's Books: A Critical Look,* University of Illinois, 1992, pp. 106-15.
Kingman, Lee, et al, *Illustrators of Children's Books, 1967-1976,* Horn Book, Inc., 1978.
Rollock, Barbara, *Black Authors & Illustrators of Children's Books,* 2nd ed., Garland Publishing, 1992, p. 70.
Smith, Irene, *The History of the Newbery and Caldecott Medals,* Viking, 1957, pp. 25-28.
Something About the Author, vol. 8, Gale Research, 1976, pp. 56-57.

Periodicals

The Horn Book Magazine, November/December 1985, pp. 685-95.
Sandlapper, Summer, 1994, pp. 46-47.
School Library Journal, February 1992.

—Gillian Wolf

Aretha Franklin

1942—

Singer, songwriter

When asked by Patricia Smith of the *Boston Globe* how she felt about being called the "Queen of Soul," Aretha Franklin's reply was characterized by grace but no false modesty. "It's an acknowledgment of my art," she mused. "It means I am excelling at my art and my first love. And I am most appreciative." Since she burst onto the public consciousness in the late 1960s with a batch of milestone recordings, Franklin has served as a standard against which all subsequent soul divas have been measured.

The combination of Franklin's gospel roots and some devastating life experiences have invested her voice with a rare—and often wrenching—authenticity. "It was like I had no idea what music was all about until I heard her sing," confessed singer-actress Bette Midler, as cited in *Ebony*. Though Franklin's work in ensuing decades has rarely matched the fire—or the sales figures—of her most celebrated singles, she has remained an enduring presence in contemporary music. The release of several CD retrospectives and the announcement in 1995 that she would publish an autobiography and start her own record label seemed to guarantee that her influ-ence would continue unabated.

Franklin was raised in Detroit, the daughter of famed minister C. L. Franklin and gospel singer Barbara Franklin, who left the family when Aretha was small and died shortly thereafter. "She was the absolute lady," the Queen of Soul told *Ebony*'s Laura B. Randolph, while at the same time admitting that her memories of her mother are few. For his part, the Reverend Franklin was no retiring clergyman; in-deed, he enjoyed the popularity and, to some degree, the lifestyle of a pop star. He immediately recognized his daughter's prodigious abilities, offering to arrange for piano lessons; the child declined, instead teaching herself to play by listening to records.

Gospel Roots

Franklin's talent as a singer was such that her father took her on the road with his traveling gospel show. She sang regularly before his congregation at Detroit's New Bethel Baptist Church as well, and it was there that her performance of "Precious Lord," among other gospel gems, was captured for posterity. She was 14 years old but already a spellbinding performer. Producer Jerry Wexler—who shepherded Franklin to greatness on behalf of Atlantic Records some years later—was stunned by the 1956 recording. "The voice was not that of a child but rather of an ecstatic hierophant [a priest in ancient Greece]," he recalled in his book *Rhythm and the Blues*.

Franklin's life was no church social, however. She became a mother at age 15 and had her second child two years later. "I still wanted to get out and hang with my friends," she recollected to *Ebony*'s Randolph, "so I wanted to be in two places at the same time. But my grandmother helped me a lot, and my sister and my cousin. They would babysit so I could get out occasionally."

Though she was first and foremost inspired by gospel music—the performance of "Peace in the Valley" by family friend Clara Ward at a funeral was a seminal influence on her desire to sing—Franklin soon became interested in non-religious music. Rather than dissuade her from this secular path, as some might have expected, her father encouraged her. In 1960 she traveled to New York, embarked on vocal and dance lessons, and hired a manager. She then began recording demonstration tapes.

While the R&B stars of Detroit's Motown label won a crossover, or white, audience by tempering their wicked grooves with a playful elegance, their southern counterparts never bothered to tone down the raw physicality of the music. Like singer-songwriter-pianist Ray Charles, who has often been credited with the invention of "soul music," Franklin brought the fire of gospel to pop music; her spiritual force in no way separated from her earthy sexuality.

Collaborations Launched Career

Celebrated Columbia Records executive John Hammond was so taken by Franklin's recordings that he signed her immediately. Her first Columbia album was issued in the fall of 1960. While a few singles made a respectable showing on the charts, it was clear that the label wasn't adequately showcasing her gifts, either in its choice of material or production. "I cherish the recordings we made together," remarked Hammond in *Rhythm and the Blues*, "but, finally, Columbia was a white company [that] misunderstood her genius."

Franklin's manager at the time, Ted White, was also her husband; they agreed that she should pursue other options when her contract expired. Wexler leapt at the opportunity to sign her to Atlantic; he originally intended to send her to Memphis to record with the staff of the legendary Stax/Volt studios, who'd already made landmark recordings with the likes of Otis Redding and Wilson Pickett. Wexler himself had his hands full with other projects, but the task of producing Franklin's first Atlantic sides ultimately fell to him, Arif Mardin, and Tom Dowd.

Wexler brought Franklin to the Florence Alabama Music Emporium (FAME) studios in Muscle Shoals, Alabama, to record with a unique group of musicians adept in soul, blues, pop, country, and rock. This able crew was stunned by Franklin's power and prowess. Accompanying herself on piano, she deftly controlled the tone and arrangement of the songs she performed; this was an integral part of Wexler's strategy to capture her natural brilliance on tape. Backing vocals were provided either by her sisters Carolyn and Erma or by the vocal group the Sweet Inspirations, which featured Cissy Houston, mother of future singing star Whitney Houston. Wexler also brought in young rock lions like guitarists Duane Allman and Eric Clapton for guest spots.

Unfortunately, only one of two songs—"I Never Loved a Man (the Way I Love You)"—was finished when White and one of the musicians had a drunken row; White grabbed Franklin and they vanished for a period of weeks. Wexler balanced jubilation with anxiety; radio programmers around the country embraced "I Never Loved a Man," and distributors clamored for an album, but the artist was nowhere to be found. At last she surfaced in New York, where she completed the unfinished "Do Right Woman, Do Right Man"; in Wexler's words, "the result was perfection."

Franklin's first album for Atlantic, I Never Loved a Man (the Way I Love You), was released in 1967; several hit-filled LPs followed. During this crucial period she enjoyed a succession of smash singles that included "I Never Loved a Man," the rollicking "Baby I Love You," the pounding groove "Chain of Fools," the supercharged "Think," which she wrote, the tender, anthemic "(You Make Me Feel Like a) Natural Woman," and a blistering take on Otis Redding's "Respect." The latter two would become Franklin's signature songs. With "Natural Woman," according to the Boston Globe's Smith, "She gathers broken women in the circle of her arms, stitches our wounds with a wondrous thread."

R-E-S-P-E-C-T

Franklin's version of "Respect," coming as it did at a crucial point for black activism, feminism, and sexual liberation, was particularly potent. Wexler noted that Franklin took Redding's more conventional take on the song and "turned it inside out, making it deeper, stronger, loading it with double entendres." What's more, he noted, "The fervor in Aretha's magnificent voice" implied not just everyday respect but "sexual attention of the highest order," as implied by the "sock it to me" backup chorus she and her sisters devised.

Writer Evelyn C. White, in an Essence piece, referred to "Respect" as a revolutionary force in her own life. Franklin's "impassioned, soulful licks and sly innuendos about sexual pleasure made me feel good about myself," she wrote, "both as a black American and as a young girl about to discover sex." Eventually, the song would become an American pop standard; its spelling out of the title word would be referenced in countless articles and commercials. At the time of its release, however, it served primarily as a fight song for social change. It scored two trophies at that year's Grammy Awards.

Franklin's voice was crucial to the soundtrack of the era, and not just as a record playing on the radio. Franklin's father was a close friend of civil rights leader Rev. Martin Luther King, Jr., and as a result, she herself was close to King and his family. When the crusading minister was assassinated in 1968, Franklin was enlisted to sing at his funeral. Wexler described her performance of "Precious Lord" as "a holy blend of truth and unspeakable tragedy."

Franklin also sang the National Anthem at the Democratic Party's riot-marred 1968 convention in Chicago. Yet even as her soulful wail soothed a number of difficult national transitions and transformations, Franklin's own changes were hidden from view. "I think of Aretha as `Our Lady of Mysterious Sorrows,'" Wexler wrote. "Her eyes are incredible, luminous eyes covering inexplicable pain. Her depressions could be as deep as the dark sea. I don't pretend to know the sources of her anguish, but anguish surrounds Aretha as surely as the glory of her musical aura."

Despite her inner turmoil, Franklin enjoyed phenomenal commercial success during these years. A number of other blockbuster Atlantic albums followed her debut on the label, and she proceeded to take home Grammys every year between 1969 and 1975. Still, she did not rest on her laurels; rather, she constantly explored rock and pop records for new material and recorded cover versions of songs by the Beatles, Elton John, the Band, Paul Simon, Jimi Hendrix, and many others. "She didn't think in terms of white or black tunes, or white or black rhythms," noted Wexler. "Her taste, like her genius, transcended categories."

In 1972 Franklin sang at the funeral of gospel giant Mahalia Jackson, which suggested her stature in the gospel world; it was no surprise when Amazing Grace, an album of church music she recorded with Wexler, soared up the pop charts that year. At the inauguration of President Jimmy Carter in 1977, she provided an a capella rendition of "God Bless America."

Triumphed Despite Turmoil

Having parted ways with husband/manager Ted White some years earlier—stories circulated in the press charging that he'd struck her in public—Franklin married actor Glynn Turman in 1978. They divorced some six years later. By the end of the 1970s, her record sales had dwindled, but she took an attention-getting turn in the *Blues Brothers* movie, in which she both acted and sang; the film and the Blues Brothers albums, recorded by *Saturday Night Live* funnymen and blues and soul fanatics Dan Aykroyd and John Belushi, helped fuel a new mainstream interest in 1960s soul.

In 1980 Franklin elected to leave Atlantic and sign with Arista Records; the label's slick production and commercial choice of material earned greater sales than she had enjoyed for some time, particularly for the single "Freeway of Love." She earned three more Grammys during the decade. Nonetheless, Dave DiMartino of *Entertainment Weekly* groused that most of her hits at Arista "have been assembled by big-name producers like Narada Michael Walden and might have easily featured another singer entirely—like, say, label mate Whitney Houston"; DiMartino also objected to the relentless pairing of Franklin with other stars for much-hyped duets, remarking, "Like ... Aretha Franklin needs a gimmick?"

> Like singer-songwriter-pianist Ray Charles, who has often been credited with the invention of "soul music," Franklin brought the fire of gospel to pop music, her spiritual force in no way separated from her earthy sexuality.

In 1979 Franklin's father was shot by a burglar in his home and fell into a coma. He died several years later, having never regained consciousness. As *Ebony's* Randolph wrote, "When you've said as many goodbyes as Aretha, it's impossible not to be palpably shaped by loss." The singer cited a point during her father's hospitalization as the most difficult decision of her life.

"We had to have a trach [a tracheotomy, a procedure that involves cutting through the vocal chords]," she confided, "and we were afraid it would affect his voice, which was certainly his living."

But beyond this and other painful incidents, further triumphs lay ahead for Franklin. She was the first woman inducted into the Rock and Roll Hall of Fame, won a Grammy for best soul gospel performance, was the subject of an all-star documentary tribute broadcast on public television, sang at the inauguration of another president, Bill Clinton, in 1993, and won a lifetime achievement Grammy in 1995. Franklin might not have been the commercial powerhouse that some of her younger acolytes, like Houston and Mariah Carey, had become—filmmaker Ron Shelton had to fight to get her on the soundtrack of his *White Men Can't Jump*—but she had become an institution; the title of Queen seemed even more appropriate as she eased into her 50s.

Franklin—who moved back to the Detroit area in the mid-1990s—announced plans for an autobiography in 1995 and also made public her intention to start a record label, which would be called World Class Records. "I'm looking for space," she told the *Boston Globe*. "I'm the CEO." She continued to perform, her band by that time featuring two of her sons, Kecalf Cunningham and Teddy Richards.

Other projects, including film and television appearances, were also in the works. "I just strive for excellence pretty much across the board, whether it's as a producer, songwriter or singer," Franklin proclaimed to *Boston Globe* writer Smith. "I give people what I feel is best, not just what everyone says is 'hot.' I want to do things that are going to be meaningful and inspiring to them one way or another." Asked by the *Detroit Free Press* if she ever got tired of singing "Respect," the Queen of Soul replied, "Actually, no. I just find new ways of refreshing the song." Similarly, Franklin's voice—forged in pain and exaltation, spirit and sensuality—continues to refresh new listeners.

Selected discography

The Great Aretha Franklin, Columbia, 1960.
The Electrifying Aretha Franklin, Columbia, 1962.
The Tender, the Moving, the Swinging Aretha Franklin, Columbia, 1962.
Aretha Franklin's Greatest Hits, Columbia, 1967.
I Never Loved a Man (the Way I Love You) (includes "I Never Loved a Man [the Way I Love You]," "Do Right Woman, Do Right Man," "Baby I Love You," and "Respect"), Atlantic, 1967.

Aretha Arrives (includes "[You Make Me Feel Like a] Natural Woman" and "Chain of Fools"), Atlantic, 1967.

Take a Look, Columbia, 1967.

Lady Soul, Atlantic, 1968.

Aretha Now, Atlantic, 1968.

Aretha in Paris, Atlantic, 1968.

Soul '69, Atlantic, 1969.

Aretha's Gold, Atlantic, 1969.

This Girl's in Love with You, Atlantic, 1970.

Spirit in the Dark, Atlantic, 1970.

Aretha Live at Fillmore West, Atlantic, 1971.

Young, Gifted and Black, Atlantic, 1972.

Amazing Grace, Atlantic, 1972.

The Beginning/The World of Aretha Franklin 1960-1967, Columbia, 1972.

Hey Now Hey (The Other Side of the Sky), Atlantic, 1973.

Let Me in Your Life, Atlantic, 1974.

Everything I Feel in Me, Atlantic, 1975.

Ten Years of Gold, Atlantic, 1977.

Sweet Passion, Atlantic, 1977.

Almighty Fire, Atlantic, 1978.

La Diva, Atlantic, 1979.

Aretha, Arista, 1980.

Jump to It, Arista, 1982.

Get It Right, Arista, 1984.

Who's Zoomin' Who? (includes "Freeway of Love"), Arista, 1985.

Aretha, Arista, 1987.

Love All the Hurt Away, Arista, 1987.

One Lord, One Faith, One Baptism, Arista, 1988.

Through the Storm, Arista, 1989.

What You See Is What You Sweat, Arista, 1991.

Queen of Soul: The Atlantic Recordings, Atlantic, 1992.

Greatest Hits: 1980-1994, Arista, 1994.

With other artists

Curtis Mayfield, *Sparkle* (soundtrack), 1976.

"Think," *The Blues Brothers* (soundtrack), 1979.

"Jumpin' Jack Flash," *Jumpin' Jack Flash* (soundtrack), 1986.

George Michael, "I Knew You Were Waiting (for Me)," Columbia, 1987.

"If I Lose", *White Men Can't Jump* (soundtrack), EMI, 1992.

All Men Are Brothers: A Tribute to Curtis Mayfield, 1994.

Sources

Books

Rees, Dafydd, and Luke Crampton, *Rock Movers & Shakers,* Billboard, 1991.

Wexler, Jerry, and David Ritz, *Rhythm and the Blues: A Life in American Music,* Knopf, 1993.

Periodicals

Boston Globe, June 14, 1991, p. 39; March 21, 1994, p. 30; September 29, 1995, p. 55.

Detroit Free Press, June 10, 1994, p. 3D; June 18, 1994, p. 2A.

Ebony, April 1995, pp. 28-33.

Entertainment Weekly, May 15, 1992, p. 64.

Essence, August 1995, pp. 73-77.

Jet, August 21, 1995, p. 33.

—Simon Glickman

Carl Franklin

1949—

Filmmaker

Describing the work of his favorite directors—Akira Kurosawa, Martin Scorsese, Charles Burnett, Francis Ford Coppola, and others—in an interview with Sheila Benson for *Premiere* magazine, Carl Franklin noted a common preoccupation. "They're not so much interested in the action of the film," he observed, "as they are in the response of the characters to the dramatic action—whether it takes them closer [to] or further from God. If that doesn't sound too pretentious."

Richmond; he never knew his father, who died before he was born. His stepfather, meanwhile, was frustrated and frequently abusive. "It was a scary situation," the filmmaker told Goldstein. "He was very loving, but when he drank he was a different person. It was worst on the weekends. If he was drunk on Friday night, he'd beat my mother up and it would go on all weekend. As a kid, it made me very terrified because these grownups twice your size are yelling at each other. It felt like the end of the world.

Franklin has earned accolades in his own work for focusing on character over plot gimmickry, exploring often dark material with both compassion and flair. Though he arrived at directing after spending many unsatisfying years as an actor, he was able to use his understanding of the actor's perspective in making his well-received features *One False Move* and *Devil in a Blue Dress* and the acclaimed television series *Laurel Avenue.* Actor Denzel Washington, who starred in *Devil,* described Franklin to Patrick Goldstein of the *Los Angeles Times* as "a history professor trapped in a movie director's body. You know he's always going to get deep into things."

Franklin was raised in the northern California town of

Richmond itself was a rough place to grow up; Franklin noted in an interview with the London *Observer,* "You had to have friends to fight with you and back you up because you'd pass through areas controlled by certain gangs and it was just too dangerous to go by yourself." Nonetheless, he survived to stand up to his stepfather and become the first member of his family to pursue a college education.

Began as an Actor

Franklin earned a scholarship to the University of California at Berkeley, arriving in the midst of the social and

At a Glance . . .

Born c. 1949, in Richmond, CA; married twice (both marriages ended in divorce); two children. *Education:* University of California, Berkeley, B.A., c. 1971; American Film Institute, M.F.A.

Appeared in productions of *Cymbeline, Timon of Athens,* and *Twelfth Night,* New York City, early 1970s; appeared in film *Five on the Black Hand Side,* 1971; appeared on television series *Caribe, Fantastic Journey, McClain's Law,* and *The A-Team;* appeared in productions of *Saint Joan* and *In the Belly of the Beast,* Los Angeles; made short film *Punk;* directed features *Nowhere to Run,* 1988, *Eye of the Eagle 2,* 1989, *Full Fathom Five,* 1990, and *One False Move,* 1991; directed television film *Laurel Avenue* for cable channel Home Box Office (HBO), 1993; adapted screenplay for and directed *Devil in a Blue Dress,* 1995.

Addresses: *Home*—Los Angeles, CA. *Studio*—Tri-Star Pictures, 10202 West Washington Blvd., Culver City, CA 90232.

political ferment that rocked the 1960s. Yet despite his exhilaration at the burgeoning Black Power movement and other progressive causes, he remained largely an observer. "It was like a dream to me," he noted to *Los Angeles Times* contributor Goldstein. "I wasn't really sophisticated enough to join a particular movement." Though initially attracted to history as a major, Franklin was drawn into the theater arts department during his junior year.

In 1971 Franklin followed the call of the stage to New York, where he appeared in small roles in producer Joseph Papp's famed Shakespeare in the Park productions. "He had us dressed up as birds and stuff—I was a cockatoo, I think," Franklin recollected to *L.A. Weekly* contributor Ella Taylor. "One guy said he didn't expect us to get any work out of that unless they were casting for *Disney on Parade.*"

Other small roles followed. Franklin gradually became more established and began earning larger parts; he has said that his finest moment onstage came in the play *In the Belly of the Beast,* presented by the trailblazing Los Angeles theater the Mark Taper Forum. Prior to this, he'd come to L.A. with a girlfriend and had gone along with her to a film audition. The film, *Five on the Black*

Hand Side, was a "blaxploitation" action picture in which he was cast without even reading for a part.

Franklin later made the transition to television, co-starring on the series *Caribe,* but he found this work generally unrewarding. Indeed, even a high-profile role on the hit 1980s program *The A-Team* didn't raise his spirits. "That was a real bad time for me in my life," Franklin said in the *Village Voice.* "I'd gotten divorced from my first wife, I was redefining myself. Acting itself wasn't fulfilling me." He described his *A-Team* character, Captain Crane, as "kind of a movable prop. I knew I didn't want to act anymore."

Even so, Franklin told the *L.A. Weekly's* Taylor, "[acting] made a director out of me." He departed The A-Team and began writing for the screen, gravitating toward "creating something from nothing, and getting involved in a different part of the production line." He began studying moviemaking at the American Film Institute and embarked on his first project, a short called *Punk.* The tale of a black kid pursued by a child molester, the film made a profound impression on Hollywood. This was fortunate; with two children to feed and alimony payments to make, Franklin needed work. He even lost his house mortgaging it to finance his film.

Corman and One False Move

Among those taken with Franklin's directorial gifts was veteran B-movie mogul Roger Corman, through whose low-budget ranks many a gifted filmmaker—including Coppola, Scorsese, Jonathan Demme, Joe Dante, Ron Howard, and many others—had risen. Corman enlisted Franklin to make a series of cheap action films in various foreign locales. "Thank God for Roger," Franklin declared to *Premiere's* Benson. "He financed my way through film school." Even so, the director has been chary of naming the features he made during this period, which include the low-budget pictures *Nowhere to Run* and *Full Fathom Five.* "A lot of people felt Corman was a springboard," said Franklin in the *L.A. Weekly.* "It's like what he said to Ron Howard—'If you do a good job for me, kid, you'll never have to work for me again.' I don't know how much I was influenced [by Corman's style]. Hopefully, not artistically."

Corman wasn't the only producer captivated by *Punk;* so was Jesse Beaton, who had developed a number of adventurous independent productions in the past. "I thought *Punk* had a very strong vision and original voice," she recalled to the *New York Times.* She was seeking a director for a gritty crime drama called *One False Move* and had met several young filmmakers who were more interested in "attitude" and style than character. "Then I met Carl," she told *L.A. Weekly* contributor Taylor, "and I knew he would be a terrific director. He so impressed me with his intelligence and articulateness, his warmth and maturity." She added that his being "African-American was not the issue, but an issue in the story."

Though*One False Move*—filmed on a $2 million budget and first released in 1991—begins with some extreme violence, Franklin has been outspoken about its moral context. "I didn't want people getting excited seeing how neat someone can be killed," he insisted in the *Observer*. "I want the audience to feel the emotional loss of life—the real violence is the loss, the violation of humanity. They've taken from us someone who had dreams, hopes, the same set of emotions we have."

Franklin's thoughtful approach to the story of three drug-dealing killers on the lam from Los Angeles to Star City, Arkansas, and to the complex undercurrents of race in the story impressed numerous critics. But *One False Move* scarcely earned uniform raves. A *Time* reviewer, for one, claimed that despite the film's "B-movie virtues," it was an overpraised and "modest melodrama." *Cineaste,* on the other hand, proclaimed that the production "extends film noir boundaries" and applauded Franklin's direction in particular. *Video* magazine—reviewing *Move's* debut on tape—hailed an "extraordinary feature film debut."

One False Move had a meager publicity budget, and it took a while for word of mouth to draw moviegoers to it. "In a left-handed way," Franklin declared to Taylor, "it worked out for the best. Every time the film would open in another major market, we would enjoy another wave of success. Critics loved the idea of championing this film." And Franklin's ethnicity was largely unknown at the time, which meant that rather than being deluged with "urban" scripts full of gangs and drugs, he was offered "all these mainstream white projects, art films, action movies—we were getting everything."

Franklin's next project, however, was directing the two-part production *Laurel Avenue* for the cable television network Home Box Office (HBO). An ambitious and dramatically complex tale of a black family in Minnesota, it earned strong reviews. *Entertainment Weekly* deemed it "a TV film that transcends the family drama" and noted that Franklin's sophisticated direction "makes this an important piece of work." *Time* ranked it among the best dramatic presentations of the year, "startling in its frankness yet leavened by a stubborn optimism, a far cry from TV's usual easy sentimentality."

Franklin remarked to *Mirabella* that while the program dealt with often sensationalized issues, he struggled to stay grounded in reality. "Drugs are a huge problem in the black community," he declared. "Not to include that would be a stupid oversight. But if the subject of drugs is introduced in the context of a hardworking family that has managed to maintain unity, and the audience sees drugs as a threat to that unity, they get a much greater understanding of the problem."

Directed Washington in Devil

A fan of mystery writer Walter Mosley, Franklin jumped at the opportunity to direct a screen adaptation of the novelist's *Devil in a Blue Dress*. With Demme executive producing and Beaton sharing production credit, he was able to secure a larger budget and at the same time avoid the creative constraints often encountered as a result of such purse strings. He adapted the screenplay himself, though he informed *Entertainment Weekly* that he "called Walter whenever there was a departure I was making, just to get feedback." *Devil* follows Ezekiel "Easy" Rawlins—played by Denzel Washington—as he embarks on a rocky career as a private detective in late-1940s Los Angeles.

> "I always look for a universal theme to unearth. My ethnicity is a plus, a tool. It gives me ammunition in terms of the way I view the world. There are certain stories in the black community that inform us all."

Franklin's historical acumen served him well in the telling of this tale; working with a gifted team of production designers and other filmic experts, he was able to reconstruct a lost South Central L.A. It was a challenge, however. "Nothing from Los Angeles in 1948 was saved," he reported in *Entertainment Weekly*. "We paid for a lot of security because we were shooting in neighborhoods that, let's just say, weren't the best." In another interview with Ella Taylor, this time for *Mirabella,* he pointed out that in "Mosley's work, you get such a strong sense of neighborhood, of history, of what black family values were. That's what you don't see on the screen about black people, those internal things that make us who we are."

Again, critics were divided over the film, though most

admitted that the recreation of the old locales bordered on the magical. Still, *Entertainment Weekly* reviewer Lisa Schwarzbaum lamented that the director "might as well be a sociologist studying 'trends and conflicts in postwar urban Negro culture' rather than igniting those trends and conflicts." Kenneth Turan of the *Los Angeles Times,* on the other hand, hailed *Devil* as "the most exotic crime entertainment of the season." Franklin himself seemed less interested in the film's standing in the thriller sweepstakes than in larger concerns. "I love film noir," he told the *New York Times,* but "this film is really social realism married to film noir. It's about people I know, people I grew up with."

Though *Devil in a Blue Dress* did not meet commercial expectations, it made a decided impression on the film community; as a result, Franklin became highly attractive to top producers and writers. He discussed in various interviews a number of projects he planned to helm, including *Reliable Sources,* from a script by Hollywood bad boy Joe Eszterhas, a film version of Russell Banks's novel *Rule of the Bone,* and an adaptation of Alexandre Dumas's classic tale *The Count of Monte Cristo.* Having established a partnership with producer Beaton, he signed a three-film deal with Tri-Star Pictures and appeared ideally positioned to pursue

his uniquely humanist vision. "I always look for a universal theme to unearth," he proclaimed to Taylor in the *L.A. Weekly.* "My ethnicity is a plus, a tool. It gives me ammunition in terms of the way I view the world. There are certain stories in the black community that inform us all."

Sources

Cineaste, Fall 1992, p. 104.
Entertainment Weekly, July 9, 1993, pp. 38-39; August 25, 1995, pp. 32-33; September 29, 1995, pp. 40-41.
L.A. Weekly, September 22, 1995, pp. 20-25.
Los Angeles Times, August 13, 1992, pp. F1, F4; September 24, 1995 (Calendar), pp. 3, 79; September 29, 1995, pp. F1, F12.
Mirabella, September 1995, p. 32.
New York Times, August 9, 1992, p. C1; October 3, 1995, pp. C1, C14.
Observer (London), April 4, 1993, Arts 2 section, p. 54.
Premiere, July 1992, p. 46.
Time, August 3, 1992, p. 75; January 3, 1994.
Video, November 1992, p. 73.
Village Voice, October 3, 1995.

—Simon Glickman

Al Freeman, Jr.

1934—

Actor, educator

Al Freeman, Jr. is a veteran of the stage and screen whose performing career spans four decades. Freeman made his stage debut as a college student in 1954, and has worked steadily ever since. His 1992 movie appearance as Elijah Muhammad in the Spike Lee film *Malcolm X* might have been the first exposure many film goers had to Freeman, but television buffs recognize him immediately for his long-running portrayal of Ed Hall on the daytime drama *One Life To Live.* An artist-in-residence at Howard University, the affable Freeman has been a respected working actor more years than his students have been alive.

Albert Cornelius Freeman, Jr. was born in San Antonio, Texas on March 21, 1934. His parents divorced when he was nine, and he rarely saw his jazz pianist father, who had moved to Columbus, Ohio. Freeman began studying acting at Los Angeles City College in 1951, but he took a hiatus from college to serve in the U.S. Air Force. After three years of military service, he returned to Los Angeles and enrolled in "every speech, broadcasting, and drama class I could take," according to the actor in *Ebony* magazine. While still a student, he had his stage debut in a 1954 Ebony Showcase Theatre production of

Detective Story.

Freeman moved to New York City in 1959, and won a role in the 1960 Broadway play *The Long Dream,* based on a novel by Richard Wright. The show closed after only five performances, but the young actor soon found other work close at hand. According to Laura B. Randolph in *Ebony,* most of Freeman's roles during the period "were as an angry young militant." For Freeman, acting in such roles served as his way of demonstrating his commitment to the civil rights struggle and to the values in which he believed.

One of Freeman's most important roles--and a personal favorite--was that of Richard Henry in the James Baldwin play *Blues for Mister Charlie,* a work loosely based on the circumstances surrounding the 1955 murder of Emmitt Till, a Chicago youth who was lynched while visiting family in the South. Freeman appeared in the first Broadway production of the play in 1964 as well as in the piece's London debut. He also took important parts in two dramas by LeRoi Jones (now Amiri Baraka), *The Slave* and *Dutchman.* The late 1960s and early 1970s found the actor juggling stage and film credits, with roles in movies such as *The Detective, The Lost Man, My Sweet Charlie, A Fable,* and *Finian's Rainbow.*

In 1972 Freeman accepted a small but continuing role as a police detective on the daytime drama *One Life To Live.* He stayed on that popular television show for 17 years, inhabiting a character whose importance to the plots became greater and greater over time. Freeman was awarded an Emmy Award in 1979, for his work as stoic police captain Ed Hall. That same year, he was chosen to portray Malcolm X in the mini-series *Roots:*

The Next Generations. He earned a second Emmy nomination for that performance. Freeman told *Ebony* that as a successful young black artist he held enormous respect for Malcolm X. "I remember him saying if a dog attacks you, whether it's a four-legged dog or a two-legged dog, you kill that dog," he recalled. "That's what I wanted to hear. I wanted to hear *stand up.* Not go out and kill anybody but *stand up and be a man.* Don't take this crap from anybody. That, I suppose, is really what Malcolm means to me: manhood."

Freeman left *One Life to Live* in 1988 for a teaching position at Howard University. By 1990, he had semi-retired from performing, preferring primarily to teach and spend time on his 40-foot sailboat moored in the Potomac basin. He was lured back into film, however, when he received a telephone call from director Spike Lee, who was casting for a new movie about Malcolm X. This time Freeman was not considered for the title role, but rather for the important supporting character of Elijah Muhammad. Freeman auditioned for the role and was thrilled when he won it. "I really didn't do the picture because of the money," he told *Ebony.* "Certainly Spike didn't pay me that much. But that wasn't the point. The point was that *it had to do with my life.* It seemed to be coming around full circle." He added: "I had gotten old enough to play Elijah, and that seemed to close the loop somehow."

> ## Veteran of the stage and screen whose performing career spans four decades.

The film *Malcolm X* was a critical and commercial success when it opened in 1993, and Freeman suddenly found himself back in the limelight. Where once he had conducted his classes at Howard in relative anonymity, he was now approached by enthusiastic students wherever he went on campus. Film critics, too, found much to praise in his performance, and several suggested he might win an Academy Award nomination. Film critic Gene Siskel told *Ebony:* "I know of more than one person who was very familiar with what the real Elijah Muhammad looked like who wondered if they were watching documentary footage of him, somehow taken in color." Perhaps the most moving reaction to Freeman's portrayal of Elijah Muhammad came from one of the granddaughters of the religious leader himself who, after seeing the film, sent Freeman a bouquet of flowers.

According to *Ebony,* with the single role of Elijah Muhammad, Freeman "has captured the admiration and respect of a whole new generation that, until now, has been largely unfamiliar with his distinguished 35-year acting career." More recently, Freeman appeared in the 1994 made-for-TV movie *Assault at West Point* and also played the role of Poppa in the film entitled *Once Upon a Time ... When We Were Colored,* that debuted in 1995. *Once Upon a Time ...,* based on the memoirs of writer Clifton L. Taulbert, chronicled the lives of African Americans in the rural south during the 1950s.

For his part, Freeman is content these days to take an occasional foray into acting while devoting most of his time to his students at Howard. "This will sound corny," he said in *Ebony,* "but these little twerps are the important people in my life. I get more from them than they get from me. Teaching really has renewed me."

Selected writings

A Fable (screenplay), MFR, 1971.
(With Ossie Davis and others) *Countdown at Kusini* (screenplay), Columbia, 1976.

Sources

Books

Contemporary Theatre, Film, and Television, Volume 7, Gale Research, Inc., 1989.

Periodicals

Ebony, March 1993, pp. 84-90.
Jet, December 11, 1989, p. 24.
Time, December 20, 1993, p. 68.
USA Today, December 21, 1992, p. D-6.
USA Weekend, January 19-21, 1996, p. 10.
Washington Post, March 1, 1992, p. B-3.

—Anne Janette Johnson

Ann Fudge

1951(?)—

Corporate executive

Ann Fudge's estimable rise through the ranks of corporate power have made her one of the most influential--while also one of the youngest--decision-making women in American business. Yet her success has gone relatively unnoticed amongst media tallies of other female movers and shakers in high positions--but that's probably not something to which the dynamic and well-regarded executive gives much thought. Named president of Maxwell House Coffee in 1994, a division of tobacco conglomerate Philip Morris's Kraft Foods division, Fudge is responsible for overseeing quality and marketing for the venerable coffee brand and its sister product General Foods International Coffees. Her achievement is all the more impressive, wrote *New York Times* reporter Judith H. Dobrzynski, because "the 44-year-old had to crash through not merely the glass ceiling that stymies white women but an all-but-insurmountable 'concrete wall' that researchers say blocks blacks and other minorities from companies' upper echelons."

Fudge was born in Washington, DC, in the early 1950s, and attended the city's Catholic schools. Witnessing the urban riots in the wake of Martin Luther King, Jr.'s assassination in 1968 helped her gain a focus. "They made me incredibly determined," she told Dobrzynski in the *New York Times.* "I wanted to do something that black people hadn't done before. When I hit roadblocks, that was what kept me going." After high school, Fudge enrolled at Simmons College to pursue a B.A. There she met Margaret Henning, author of the influential book *The Managerial Woman,* and later a founder of the college's school of business. As her adviser, Henning told the undergraduate Fudge that she recognized in her some of the skills crucial to becoming a corporate executive, and that she should pursue it as a career.

Balanced Personal and Career Goals

While at Simmons, Fudge also met her future husband, Richard, and the two married and had their first child while she was still an undergraduate. After earning her B.A. in 1973, Fudge worked as a personnel executive for General Electric, and she began to take on the demanding lifestyle required of working mothers--her family now included a second son. A business degree was next. After graduating from Harvard Business School with an M.B.A. in 1977, Fudge was hired by the Minneapolis, Minnesota-based General Mills company. She then set for herself a timetable of professional goals, including becoming the general manager of a brand by the age of 40.

In her first position at General Mills, Fudge was a marketing assistant for brands made by this sixth-largest food manufacturing company in the United States. By 1978, Fudge had begun moving quickly up the corporate ranks, becoming assistant product manager that year and product manager in 1980, and finally a

At a Glance . . .

Full name, Ann Marie Fudge; born c. 1951, in Washington, DC; daughter of a U.S. Postal Service administrator and a National Security Agency manager; married Richard Fudge, Sr. (an educational and training consultant to businesses and nonprofit groups), c. 1970; children: Richard Jr., Kevin. *Education:* Simmons College, B.A. (honors), 1973; Harvard Business School, M.B.A., 1977.

General Electric Company, manpower specialist, 1973-75; General Mills Corporation, Minneapolis, MN, marketing assistant, 1977-78, assistant product manager, 1978-80, product manager, 1980-83, marketing director, 1983-86; Kraft General Foods, White Plains, NY, associate director of strategic planning, 1986-89, vice-president for marketing and development in the Dinners and Enhancers division, 1989-91, general manager of same division, 1991-93, executive vice-president, 1993--, president of Maxwell House Coffee division, 1994--.

Member: National Black MBA Association, 1981--; Junior League, 1981--; Executive Leadership Council (has served as vice-president and president); member of board of directors of Allied Signal, Inc., and Liz Claiborne, Inc., both since 1993, and of Simmons College, Harvard Business School Alumni Association, and the Catalyst Advisory Board.

Awards: COGME Fellow, 1975-76; Young Women's Christian Association Leadership Award, 1979.

Addresses: *Home--*Westport, CT.*Office--*Maxwell House Coffee Company, 250 North St., White Plains, NY 10605.

That job offer was at Kraft General Foods in White Plains, NY, a subsidiary of Philip Morris, Inc. and the nation's largest consumables manufacturer. For its products, the parent company has an advertising budget of over $2 billion, one of the deepest pocketbooks in American business. Fudge became responsible for some of that ad budget when she was promoted to brand manager of the Dinners and Enhancers Division in 1991. In her new position, Fudge oversaw longtime company staples such as Log Cabin Syrup, Minute Rice, and Stove Top Stuffing. Such brands had a high consumer recognition factor, but were meeting fierce competition from cheaper private-label goods.

Marketed Classic Brands

At Kraft General Foods, Fudge quickly became known for having a special skill for reviving older brands and repositioning them on the market. One example of Fudge's success in the Dinners and Enhancers division was Shake 'N Bake, a mixture of seasoning and bread crumbs that came in specially-designed pouches. Consumers added meat such as chicken drumsticks to the bag, tossed it around, and then removed the meat and baked it. The brand had not warranted a high-profile television advertising campaign in several years, and Fudge and her team came up with the slogan "Why Fry?" to reintroduce the product. They also revamped the print ad campaign. Within months, Shake 'N Bake sales saw double-digit growth.

> "I encourage my team to challenge the status quo....I'm convinced that everything we do can be done better."

A similar strategy was used with Stove Top Stuffing, which also yielded an immediate jump in sales. When *Black Enterprise* magazine named her one of the country's "21 Women of Power and Influence" in 1991, Fudge was modest about her achievements at Kraft General Foods. "I encourage my team to challenge the status quo," she told the magazine that year. "I'm convinced that everything we do can be done better."

Fostering that cooperative spirit seems to work best for Fudge. "As a business leader, Ann combines a very forceful personality with a great sensitivity to people,"

director of marketing by 1983, responsible for four brands at once. During her tenure, she headed a team that developed and introduced to the consumer market a new breakfast cereal--Honey Nut Cheerios, which quickly became one of the division's top performers. On the verge of a promotion to general manager in 1986, Fudge instead accepted another job offer in order to be closer to her ailing mother on the other side of the country.

her boss, General Foods president Robert S. Morrison, told *Black Enterprise* writer Ronda Reynolds. "She relies heavily on a team approach to achieving business goals." He went on to say that Fudge had positively impacted every area she worked at within the company. In 1991, she was promoted to general manager of the brand division, a year ahead of her goal.

The promotion was also teamed with Fudge's ascension to executive vice president at Kraft General Foods. Her rise up the corporate ladder was not without sacrifice, however. She once turned down a top job offer that entailed a move to another city. "It would have meant relocating just as my son was entering his senior year in high school," she told *National Executive* writers Deborah J. Swiss and Judith P. Walker. "I didn't think it would be right to move him that year. And I did not want to be a commuter wife and mom."

Moved Into Senior Offices

In 1993 Fudge's success in the Dinners and Enhancers division--which included double-digit growth and an increased market share for many of the products whose images she retooled--was responsible for her promotion to executive vice president within the company. The following year, her skills brought her an even tougher assignment--taking over the presidency of Kraft's ailing Maxwell House Coffee brand. The canned coffee product held the number two market spot, after Procter & Gamble's Folgers, but such supermarket coffee products were becoming increasingly overshadowed by a consumer preference for more sophisticated beans and specialty brands.

Fudge started off her new job by visiting the nation's home of the nineties' coffee craze, Seattle. Younger consumers are more apt to buy pricey beans from specialty gourmet coffee retailers such as Starbucks than to purchase a can of Maxwell House. Fudge's plan was to revamp advertising and reposition the brand to make it more attractive to this segment of the market. She faced a tough job--Maxwell House had tried this

approach before, and failed, in part because their "marketing strategies did not have enough finesse," Ted R. Lingle, executive director of the Specialty Coffee Association of America told Reynolds in *Black Enterprise*. "And [General Foods] does so much by committee." Fudge's plan was to emphasize the durability and retro-chic of the brand by bringing back some elements of its old advertising campaigns, a position opposed by Kraft executives above her. Lingle, however, noted that Fudge's qualifications and previous successes gave her the edge to make her strategy a success.

Fudge's achievements have caused some to predict that she will be the first African American woman to run a major company in the United States. Large companies are attempting to add diversity to all facets of their workforce, including the highest corporate offices. Fudge's astounding success and business demeanor have attracted attention from corporate headhunters, and it seems assured that the next 20 years of her career will bring an even higher degree of achievement--and accolades. In 1993 Fudge was invited to sit on the boards of Allied Signal and Liz Claiborne, Inc.

Fudge also manages to balance the personal and professional with the charitable. She is a member of a number of organizations, including the Executive Leadership Council, a non-profit group of high-level African American leaders in business. In all of the positions, Fudge uses her skills and experience to increase African American presence in the upper ranks of corporate America. "Ann wears nice kid gloves that mask an iron fist," a colleague of hers on the boards of some professional and charitable organizations told Reynolds in *Black Enterprise*. "She's eminently qualified and a terrific leader."

Sources

Black Enterprise, August 1991, p. 52; February 1993, p. 94; June 1994, p. 63; August 1994, p. 68.
Essence, May 1995, p. 114.
National Executive, November 1993, p. 44.
New York Times, May 11, 1995.

—Carol Brennan

Lenora Fulani

1950—

Political party leader, psychologist, social therapist

For more than 20 years, Dr. Lenora Branch Fulani has established herself as one of the leading voices in national independent politics and working class advocacy. She is a community organizer against discrimination and violence. She is the first woman and first African American to have appeared as a presidential candidate on all U.S. ballots. She also practices social therapy in order to make a difference on an individual level.

Fulani was one of the founders of the Barbara Taylor school in New York City. This independent school adopted the social development model first outlined by Soviet psychologist Lev Vygotski who specialized in child development and the learning process. She is a main supporter of the Castillo Cultural Center in Manhattan, founded in 1984, which supports multicultural art and theater. Fulani is the founder and co-producer of the "All Stars Talent Show Network," an anti-violence television program for urban children in the United States.

"When," Not "If"

Lenora Fulani was born just outside of Philadelphia in the working class city of Chester, Pennsylvania. She spent her first 18 years in Chester progressing through the public school system and attending church. According to an article published in *Ms. Black Shopper International Network,* Fulani first became interested in changing the world at the age of 12, when her father, Charles Branch, "died of a seizure after her family could not get an ambulance to come into their neighborhood in Chester." Even at such a young age, she was aware that the economic considerations of others had an effect on the health and well-being of African Americans.

In her book, *The Making of a Fringe Candidate, 1992,* Fulani explained that the firing of her church's choir director also convinced her to assist people whom she terms "disenfranchised." "Everybody sort of knew [the choir director] was gay, but nobody said anything about it until they decided to replace him so they could do something else with his salary line. They used his homosexuality as an excuse to get rid of him." The injustice of the situation enraged the young Fulani so much that she advocated his retention, even against the urging of her mother to simply participate in "`prayer meetings ... like

At a Glance . . .

Born Lenora Branch on April 25, 1950, in Chester, PA; daughter of Charles (a railroad worker) and Pearl Branch (a licensed practical nurse); changed name to Lenora Branch Fulani, 1973; divorced; children: Ainka (daughter) and Amani (son). *Education:* Hofstra University, B.A.; Columbia University Teachers College, M.A.; City University of New York, Graduate Center, Ph.D.; New York Institute for Social Therapy and Research, post-graduate training in social therapy.

East Side Center for Short Term Psychotherapy, New York City, psychotherapist; National Alliance Party, founder, presidential candidate, 1988 and 1992; *Independent Black Leadership in America,* Castillo International, contributor, 1990; "This Way for Black Empowerment" newspaper column, columnist; All-Stars Talent Show Network, founder; "Fulani!," television show, host. Author: *The Making of a Fringe Candidate, 1992.*

Member: Transnational Radical Party, General Council; Committee for a Unified Independent Party, Chair; Patriot Party, co-founder, 1994.

Addresses: *Office*—Committee for a Unified Independent Party, 200 W. 72nd St. Suite 37, New York, NY 10023. *Agent*—Castillo International, 500 Greenwich St., Suite 201, New York, NY 10013, (212) 941-5800.

everyone else.'"

Another example of Fulani's early activism was related in the *Philadelphia Inquirer Daily Magazine.* "As a senior at predominantly black Chester High in 1968, she [threatened] to organize a walkout if her class were forced to integrate its all black class cabinet, the first in the school's history. The administration backed down." Fulani's cousin, Yvonne Mann, was quoted as saying in the article: "All her life she knew she was going somewhere.... She thought about `when,' not `if.'"

Fulani told of her time at Hofstra University in *The Making of a Fringe Candidate, 1992* as one of growth. While there she learned about her own prejudices and how to overcome them. She noticed that women and their contributions to society and the civil rights movement remained in the shadows of men. Fulani did not

enjoy this unequal treatment, but she was unsure about what she could do to change anything as prevalent as sexism.

During the early 1970s Fulani married. The two children from this relationship--a daughter, Ainka, and a son, Amani--received the majority Fulani's attention while she also worked to support the family and complete her various degrees. As she acknowledged in her book, the effort was taxing, but it made her stronger. The hard work and desire for change lead Fulani in new directions.

Fulani began exploring activism and social change in the 1970s. While completing her doctorate work and working at the Rockefeller Institute in New York City, she attended a therapy group run by Dr. Fred Newman, a psychologist who practices what he calls social therapy. The group helped her eradicate her prejudices against different kinds of people. She wrote in *The Making of a Fringe Candidate, 1992* that "what I had learned about [people different from myself] was a pile of bull and very hurtful. I worked aggressively to do something about that." With Dr. Newman's help, she recognized that she had been raised with "certain expressions [and] attitudes" that were unfair assessments of people she did not know. "[Prejudices are] so deeply embedded in how you think that they make you insensitive and hurtful even to people you love very much. I worked hard in that group to provide leadership around these issues...."

Dr. Newman has continued to play an important role in Fulani's life outside of the therapy group by serving as campaign manager during most of her political campaigns. As Fulani admitted in her book, she consults Newman about her most pressing concerns because he shares Fulani's hope of improving the lot of disenfranchised people through political means.

Independent Politics

After finishing her doctoral work, Fulani chose to remain with the New York Institute for Social Therapy and Research. She began her therapy practice working with people in Harlem. Fulani also founded a political party known as the National Alliance Party (NAP) in order to effect political change without resorting to the policies of the Republican or Democratic parties. As an independent party, she looked for support wherever she could find it, but the majority of NAP's original followers were women and African Americans from Fulani's work place and the local community.

As Fulani's and others' political starting point, the NAP

described itself, according to the *Philadelphia Inquirer,* as "black-led, multiracial, pro-gay, and pro-socialist." Over the years Fulani often served the party as its standard bearer in elections. She campaigned for lieutenant governor of New York in 1982, mayor of New York City in 1985, governor of New York in 1986 and 1990, and president of the United States in 1988 and 1992. In her run for the presidency, she distinguished herself by becoming the first woman and the first African American to qualify for the ballot in all 50 states. She also became the first woman to qualify for federal primary matching funds during her 1992 bid. In fact, she was so successful in 1992 that she garnered more in matching funds than mainstream candidates Jerry Brown and Douglas Wilder.

Fulani's brand of independent politics has involved many tactics. She has led drives for voter registration. She has initiated lawsuits to open up ballot access to independent parties. Fulani has fought to be included in debates with major candidates on the state and national levels.

During her bids for public office, Fulani received endorsements from disparate people and groups. One of her supporters over the years has been the controversial minister Louis Farrakhan. Fulani has endured a great deal of criticism from more mainstream politicians because she has refused to denounce Farrakhan. Fulani stated in *The Making of a Fringe Candidate, 1992,* however, that "black leaders--like white leaders--have the right to have differences without having to repudiate each other." She also received a great deal of bad publicity for her support of gay rights.

Fulani insists, though, that it is possible to derive support from these very different sectors of the country and build a movement that is unified in its thinking. In her run for the Democratic party's nomination for governor of New York in 1994, she showed this statement to be true by collecting 21 percent of the total vote in the primary elections. She gathered more than 30 percent of the vote in many black majority areas and more than 40 percent of the vote in the six northern New York counties where industrialist Ross Perot scored very high percentages of the vote in the 1992 presidential election.

Worked the Streets

In addition to her grassroots runs for political office, Fulani has often taken to the streets to push for action issues or solve problems of the working class. She has played a major role in attempting to serve justice in the rape case of 15-year-old Tawana Brawley in which she

originally implicated three white men, was defended by black social activist Al Sharpton, but eventually admitted that she fabricated the story. Fulani organized marches, again with Reverend Al Sharpton, in regards to the Howard Beach, New York, incident in which three black men with car problems were severely beaten, one fatally, by whites in a white neighborhood for just being there. Fulani took to the streets for more than 25 marches through the the predominantly white Bensonhurst section of Brooklyn, New York, in which Yusuf Hawkins, a black youth, was killed. She spent several hours in the streets of the Crown Heights section of Brooklyn "helping to avert a bloodbath [between African American and Jewish residents] in the wake of the death of Gavin Cato [a black child run over by a car]," according to *Ms. Black Shopper.* This event led to her endorsement in the 1990 gubernatorial race by the Guardian Association of the New York City Police Department.

> "[Prejudices are] so deeply embedded in how you think that they make you insensitive and hurtful even to people you love very much."

Fulani continues her work with what she calls "the overtaxed and under served population" in her political activities, said her spokesperson Madelyn Chapman. In 1994, Fulani assisted in forming a unified front of the disenfranchised and other independent voters who supported the presidential campaign of Ross Perot. At a meeting that year of the Federation of Independent Voters in Arlington, Virginia, the Patriot Party was born through this organizing effort. The NAP has since folded itself into the Patriot Party for the 1996 elections, hoping to strengthen the power of independent voters.

Although Fulani has achieved great success in organizing independent voters, it has not been without obstacles. Both Political Research Associates of Cambridge, Massachusetts, and *Nation* magazine have published material highly critical of Fulani and the NAP. *Nation* likened the party to a cult run by Dr. Newman. According to the *Philadelphia Inquirer,* however, "Fulani's followers have heard all the criticism and remain fiercely loyal. Many of the most ardent, from the most disaffected quarters of society, say she has revived their interest in politics."

However she is viewed by others, Fulani is sure to persist in working hard for independent politics and the reform of the current system. In 1996 she reached out to people through a newspaper column carried in more than 140 newspapers, entitled "This Way for Black Empowerment." She also is the host of her own cable television show, "FULANI!," seen in more than 20 cities each week. In these ways, Lenora Fulani has expanded her efforts to include everyone in the democratic process.

Sources

Books

Fulani, Lenora B., *The Making of a Fringe Candidate, 1992,* Castillo International, 1993.
Salit, Jacqueline and Gabrielle Kurlander, *Independent Black Leadership in America,* Castillo International Publications, 1990.

Periodicals

Ms., May/June 1992, pp. 86-88.
Ms. Black Shopper International Network, January 1995, p. 3.
Nation, May 4, 1992, pp. 385-94; May 30, 1994, pp. 746-47.
New York Amsterdam News, January 30, 1993, p. 4.
Philadelphia Inquirer Daily Magazine, April 6, 1992, p. C1.

Additional information for this profile was obtained through a November of 1995 press release from Castillo International Publications.

—Stephen Stratton

Paula Giddings

1947—

Editor, educator, journalist, social historian

Paula Giddings has made her name and reputation carrying out a simple but formidable project, recovering the lost voices of silent generations of American black women. Giddings has put her strongest efforts into restoring and understanding the perspective of others in her two well-received, major books of social history, *When and Where I Enter: The Impact of Black Women on Race and Sex in America* and *In Search of Sisterhood: Delta Sigma Theta and the Challenge of the Black Sorority Movement.* Giddings credits her interest in language to her mother who taught her the importance of having a voice. Giddings has been recognized for her hard work by many group, including the National Coalition of 100 Black Women, the New York Urban League, and Bennett College in Greensboro, North Carolina--awarded her an honorary doctorate in human letters in 1990.

Silenced by Classmates' Racism

In *Essence* Giddings recalled one particularly formative experience from her childhood in the 1950s. She was the first black child to go to her privately run elementary

school; the other children made fun of her African looks and taunted her with racial epithets, but Giddings did not respond. Her diffidence bothers her to this day. She wrote in *Essence,* "It was my first experience with the politics of difference, and my reaction, I am ashamed to say, was one of stunned silence." In a process similar to ones she would document in her later work, she found her voice suddenly muted.

The white administrators were sympathetic enough to Giddings plight but were ineffectual in dealing with the childrens' cruelty. Not knowing what to do, they approached Giddings's mother, perhaps silently hoping she would remove her daughter from the school. Instead Mrs. Giddings asked to address the class. For the future writer, it was an important lesson. The author recollected in *Essence,* "She exuded such authority ... that the kids fell in line right away." Her mother a children's book about dealing with differences to the class.

After finishing the book, Mrs. Giddings encouraged the children to speak up about their feelings of race. The youngsters, un-used to receiving such respect from an adult on such an important issue, were allowed to

At a Glance . . .

Born Paula Jane Giddings, November 16, 1947, in Yonkers, NY; daughter of Curtis G. (a guidance counselor and school teacher) and Virginia (Stokes; a guidance counselor) Giddings. *Education:* Howard University, BA, 1969.

Random House, editorial assistant, 1969-70, copy editor, 1970-72; Howard University Press, associate book editor, 1972-75; *Encore America/Worldwide News,* Paris bureau chief, Paris, France, 1975-77, associate editor, New York, NY, 1977-79; *Essence,* contributing and book review editor, 1985-90; Spelman College, distinguished United Negro College Fund (UNCF) scholar, 1986-87, visiting scholar, 1991-92; Rutgers University/Douglass College, Laurie New Jersey chair in women's studies, 1989-91; Princeton University, visiting professor, 1992-93; Phi Beta Kappa visiting scholar, 1995-96. Fellow, Barnard Center for Research on Women, 1990-93, New York University Institute for the Humanities, 1991–, John Simon Guggenheim Foundation, 1993-94, National Humanities Center, Research Triangle Park, NC, 1993-95.

Member: Delta Sigma Theta, 1967–; National Coalition of 100 Black Women, 1985; American Historical Association, 1990–; International Association of Poets, Playwrights, Editors, Essayists, and Novelists (PEN; board member), 1990–; Author's Guild of America (treasurer), 1991; Century Club; Association of Black Women Historians; National Women's Studies Association; Author's League Foundation (board member); Organization of American Historians; Women's WORLD (World Organization for Rights, Literature, and Development; cofounder and board member).

Awards: Ford Foundation Grant, 1982; Candace Award, National Coalition of 100 Black Women, 1985; Alumni Award, Howard University, 1985; Westchester Black Women's Political Caucus Award, 1986; Building Brick Award, New York Urban League, 1986; Anna Julia Cooper Award, *Sage: A Scholarly Journal on Black Women,* 1990, Bennett College, Greensboro, NC, honorary doctorate in humane letters 1990.

Addresses: *Home*–New York, NY.

express openly the fears and prejudices that they were usually forced to suppress. The mother who had come in to help her daughter "find her voice" also performed the same service for her child's tormentors.

When the dark feelings of the other children were brought out into the open and dealt with, they lost most of their virulence. Giddings compared what her mother did to an exorcism of "the monstrous images" that had come to dominate the children's understanding of black people. It was an extraordinary experience, bringing the children to feel true remorse for the inhuman way they had been treating another human being; and for the little girl, Paula, the encounter between her mother and her classmates became an emblem for the dignity of the human voice and the power of the story teller's art.

Giddings mother was no stranger to the educational system. The Giddings family had been active in education and civil rights for generations. Paula's great-great-grandmother, a slave and daughter of her Virginia slave master, was taught "the rudiments of education, fine embroidery, and music, as well as the harsher lessons of being black and a woman in America," according to the preface to Giddings' *Where and When I Enter.* Both Paula's parents were college educated, and both taught in the public school system. Her father also founded the local chapter of the Congress of Racial Equality (CORE) in Yonkers, New York. From a young age, Paula knew she wanted to write. She went to Howard University in Washington, DC, and became editor of the literary magazine *Afro-American Review,* but about this time she also began to move away from her own creative writing towards journalism and social history. Giddings graduated with an undergraduate degree in English in 1969.

The 1970s were a period of search for Giddings. After graduating, she worked as a Random House copy editor during an exciting time there, when its authors included the black political activists, Angela Davis and Stokely Carmichael. Toni Morrison, the eventual author of such acclaimed novels as *Beloved,* was also an editor there at the same time. After a couple of years Giddings and her mentor at Random House, Charles Harris, went to Howard University Press where she helped develop book ideas and took part in deciding what should be published as well as performing the usual grunge work associated with preparing a manuscript for publication.

The job was satisfying to her in many way, but Giddings remained restless. A desire to work overseas led her to open the Paris bureau of *Encore American & World Wide News* for famed publisher Ida Lewis in 1975. From Paris, Giddings not only covered Europe, she also traveled through Africa, reporting on news and interviewing such personages as Uganda's notorious dictator, Idi Amin, and South African activist under apartheid, Winnie Mandela. *Encore* brought her back to New York in 1977 to work as an associate editor.

Reached Career Turning Point

In 1979 Giddings reached an important turning point.

While working on a program initiated by the U.S. government to produce a series of books on the historical experience of black women in America, Giddings came to realize how dramatically small was the documentation of the black female voice in our history. She became determined to do what she could to rectify the situation, and so began the research into the book that five years later would come out under the title, *When and Where I Enter: The Impact of Black Women on Race and Sex in America.* To write the book, Giddings searched out the hidden primary sources of the past, from diaries to letters and even to obscure novels. Along the way she received a Ford Foundation Grant to help her complete the project.

In the preface to *When and Where I Enter* Giddings noted that "despite the range and significance of our [black women's] history, we have been perceived as token women in black texts and as token blacks in feminist ones." Emergent themes in Giddings work include the relationship between sexism and racism, the effect of "double discrimination" on the basis of gender and race on black women, and the relevance of historical issues to contemporary life. Writing in the*New York Times Book Review,* Gloria Naylor described *When and Where I Enter* as the "narrative history of black women from the seventeenth century to the present" as "a labor of commitment and love—and it shows." Naylor went on in her glowing review to call the work "jarringly fresh and challenging...." In fitting tribute to the woman who had protected her voice, Paula Giddings dedicated the book to her mother.

The response to the book was strong and very favorable. Her former colleague, Toni Morrison called *When and Where I Enter,* "History at its best."*Publishers Weekly* predicted correctly that it would become a standard in its field and *The Women's Review of Books* went so far as to call it the "best interpretation of black women and race and sex that we have." The Book of the Month Club made it an alternate selection, and *When and Where I Enter* was translated into several foreign languages. The success of the book not only made her a speaker much in demand on the lecture circuit, it also launched an academic career for her.

Dabbled in Academics

Giddings first academic post came in the mid-1980s at Atlanta's Spelman College, where she was a United Negro College Fund Distinguished Scholar. Giddings also deeply immersed herself in traditional journalistic work. She went to work at *Essence,* a magazine aimed at black women, as both a contributing editor and editor

of the publication's book section. In 1987, the prestigious journal*Harper's,* edited by Lewis Lapham, invited Giddings to take part in a forum on whether or not conditions for African Americans in the United States were improving.

Giddings comments in *Harper's* tended to focus on the wedge that was perceived to be growing between middle class blacks and their underclass brothers and sisters. Troubled by this development, she pointed out that the differences between the classes were to some degree illusory since the "fate of all blacks is inseparable by class.... The black middle class will remain fragile as long as there's a large and growing underclass."

> "Despite the range and significance of black women's history, we have been perceived as token women in black texts and as token blacks in feminist ones."

In 1988, Giddings followed up *When and Where I Enter* with *In Search of Sisterhood: Delta Sigma Theta and the Challenge of the Black Sorority.* The sorority differed from the "Greek" organization stereotype of initiation rituals, or hazing and raucous toga parties. Instead, Delta Sigma Theta, founded at Howard University in 1913, took the education of its members concerning political change and civil rights legislation as its mission from the very beginning

In the first year of its existence, the "Delts" joined 5,000 female protesters marching up Washington, DC's Pennsylvania Avenue to bring to the government their demand that women receive the right to vote. A member herself, other famous members of Delta Sigma Theta include Barbara Jordan, a professor and former congresswoman from Texas, singer Lena Horne, and the opera diva Leontyne Price. A more obscure but no less impressive alumna of the sorority is Sadie T. M. Alexander, the first woman of color to earn a doctorate in the United States.

Critics were quick to praise *In Search of Sisterhood.* Writing in *The Washington Post,* Dorothy Gilliam gave Giddings "a hearty cheer for bringing to the fore yet another piece of overlooked black women's history." *The Los Angeles Times* said, the book "succeeds as a detailed study of an organization that has touched the lives of some of the most prominent black women in

The Los Angeles Times said, the book "succeeds as a detailed study of an organization that has touched the lives of some of the most prominent black women in America."

Ventured into Creative Writing

In the early 1990s, Giddings continued to juggle writing and teaching, beginning with a three-year fellowship at the Barnard Center for Research on Women. In 1991, the Women's Project Productions of New York City commissioned her to write a one-act play, *The Reunion,* which was given a staged reading at one of New York City's most famous theaters, the Judith Anderson. The same year, Giddings was invited back to Spelman as a visiting scholar, Rutgers University's Douglass College asked her to chair their women's studies program, and she was honored with a fellowship at the New York University Institute for Humanities.

Giddings spent 1992 as a visiting professor at Princeton University, a distinct honor in light of the fact she'd never earned an advanced degree and most Ivy League institutions usually hire graduate-degree wielding scholars. Other fellowships were bestowed upon her during the next few years, including one-year associations with the John Simon Guggenheim Foundation and the National Humanities Center in Research Triangle Park in North Carolina. The culmination of these experiences was an academic year spent as a visiting scholar with Phi Beta Kappa in 1995 to 1996.

An energetic woman, Giddings still found the time throughout her career participate as a high ranking member of such esteemed organizations as the International Association of Poets, Playwrights, Editors, Essayists, and Novelists (PEN); the Author's League Foundation; the Author's Guild of America; and Women's WORLD (World Organization for Rights, Literature and Development), the latter being an anti-censorship group that she cofounded. After helping the National Book Award committee judge the nonfiction output of 1989, she also sat on the judging committee's for PEN's Gerard Fund Award in 1992 and the National Association of Colored People (NAACP) ACT-SO award as well as serving on various advisory committees for a number of academic institutions.

Despite all her other obligations, expressing herself with words remained Giddings number one priority and love. "For a black woman to write about black women is at once personal and an objective undertaking. It is personal," she explained in the preface to *When and Where I Enter,* "because the women whose blood runs through my veins breathe admist the statistics. [It] is also an objective enterprise because one must put such experiences into historical context, find in them a rational meaning so that the forces that shape our own lives may be understood." With that ethic in mind, Giddings was planning a biography of the former slave, outspoken journalist, and anti-lynching crusader Ida B. Wells-Barnett, who died in 1931. Always in the midst of a project, she also co-edited, with social critic Cornel West, an anthology of essays about Malcolm X entitled *Regarding Malcolm X.* As Giddings noted in an interview with *Notable Black American Women,* "I will write 'till I say goodbye to this world."

Selected writings

Books

When and Where I Enter: The Impact of Black Women on Race and Sex in America, William Morrow, 1984, Bantam, 1985.
In Search of Sisterhood: Delta Sigma Theta and the Challenge of the Black Sorority, William Morrow, 1988, Quill, 1995.
(With Cornel West) *Regarding Malcolm X,* Amistad Press, 1994.

Plays

The Reunion, reading at Judith Anderson Theater, New York City, 1991.

Sources

Books

Giddings, Paula, *When and Where I Enter: The Impact of Black Women on Race and Sex in America,* William Morrow, 1984, pp. 1, 5-8.
Notable Black American Women, edited by Jessie Carney Smith, Gale, 1992, pp. 402-03.

Periodicals

Booklist, August 1988, p. 1872.
Essence, May 1995, pp. 196-98.
Harper's, February 1987, p. 35ff.
Los Angeles Times Book Review, July 31, 1988, p. 1.
New Directions for Women, March 1989, p. 18.
New York Times Book Review, July 8, 1984, p. 10.
Publishers Weekly, July 8, 1988, p. 44.
Washington Post, August 12, 1988.

Additional information for this profile was obtained via information provided to *CBB* by Paula Giddings on January 4, 1996.

—*Jim McDermott*

Simon Gourdine

1940—

Sports executive, labor negotiator, city government official, attorney

In the summer of 1995, Simon Gourdine undertook the difficult task of negotiating a new contract for National Basketball Association (NBA) players. As executive director of the National Basketball Players Association, he had the unenviable task of acting as mediator between a divided players' union and the NBA owners--a seemingly no-win situation that he handled with calm professionalism.

Gourdine is a true pioneer in professional sports, not for what he has done on the court, but for what he has accomplished in a series of important offices. He was deputy commissioner of the NBA for seven years from 1974 to 1981, and was, at that time, the most powerful black executive in professional sports. His significant expertise was put to use by the Players Association, placing him once again in a position of authority and influence.

Gourdine has said that he identifies with pro basketball players, most of whom are black, because he grew up in similar circumstances. He was born in 1940, in Jersey City, New Jersey, but grew up in the Harlem section of New York City. He earned his bachelor's degree from the City College of New York in 1962. As an enterpris-

ing student, Gourdine interviewed his hero, black nationalist Malcolm X, for the City College newspaper. Malcolm urged Gourdine to be fair in his coverage of their conversation, and Gourdine tried hard to comply. Gourdine found that he shared many of Malcolm's concerns about the future of blacks in the United States. "I grew up in the middle of the civil rights struggle," Gourdine told *Sports Illustrated*. "A moderate was someone who maybe was too accommodating, who wasn't pushing hard enough."

A Different Kind of NBA Career

Gourdine worked extremely hard. After finishing his bachelor's degree, he entered the Fordham University School of Law. Upon finishing his law studies in 1965, he entered the U.S. Army and completed a two-year tour of duty. The army promoted him to captain and awarded him the prestigious Army Commendation Medal.

When Gourdine finished his military service, he returned to New York City and briefly took a job with the U.S.

At a Glance . . .

Born Simon Peter Gourdine, July 30, 1940, in Jersey City, NJ; son of Simon Samuel and Laura Emily (Rembert) Gourdine; married Patricia Campbell, 1964; children: David Laurence, Peter Christopher, Laura Allison. *Education:* City College of New York, B.A., 1962; Fordham University School of Law, J.D., 1965; attended Harvard University Graduate School of Business, 1979.

Southern District of New York, assistant U.S. attorney, 1967-69; National Basketball Association, New York, NY, assistant to the commissioner, 1970-72, vice president of administration, 1973-74, deputy commissioner, 1974-81; New York City Department of Consumer Affairs, commissioner, 1982-84; The Rockefeller Foundation, New York, NY, secretary, 1984-86; Metropolitan Transportation Authority, New York, NY, director of labor relations, 1986-90; National Basketball Players Association, New York, NY, general counsel, 1990-95, executive director, 1995-96. *Military service:* U.S. Army, 1965-67, became captain; received Army Commendation Medal.

Member: Member of board of directors, Police Athletic League, 1974– and Fresh Air Fund, 1985–; member, New York State Banking Board, 1979-90; New York State Bar Association; U.S. District Court Bar Association; U.S. Supreme Court Bar Association.

Addresses: *Office*–National Basketball Players Association, 1775 Broadway, New York, NY 10019.

Attorney's office. In 1970, he was hired by the NBA as assistant to the commissioner. The job was high-profile with many important responsibilities, and Gourdine was the first black hired to such a position in the history of professional sports. "I had to get [the job] on merit because I had no sports connections at all," Gourdine noted in the *Washington Post*, "There was a value in my being black, but I certainly wasn't hired because I was black." At the same time, Gourdine told the *New York Times*, he "brought a black perspective to the job" in a time when more and more minority players were being hired by the NBA.

In 1974, Lawrence O'Brien assumed the duties of NBA commissioner. He named Gourdine deputy commissioner, making him the highest ranking black executive in sports. Wrote Steve Marcus in *Newsday*, "Here was a black with important duties during a volatile time in the league's history. He helped develop the 1976 collective bargaining agreement that led to free agency and worked on the merger between the ABA (American Basketball Association) and the NBA." For his part, Gourdine told the *Washington Post*, "Being black and being in this position hits you at times. It makes you feel good. What I don't ever forget is that I've got to be as good as I can be all of the time.... I owe much to black people, so the record has to be good."

In 1981 the *Los Angeles Times* published a controversial article about cocaine use in the NBA. The newspaper story contended that as much as 75 percent of NBA players were using the drug. Commissioner O'Brien was out of the country when the story broke, and Gourdine had to answer the allegations on behalf of the NBA. He quickly suggested that the report was racially motivated. "75 percent happens to be the proportion of blacks in the NBA," he said in the *New York Times*, "If someone chose to, they could have concluded that 100 percent of the black players were involved with drugs. Anytime there are social problems like drugs and alcohol, the perception is that it's black players involved. That concerns me. Sometimes perception becomes reality. You have to go out aggressively and fight those perceptions."

> "Being black and in a position of power hits you at times. What I don't ever forget is that I've got to be as good as I can be all of the time. The record has to be good."

Gourdine had high hopes that he would be named NBA commissioner at some point, but as the years passed, he began to feel he had hit a glass ceiling as deputy commissioner. In 1981, he stepped down. "This is not a midlife crisis," he told the *New York Times* at the time. "Government has always been a great interest of mine. It may be time to take my license out, dust it off and practice law again." Asked if he felt he would never be named commissioner because he was black, Gourdine responded: "If sports ever has a black commissioner, it will be in basketball."

Beckoned by New Challenges

Gourdine did not find himself idle after leaving the NBA.

In 1982, he became commissioner of New York City's Department of Consumer Affairs. Two years later, he moved to the Rockefeller Foundation as secretary. He served as director of labor relations for Manhattan's Metropolitan Transportation Authority in 1986. In addition to his professional duties, Gourdine devoted a good deal of time to charitable causes, including the Police Athletic League and the Fresh Air Fund.

The business side of sports still appealed to Gourdine, however, and he was thrilled when executives from Major League Baseball began courting him as the possible president of the National League. According to Manny Topol of *Newsday,* Gourdine "was the leading candidate for many months." In the end, the committee chose another black man, Bill White, for the job. "I am, of course, disappointed," Gourdine said in *Newsday.* "I certainly was in the selection process right to the end. But I understand that there could be only one winner."

Gourdine's experience as a top sports executive and labor negotiator brought him another opportunity in 1990. He returned to professional basketball, this time as general counsel for the National Basketball Players Association. His new duties involved negotiating contracts and resolving disputes on behalf of NBA players. NBA commissioner David Stern commented that Gourdine's appointment would bring the Players Association "an excellent lawyer and a tough advocate." Stern added, as quoted in the *New York Times,* "The players are lucky to have someone with Simon's knowledge of the game, its history, and the players and owners working together for the continued growth of the sport." In the same newspaper piece, Gourdine said, "I'm quite excited about coming back into pro basketball, even if it's on the other side."

Forged Contracts, Dealt with "Dissidents"

In the spring of 1995, during a bitter labor dispute between the NBA players and owners, Gourdine assumed the executive directorship of the Players Association. This proved to be an unenviable task. Gourdine took the top post after disgruntled players forced out negotiator Charles Grantham. When Gourdine appeared more moderate than Grantham, the players accused him of cooperating with his old cohorts in the league offices. While the NBA players endured an 80-day lockout imposed by the owners, Gourdine struggled to forge a new collective bargaining agreement between the two parties. Unfortunately, the deal he negotiated with the league did not satisfy many players, among them high-profile "dissident" stars like Patrick Ewing and Michael Jordan. At one point in July of 1995, sentiment was so high against Gourdine that 180 players signed a petition for an election to decertify the Players Association. Gourdine persisted and the decertification attempt failed.

The NBA lockout ended in time for the 1995-96 season, and Gourdine continued to iron out the details of a new six-year contract for the players. At the beginning of 1996, the executive board of the Players Association extended Gourdine's contract through October of 1997. However, some of Gourdine's harshest critics forced a vote on the contract. NBA player representatives met at the end of January of 1996 and voted to replace Gourdine.

Sources

Boston Globe, July 13, 1995, p. 62.
Newsday (Long Island, NY), November 27, 1988, p. 11; February 3, 1989, p. 159.
New York Times, June 27, 1981, p. 15; February 13, 1990, p. 12B.
Rocky Mountain News, January 14, 1996, p. 14B.
Seattle Times, January 21, 1996, p. 4F.
Sports Illustrated, May 8, 1995, p. 76.
Washington Post, July 1, 1979, p. 4E.

—*Mark Kram*

William Leo Hansberry

1894–1965

Historian, professor

William Leo Hansberry was a man born one generation too soon. A pioneer in the study of ancient African history, he started his career at Howard University in 1922. It was a time when the black academic community was far more concerned with creating a livable present than with resurrecting an ancestral past. It was also a time when many white scholars were still mired in the racist tradition that saw all blacks as intellectual inferiors. Therefore, Hansberry's insistence on studying long-gone communities at first earned him little support from either camp.

Recognition finally came in the early 1950s. During this time, many African countries, long held under colonial rule, began their conversion to self-governance. Searching for proof that African societies had, at one time, a sophisticated cultural history, and could reach these heights again, these new regimes treated Hansberry's research into their societies with deep respect. The international attention he received prompted his U.S. colleagues to take a second look at his work, and to acknowledge, at last, his contribution to the study of ancient African culture.

The direction of Hansberry's life was set by his father, Elden Hansberry, who taught history at Alcorn College in Gloster, Mississippi. The elder Hansberry died when his son was scarcely three years old, but he left him the priceless legacy of a library on culture and customs of the ancient world. Young Leo enjoyed reading his late

father's collection of books. He could not help wondering, however, why they held so much information about the glorious histories of Greece, Rome, and even far-away China, but so little about Africa, the home of his own ancestors.

Formed a Lifelong Belief

In 1915 Hansberry entered Atlanta University as a freshman. The history of the ancient world continued to fascinate him, but the mystery of Africa's shadowy past was not solved by his course work. Extra-curricular reading proved no more enlightening, for only two types of information seemed to be available. The first, as represented by the Old Testament of the Bible, mentioned such countries as Kush and Ethiopia, but gave no details of their inhabitants' lives. The second category of African history tended to emphasize either the supposedly civilizing influence of the slave trade or the rescue of the indigenous population from hopeless ignorance by white colonial missionaries.

An example of this parochial thinking appears in a book called *Howard University Department of History, 1913-1973,* written by faculty member Michael Winston. To show how the Jim Crow laws of the late 19th century perpetuated such so-called white superiority, Winston resurrected the following opinion of "the arche-typal black person" aired during a U.S. Senate session

At a Glance . . .

Born William Leo Hansberry, February 25, 1894, in Gloster, MS; died of cerebral hemorrhage, November 3, 1965, in Chicago, IL; son of Elden Hayes and Pauline (Bailey) Hansberry; married Myrtle Kelso, 1937; children: Gail Adelle, Myrtle Kay. *Education:* Harvard University, B.A., 1921, M.A., 1932. Attended Oriental Institute, University of Chicago, 1936-37; Oxford University, 1937-38; Cairo University, 1953.

Howard University, professor of history, 1922-59; University of Nigeria, visiting professor, 1963.

Awards: Award of Honor, African Student Association of the U. S. and Africa, 1951, 1959, 1963; Fullbright Scholarship, 1953; Bronze Citation for "Forty Years of Service in the Cause of African Freedom," United Friends of Africa, 1961; Achievement Award, Omega Psi Phi Fraternity, 1961; Hansberry Institute of African Studies, University of Nigeria, established in his name, 1963; First African Research Award, Haile Selassie I Prize Trust, 1964. Honorary degrees include: Doctor of Letters, University of Nigeria; Doctor of Laws, Morgan College.

of February 1914 by then-Senator James K. Vardaman of Mississippi. "He has never had any civilization except that which has been inculcated by a superior race," said Vardaman. "And it is lamentable that his civilization lasts only so long as he is in the hands of the white man who inculcates it ...."

Hansberry was unconvinced by Vardaman's assertion that Africa's entire indigenous population owed all the wisdom they possessed to their European conquerors. He could find no respected social scientist to support his own dissent until 1916, when a new volume of essays on race was published by Atlanta University's Department of Sociology. In two of the essays, "Old African Civilizations" by Franz Boas, then an anthropology professor at Columbia University, and "The Contribution of the Negro to Human Civilization" by A. F. Chamberlain, did Hansberry finally find confirmation of his opinion that the modern march of progress owed much to Africa and her ancient societies. Later that year he found another source of support in the work of activist W. E. B. Du Bois. The first black scholar to gain a Ph.D. from Harvard University, Du Bois was well known nation-wide as a founder of the National Association for the Advance-

ment of Colored People (NAACP) and editor of the NAACP's journal entitled *The Crisis.*

Du Bois had also recently gained attention as the author of a new book called *The Negro.* A devoted follower of Du Bois' trailblazing work, Hansberry bought a copy of the new book and read it immediately. As he had hoped, Du Bois mentioned not only the Greek historian Herodotus, but also several Latin writers who had acknowledged the existence of Kushite, Ethiopian, and other sophisticated African kingdoms predating their own Roman Empire by centuries. Eagerly he rushed to the library to request each precious reference that Du Bois had cited. But Atlanta University was not equipped for detailed study of the more obscure antiquities. Its shelves offered a meager selection so disappointing to him that he decided to transfer to the best-equipped academic institution open to blacks that he could find. Two weeks into his sophomore year he left Atlanta to attend Harvard University, in Cambridge, Massachusetts.

A Student and a Teacher

Hansberry arrived in Cambridge in February of 1917, and plunged immediately into the work that was to occupy him for the rest of his life. African archeology, anthropology, ethnology, and paleontology became the focus of his existence, with courses in the history of science providing a systematic backbone for future research. Yet, while he found encouragement and friendship from Dr. E. A. Hooton of Harvard's renowned Peabody Museum, he found little support for his conviction that indigenous African people had played the most important roles in the shaping of their own communities. Even at Harvard, he noted, the prevailing scholarly belief of the time was that the Africans who had made contributions to civilization were not blacks at all. Instead, it was thought that they, similar to the inhabitants of India, were members of predominantly brown races.

In 1921 Hansberry left Harvard with a bachelor's degree in anthropology, and a burning determination to stamp out American ignorance of what was derogatorily known as the Dark Continent. As a first step he designed a flier called "Announcing an Effort to Promote the Study and Facilitate the Teaching of the Fundamentals of Negro Life and History." He mailed it to several black schools and colleges to express his interest in helping those institutions replace what he considered to be the dangerous revisionist history they were teaching. He wanted to encourage educators to teach black students about their real roots. He felt such instruction could lift students out of the humiliating bigotry that was a part of their lives, and give them some badly needed pride in their heritage.

Hansberry picked a good time to launch his project. A consciousness surrounding black-influenced culture was awakening, thanks to the emergence of the back-to-Africa movement of Marcus Garvey, the newly-popular black-inspired jazz music and dance scene, and the Harlem Renaissance period of talented writers and artists. Nevertheless, many white Americans who enjoyed these novel additions to their culture were unaware of the ancient African roots from which they sprang. Several recipients of Hansberry's flier conceded this point and offered him cordial invitations to visit their schools and colleges.

Among the invitations Hansberry received were three offers of long term employment. One offer, that was impossible to pass up, came from Howard University. Situated just a stone's throw from the great Library of Congress in Washington, D.C., well-entrenched on the educational front since 1867, and reasonably well-funded, the university informed him that they were planning to expand their history curriculum by adding a new section on African studies. Howard added that a teaching post would soon be available if Hansberry chose to consider it.

Pausing only to honor a year-long teaching contract at Straight College in Atlanta, Hansberry arrived at Howard University in 1922, and quickly established three new courses. "Negro Peoples in the Cultures and Civilizations of Prehistoric and Proto-Historic Times" was a general survey, based partly on archeological and anthropological finds in Paleolithic and Neolithic cultures of Africa. "The Ancient Civilizations of Ethiopia" covered the present-day Sudan and Egyptian areas, while "The Civilization of West Africa in Medieval and Early Modern Times" moved the student ahead to the fifteenth century and beyond. Each of these programs was based on his profound belief that the earliest beginnings of higher human culture sprang not from Asia, as the prevailing theory of the time specified, but from Africa. His theory proved vastly popular with Howard's history students, and by 1925 the department's new section of African Studies boasted upward of 800 undergraduates.

The Dark Before the Dawn

Hansberry's success did not bring universal approval, however. In fact, two distinguished faculty members went to then-Howard University president Stanley Durkee and accused Hansberry of endangering Howard's reputation by teaching subject matter for which he had no proof. As a result the university's board of trustees came perilously close to closing his program. To prevent this, Hansberry justified his opinions with a sheaf of detailed documents, among them a meticulously annotated bibliography he had amassed while chronicling the passing centuries of Africa's history. Arranged by subject, the list covered a dazzling array of primary sources ranging from the diaries of Roman travelers such as Pliny the Elder through the Amharic and Coptic accounts of the Middle Ages. His documents also included up-to-the-minute papers written by the modern Egyptologists responsible for the excavation of the tomb of Egyptian pharaoh King Tutankhamen in 1922. His list was an impressive achievement. Hansberry knew however, it was not enough to prove his academic integrity so he also took care to spell out for the board his long term goal--to use these sources to produce a narrative, chronological, history of ancient and medieval Africa. This effort to save his career, though diligent, was only moderately successful.

In the end, the Howard board of trustees rescinded its decision to discontinue African Studies, but refused to reinstate Hansberry's former financial support. His tainted status marred the rest of his 30-plus years at Howard. As a little-respected member of the university faculty, he found reimbursements for classroom equipment suddenly unavailable. Study grants and work-related travel expenses became bureaucratically impossible to obtain. Even a hard-earned promotion was systematically denied him until 1938, when he was at last elevated to an assistant professorship. Still, he refused to let these problems intimidate him. Philosophically he put the opposition down to public ignorance of the widely scattered and extremely technical sources he had used to reach his conclusions. Therefore, he set for himself the mammoth task of bringing the contents of his research out of arcane obscurity, so that anyone interested could understand what he was trying to achieve.

Tried to Move On

While the 1920s could be characterized as the direction-finding decade of Hansberry's career, the 1930s signaled a concern with his own continuing education. In 1932 he went back to Harvard University for a master's degree in anthropology and history, following up in 1936 to 1937 with further post-graduate study at the University of Chicago's renowned Oriental Institute. Next, he was awarded a two-year Rockefeller Foundation grant that enabled him to study at Oxford University in England. This small breakthrough proved temporary, however, for the grant was abruptly terminated without explanation after just one year. Hansberry chose to regard this unexpected free time as a bonus, attending

European conferences and visiting museums, where he carried out in-depth studies of artifacts gathered by the Leakey family and other eminent scholars of the time.

Hansberry tried to get other financial grants that would support him while he furthered his research, but he was largely unsuccessful. Two possible reasons have been cited for this frustrating failure. The first may have been due to the general academic trend, which was still following the tenets of *A Study of History* by the influential Arnold Toynbee. First published in 1934, it expressed his blunt opinion that "the only primary race that has not made a creative contribution to any civilization is the Black Race," a view that stood unaltered on page 233 of a condensed 1962 edition, in proud defiance of the growing civil rights movement.

The second possible obstacle to grant money for Hansberry resulted from the new modus operandi of the universities that catered to black students. The accreditation of these schools became a crucial issue in terms of both federal funding and the post-graduate opportunities open to their alumnae. For these reasons, these colleges became increasingly unwilling to employ faculty members who had not earned Ph.D. degrees. Lacking this tangible badge of academic excellence, Hansberry was at a competitive disadvantage when grant money was being awarded.

The situation seemed unfair. It was not as if Hansberry had not tried to fill this gap, as a supporting letter from his loyal Harvard mentor, Earnest Hooton, showed. "He [Hansberry] has been unable to take the Ph.D. degree … because … there is no university or institution that has manifested a really profound interest in this subject," wrote Hooton to the generous Rosenwald Foundation. He added, "no present day scholar has developed anything like the knowledge of this field that Hansberry has developed.…" Nevertheless, like several others, this grant did not materialize.

Networked for Newcomers

Stymied on two fronts, Hansberry was still an associate professor without tenure as World War II came to an end. But when the century-long colonial stranglehold on Africa began to loosen in the 1950s, his value to the university began to rise. Howard University had long been an educational leader with an international reputation, which made it a natural choice for black undergraduates coming to the United States to study. Now, as nationalism became a closer reality for many African countries and the need for an educated leadership increased, the numbers of foreign students escalated,

adding to both Howard's coffers and its luster.

Unfortunately, not all the newcomers found this adventure to be a happy one. Many foreign students did not have enough money to live on. Most faced the challenges of fitting themselves into an educational and social system completely different from their own, and then transporting their new knowledge into the completely virgin territory of their homelands. Upon return to Africa, they then had to readjust socially, and fit their new cultural knowledge into their former indigenous setting.

> The great contributions Hansberry made to the historical study of African culture will live on to the benefit of all future generations.

Nobody understood these students' dilemma better Hansberry, who had studied their customs since his youth. His expertise now made him indispensable to the university authorities, who assigned him to the position of faculty advisor to African students in 1946, and followed up in 1950 by appointing him to Howard's Emergency Aid to the African Students' Committee. Quietly he took on these added responsibilities. For example, without benefit of secretarial help or typewriter, he wrote hundreds of letters and smoothed out emergencies. In one case, as requested, he even saw to it that the heart of a deceased undergraduate was excised and returned to his Nigerian homeland. Hansberry's proteges called him the "father of African students," and several made sure they kept in touch with him after graduation.

The Father of African Students

With the dawn of the U.S. civil rights movement in the 1950s, knowledge of African American roots became essential to Howard University. Finally, Hansberry's vast knowledge of Africa and her history became more valuable to the university than his role as the "father of African students." This may have been the reason why the Fulbright Scholarship for 1953 was awarded to him, finally giving him the means to do fieldwork in Egypt, the Sudan and Ethiopia, to deliver lectures requested by former students in many parts of Africa, and to serve as a team member on trips to Kenya, Uganda and the mighty Zimbabwe Ruins in what was then Southern Rhodesia. On the negative side however, in his absence, the Ford Foundation had awarded the university a grant to further its African Studies program, from which he had been excluded, despite his 27 years of service.

It is not surprising that his retirement in 1959 brought Hansberry the first real distinction he had ever known. Free to travel as he wished, in 1960, Hansberry accepted an invitation by the government of Ghana to the ceremonies celebrating the establishment of the Republic. That same year, he also made a point of accepting an invitation to visit Nigeria when the country received its independence, and watched with pride as a former student named Nndami Azikiwe became that country's first president. Ties with Nigeria remained so close that Hansberry was on hand in 1963 as a distinguished visiting professor to inaugurate the Hansberry College of African Studies.

Hansberry took great pleasure in traveling until, when in November of 1965, he died as a result of a cerebral hemorrhage while visiting relatives in Chicago. He never knew of the honor finally paid him by Howard University—a lecture hall bearing his name--dedicated in 1972 to mark his 50 years of association with the university's Department of History. Regardless, the great contributions he made to the historical study of African culture will live on to the benefit of all future generations.

Selected writings

Pillars in Ethiopian History: The William Leo Hans

berry African History Notebook, vol. I, edited by Joseph E. Harris, Howard University Press, 1974.

Africa and Africans As Seen by Classical Writers: The William Leo Hansberry History Notebook, vol. II, edited by Joseph E. Harris, Howard University Press, 1977.

Sources

Books

Davis, John P., *American Negro Reference Book,* Prentice-Hall, 1966, p. 677.

Dictionary of American Negro Biography, Logan, Rayford W. and Winston, Michael R., *eds.,* W. W. Norton, 1982, p. 284.

Page, James A., *Selected Black American Authors: An Illustrated Bio-Bibliography,* G. K. Hall, 1977, p. 112-13.

Winston, Michael R., *Howard University Department of History, 1913-1973,* Department of History, Howard University, 1973.

Periodicals

Current Bibliography on African Affairs, November/December 1970, p. 25.

Daedalus, Summer 1971, p. 678.

Ebony, February 1961, p. 62, October 1964, p. 28.

Freedomways, Second Quarter, 1966, p. 161.

Negro History Bulletin, December 1965, p. 63.

—Gillian Wolf

Frances Ellen Watkins Harper

1825–1911

Poet, writer, lecturer, activist

Frances Ellen Watkins Harper was the most popular black poet of her day. She was known internationally during the mid- to late 1800s as a poet, writer, lecturer, abolitionist, and proponent of temperance and women's rights. Although she was a highly sought after speaker and a best-selling author, her works fell into obscurity after her death in 1911. In the introduction to her book *"A Brighter Coming Day,"* Harper scholar Frances S. Foster suggests that racism and sexism—specifically as they manifested themselves in attitudes toward the emancipation of blacks and the suffragette movement of the turn of the century—kept Harper out of America's literary canon.

Frances Ellen Watkins was born to free parents in the slave city of Baltimore, Maryland, on September 24, 1825. By the time she was three both of her parents had died. She was subsequently taken in by an aunt and uncle active in the antislavery movement. Although living free among slaves was not easy, Harper was extremely privileged for her time. She attended the school founded by her uncle, the William Watkins Academy for Negro Youth. The school's emphasis on bible studies, public speaking, and classic literature, as well as

an encouragement of political leadership and social service work for its graduates strongly influenced the young girl.

Privileged Upbringing Did Not Stave Off Loneliness

Apparently, Harper was a lonely child. Foster quotes a letter Harper wrote to a friend in which she laments, "Have I yearned for a mother's love? The grave was my robber. Before three years had scattered their blight around my path, death had won my mother from me. Would the strong arm of a brother have been welcome? I was my mother's only child." As a youth she was considered industrious and intelligent, often given to movements of quiet reflection. She was also profoundly affected by her school's abolitionist teachings.

When she was 14 years old it became necessary for Harper to seek employment. She had already established a reputation as a writer and scholar, and she had enjoyed an education as good or better than that of most women of the period—regardless of class or color. Nonetheless, the best job she could find was as a housekeeper, seamstress, and babysitter for a family

At a Glance . . .

Born September 24, 1825, in Baltimore, MD; died of a heart ailment, February 20, 1911; married Fenton Harper, 1860; children: Mary.

Began writing essays and poems in her early teens; worked as housekeeper, seamstress, and babysitter, c. 1839; taught school in various cities, c. 1850-54; first lectured on abolitionism, 1854; published first volume of poetry, *Forest Leaves*, c. 1845; gained widespread recognition with *Poems on Miscellaneous Subjects*, 1854; published first short story, "The Two Offers," 1859; published novel *Iola Leroy*, 1892; superintendent of the Colored Branch of the Philadelphia and Pennsylvania Chapters of the Woman's Christian Temperance Union, 1875-82; directed Northern United States Temperance Union, 1883-90. Lectured extensively on abolitionism, temperance, and equal rights for women and African Americans, 1854-c. 1900.

who owned a bookstore. She spent her spare time reading in order to further her education. By that time she had written an essay and composed several poems.

In 1850 Harper's uncle closed his school and moved to Canada. Baltimore had become a dangerous place for free blacks, so Harper moved to Ohio, where she taught at the African Methodist Episcopal's (AME) Union Seminary near Columbus. The seminary eventually became part of Wilberforce University. Harper was the first woman faculty member there; she taught what was then called domestic science, essentially housekeeping skills.

In 1852 Harper moved to Little York, Pennsylvania, to teach a class of what she called "fifty-three untrained little urchins," according to Ann Shockley in *Afro-American Women Writers*. But she soon quit that miserable job. She found herself increasingly depressed due to a combination of outrage at slavery and longing for Baltimore. The latter was intensified in 1853 when it became impossible for her to return to the city of her youth. Maryland had passed a law forbidding free blacks from entering the state—going back would have meant imprisonment or enslavement. For the next several years Harper moved frequently, devoting herself to the abolitionist cause. In 1853 she relocated to Philadelphia, where she lived with the family of William Still, whose house was the main stop on the Philadel-

phia portion of the Underground Railroad. The "railroad" was a secret network of hiding places where escaped slaves were aided in their escape to freedom in Canada.

Lectured in Support of Antislavery Movement

Harper spent much of her time traveling to antislavery offices in Philadelphia, Boston, and New Bedford, New Hampshire, learning the abolition movement's theories and practices. She gave her first speech in 1854 in New Bedford. She was so incensed by the horrors of slavery that she became a permanent lecturer for the Maine Anti-slavery Society. Harper traveled throughout New England, southern Canada, and parts of the Midwest speaking on antislavery and civil rights. She would frequently give three lectures in a day. She was an excellent speaker, described as fiery yet dignified. Some people were so impressed, but still so stubborn in their racist convictions, that they insisted Harper could not be genuine. "You would be amused," she wrote to a friend, as quoted in Hallie Q. Brown's *Homespun Heroines and other Women of Distinction*, "to hear some of the remarks which my lectures call forth. 'She is a man.' 'She is not colored, she is white. She is painted.'"

Harper's poetry was often interspersed throughout her lectures. She also began publishing poems regularly in newspapers and magazines, gaining a national reputation in the process. She had published her first volume of poetry in Baltimore around 1845 when she was just 21 years old. Copies of this small collection, entitled *Forest Leaves*—also published as *Autumn Leaves*—have long since disappeared. The book that truly launched her literary career, however, was *Poems on Miscellaneous Subjects*, printed in both Philadelphia and Boston in 1854. It contained a preface by well-known abolitionist William Lloyd Garrison. The book's success was prodigious; it sold over 10,000 copies in three years and was enlarged and reissued in 1857 and reprinted again in 1858, 1864, and 1871, making Harper the most popular black American poet of the time.

It is not surprising that Harper is most often referred to as an abolitionist poet, but her volumes of poetry actually contained works on a variety of topics, including religion, heroism, women's rights, black achievement, and temperance. Her poems also took the form of responses to contemporary writers like Harriet Beecher Stowe and Charles Dickens, new readings of bible stories, and commentaries on current events. In 1859

Harper became the first black American woman to publish a short story when "The Two Offers" was published in the *Anglo-African.*

Harper married Fenton Harper, a young widower with three children, on November 22, 1860, in Cincinnati. Savings from lectures and book sales allowed her to buy a farm outside of Columbus, where she and her husband set up house. They had one child together, a daughter named Mary. The responsibilities of married life and family allowed Harper little time to write or lecture, but she continued to speak out against the atrocities of slavery and published occasionally during the Civil War.

Fenton Harper died during the spring of 1864, which sent Frances immediately back out on the lecture circuit, where she began advocating equal rights for the newly emancipated slaves. In 1867 she financed her own speaking tour and from 1867 through 1871 she lectured daily throughout the North and war-torn South. She worked hard for the Reconstruction effort, espousing the necessity of racial uplift, moral reform, and women's rights. Among the titles of her speeches were "Enlightened Motherhood," "Racial Literature," and "The Demands of the Colored Race in the Work of Reconstruction." As women's clubs became popular, Harper became a favorite speaker on the women's movement

Pioneering Use of Dialect and Folk Characters

During this period Harper tried her hand at her most experimental writing. In 1869 the *Christian Recorder* published her serialized novella, *"Minnie's Sacrifice."* That year she also published "Moses: A Story of the Nile," an extended dramatic poem retelling the bible story of the Hebrews' enslavement in Egypt and their subsequent exodus to the promised land. Still, many critics consider Harper's *Sketches of Southern Life* her most inventive and best literary piece. Published in 1872, it is comprised of a series of poems by "Aunt Chloe" telling stories of slavery and reconstruction. It is considered a pioneering effort in its use of African American dialect and folk characters. Harper's more innovative works did not replace her lyrical balladry, however; in 1871, while arranging for the twentieth edition of *Poems on Miscellaneous Subjects,* Harper published *Poems,* her first new volume of verse in over ten years.

From 1875 to 1882 Harper served as superintendent of the Colored Branch of the Philadelphia and Pennsylvania Chapters of the Woman's Christian Temperance Union. Although she had recently purchased a home in Philadelphia, she was rarely there as demands for her speech-making talents grew. Her daughter, Mary, who never married and was extremely close to her mother, often traveled with her.

Harper developed Sunday schools and YMCAs in the black community, as well as helping to rehabilitate juvenile delinquents and working for the security of the aged. In 1873 she wrote a series of pieces entitled "Fancy Etchings" for the *Christian Reader,* the characters in which discuss current events and various issues supported by Harper. From 1883 to 1890 she directed the Northern United States Temperance Union.

Challenged Racism of Fellow Suffragettes

Three years later Harper joined with colleagues Fannie Barrier Williams, Anna Julia Cooper, Fannie Jackson Coppin, Sarah J. Earley, and Hallie Q. Brown to charge the international gathering of women assembled at the World's Congress of Representative Women in Chicago with racism. The attitudes of celebrated suffragettes Elizabeth Cady Stanton and Susan B. Anthony and other white feminists who made racist remarks about black men was something black feminists would not tolerate. They had depended on the suffrage movement to represent black women as well, but they ultimately realized that they would be forced to organize separately. Harper became the vice-president of the group she helped to form, the National Association of Colored Women.

Still, though the Fifteenth Amendment, which would allow blacks the right to vote, did not include women, Harper pushed to have it passed. When forced to choose, she felt that rights for black Americans were more important than rights for women and that if *any* black person could progress, she would encourage the effort. Harper insisted in her lectures that the burdens of one group were the burdens of all. In a poem entitled "The Burdens of All" she wrote, "The burdens will always be heavy/ The sunshine fade into night/ Till mercy and justice shall cement/ The black, the brown and the white." Neither an advocate of assimilation nor of separatism, Harper championed the value of education in achieving change and did not condone violence.

In 1892 Harper published her only novel; she was just the second African American woman to boast such an accomplishment.*Iola Leroy, or Shadows Uplifted* tells the story of a young woman growing up in post-Civil War America, when women were subjugated and African Americans were restricted and abused despite their freedom. *Publishers Weekly* called it "a classic of 19th century African-American women's fiction." The book was well received and reached a wide audience. But *Iola Leroy* would be Harper's last long literary project (most volumes published later were rearrangements of already published work with some previously uncollected writings added). Toward the end of her life Harper was often ill; she therefore traveled and published less frequently. Mary Harper died in 1909. Constant offers of help were forwarded, but Harper had always been independent and would remain so. She died of a heart ailment on February 20, 1911, at the age of 87.

In *Library Journal's* review of Frances Foster's *"A Brighter Coming Day,"* Veronica Mitchell noted that "Harper was the most popular African-American poet of her time; the first paid black abolitionist lecturer and short story writer; the first to experiment with dialect in the speech of her characters to express the sensibilities of the oppressed; and the first to develop heroic black characters." In 1994 Foster edited *Minnie's Sacrifice; Sowing and Reaping; Trial and Triumph: Three Rediscovered Novels by Frances E. W. Harper* (though the three titular works are generally considered novellas, not novels). *Metro Times Literary Quarterly* contributor Kierna Mayo Dawsey called the trio "buried treasures," remarking on Foster's "tremendous contribution ... in searching for and reprinting Harper's works."

"You would be amused to hear some of the remarks which my lectures call forth. 'She is a man.' 'She is not colored, she is white. She is painted.'"

Dawsey pointed out that "[Harper's] accomplishments as a writer and speaker dedicated to abolition, women's rights and religion earned her national recognition, but ironically did not prevent a significant portion of her work from being lost and forgotten upon her death." It wasn't until the end of the twentieth century, when the contributions of Africa American women to the literary canon began to be studied in earnest that Harper's rightful place among major writers of the nineteenth century commenced to reassert itself. Frances E. W. Harper would have been considered exemplary in any century, but to accomplish what she did during a time when both blacks and women were institutionally oppressed is truly remarkable.

Selected writings

Forest Leaves (also published as *Autumn Leaves*), c. 1845.
Poems on Miscellaneous Subjects, 1854.
"The Two Offers," 1859.
Moses: A Story of the Nile, 1869.
"Minnie's Sacrifice," 1869.
Poems, 1871.
Sketches of Southern Life, 1872.
"Fancy Etchings," 1873.
"Fancy Sketches," 1874.
"Sowing and Reaping: A Temperance Story," 1876-77 (serialized).
"Trial and Triumph," 1888-89 (serialized).
"The Woman's Christian Temperance Union and the Colored Woman," 1888.
Iola Leroy, or Shadows Uplifted, 1892.
The Sparrow's Fall and Other Poems, c. 1894.
Atlanta Offering: Poems, 1895.
Martyr of Alabama and Other Poems, c. 1895.
Poems, 1900.
Light beyond the Darkness.

Sources

Books

Baym, Nina, *Woman's Fiction: A Guide to Novels by and about Women in America 1820-1870,* Cornell University Press, 1978.
"A Brighter Coming Day": A Frances Ellen Watkins Harper Reader, edited by Frances Smith Foster, Feminist Press, 1990.
Brown, Hallie Q., *Homespun Heroines and Other Women of Distinction,* Aldine Publishing Co., 1926, pp. 97-103.
Carby, Hazel, in the introduction to *Iola Leroy,* edited by Deborah E. McDowell, Beacon Press, 1987, pp. 1-20.
Carby, Hazel, *Reconstruction Womanhood: The Emergence of the Afro-American Woman Novelist,* 1987.
Cavalcade: Negro American Writing from 1760 to the Present, edited by Arthur P. Davis and J. Saunders Redding, Houghton Mifflin, 1971.
Christian, Barbara, *Black Woman Novelists: The Development of a Tradition, 1892-1976,* 1980.
Foster, Frances Smith, in the introduction to *Iola Leroy,* edited by Henry Louis Gates, Jr., Oxford University Press, 1988.
Invented Lives: Narratives of Black Women, 1860-1960, edited by Mary Helen Washington, 1988.
Notable Black American Women, Gale, 1992.
Lerner, Gerda, *Black Women in White America: A*

Documentary History, 1973.

Montgomery, J. W., *A Comparative Analysis of the Rhetoric of Two Negro Women Orators—Sojourner Truth and F. E. W. Harper,* 1968.

Redding, J. Saunders, *To Make a Poet Black,* 1939.

Robinson, W. H., *Early Black American Poets,* 1971.

Sherman, Joan R., *Invisible Poets: Afro-Americans of the Nineteenth Century,* 2nd edition, University of Illinois Press, 1989, pp. 62-74.

Shockley, Ann Allen, *Afro-American Women Writers 1746-1933,* G. K. Hall, 1988, pp. 56-61.

Sillen, S., *Women against Slavery,* 1955.

Still, William G., in the introduction to the second edition of *Iola Leroy,* Garigues Brothers, 1892.

Still, William G., *The Underground Railroad,* 1872.

Williams, Kenny J., *They Also Spoke: An Essay on Negro Literature in America,* 1970.

Periodicals

American Visions, October 1994, p. 38.

Boston Globe, August 30, 1994, p. 34.

Library Journal, March 15, 1990, p. 90.

Metro Times Literary Quarterly, February 15, 1995, p. 6.

New Literary History, Winter 1987.

New York Times Book Review, September 23, 1990, p. 38.

Pennsylvania Magazine of History and Biography, January 1989.

Publishers Weekly, May 16, 1994, p. 52.

—Joanna Rubiner

Beverly Harvard

1950—

Law enforcement executive

The image of the big-city police chief has undergone some revision of late. With Los Angeles's Daryl Gates in the news following the 1992 riots and Detroit's William Hart forced to resign the following year after being indicted on embezzlement charges, the position itself has become a center of controversy. In late 1994 when Beverly Harvard--a 21-year veteran of the Atlanta Police Department--was appointed chief of police, a new face and a new image were attached to this public office. Not only is Harvard one of the few female police executives in the United States (joined by Betsy Watson in Houston and Austin, Texas, and Penny Harrington in Portland, Oregon), she is also the first African American woman to head a major police force.

According to Ronald Smothers, writing in the New York Times, Harvard's new office, "with its gleaming, stained oak paneling and view of midtown Atlanta, is a far cry from her hometown of Macon, [Georgia,] ... where she was raised in a sheltered environment with little knowledge of police or of crime." Harvard was born in 1950 as the youngest of seven children. Her birth order allowed her to be the much-protected baby of the family.

Grueling Education

Taken with public service from her early adult years, Harvard earned a bachelor's degree in sociology in 1972 from Morris Brown College. In 1980 she earned a master of science degree in urban government and administration from Georgia State University. Later on, Harvard earned a degree from the Federal Bureau of Investigation's (FBI) National Academy in Quantico, Virginia.

Education of another sort began in 1973. One day while Harvard's husband and his friends were discussing the possibility of female police officers, they suggested the kind of women suited to police work would have to "be 6 foot 2 inches tall, weigh 200 pounds, and have deep voices," recalled Harvard to Smothers. While she hardly measured up to those dimensions, she did have her opinion of a woman's place in the police force. "I thought [my husband and his friends] were just being ridiculous, and I was upset because my husband didn't defend me and women in general more," she added. "I just wanted to get this piece of paper and wave it in their

At a Glance . . .

Born Beverly Joyce Bailey in 1950 in Macon, GA; married Jim Harvard; children: Christa. *Education:* Morris Brown College, B.A., 1972; Georgia State University, M.S., 1980; Federal Bureau of Investigation (FBI) National Academy, graduate, 1983.

Atlanta Police Department, Atlanta, GA, officer, 1973-79; Atlanta Department of Public Safety, affirmative action specialist, 1979-80, director of public affairs, 1980-82; Atlanta Police Department, deputy chief of police, 1982-94, acting chief of police, April-October 1994, chief of police, October 1994–.

Member: International Association of Chiefs of Police; National Organization of Law Enforcement Executives; Georgia Association of Chiefs of Police; Leadership Atlanta (member of board of trustees); American Red Cross (board of directors); Council on Battered Women (board of directors); Commission on Accreditation for Law Enforcement Agencies.

Selected awards Outstanding Atlantan, 1983; Alumni of the Year, Morris Brown College, 1985; Woman of the Year, Atlanta City Government; named one of Atlanta's Top 100 Powers to Be by *Atlanta* magazine; one of five Women of the Year on CBS's "Good Morning" television program, 1995.

Addresses: *Office*–Chief of Police, Atlanta Police Department, 175 Decatur Street SE, Atlanta, GA 30335.

"Maynard Jackson was about to win election as [Atlanta's] first black mayor, in part on a platform that police brutality aimed at black residents was common among the predominantly white police force."

The Beat and Beyond

Despite the social and political turmoil, Harvard entered the Atlanta police department as an officer in 1973. She cut her teeth on street patrol, walking a beat for two years. Moving up the ranks over the next two decades, Harvard served as affirmative action specialist, director of public affairs, and deputy chief of police in three divisions--Career Development, Criminal Investigations, and Administrative Services. In April of 1994, her long and distinguished service was rewarded; she became acting chief of police for the city of Atlanta. On October 26, 1994, Mayor Bill Campbell formally announced Harvard's promotion to chief of police.

> "Halfway through academy training, an enduring bond between Harvard and law enforcement was cemented when she discovered that as a police officer she could fulfill her desire to help people and to work in the public service arena."

Among those who monitor police policy, Harvard is known as a gifted administrator, able to "get more out of less," as Smothers wrote, and to motivate her peers. "What Beverly brings is more of an openness to new ideas and a management style that is more in line with the more educated police officers that we are trying to attract," Mayor Campbell told Smothers in the *New York Times.* Harvard regularly solicits feedback from the force and feels that cops should be problem solvers versed in community outreach. "The ideal officer, first of all, has to care about people," Harvard noted in *Ebony.* Whetstone wrote in the same article, "In Harvard's opinion, the police department can best combat crime by joining forces with the community to prevent [crimes] from occurring in the first place."

faces. If I had known then all that was involved, I wouldn't have done it, but nobody told me."

After betting her husband $100 that she could graduate from the police academy, Harvard undertook the intense physical and mental training that *every* officer must face. "Halfway through academy training," Muriel L. Whetstone noted in *Ebony,* "an enduring bond between Harvard and law enforcement was cemented when she discovered that as a police officer she could fulfill her desire to help people and to work in the public service arena." In those days, however, African Americans--especially women--weren't quickly accepted as police material. Harvard came into the force "at a time of political upheaval in the city," Smothers continued.

Harvard had her work cut out for her almost immediately. In early 1995, she had to prepare the city's police force for Freaknik, an annual festival which brings approximately 100,000 college students from predominantly black colleges to Atlanta. As if the challenge of patrolling thousands of excited, vacationing young people were not enough, she was charged with keeping a tight rein on Atlanta when the Summer Olympic Games came to the city in 1996. Few who have seen Harvard at work would doubt her ability, though. Hubert Williams, president of the Police Foundation, summed it up when he told Smothers, "The fact of the matter is that she has been a good professional and a strong police leader for a number of years now. Everyone knows it."

Sources

Atlanta Constitution, November 17, 1994, p. C2; January 3, 1995, p. D1; February 9, 1995, p. C6; April 7, 1995, p. C2.

Atlanta Journal and Atlanta Constitution, October 29, 1994, p. A2; April 23, 1995, p. D8; May 6, 1995, p. A2.

Ebony, March 1995, p. 92.

Jet, November 14, 1994, p. 22; April 15, 1995, p. 46.

New York Times, November 30, 1994, p. C1.

USA Today, October 27, 1994, p. A4.

U.S. News and World Report, December 26, 1994, pp. 82-83.

Additional information for this profile was obtained from a City of Atlanta news release, 1994.

—Susan Salter

Fred Hickman

1951—

Television sportscaster

Fred Hickman's polished and urbane sportscasting for the Cable News Network (CNN) has helped to develop a sports identity for cable television. Teamed with Nick Charles as the co-host of *Sports Tonight* since 1980, Hickman has been part of the longest-running anchor team in the history of television--sports or otherwise. *San Diego Union-Tribune* columnist Fritz Quindt cites *Sports Tonight* as a "stand-out franchise," largely due to the "creamy-smooth delivery, witty personality, [and] free-formed-ness" that Hickman and Charles exhibit. Indeed, going head-to-head with sports highlight shows on other cable networks, Hickman and Charles have been able to sustain high ratings and a large fan base through more than 3,300 broadcasts. Hickman described *Sports Tonight* in the *Baltimore Sun* as "hard to find, but it's worth it when you get there." He added: "I think our viewers feel that way. We wouldn't have 3,000 shows if they didn't. There may not be a lot of viewers, but they are nice people who want something different. I hope we give them that."

Frederick Douglass Hickman was born and raised in Springfield, Illinois. From an early age he was a good athlete and a "ham" who liked to clown in front of the camera. Ironically, one of his heroes was a local Spring-

field sportscaster named Nick Charles. The first time the two men occupied the same television screen was in 1970--Charles, 24 at the time, was reporting on a high school football game from the field; Hickman, a freshman at the school, was waving from the stands.

After graduating from Springfield Southeast High School in 1974, Hickman attended Coe College, in Cedar Rapids, Iowa, where he studied broadcasting. Like many radio and television personalities, he did not stay to finish his degree because he was able to land a job without it. In 1977 he began his professional career at radio station KLWW in Cedar Rapids. Less than one year later he found a broadcasting job in his home town, with WFMB Radio. By 1978 he was on television at WICS-TV in Springfield, the same station that had employed Nick Charles. Although only 22 at the time, Hickman quickly established himself as a serious and dependable anchor person. Most days he was responsible for the sports report, but on some occasions he anchored the entire

At a Glance . . .

Full name Frederick Douglass Hickman; born October 17, 1951, in Springfield, IL; son of George Henry and Louise Winifred Hickman; married second wife, Judith Tillman (an attorney), February 20, 1989; children: one. *Education:* Attended Coe College, Cedar Rapids, IA, 1974-77.

KLWW Radio, Cedar Rapids, IA, news anchor, 1977; WFMB-FM Radio, Springfield, IL, news and sports anchor, 1977-78; WICS-TV, Springfield, sports director, 1978-80; CNN/Turner Broadcasting, Atlanta, GA, sportscaster/commentator, 1980-84; WDIV-TV, Detroit, MI, sportscaster, 1984-86; CNN/Turner Broadcasting, Atlanta, sportscaster and cohost of *Sports Tonight,* 1986-

Selected awards: Cable ACE Award nominee, 1988, 1989, 1990, 1991, 1992, 1993; Cable ACE award winner, 1989 and 1993; named "sexiest sportscaster" by U.S. Television Fan Association, 1993.

Address: *Office*–Turner Broadcasting System, Inc., One CNN Center, Box 105366, Atlanta, GA 30348-5366.

nightly news show including news, sports, and weather.

A Pioneer at CNN

In 1980 Hickman accepted a job with fledgling cable television company Turner Broadcasting, based in Atlanta. There he joined his former hero, Nick Charles, as part of a four-person sports department working for the Cable News Network. On June 1, 1980, Hickman and Charles took to the air with *Sports Tonight,* an "unpromoted show on an unknown network," to quote *Star Tribune* reporter Rachel Blount. Even then the camaraderie between the two cohosts was evident. "We had to develop something consistent and something consistently different from ESPN," Hickman recalled in the *Star Tribune.* "We also catered to an audience that was interested in finance, world affairs, and the body politic. But all those people graduated from some school, and many of them were interested in sports. That gave us a chance to develop a show where we could bring in our

personalities."

Sports Tonight developed as a nightly sports wrap-up show in which Hickman and Charles reported scores and events, selected a "play of the day," and showed highlights of college and pro games. "We had good chemistry," Charles remembered in *Sports Illustrated* of those early days in Atlanta. On the air, the two anchors projected an image of polish and wit with just a hint of playfulness, and sure enough theirs was a departure image for the sports television industry.

In 1984 Hickman was offered a job as the weekend sports anchor at WDIV-TV in Detroit, and he accepted it. He thought the move to Detroit would establish him in a major metropolitan market and thus enhance his career. Instead it proved a fiasco that almost sent him into early retirement.

Beat a Cocaine Habit

Reflecting on his decision to leave CNN in 1984, Hickman told *Sports Illustrated:* "I wanted to go out by myself into the desert. But I picked the wrong desert." Lonely and unhappy in the Motor City, he began using cocaine and soon found himself overcome by a $400-a-week habit. His first marriage dissolved, and--although none of his viewers or coworkers ever detected it--he succumbed to a deep addiction. "It was one of those things where--I don't like to make excuses about it--but where I was a young kid, and I was in a city that I didn't particularly like," Hickman said in the *Akron Beacon Journal.* "It was a bad choice of career moves."

> Hickman's polished and urbane sportcasting has helped to develop a sports identity for cable television.

One early morning in 1985, Hickman found himself weeping uncontrollably at the wheel of his car. "The valley was incredibly low," he recalled in a Knight-Ridder wire story. "I knew I needed to go to a rehab center." He checked himself into a treatment facility and spent one month there overcoming his addiction and exploring the personal issues that had caused it to happen. Today he cites low self-esteem as the source of his troubles. "I didn't get into the [broadcasting] business to be any kind of star," he declared in the *Akron Beacon-Journal.* "All of a sudden people are asking for autographs, interviewing you.... I never knew whether people wanted to hang out with me because they liked Fred or because they were trying to get free tickets."

Hickman returned to his sports anchor duties at WDIV, but within a few weeks he quit and left Detroit. He thought he would have no trouble finding another television job, but the publicity surrounding his drug treatment made it impossible for him to get work. Finally, it was his old friend Nick Charles who convinced the executives at Turner Broadcasting to give Hickman another chance. Hickman and Charles were reunited at the *Sports Tonight* desk for CNN in November of 1986 and have been working together consistently ever since.

The Hickman-Charles duo has been described as everything from "the Lucy and Ricky Ricardo of sports broadcasting" to comedic team "Laurel and Hardy." Hickman himself joked in the *Baltimore Sun* of his relationship with Charles: "We're still on our honeymoon." That "honeymoon" has lasted through a decade of continuous broadcasting and close daily association. In addition to the nightly *Sports Tonight* shows, Hickman and Charles hosted the 1992 and 1994 Olympic Games for CNN and have worked the Goodwill Games as well. Their broadcast of the 1992 Olympics from Barcelona

was the first time the Olympics had ever received major coverage on cable television.

Hickman has been nominated for the Cable ACE sportscasting award numerous times and has won it twice, in 1989 and 1993. Married again to an Atlanta attorney, he is the father of a young child. Reluctant to give interviews or discuss his past in the press, Hickman nonetheless told the *Akron Beacon-Journal:* "I'm a walking miracle. I came out of that [drug] thing a lot better human being than I was before I went in. So, thanks to God, things always happen for a reason."

Sources

Akron Beacon-Journal, July 30, 1993, p. 1A.
Baltimore Sun, November 10, 1994, p. 2C.
Sports Illustrated, June 26, 1989, p. 74; November 21, 1994, p. 52.
Star Tribune (Kansas City, MO), November 11, 1994, p. 8C.
USA Today, June 10, 1988, p. 3C.

Additional information supplied by Turner Broadcasting Company, Inc. and a Knight-Ridder wire story, February 9, 1992.

—Anne Janette Johnson

Robert Holland, Jr.

1940—

Business executive

In June of 1994 famed ice cream purveyors Ben & Jerry launched a contest to replace retiring chief executive Ben (Bennett R. Cohen). Their "Yo! I'm Your C.E.O." contest asked competitors to convince them why they—the competitors—should personally replace Cohen in one hundred words or less. It caused a media brouhaha, and when the dust had settled, Robert Holland, Jr., was the winner and new chief executive of Ben & Jerry's Homemade Ice Cream, Inc.

father contracted tuberculosis and died. "Essentially, I was the man of the house," Holland told Lowery. "My mother was our rock." Holland went on to complete the education so dear to his parents. He attended Union College in Schenectady, New York, where he earned a bachelor of science degree in mechanical engineering. He told Lowery, "I got on the bus to go to Union College [a 26-hour ride]. It was the first time I'd been out of Michigan. That was not the last blind journey I would take, but the first of many."

Bob Holland could never have guessed that his path would lead down this rocky road. But none of his career moves have been planned much in advance. Holland was born in Michigan in 1940 and raised in the small college town of Albion, the third of five children. Neither of his parents were formally educated, but they insisted that all of their children get a good education. To Mark Lowery of *Black Enterprise* Holland reminisced, "My dad knew more about the law than I'm sure most lawyers know."

Holland's father, an Albion city councilman, made his living in a foundry. While Holland was still young his

From there Holland went on to Manhattan's Bernard Baruch Graduate School, receiving a masters of business administration in international marketing. Although his father was not there for moral support, "There were a lot of people who felt they were responsible for you," he explained. "That helped me to keep going."

Corporate Climb

In 1968, after working as an engineer and sales manager for Mobil Oil Co., Holland took a job with the New York-based consulting firm McKinsey & Co. As an

At a Glance . . .

B orn in April, 1940, in Michigan; son of Robert (a foundry worker) Holland, Sr.; wife's name, Barbara; children: Robb, Kheri, Jackie. *Education:* B.S. in mechanical engineering, Union College, c. 1961; M.B.A. in international marketing, Bernard Baruch Graduate School, c. 1963.

Engineer and sales manager, Mobil Oil Co., until 1968; associate, then partner, McKinsey & Co. (marketing consultants), 1968-81; chief executive officer, City Marketing, 1981-87; chairman, Gilreath Manufacturing, Inc., 1987-91; owner and chief executive officer, Rokher-J Inc., 1991-94; president and chief executive officer, Ben & Jerry's Homemade Ice Cream, Inc., 1994—. Chairman of board of trustees, Spelman College; member of board of directors, Harlem Junior Tennis Program and UNC Ventures; trustee, Atlanta University Center.

Addresses: *Office*—Ben & Jerry's, P.O. Box 240, Waterbury, VT 05676.

associate and partner until 1981 he managed projects for global marketing accounts. During that time he became known throughout the corporate world as a "turnaround expert," someone who helps struggling companies return from the brink of bankruptcy and flourish. Holland spent two years in Amsterdam, the Netherlands, and worked in England, Mexico, and Brazil as well.

Then it was back to Michigan—Detroit this time—as CEO of City Marketing, a beverage distributor. From 1987 to 1991, Holland acted as chairman of Gilreath Manufacturing, Inc., in Howell, Michigan, where he performed his turnaround magic once again, helping to rescue this maker of plastic injection molds. In 1991 Holland started his own company, Rokher-J Inc., in White Plains, New York, where he waged leveraged buyouts of service-oriented companies, buying them when they weren't doing well, turning them around, and selling them.

It was during his tenure at the helm of Rokher-J that "headhunters"—in this case the blue-chip New York recruiting firm Russell Reynolds Associates—discovered him and referred him to Ben & Jerry's. In truth, Holland had not actually entered the company's "We Want You

To Be Our CEO" contest, though nearly 22,500 others did when the contest was announced on June 13, 1994. The company insisted the competition was not a publicity stunt, but rather, as Ben & Jerry's director of investor relations told Joseph Pereira and Joann S. Lublin in the *Wall Street Journal,* "a way to cast a wide net and not exclude anyone. If someone chose to call that a marketing gimmick, so be it. It was in the spirit of fun that Ben & Jerry's has always been known for."

Indeed, the often wacky ice cream company has become famous not only for their luscious and decadent desserts, but for their sense of whimsy. Such evocative ice cream names as Cherry Garcia (named for Jerry Garcia, leader of the legendary band the Grateful Dead), Wavy Gravy (named for another late 1960s San Francisco music scenester), and Chunky Monkey helped earn Ben & Jerry's their fun-loving reputation. The company—represented in their logo by friendly-looking Holstein cows and the smiling faces of the founders—was established in 1978 when ex-hippies Ben Cohen and Jerry Greenfield set up shop in Waterbury, Vermont. Over time it grew to be the biggest vendor of premium ice cream, reaching profits in the $100 millions. And Ben & Jerry's is considered a leader in the trend toward socially responsible business practices; among their pet causes are saving the rain forests and aiding the homeless.

Protested Racism

"After the first five minutes of a 10-minute conversation," remembered Russell Reynolds managing director Melanie Kusin in *Black Enterprise,* "I walked out to my secretary and said `I think I just talked to a successful candidate.' He has perspective and an extremely high intellect." Ben & Jerry's search committee recommended Holland and another finalist once they had interviewed the four leading contenders. It was only after he was selected as a finalist that Holland was asked to write the essay. Being a poet hobbyist, he chose to submit his entry in verse form. Getting around the one hundred word requirement, Holland suggested that his poem was "only 100 words before translation from the language of Chunky Mandarin Orange with natural wild Brazil nuts."

In his poem, entitled "Time, Values and Ice Cream," Holland extols America, yet bitterly remembers being barred from his hometown ice cream shop as a youth due to the color of his skin: "Yet, some nostalgia stayed 'yond one's grasp/ like Sullivan's,/ the ice cream place on Main—Swivel stools, cozy booths, and/ sweet, sweet smells with no sitting place for all of some of us." Holland pointed out to *Black Enterprise*'s Lowery, "You have to realize that Michigan was the only state north of the Mason Dixon line that voted for [former Alabama Gov. George] Wallace when he ran for president on a 'segregation now and forever' platform. So that's the environment I grew up in, and that was not an incident; it was a continuum."

To this day Holland will not eat a banana split sundae. Because African Americans were not allowed to sit in Sullivan's dining room, they were not able to partake of the banana splits that were only served there—they were limited to a cone to go. "The banana split was the thing to have," Holland told Mark Mayes in the *Battle Creek Enquirer.* "It was a measure of something, and we never got one."

Nor will Holland shop at Woolworth's, because they did not sell to blacks in his youth. And he will never erase the pain of seeing a cross burn on the lawn of his family's home in the early 1940s after his parents purchased a house on an all-white street. "My dad was angry," Holland recalled to Mayes. "He wasn't nervous or scared by all this. He was angry that we had to see this." He told Mayes that he thought he had been strong enough to keep the racism from dragging him down, but remarked, "The probability of leaving all these psychological scars and social scars and physiological scars behind to sort of participate in the American Dream, that's the hopelessness. I think the consequences of much of this prejudice and racism is enormous. It's mindbending."

Sources suggest that Holland, an ardent ice cream fan, prevailed over a co-finalist in the Ben & Jerry's race due to the other candidate's preference for frozen yogurt. Apparently, in the course of interviews with Ben Cohen, Holland impressed the ice creamery's founder with his capacity for consuming the sweet stuff. On the record, of course, Ben & Jerry's board offered other reasons for Holland's hiring. Several sources cited the news conference in which Cohen said, "Bob Holland is the board's unanimous choice to be our new CEO. We were very impressed, not only with Bob's operational expertise, but with his social commitment." During that conference, Cohen performed a ceremony wherein he removed a hat shaped like a Ben & Jerry's pint of ice cream from his head and placed it on Holland's.

Shares Company's Commitment

Holland's commitment to social causes has been expressed in numerous activities, including a program to help 30 struggling Detroit students finish high school and enroll in college. His credentials in this area also include

serving as chairman of the board of trustees of Atlanta's Spelman College; additionally, he is a trustee of Atlanta University Center and sits on the board of the Harlem Junior Tennis Program and UNC Ventures, a Boston-based minority venture capital fund. "In terms of character and integrity, Bob seems like the right person for the job at the right time," Cohen told the *Wall Street Journal.* "If you can imagine a company that cares about people going to bed hungry and wants to do something about it—that's what I hope will be the epitaph for my whole life," Holland told Lowery, "to be part of a company which has that as a part of their credo—this is [like having] died and gone to heaven."

Holland would have his work cut out for him at Ben & Jerry's, however. Though when he began at the company it was enjoying a 40 percent share of the premium ice cream business, its executives were also reporting a five percent decline in sales and a major quarterly loss, their first since the company's shares went public in 1984. Much of the loss was due to delays in opening a state-of-the-art ice cream production facility near the home office; computer problems had kept its unveiling months behind schedule. Losses were also attributed to consumers abandoning high-fat luxury food items for health reasons in the 1990s.

> "Yet, some nostalgia stayed 'yond one's grasp/ like Sullivan's,/the ice cream place on Main— Swivel stools, cozy booths, and/sweet, sweet smells with no sitting place for all of some of us."

Analysts were mixed in their assessment of how Holland would fare at his new post. Many cited his history as "turnaround king," but some, like Lewis Alton, a securities analyst, told Glenn Collins in the *New York Times,* "His résumé doesn't come across to me as that of a marketing genius with a lot of experience with consumer products. How do you transfer experience from plastic injection molding to Ben & Jerry's?" Alton also voiced reservations to Jesus Sanches in the *Los Angles Times,* venturing, "With people concerned in this country over fat, it's hard to know what sort of future exists for high-butter-fat-content ice cream." But Cohen told Pereira and Lublin in the *Wall Street Journal,* "Bob's key talents and abilities aren't related to making ice cream but more to leadership, management and strategic planning."

As to Holland's own take on the issue, he told Pereira and Lublin, "The biggest challenge for Ben & Jerry's is to get growth started up again." Ben & Jerry's sells primarily through grocery stores but has 100 "scoop shops" in the U.S., Canada, Israel, and Russia. Holland told Lowery that "half of the ice cream-eating world doesn't even know Ben & Jerry's exists, so it's an incredibly fertile opportunity to expand to the overseas market." Holland also noted that Ben & Jerry's was not in "a turnaround situation," informing the *Wall Street Journal*, "I'm approaching my job with this attitude. If it ain't broke, don't fix it."

Though Holland is the first African-American to be recruited as CEO of a majority-owned franchise company, he denied that there is a racial significance to his appointment. He did concede, nonetheless, that it was a nice sign of changing trends, stating his belief that in 20 years the color of a newly appointed CEO will not inspire comment. For now, though, the progress he sees toward equality in corporate America is too slow. While three other choice executive positions were filled by blacks around the same time that Holland took on his new role, he noted to the *Wall Street Journal* that the percentage of black executives in top corporate positions is "not even close" to matching blacks' representation in the population, which is about 13 percent.

One can only hope that this situation will be remedied through the efforts of people like Bob Holland, people who make strong social commitments and give back to the community in the best way they can: with their time and their love. Perhaps Holland has been partly inspired to continue his efforts toward social equality because of his strong connections to the community that nurtured him, despite its shortcomings "He's still down-to-earth Bobby Holland," a childhood friend told the *Battle Creek Enquirer.* "He never forgets home. He never forgets anyone he grew up with."

Sources

Atlanta Business Chronicle, April 21, 1995, p. C1.
Atlanta Constitution, February 2, 1995, p. F7; June 28, 1995, p. E2.
Atlanta Journal and Constitution, February 5, 1995, p. D6; June 24, 1995, p. B3.
Battle Creek Enquirer (Battle Creek, MI), August 12, 1995, p. 1.
Black Enterprise, April 1995, p. 60.
Boston Globe, February 2, 1995, p. 35; February 16, 1995, p. 56; March 1, 1995, p. 1; June 25, 1995, p. 57.
Chicago Tribune, August 12, 1995.
Daily Review (Hayward, GA), June 19, 1995.
Jet, February 20, 1995, p. 32.
Los Angeles Times, February 2, 1995, p. D1.
New York Times, February 2, 1995, p. D1.
People, February 20, 1995, p. 54.
USA Today, February 2, 1995, p. B2.
Wall Street Journal, February 2, 1995, p. D11; February 3, 1995, p. B1; June 20, 1995, p. B9; August 2, 1995, p. B4.

Additional information for this profile was obtained from Ben & Jerry's Homemade Ice Cream, Inc.'s 1994 annual report to stockholders.

—Joanna Rubiner

Iceberg Slim

1918–1992

Novelist

Robert Beck, better known as Iceberg Slim, sold more than six million books before he died in 1992. At one time he was said to be the best-selling African American novelist ever. Before he became a writer Beck was a "manager" of prostitutes, or a pimp for nearly 30 years. When his first book, *Pimp: The Story of My Life,* came out in 1967, it held nothing back. Beck became an underground cult figure. He would influence numerous writers, rappers, filmmakers, and criminals over the years.

Robert Beck was born on August 4, 1918, in Chicago, Illinois. In his books he praised his mother for not leaving him in a dumpster when he was an infant. Beck was abandoned by his father. Somehow, he and his mother managed to survive, moving frequently around the Midwest. Beck spent most of his childhood in Milwaukee, Wisconsin, and Rockford, Illinois. His mother worked as a maid and operated a beauty shop. She was exploited by a series of men who drifted in and out of her life. Still, it seems she was able to provide Beck with some semblance of luxury; he once said that his mother helped pave the way for his life as a pimp by pampering him.

"Street-Poisoned at an Early Age"

Beck returned to the rough South Side of Chicago as a teenager. The only people with money in his circle were pimps. His mother wanted him to become a lawyer. "But," he told *Answer Me!,* "the environment poisoned me, street-poisoned me at an early age." For Beck, these affluent pimps had everything; they were fashionable, smooth-talking, dripping with gold and diamonds, and they drove El Dorados. They would come for manicures at his mother's beauty shop. "They seemed so glamorous and so worldly and so polished and sophisticated. So this is what molded my thinking, and I wanted to be a pimp. I used to just dream about being a pimp and having all those sexy women givin' me money."

Beck attended Alabama's prestigious Tuskegee Institute for a time in the 1930s—he was there at the same time as writer Ralph Ellison—but he did not earn a degree. Prison officials once measured Beck's IQ at 175—an extremely high score. His innate intelligence notwithstanding, by 19 Beck was getting his start as a pimp on the streets of the South Side. There he met a

At a Glance . . .

B orn Robert Beck, August 4, 1918, in Chicago, IL;
died April 28, 1992, in Los Angeles, CA; married
a woman named Catherine, early 1960s, and had four
children. *Education:* Attended Tuskegee Institute, c.
1937.

Pimp (a manager of prostitutes), c. 1937-62; insecticide
salesman, mid-1960s; published *Pimp: The Story of My
Life,* c. 1967 (according to most sources); novelist and
lecturer, 1967-1980s.

hustler named Party Time who showed him the ropes.
Clever and keen, Beck was nonetheless naive and was
arrested when his first prostitute was servicing her
second client. In jail Beck met a man named Sweet
Jones, an older pimp of some renown who taught him
the real tricks of the trade.

In *Pimp* Beck quotes some of Sweet's advice: "A good
pimp is always alone. You gotta always be a puzzle, a
mystery to them. That's how you hold a whore." Beck
was clever and well spoken; he quickly rose through the
ranks toward his goal of being "Pimp of all Pimps."
Pimp chronicles his years in "the life." During his career
he had over 400 women, both black and white, working
for him. He was known for his frosty temperament, and
and at six feet, three inches tall and 180 pounds, he was
indeed slim. He also had a reputation for icy calm in
sticky situations. He thus earned the street name
Iceberg Slim. When verbal instruction and psychological
manipulation failed to keep his women in line, he beat
them with wire hangers; his autobiography makes no
bones about his being a ruthless, vicious man.

"Pimp of All Pimps"

As such, Iceberg Slim ascended to the top of his game.
He made sure his girls gave him all the money they
earned. He doled their cuts out in rations as he saw fit.
Payment often took the form of drugs, on which many of
his prostitutes were hooked. This helped keep him in
control. He was a heroin addict himself, though apparently few knew it. Slim concentrated most of his efforts
in the Chicago area, but he worked women throughout
the Midwest. He served a total of seven years in jail for
various offenses—including time at the Leavenworth
federal penitentiary in Kansas, the Cook County (Illinois)
House of Corrections, and Waupan State Prison in
Wisconsin.

During his second to last incarceration Slim was able to
escape. He just disappeared like a wisp of smoke, as he
often liked to say. He pimped for 13 more years before
he was recaptured in 1960 and placed in solitary
confinement at Cook County. For nearly a year he lived
in a cell no more than eight feet deep and four feet wide;
he described it as a steel casket. The food was often
infested with worms, but he ate it anyway, deeming the
pests protein after much self-persuasion.

Slim did a lot of soul-searching in that metal box. He
decided he was getting too old to pimp. He was 43 and
there were younger, tougher pimps on the street. In
Pimp he wrote, "I got out of it because I was old. I did
not want to be teased, tormented and brutalized by
young whores." *The Nation's* Monroe Anderson quoted him as saying, "I realized I had been stupid. I was
elderly and tired. I had the revelation that pimping, after
all, was not the most magnificent profession. I had a
feeling that I had wasted myself."

On his release from prison Slim retired from street life
and moved to Los Angeles, California, where he attempted to reconcile with his mother. He spent a heart-
wrenching six months at her oxygen-tent-covered bed-
side, where she lay slowly dying of complications from
diabetes. Her death was a great blow; it proved to be
what he needed to quit heroin, which he did cold turkey,
completely and abruptly.

Began New Life

By 1962 Slim was seeking work anywhere he could. He
finally got a job selling insecticide for $75 a week. He
had been a natural salesman all of his life. He also met
and married a women named Catherine who was 20
years his junior. By all accounts, though, Slim often
seemed and looked half his age. When *Sepia's* Bob
Moore asked how he could marry after having so hard-
heartedly exploited the 400 women that he had "managed," Slim replied: "I got married because I found a
woman who obviously has a lot of common sense and
who understands the kinds of changes that I was going
through, and who is highly intelligent and extremely
lovable, and who just seems to understand—has a sixth
sense about what I had gone through." He also admitted
that he needed a little taking care of, that marriage was
an important positive step, and that he thought children
would be good for him.

For four years Slim sold insecticide. While making a
pitch to a college professor, he mentioned that he had
been a pimp. The professor offered to collaborate with
Slim on an autobiography, but after the interviews had

been taped, Slim discovered that he would only receive a minimal percentage of the book's royalties. Spurred on by the need to beat the professor before he stole his life story, Slim wrote his own book, *Pimp: The Story of My Life,* in three months. He insisted that real creativity had not been a factor, that all he had done was remember, but *The Nation* dismissed this notion, reporting, "There were perception and introspection, ... in the book Beck bares his mind and the pimp psychology to the reader while writing in the argot of the ghetto with descriptions to match."

Bentley Morriss of Holloway House publishers in Los Angeles recognized Slim's talent and worked with him on publishing all of his subsequent novels. *Pimp* was published in 1967 (though sources vary on this). It shocked the public and sold like hotcakes. And despite Slim's efforts to dissuade young men from going into "the life," the book reportedly had the opposite effect on some, who figured they'd be slicker than Iceberg Slim.

Contributed to Black Culture

Reviews of *Pimp* were mixed, but no one denied the importance of the book. In a piece on pulp fiction in *The Source,* Ronin Ro gave credit where credit was due: "The original storytellers from the 'hood weren't today's rap artists, but the prolific black 'pulp fiction' novelists such as Chester Himes, Iceberg Slim and Donald Goines, who created worlds of pimps, whores, druggies, stooges, lay persons and ghetto heroes." He points to director Quentin Tarantino's 1994 film *Pulp Fiction,* for which the filmmaker won best screenplay honors, as a contemporary work influenced by these writers. Several rap stars—Ice T, Ice Cube, and Vanilla Ice— adopted stage names that owed an obvious debt to Iceberg Slim. Ice T readily admitted he "borrowed" part of Slim's name in order to reinforce his reputation as a cold-blooded player on the scene. Slim appears again and again as the source for words and phrases in dictionaries of slang and books on black English. Indeed, his books were published with glossaries.

"Instead of the million dollar mansions where white crime novel types like Sam Spade met employers," Ro continued, "[the black novelists] took readers to the dilapidated tenements, where [the] employees lived." In the *San Jose Mercury-News* Fred Dickey wrote that Slim "has been places that shouldn't be allowed to exist and he's done things that people shouldn't be allowed to do, but because they do and he did, his telling us about them fulfills an important literary function."

After *Pimp,* Slim published *Trick Baby,* a book of essays

called *The Naked Soul of Iceberg Slim, Mama Black Widow,* and *Death Wish.* "Though his writing voice grew angrier, his characters started to seem like far-fetched jive turkeys," Ro asserted. "Trick Baby was a preposterous 'blue-eyed, light-haired, white-skinned Negro.' *Mama Black Widow*'s Otis Tilson was a Black homosexual living in the Deep South who battled sadistic pimps and white sheriffs. *Death Wish*'s Don Jimmy Collucci was an Italian hitman 'who wants nothing less than to rule the "Honored Society."'" His corny plots, however, didn't stop Hollywood from filming *Trick Baby* and buying the rights to *Pimp.*"

> "I realized I had been stupid. I was elderly and tired. I had the revelation that pimping, after all, was not the most magnificent profession. I had a feeling that I had wasted myself."

In the early 1970s Slim became acquainted with the militant Black Panthers, whom he admired very much. The Panthers, however, were not as enthralled by Slim, who they felt had exploited his people. Slim stopped writing after meeting the Panthers, instead spending a great deal of time on the lecture circuit, trying to keep black youths from going astray.

Remained in the Ghetto

The retired pimp was by then largely a changed man. He still dressed immaculately and conversed in an articulate, often compelling, manner, but except for a still slightly sexist attitude evident in interviews, he had completely reformed his old ways. He lived with his wife and their four children in the black community of South Central Los Angeles. He resided in the ghetto by choice; he couldn't imagine continuing in his work to educate young black people without living among them. He wanted constant reminders of where he had been.

Iceberg Slim died on April 28, 1992, just as Holloway House was issuing a silver-bound twenty-fifth-anniversary edition of *Pimp.* During the last year of his life sales of his books increased as interest in all forms of black literature continued to grow. African American studies courses began teaching his works more widely, but as Phil Patton wrote in *Esquire,* "they should be taught elsewhere as well." To be sure, Iceberg Slim and his contemporaries are often overlooked when it comes to acknowledgement and acclaim from the black community, mostly because their milieu was so ugly. But their work is inextricable from the black experience; it records history and pain and its very existence represents a triumph over adversity.

Iceberg Slim said as much in *Answer Me!:* "The truth is, I feel so triumphant that ... I've survived, 'cause I've got news for you, rhetorically: If a nigger, if a male nigger is able to survive in this society to be almost 72, friend, he has accomplished one hell of a miracle. Believe me. Believe me."

Selected writings

Published by Holloway House

Pimp: The Story of My Life, (most sources say) 1967.
Trick Baby, 1967.
Mama Black Widow, 1970.
The Naked Soul of Iceberg Slim, 1971.
Death Wish, c. early 1970s.

Sources

Amsterdam News (New York, NY), February 3, 1973.
Answer Me!, vol. 1, no. 1, pp. 20-21.
Black World, May 1972, pp. 79-80.
Chicago Defender, December 16, 1972, p. 3.
Dawn Magazine, March 1983, p. 4.
Entertainment Weekly, February 3, 1995.
Esquire, October 1992, p. 76.
Los Angeles Free Press, February 25, 1972, pp. 3-5.
Nation, December 4, 1971.
San Jose Mercury-News, April 30, 1972, p. 8F.
Sepia, February 1972, pp. 52-58.
The Source, March 1995, pp. 46-48.

—Joanna Rubiner

Sir Dawda Kairaba Jawara

1924—

Former Gambian statesman

It was author Alex Haley who drew the world's attention to Gambian president Dawda Jawara and his struggle to achieve independence for his small, democratic government in 1965. Prior to Haley's 1977 visit in search of his ancestral roots, Gambia was only a remote and unknown dot on the West African map. But after the noted author spurred interest in the country, that changed. Maps attached to newspaper articles chronicling Jawara's career would delineate a country divided in two: the riverbanks, dotted with tribal communities and small towns, which bear the collective name the Protectorate, and the capital city of Banjul--known as Bathurst until 1973.

A modest, retiring man, Jawara expected to spend his life after college in his chosen field of veterinary science. "There's not a cow in the Gambia that doesn't know me personally," he once said in a comment that soon became part of local folklore. Jawara was not destined to spend his life ministering to animals, however. Convinced that Gambia must follow the example of nearby Ghana and become independent of British rule, he abandoned his profession in 1960 to enter politics. Jawara adopted the name Dawda in 1965 and em-

braced the Islam heritage shared by most Gambians. As a Muslim politician, he maintained staunch ties to the international Arab community while vehemently opposing radical or violent political action.

Modest Beginnings

Jawara was born May 16, 1924, in the small town of Barajally. His father, a prosperous Mandinka farmer, selected him from among his six sons as best fitted for education and sent him to the local Islamic primary school. In 1945, after graduating from the Methodist Boys' High School in the capital city of Bathurst, Jawara went to Ghana and studied science at Achimota College for two years before departing for Scotland and the University of Glasgow to gain a degree in veterinary surgery. In 1954 the young man came home to take an appointment as the government's animal physician. He spent most of his working hours in the rural areas of the Protectorate where agricultural disease control programs were sorely needed.

Jawara's leisure time was spent in Bathurst. Deeply interested in politics, he joined the newly-established

At a Glance . . .

Born David Kairaba Jawara, May 16, 1924, in Bara jally, Gambia; son of Almamy (a farmer) and Mama Jawara; married Augusta Mahoney, 1955 (divorced, 1967), remarried; children: (first marriage) three boys and two girls. *Education:* Achimota College, B.S., 1949; Glasgow University, graduated as a veterinary surgeon, 1954. *Religion:* Islam.

Veterinary surgeon, Protectorate Area, Gambia, 1954-60; Gambian government, Protectorate Area, Minister of Education, 1962-64, Prime Minister, 1962-70, then President, 1970—.

Awards: Knighted by Queen Elizabeth II of Great Britain, 1966; Agricolan Medal, United Nations, 1980.

Protectorate People's Society (PPS), an association popular with his civil service colleagues. The PPS had a mission Jawara fully endorsed: improving the lot of rural black Gambians who endured a primitive lifestyle that city-dwellers would never have tolerated. Mud roads and inadequate medical facilities were just two of the many inconveniences with which country-dwellers were forced to live. Perhaps more limiting was the extreme poverty of the rural educational system and the resultant high rate of illiteracy.

Developed a Social Conscience

Social services were desperately needed in Gambia's Protectorate area, but the PPS was unable to inspire either the governor or the legislative council with their own sense of urgency. In 1958, when a multi-party conference was held to discuss ways in which Gambia might break away from Britain and achieve self-government, the PPS decided it was time to voice its concerns. The fledgling party outlined a plan of action for addressing the country's main concerns and chose Jawara as its represeentative for the conference.

Unfazed by the occasion's importance, Jawara made his political debut at the meeting. He outlined the PPS's findings about rural Gambian life while stressing his own belief that only indigenous Gambian legislators would care enough about improvement to plan specific projects and carry them through. His conclusion was simple—it was time to form a political party.

The People's Progressive Party (PPP) was organized in time to contest the 1960 elections. It set out to attract

Protectorate supporters by allocating a separate party branch to each ward or village, and heading each unit with an executive committee elected from the local population. At 35, Jawara was one of Gambia's most highly-educated citizens and was knowledgeable about the inner workings of democracy. He had many friends among the influential civil servants who ran the country. Furthermore, as the chief planner of cattle-disease control programs, Jawara's presence was reassuringly familiar to the rural people who were the party's targeted supporters. With such credentials, it came as no surprise that Jawara was the unanimous choice as party leader.

Because the rival political parties--the Gambia Muslim Congress and the Democratic Party--had been in existence since 1945, and the popular United Party had been around since 1951, the PPP hardly expected to sweep the boards in its first election. Nevertheless the fledgling political party captured eight of 12 seats in the Protectorate, and one of seven in the Colony area around Bathurst. Two years later, even this triumph was topped when the PPP captured 19 of the 33 available seats.

Having served briefly as Minister of Education, Jawara stepped into the prime minister's post where he found the challenges immense. There were only 80 schools existed nationwide with a total of just 13,000 students; the agriculture-based economy reflected untapped opportunities for expansion into different crops; and the embryonic tourist industry catered to far too few sun worshippers. Each of these fields merited immediate development, but none were as urgent as the demands from the 316,000 Gambians impatient for the social services they expected to receive as soon as independence came. Patiently the prime minister registered the complaints and cautioned people not to expect miracles. "Independence is not a magic formula that will turn our ground nuts into diamonds," he warned.

Britain was not surprised by the growing Gambian insistence on independence. Kenya, Ghana, Guinea, and Nigeria had all chosen the same difficult path in the early 1960s, and logic decreed that other colonies would soon follow them. Besides, distinct financial advantages could be obtained by loosening the Gambian tie. With its meager agricultural output based mainly on ground nuts, the deficit of the little West African colony had long been a drain on the British treasury.

Road to Independence

In 1889 the territory now encompassing Senegal and Gambia was divided between the French and British.

During the next 70 years, the French imposed prohibitive tariffs on imports into Senegal while the British encouraged imports into Gambia by fixing low tariffs. Furthermore, the Senegalese government was compelled to obtain two-thirds of their imports from France in exchange for preferential prices on their peanut crop. These policies--plus the completely-enveloping Senegalese border--tempted many unscrupulous importers to smuggle goods across the Gambian border. Over the years the two countries thus became economic losers; Gambia's coffers were never full and Senegal had one of the highest cost-of-living rates in Africa.

Both Jawara and President Leopold Senghor of Senegal wanted the economic healing that a closer alliance could bring. In early 1962 they sent a joint request to the United Nations (UN) asking for ways in which affiliation might be achieved. A four-person UN research team came up with three alternatives. Gambia could be fully incorporated into Senegal, each state could retain its own sovereignty while helping to form a central organization to deal with matters of interest to both, or each state could retain its sovereignty while drawing up treaties of friendship and cooperation in specific areas of interest.

Gambians examined their options and voiced their opinions for almost a year. Sentiments ranged from pride in British heritage to fear of being overlooked in the event of becoming part of the larger Senegalese population. Jawara reviewed the many factions and came to the conclusion that Gambians did not want to lose their autonomy, an opinion with which he agreed completely. Early in 1964 he went to Dakar, the capital of Senegal, for talks with President Senghor. Polite but inflexible, he refused to consider incorporating Gambia with Senegal and spoke against the formation of a central organization. In the end, he agreed to a Senegambian coalition for cooperation for defense, foreign affairs, and overseas representation as the change least likely to jeopardize Gambian autonomy.

Independent Gambia

On February 18, 1965, Gambia became Africa's 36th independent state and its most financially troubled democracy. Though a change to republic status was proposed at this time, it was rejected by voters until 1970, when Jawara became the Republic of Gambia's first president. In April of that year he shouldered his new position with few illusions about the economic and social problems awaiting him. However, he was surprised to meet another unexpected challenge—escalating friction with Senegal.

Though Senegal and Gambia cooperated on several fronts, they retained different domestic economic agendas. Many Senegalese farmers smuggled their crops into Gambia to capitalize on its cash markets in favor of Senegal's government-issue promissory notes. As a result, the Senegalese government accused Gambia of "economic aggression." Grassroots discontent in both countries bubbled to the surface in early 1971 after Gambia informed the UN that a Senegalese army patrol crossed the border, snatched a village headman and his son, and severely beat them. Senegal denied the allegation and, while the incident left an atmosphere of tension, the diplomatic friendship held. This proved fortunate, since the early 1980s found President Jawara in need of his neighbor's staunch support.

Coup Attempt and Confederation

After the murder of a Gambian field service officer in 1980 by one of his own men, investigators learned that Libya, a North African Arabic nation, had been recruiting young Gambian men and persuading them to go to Libya's capital for training in guerilla tactics. At first the Gambian government found it hard to see Libya's hand in either of these events. Tripoli had always been an ally, invested heavily in Gambia, and maintained a large staff at Banjul's Libyan Embassy. All doubt vanished in December of that year, however, when 22 young Gambian men described the guerrilla training they had received. Jawara swiftly severed all diplomatic ties with the Libyans.

On July 30th, 1981, the Movement for Justice in Africa, a small Gambian radical group organized by Libyans, attempted a coup d'état in Banjul. At the peak of its violence, a mob rampaged through the streets, looting stores, liberating prisoners, and injuring bystanders. Jawara, who had been in London for Prince Charles's wedding, flew to Dakar to invoke the 1967 Senegambian defense treaty and bring troops to Gambia's aid.

By August 2, the uprising was over, but at a cost of more than 600 lives. Again firmly in control, Jawara launched the reconstruction of a shattered Banjul and instituted a prudent curfew. Aware that he could not have stayed in power without Senegal's help, he toured Gambia to explain that more active and closer ties with their neighbors were vitally needed.

The Confederation of Senegambia came into official existence on February 1, 1982, with Senegal's President Abdou Diouf at its head and Jawara as its vice-president. Formed specifically for collaboration in external, military, and economic affairs, its main concerns were simple: the integration of troops for mutual security, progress towards an economic unity that would curb smuggling and allow both countries to use the same currency, and coordination of foreign policies and communication services.

The most successfully handled items were transportation and communications. A private ferry boat and water transport company was soon set up in Gambia with support from Senegalese shareholders; roads were extended through both areas; and a common driver's license served both countries. Otherwise, the Confederation's path was a thorny one, with the military alliance the most difficult. Having disbanded its Field Service after the coup attempt, Gambia lacked an army. French-trained Senegalese troops were called in to train new Gambian soldiers, protect Jawara, and guard strategic buildings and military installations at Gambia's ports. Initially this arrangement seemed ideal, but Gambians soon began to resent the strangers, fearing that their power could topple Jawara's government. In 1986, heeding the voice of his people, Jawara requested that the defence agreement be amended so that troops could not be mobilized without orders from both presidents.

The most important reason for the Confederation's failure was that neither government had organized a referendum to monitor the support of their citizens. Lacking democratic support, the new organization was regarded as a personal collaboration between two rulers rather than as a friendly alliance between two complete states. In August of 1989, President Diouf acknowledged the Confederation's failure and proposed that it be frozen. At the same time, the 300 Senegalese soldiers serving in Gambia were suddenly withdrawn.

Bloodless Coup Ends Reign

Despite this disappointment, by the 1990s, Jawara and his regime had reason to be proud of their achievements. They had received about $53 million in annual foreign aid throughout the 1980s, but sensible handling of the money--as well as loans from the World Bank, Africa Development Bank, and other Islamic financial institutions--ensured that almost 70 percent of younger children were enrolled in grammar schools across the country. Ten hospitals and more than 60 dispensaries provided health care nationwide. The domestic economy, too, had expanded, with more than 100,000 visitors arriving from Europe and North America during the 1989-90 season alone. In addition, the fishing industry was thriving and rice, cotton, millet, and other crops broadened the country's agricultural output.

After 30 years as Gambia's leader, Jawara felt it was time for a change. In 1992, he suggested that his party start looking for a new candidate. Such panic greeted this proposition, however, that he consented to stand for election yet again. The question of his retirement continued to loom over Gambia's political future, however, and dissention mounted.

> Patiently Jawara registered the complaint and cautioned people not to expect miracles. "Independence is not a magic formula that will turn our ground nuts into diamonds," he warned.

Starting on July 22, 1994, a group of Gambian soldiers led by Yahal Jammeh stormed the capital city of Banjul. Compared with the previous attempt to overthrow Jawara, though, this coup was deemed "bloodless." Even Jawara escaped unharmed: he was taken to Senegal by a U.S. warship that was conveniently in the area when the coup began. Jawara had hoped that his work as the country's head politician would create an economically prosperous society based on his priorities--democracy, unity, and tolerance for personal differences. The new government, however, seemed to have different aspirations--or at least different means of achieving those goals. The self-appointed, five-man ruling council dissolved the constitution and established a nationwide curfew until democracy was reinstated. From his political asylum in Senegal, Jawara could only hope that they would uphold their promise of renewed democracy.

Sources

Books

Africa Contemporary Record: Annual Survey and Documents, Africana Publishing, 1982-83, 1984, 1988-89, 1990.

Africa Today, second edition, Africa Books, 1991.

Gailey, Harvey A., *Historical Dictionary of the Gambia,* second edition, Scarecrow Press, 1967.

Rice, Berkeley, *Enter Gambia: The Birth of an Improbable Nation,* Houghton, 1967.

Periodicals

Africa Report, May 1972, p. 4; July/August 1984, p. 37; March/April 1991, p. 45; March/April 1992, p.

34.

Boston Globe, July 24, 1994, p. 5.

Christian Science Monitor, Nov. 22, 1985, p. H35; May 5, 1988, p. 7; July 19, 1990, p. 8.

Contemporary Review, Volume 254, May 1989, p. 258; Volume 257 September 1990, p. 133.

Foroyya, Nov. 15, 1992, p. 14.

Los Angeles Times, July 24, 1994, p. A16.

New York Times, Feb. 18, 1965, p. 9; July 24, 1994, p. 9.

Wall Street Journal, July 25, 1994, p. A1.

West Africa, February 14, 1987, p. 292.

—Gillian Wolf

Adrienne Kennedy

1931—

Playwright, writer

In 1995, the *Village Voice* observed that "with Beckett gone, Adrienne Kennedy (pronounced with a short "a" as in "had") is probably the boldest artist now writing for the theater." Since her *Funnyhouse of a Negro* was first produced off Broadway in 1964, Kennedy has generated a remarkable repertoire of highly acclaimed avant-garde plays that challenge traditional ideas regarding character, dialogue, and plot. Alisa Solomon commented in her foreword to Kennedy's 1992 collection, *The Alexander Plays,* "Character is frequently split in Kennedy's work, her protagonists projected through myriad personae--centuries-old royalty, contemporary revolutionaries, Hollywood movie stars, even owls and rats. Dialogue takes place not through conversational exchange of characters addressing each other, but through the fluid interplay of visual and verbal imagery. And plot, in its conventional sense, does not even exist." Writing in *American Theatre,* Scott T. Cummings described Kennedy's early plays as "interior monologues for the stage. Dense and violent in their imagery, often dazzling and bizarre in their theatricality, they are psychic collages governed by a troubled and erratic stream of consciousness. Each of these plays operates like a prism, which refracts its heroine into fragments, giving her multiple identities which resist reintegration."

Kennedy's nonlinear, surrealistic short plays have consistently pushed beyond the boundaries of experimental theater. The *New York Times* noted in 1995 that "her work, which blends time frames and historical charac-ters, has been called upsetting and mysterious, often powerful on a visceral level, but not always easy to follow." As a result, critical reaction has been sharply divided; from the beginning it has been clear that while some critics love Kennedy's fragmented, hallucinogenic style, others hate it. This extreme response is clearly illustrated by the reviews of *Funnyhouse* in 1964. Called a disaster by one reviewer, the play closed after 46 performances, but won a prestigious Obie award for "most distinguished play."

In the more than 30 years that Kennedy has been writing for the theater, her one-act plays have more often been studied in college courses and produced in workshops or on European stages rather than produced in resident theaters of the United States. Nevertheless, this unique artist, a pioneer of the off off Broadway movement of the sixties, has continued to write. Reviewer Nicole King, writing in the *Theatre Journal,* noted in 1993 that Kennedy has been "credited with creating and delivering 'performance art' long before the term was conceived."

Kennedy's memoir provides valuable insight to the themes of her work. A reviewer for *Theatre Journal* wrote in 1991 that "this journey through Kennedy's interior landscape creates a fascinating portrait of a highly impressionable, brilliant individual, who never

At a Glance . . .

Born Adrienne Lita Hawkins on September 13, 1931, in Pittsburgh, PA; daughter of Cornell Wallace (a social worker) and Etta (Haugabook) Hawkins (a teacher); married Joseph C. Kennedy, 1953, (divorced 1966); two children, Joseph C., Jr. and Adam Patrice. *Education:* Ohio State University, B.S. 1953; Attended Columbia University, 1954-56; New School of Social Research, American Theatre Wing, Circle in the Square Theatre School, 1957-58, 1962.

Playwright, lecturer, writer. Yale University, lecturer, 1972-74, Princeton University, lecturer, 1977; Brown University, visiting associate professor, 1979-80; Harvard University, 1990-91; Actor's Studio, New York City, member, playwriting unit, 1962-65; International Theatre Institute representative, Budapest, 1978; University of California at Berkeley, Distinguished Lecturer, 1980, 1986.

Selected awards: Obie award, *Village Voice,* for *Funnyhouse of a Negro,* 1964; Pierre Lecomte du Novy award, Lincoln Center, 1994; fellow, Guggenheim Foundation, 1968; Rockefeller Foundation grants, 1967-69, 1974, 1976; National Endowment for the Arts grant, 1973; CBS fellow, School of Drama, 1973; Lila Wallace Reader's Digest grant, 1994; Yale fellow, 1974-75; Creative Artists Public Service grant, 1974.

Addresses: *Agent*–Bridget Aschenberg, 40 West 57th Street, New York, New York, 10019.

loses the intense wonder of a child."

Raised in a Melting Pot

Kennedy was born Adrienne Lita Hawkins on September 13, 1931, in Pittsburgh. She was a precocious child who learned to read at the age of three and grew up in a middle-class family in Cleveland, Ohio, where her parents had moved from the small Georgia town of Montezuma. Her father, Cornell Wallace Hawkins, was a social worker and executive secretary of the Young Men's Christian Association. Her mother, Etta Haugabook Hawkins, was a teacher. Both were college-educated and prominent members of Cleveland's black community. Adrienne and her brother, Cornell, led fairly sheltered childhoods, growing up in an integrated, culturally diverse neighborhood. Kennedy attended Cleveland's public schools and was encouraged by her parents to meet high standards of achievement. She began writing as a child, keeping diaries on the members of her family. However, she did not begin to write seriously until she was a senior in college.

During their childhood, Kennedy and her brother often took train trips back to Montezuma to visit their grandparents. They were required to travel by Jim Crow car south of Cincinnati on these trips. Her maternal grandfather was a wealthy white peach grower. Kennedy wrote in *People Who Led to My Plays,* "My mother often said that most of the white people of Montezuma's families came from England. I realized dimly that this meant some of our ancestors too had come from England since, like most 'Negro' families in the town, we had white relations as well as 'Negro.' I became very interested in 'England.'"

Kennedy did not encounter overt racism until she went to Columbus to attend Ohio State University. She was amazed that the intolerant atmosphere at Ohio State so closely mirrored the deep South rather than her native northern Ohio. The impact of this racism scarred Kennedy for life, prompting her to examine issues of race in her plays. She majored in education at Ohio State and, in general, found college to be very boring. As a senior, she took a course that surveyed twentieth-century drama. It piqued her interest, and she began writing.

Graduating in 1953, she married Joseph C. Kennedy one month later. Eventually, her husband was sent overseas to fight in the Korean War. While he was away, Kennedy lived with her parents, gave birth to she and her husband's first son, Joseph, Jr., and continued to write. In 1955, her husband returned from Korea and moved the family to New York, where he attended graduate school. While her husband was in school, Kennedy began devoting more time to developing her literary talents, attending writing classes at the American Theatre Wing and Columbia University. She wrote her first play while in New York. That play, *Pale Blue Flowers,* was never published or produced, although not for lack of trying.

Found Voice in West Africa

Many people encouraged Kennedy in those early years, particularly her husband, whom Kennedy credits with unflagging interest and support. But in seven years of writing plays, short stories, and a novel, Kennedy remained unpublished. Her despondency reached new lows. In 1960 her husband, by then a professor at Hunter College, received a grant from the Africa Research Foundation. The Kennedys traveled first to Europe and then to Ghana. The journey was the key to a critical turning point in Kennedy's writing. Suddenly it was more focused, more powerful, more original. After arriving in Ghana, Kennedy discovered the literary magazine, *Black Orpheus,* and decided to submit a story she had finished on the trip, "Because of the King of France." It was accepted and, after ten years of effort, Kennedy was published.

While the Kennedys lived in Ghana, the African liberation leader Patrice Lumumba of the Congo (now Zaire) was assassinated. This event affected Kennedy deeply. "Just when I had discovered the place of my ancestors, just when I had discovered this African hero," Kennedy wrote in her autobiography, *People Who Led to My Plays,* "he had been murdered .... I felt I had been struck a blow. He became a character in my play ... a man with a shattered head." Another significant influence of the West African sojourn was Kennedy's discovery of masks, which would mark many of her plays. Kennedy explained in *People Who Led to My Plays,* "A few years before, [Spanish artist Pablo] Picasso's work had inspired me to exaggerate the physical appearances of my characters, but not until I bought a great African mask from a vendor on the streets of Accra [Ghana], of a woman with a bird flying through her forehead, did I totally break from realistic-looking characters." Owls in the trees at night during her confined pregnancy in Ghana would figure as a character in 1965's *The Owl Answers.* The shocking news of her parents' separation at that time also caused Kennedy to reshape her vision of Jesus. A cruel Jesus would also figure prominently in her future work.

When she was 29, Kennedy wrote *Funnyhouse of a Negro.* The one-act play is about Sarah, a biracial girl, and her psychological agony over her mixed heritage. She is visited in her room by several historical personages: the Duchess of Hapsburg, Queen Victoria, Patrice Lamumba, and a hunchbacked Jesus, all of whom are described as "herselves." The play was selected by Edward Albee to be produced in his workshop at New York City's Circle in the Square and was thereafter produced at the Actors Studio in New York. It was co-produced by Albee and others at the East End Theatre in New York and ran from January 14, 1964, to February 9, 1964, with Michael Kahn directing. Criticism was mixed. Unprepared to deal with this stunning piece of experimental theater, some mainstream critics

dismissed the work as irrelevant. Kennedy was also praised for her imaginative genius, and the play won one of the year's Obie awards, but the harsh criticism instilled in Kennedy a lifelong dread of opening night.

Creative Period Followed

Following the success of *Funnyhouse,* Kennedy's play *The Owl Answers* was produced in 1965. Written in 1963 soon after *Funnyhouse,* the play is another avant-garde tale, the story of Clara Passmore, a Mulatto girl who is told she came from the owls, a girl who fits into neither white nor black society. On a subway train she encounters her ancestors, among them seventeenth-century poet and playwright William Shakespeare and sixteenth-century Queen of England Anne Boleyn. Werner Sollors wrote in *American Literature* that "Kennedy's bird imagery ... manages to remain evocative and does not settle on one meaning." *The Owl Answers,* like *Funnyhouse,* won a Stanley award from Staten Island's Wagner College. In the decade following *Funnyhouse,* Kennedy wrote several other one-act plays, including *A Rat's Mass, A Lesson in Dead Language, A Beast's Story,* Sun, and *An Evening with Dead Essex.* She stated in *Interviews with Contemporary Women Playwrights,* "It was a confident period.... I felt confident because I knew I had revealed my obsessions in *Funnyhouse....* I was riding an emotional crest. After all those years of rejection slips, people suddenly wanted to do my plays.... It made me very productive."

A Rat's Mass, the story of two light-skinned black children, siblings who are literally half human and half rat, was first produced in Rome and then by the Theatre Company of Boston in 1966. It was produced off Broadway by La Mama E.T.C. in 1969 and again in 1976. *A Lesson in Dead Language* finds a white dog teaching a class of adolescent girls. The central image is menstrual blood and its inherent trauma. It was first produced in London in 1968. *A Beast's Story* was first produced in New York in 1965. This drama about a black woman's sexual fears was also produced on a double bill with *The Owl Answers,* under the title *Cities in Bezique* in 1969. *Cities in Bezique* ran for 67 performances and was directed by Gerald Freedman.

The successes of these early works led to several grants, including a Guggenheim fellowship and several Rockefeller grants. In 1966, Kennedy divorced her husband, although they remain friendly. Commissioned by the Royal Court to write a play, Kennedy went to London, where she lived for the next three years. She recalled her time in London as "a very pleasurable living experience because of the literary community there. I met writers," she told an interviewer in 1987 *Interviews with Contemporary Women Playwrights*, "I could write every day. And I met many people in theater. ...it was a heyday for Americans in London." Kennedy, working with Victor Spinetti, adapted John Lennon's *In His Own Write* and *A Spaniard in the Works* to create *The Lennon Play: In His Own Write* in 1967. This celebration of wordplay was a simply staged exploration of growing up based on Lennon's stories and poems. It was first produced in London by the National Theatre in 1967. *Sun: A Poem for Malcolm X Inspired by His Murder,* a memorial monologue, was the result of the Royal Court commission. It was first produced at the Royal Court Theatre in London's West End in 1969. *Boats* was produced at the Mark Taper Forum in Los Angeles in 1969.

Although less visible during the seventies and eighties, Kennedy continued to write plays while also teaching at various universities. She was a lecturer at Yale University from 1972 to 1974. During that time her play, *An Evening with Dead Essex,* a memorial to Mark Essex, a sniper slain by New Orleans police, was produced off Broadway at the American Place Theatre. In 1974, it became the first play by a woman to be produced by the Yale Repertory Theatre. *A Rat's Mass* was adapted and staged as a jazz opera by Cecil Taylor in 1976, running for six weeks. *A Movie Star Has to Star in Black and White* (1976) was first staged Off Off Broadway as an experimental workshop production, directed by Joseph Chaikin. In 1980, the Julliard Conservatory commissioned Kennedy to adapt the Greek classics, *Electra* and *Orestes.* Commissioned by the Empire State Youth Theatre, *A Lancashire Lad* was produced in Albany in May of 1980. The *New York Times* praised this fictionalized, Dickensian account of Charlie Chaplin's childhood as "a beautiful play of great poetry and feeling." In November of 1980, her play *Black Children's Day*--commissioned by Brown University while Kennedy was artist-in-residence there--was produced at Brown's Rites and Reason in Providence, Rhode Island. In 1985, Joseph Chaikin staged excerpts of three of Kennedy's plays under the title *Solo Voyages.* Mel Gussow wrote in the *New York Times,* "All three plays--and *Solo Voyages* itself--share a landscape of imagery that is alternately lofty and earthy."

Serenity Mellowed Work

Kennedy published heavily during the end of the 1980s and into the next decade, starting with her scrapbook memoir, *People Who Led to My Plays* in 1987. A *Theatre Journal* reviewer described the autobiography as a "journey through Kennedy's interior landscape [that] creates a fascinating portrait of a highly impressionable, brilliant individual, who never loses the intense wonder of a child. One year later, eight of Kennedy's plays were collected in the volume *In One Act.* In 1990, the prose novella *Deadly Triplets: A Theatre Mystery and Journal* appeared, followed by a collection of four new plays--*She Talks to Beethoven, The Ohio State Murders, The Film Club,* and *The Dramatic Circle*-- in 1992.

Known collectively as *The Alexander Plays,* the four dramas share a central character in the fictional personage of Suzanne Alexander, a writer. Alisa Solomon noted in her foreword to *The Alexander Plays,* "If in the early plays, Kennedy's protagonists were hallucinators whose tortured psychosexual lives were being blasted open into a raw, relentless vision, in *The Alexander Plays,* the protagonist has stopped dreaming openly and started recounting." Kennedy herself attributes this mellower tone to the self-reflective nature of her work.

Commenting on her life changes in the June 1992 issue of *American Theatre* Kennedy remarked, "I wouldn't be alive if I had remained as fragmented as that person who wrote *Funnyhouse* and *The Owl Answers.* Over the years, these people came together inside me." That view coincided with statements Kennedy made in 1977 in *The Drama Review,* when she explained that "Autobiographical work is the only thing that interests me, apparently because that is what I do best."

> "With Beckett gone, Adrienne Kennedy is probably the boldest artist writing for the theater."

The 1990s also saw a renewed interest in the staging of Kennedy's works. In 1992, the Great Lakes Theatre Festival organized a month long celebration of her work, which included the official premiere of *The Ohio State Murders* and a one-day Kennedy symposium at Cleveland State University. A few years later The Signature Theatre Company honored Kennedy as playwright for its fall season, selecting seven of her plays to produce.

Although both Kennedy and her work have found acceptance, praise, and a new tranquillity in her search for identity, her successes still feel hollow to her. The *New York Times* quoted her as saying in 1995: "I feel that white America is against me in a struggle to take away my birthright. My only salvation is to write."

Selected writings

Plays

Funnyhouse of a Negro (produced New York, 1964, London, 1968, New York, 1995), French, 1969.

The Owl Answers (produced, Westport, CT, and New York, 1965).

A Rat's Mass (produced Rome, 1966, Boston, 1966, New York and London, 1970).

A Beast's Story (produced New York, 1965, 1969).

(With John Lennon and Victor Spinetti) *The Lennon Play: In His Own Write,* adaptation of works by Lennon (produced London, 1967; revised version produced London, 1968; Albany, NY, 1969), Cape, 1968; Simon & Schuster, 1969.

A Lesson in Dead Language (produced New York and London, 1968).

Boats (produced Los Angeles, 1969).

Sun: A Poem for Malcolm X Inspired by His Murder (produced London, 1969).

Cities in Bezique: 2 One-Act Plays: The Owl Answers and A Beast's Story, French, 1969.

An Evening With Dead Essex (produced New York, 1973).

A Movie Star Has to Star in Black and White (produced New York, 1976 and 1995).

Orestes and *Electra* (produced New York, 1980).

Black Children's Day (produced Providence, RI, 1980).

A Lancashire Lad (for children; produced Albany, NY, 1980).

Solo Voyages (contains excerpts from *The Owl Answers, A Rat's Mass,* and *A Movie Star Has to Star in Black and White,* produced New York, 1985).

Diary of Lights (produced New York, 1987).

In One Act (includes *Funnyhouse of a Negro, The Owl Answers, A Lesson in Dead Language, A Rat's Mass, Sun, A Movie Star Has to Star in Black and White, Electra, Orestes*), University of Minnesota Press, 1988.

The Alexander Plays (includes *She Talks to Beethoven, The Ohio State Murders, The Film Club, The Dramatic Circle*), University of Minnesota Press, 1992.

Other

People Who Led to My Plays (autobiography) Knopf, 1987.

Deadly Triplets: A Theatre Mystery and Journal (novella) University of Minnesota Press, 1990.

Sources

Books

Intersecting Boundaries: The Theatre of Adrienne Kennedy, edited by Paul K. Bryant-Jackson and Lois More Overbeck, University of Minnesota Press, 1992.

Interviews with Women Playwrights, edited by Kathleen Betsko and Rachel Koenig, Beech Tree Books/William Morrow, 1987.

Kennedy, Adrienne, *People Who Led to My Plays,* Knopf, 1987.

Kennedy, Adrienne, *The Alexander Plays,* University of Minnesota Press, 1992.

Peterson, Bernard L., Jr., *Contemporary Black American Playwrights and Their Plays,* Greenwood Press, 1988.

Periodicals

African American Review, Summer 1994, pp. 293-304.

American Literature, September 1991.

American Theatre, June 1992, pp. 32-33.

Drama Review, December 1977, pp. 42-46.

Kenyon Review, Spring, 1993, pp. 86-99.

Library Journal, May 1, 1990, p. 114; August 1992, p. 99.

Los Angeles Times Book Review, July 12, 1987, p. 4.

Melus, Fall, 1985.

Modern Drama, December 1990, pp. 581-83.

New York Times, May 21, 1980, p. C30; September 20, 1985, p. C2; July 25, 1995, p. C13.

Theatre Journal, March 1991, pp. 125-28; March 1992, pp. 67-86; October 1993, pp. 406-08.

Village Voice, October 3, 1995, p. 93.

—Ellen Dennis French

Alan L. Keyes

1950—

Politician, lecturer, author

After a decade of service in the U.S. Department of State, two unsuccessful bids for the U.S. Senate, and a vigorous campaign for the Republican Party presidential nomination, Alan Keyes still refused to describe himself as a politician. Calling himself instead a "moral populist," Keyes has used the fiery oratorical style of an old-time revival preacher to bring his message of conservative family values to the American public. It is a message that captured the interest of many people disillusioned with the state of American society.

An Early Champion of Conservative Causes

Keyes was born the youngest of five children on August 7, 1950, in New York City. As a member of a military family, Keyes lived in several locations in the United States and Italy during his childhood. The Keyes family stressed education, and Alan was a high achiever from the start. At his high school in San Antonio, Texas, Keyes was president of the student council. By the time he was a teenager, Keyes had already embraced conservative political views. At the age of 16, he was elected president of the American Legion Boys Nation, the first African American ever to hold that post. He used that position to deliver resounding speeches in support of the Vietnam War. Keyes's speech "The Blessings of Liberty, the Blessings of Life" won the Legion's annual contest during his junior year in high school.

Upon graduation from high school, Keyes enrolled at Cornell University, where he became a disciple of Allan Bloom, author of the best-selling book, *The Closing of the American Mind.* In 1969, Keyes's freshman year, black militants took over the student center at Cornell. Keyes chose to speak out against the takeover. Taken aback by the tactics employed by the militants, he quit the university's African American Society. Keyes's opposition to the militancy on campus did not go over well with some activists, and, after receiving threats from fellow black students, Keyes left Cornell.

After spending a year in Paris, Keyes returned to the United States and enrolled at Harvard. He spent most of the next decade at Harvard, eventually earning a Ph.D. in political science. Upon completing his graduate studies, Keyes went to work for the U.S. State Depart-

At a Glance . . .

Born Alan Lee Keyes, August 7, 1950, in New York, NY; married Jocelyn Marcel, 1981; children: Francis, Maya, Andrew. *Education:* Harvard University, B.A., 1972, Ph.D., 1979.*Politics:* Republican.*Religion:* Catholic.

U.S. Department of State, foreign service officer, 1978, consular office, Bombay, India, 1979-80, desk officer, Zimbabwe, 1980-81, policy planning staff, 1981-83, U.S. representative to the United Nations Economic and Social Council (UNESCO), 1983-85, assistant secretary of state for International Organization Affairs, 1985-88; Republican nominee for U.S. Senate from Maryland, 1988, 1992; Citizens Against Government Waste, president, 1989-91; public speaker, lecturer, 1990- ; Alabama A&M University, interim president, 1991; WCBM Radio, Owings Mills, MD, host of nationally syndicated "America's Wake-Up Call" show; candidate for president of the United States, 1995-96.

Addresses: *Office*–Alan Keyes for Pres. '96, 611 Pennsylvania Ave, Ste 1150, Washington, DC 20003-4303.

Post as stating that Keyes was merely the black man that the Reagan administration liked to "trot out" to put forth policies "hated by the overwhelming majority of blacks."

> Calling himself a "moral populist," Keyes has urged the fiery oratorical style of an old-time revival preacher to bring his message of conservative family values to the American public.

In 1987, Keyes was the highest ranking African American in the State Department. However, he abruptly resigned after a confrontation with deputy secretary of state John C. Whitehead. The dispute focused around the issue of how U.S. funds should be allocated to different agencies within the UN. Keyes also believed that Whitehead snubbed him at a meeting, addressing questions to his white subordinates rather than directly to Keyes.

A Thirst for Political Office

In 1988, Keyes ran for the U.S. Senate against Maryland Democrat Paul Sarbanes, a popular incumbent in a heavily Democratic state. The Senate campaign was managed by William Kristol, Keyes's roommate at Harvard. Kristol, who resigned as Secretary of Education William Bennett's chief of staff to direct the campaign, would later become chief of staff for Vice President Dan Quayle and a top Republican Party strategist. Keyes lost the election, receiving only 38 percent of the vote. However, he became a more recognizable figure outside of the diplomatic arena.

Keyes served as president of Citizens Against Government Waste, a Washington-based organization founded by newspaper columnist Jack Anderson and businessman J. Peter Grace, from 1989 until 1991. He also worked extensively as a public speaker, a role in which he had always excelled. According to the *Washington Post*, Jeane Kirkpatrick referred to Keyes as "one of the most dramatically articulate people I've ever known in my life." Richard Kennedy, a New Hampshire State Representative, remarked in the *New York Times* that Keyes "makes [Jesse Jackson] sound like he stutters."

ment in 1978. The big break in his diplomatic career came within a couple of years, when he was serving as U.S. vice consul in Bombay, India. When visiting diplomat Jeane Kirkpatrick came under verbal attack during a meeting, Keyes used his rhetorical skills to defend her. She returned the favor by serving as a mentor to Keyes. By the time Kirkpatrick became the U.S. ambassador to the United Nations (UN)in 1981, Keyes's career was on the fast track.

His meteoric rise in the State Department included a spot as desk officer for southern African affairs, membership on the department's Policy Planning Council, a stint as ambassador to the United Nations Educational, Scientific, and Cultural Organization (UNESCO), and a position as assistant secretary of state for International Organizational Affairs. At the State Department, Keyes was an ardent supporter of U.S. president Ronald Reagan's policies concerning South Africa, and he was often chosen to articulate the administration's argument against imposing economic sanctions. Because of his support for Reagan, Keyes was frequently criticized by African American leaders. Rep. George Crockett of Michigan, for example, was quoted in the *Washington*

Keyes was able to command as much as $7,500 for each speaking engagement.

In 1992, Keyes made another run for the U.S. Senate against Barbara Mikulski, a Democratic incumbent from Maryland. He was defeated again, receiving only 29 percent of the vote. Following the 1992 election, Keyes was criticized for his handling of campaign finances. Many contributors became angry when it was revealed that Keyes paid himself a generous salary of $8,500 per month from the campaign fund. In addition, a campaign debt of about $44,500 was never repaid, much to the dismay of businesses that had provided Keyes's campaign team with essential services.

Following his second unsuccessful Senate campaign, Keyes decided to try a new outlet for his oratorical skills. He became host of his own talk radio show, "America's Wake-Up Call: The Alan Keyes Show," at WCBM Radio in Baltimore. Airing weekdays from 9:00 AM until noon, the show provided Keyes with a forum for his staunchly conservative views on everything from foreign policy to the deterioration of the family structure in the United States.

An Unlikely Presidential Candidate

As a result of his radio show, Keyes was able to drum up tremendous grass roots support for his conservative causes. On March 26, 1995, he formally announced his candidacy for president. By entering the race, Keyes became the first African American in the twentieth century to run for president as a Republican. In his campaign rhetoric, Keyes tended to focus almost entirely on moral issues and the decline of family life in the United States. His key campaign platform was his adamant opposition to abortion. Drawing from his background as both a devout Catholic and a career diplomat, Keyes's speeches were likely to invoke the Bible and the Declaration of Independence with equal frequency.

Keyes's presidential campaign gained new supporters when a February of 1995 speech he delivered in New Hampshire was replayed on the Christian radio show "Focus on the Family" by its host, James Dobson. The speech, in which Keyes decried the decline of morality in the United States, aired on approximately 1,500 stations nationwide and sparked a flood of supportive phone calls to the show. Throughout the campaign, Keyes received his strongest support from members of the Christian right, a group that is almost entirely white and Protestant. To those familiar with Keyes and his constant willingness to go against the political grain, that odd marriage made perfect sense.

Selected writings

Masters of the Dream: The Strength and Betrayal of Black America, Morrow, 1995.

Sources

Congressional Quarterly Weekly Report, May 20, 1995, p. 1446.
Jet, April 17, 1995, p. 6.
Los Angeles Times, June 5, 1995, p. A1.
MultiCultural Review, September 1995, pp. 24-27, 53-56.
Nation, October 30, 1995, pp. 500-503.
National Review, May 1, 1995, pp. 30-32.
New Republic, April 17, 1995, pp. 16-18.
New York Times, September 18, 1987, p. A3; March 27, 1995, p. A8; August 9, 1995, p. A16.
Washington Post, September 18, 1987; September 11, 1988; August 25, 1992, p. B1.

—Robert R. Jacobson

Ron Kirk

1954—

Attorney, politician

Ron Kirk would rather not be known as the first black mayor in the history of the city of Dallas, Texas. Nevertheless, his 1995 election landslide--which included support from blacks and whites, Democrats and Republicans--signalled a new era in Dallas, a new impetus to improve everything from city services to race relations. Kirk campaigned on a platform that promised increased economic prosperity, a lower crime rate,*and* the important notion of uniting Dallas's diverse ethnic and racial population in order to improve the city. As he told *Ebony* magazine soon after his election: "It doesn't matter whether your ancestors came over on the Mayflower [17th century ship that carried European settlers to North America] or a slave ship. We're all in the same boat now." That "boat," in Kirk's case, is the seventh largest city in United States.

No stranger to Texas politics, Kirk has held important positions in the state, including a stint as secretary of state in the administration of former-Governor Ann Richards. He has also served as a lobbyist on behalf of the city of Dallas before the Texas legislature and has served numerous local and national charities. According to*Washington Post* correspondent Sue Anne Pressley,

what Kirk brought to his successful mayoral race "was an impressive career record and an outgoing personality that many powerful whites find appealing while also standing as a progressive symbol that Dallas is no longer mired in the 1950s." Former Dallas Cowboys football team superstar quarterback Roger Staubach--now a Texas businessman--perhaps best described the optimism surrounding Kirk's election. "From the inner city to the corporate board room, from the Dallas Zoo and Cotton Bowl [football stadium] to the granite dome of the Texas Capitol, Ron has a lifetime history of getting the job done for Dallas," Staubach wrote in the *Dallas Morning News.* "He is a leader who brings people together, instead of looking for someone to blame."

An Early Interest in Public Service

The youngest of four children, Kirk was born and raised in Austin, Texas. His family knew its share of adversity, but both of his parents were politically attuned and active in their predominantly black community. Kirk's father was a college graduate who, although he was

At a Glance . . .

Born June 27, 1954, in Austin, TX; son of a U.S. postal worker and a school teacher; wife's name Matrice; children: Elizabeth Alexandra, Catherine Victoria. *Education:* Austin College, B.A., 1976; University of Texas School of Law, J.D., 1979. *Politics:* Democrat. *Religion:* Methodist.

David Cain (law firm), Dallas, TX, private practice lawyer, 1979-81; Office of Senator Lloyd Bentsen, Washington, DC, legislative assistant, 1981-83; City of Dallas, assistant city attorney and chief lobbyist, 1983-89; Johnson & Gibbs, P.C. (law firm), Dallas, shareholder, 1989-94; Secretary of State, Austin, TX, 1994; Gardere & Wynne, L.L.P. (law firm), Dallas, partner, 1994–; City of Dallas, mayor, 1995–. Executive committee member, Dallas Regional Mobility Commission, 1992-94; member of board of directors, State Fair of Texas, 1993–.

Member: National Bar Association, Big Brothers/Big Sisters of Dallas, North Texas Food Bank, Leadership of Dallas Alumni Association.

Selected awards Volunteer of the Year Award, Big Brothers/Big Sisters of Dallas, 1992; Distinguished Alumni Award, Austin College Alumni Association, 1992; named "Citizen of the Year" by Omega Psi Phi, 1994; C. B. Bunkley Community Service Award, Turner Legal Association, 1994.

Address: *Office*–Office of the Mayor, City Hall, 1500 Manilla, Dallas, TX 75201.

In addition to the ideals of hard work and social commitment, Kirk's parents stressed Christian values such as helping the needy and being supportive to family and friends in troubled times. Kirk noted in the *Dallas Morning News* that, then and now, his family believed the African proverb, "It takes a whole village to raise a child." Kirk attended public schools, where he earned good grades, played sports, and sang in the school choir. Even though he was a student during the disruptive early years of desegregation in Austin's schools, he was rarely affected personally by racial strife. In fact he was elected student body president as a high school senior. The issue of race became more important to him when he entered Austin College in Sherman, Texas. He was one of only a few blacks on campus at the time, and, as he told the *Dallas Morning News,* he finally underwent an identity crisis. "I got called Uncle Tom [overeager to win the approval of whites] so much it made me wonder who I was," he explained. His response to the personal confusion was to leave the school during his sophomore year.

The hiatus from college was temporary, however. While home with his family, Kirk received an internship as a legislative aide to the Texas Constitutional Convention of 1974. He became so fascinated by the political process that he returned to Austin College and completed his degree in political science and sociology in 1976. From there he went directly to the University of Texas School of Law, earning his law degree in 1979. Kirk admitted in the *Dallas Morning News* that he was an "undistinguished" student, both as an undergraduate and in law school. "I was much more interested in politics and law practice than law school," he explained.

Lawyer and Lobbyist

Having worked as an intern with the Texas legislature even during his law school days, Kirk naturally gravitated toward the political arena. After only two years as a private practice attorney, he took a job in the office of then-U.S. Senator Lloyd Bentsen, a popular and well-connected Washington insider. Kirk worked in Bentsen's Capitol Hill office for two years, from 1981 until 1983, and then returned to Texas with a clear vision of the political process. He joined the staff at the Dallas City Attorney's office, rising quickly to the position of chief lobbyist for Dallas. As Stahl and Moreno put it, Kirk's job "was to push the city's legislative agenda with state legislators in Austin." Among his other initiatives, Kirk helped to persuade the state legislature to toughen penalties on the most serious criminals and saw bills enacted to enhance economic opportunities for women and minorities. At home in Dallas he also worked as an attorney for the firm Johnson & Gibbs and played an

accepted at two medical schools, had to give up his dream of being a doctor because he could not afford the tuition. Instead, the elder Mr. Kirk took a job with the U.S. Postal Service, becoming "a racial ground-breaker of sorts ... as the first black civil service employee in Austin," to quote *Dallas Morning News* reporters Lori Stahl and Sylvia Moreno. The postal job might have been an important step for black Texans, but Ron Kirk recalled in the *Dallas Morning News* that his father became extremely frustrated working "35 years in a career that was below his intellectual ability." Kirk added: "He stayed there, and he endured.... There was an expectation from everyone that we are going to have it better."

active role in the Dallas chapter of Big Brothers/Big Sisters of America, a volunteer organization linking children with adult role models.

The opportunity that put Kirk on the political map permanently occurred in 1994. Early in that year, then-Texas Secretary of State John Hannah resigned to accept a federal judgeship. Governor Ann Richards appointed Kirk as Hannah's replacement. Kirk agreed to become the new secretary of state but declared that he would only fill the remainder of Hannah's term. By that time, Ron Kirk had his eye on another, even more high-profile political prize.

Prayers and a Serious Agenda

Over the years, Kirk became convinced that the federal government had become so mired in bureaucracy that real political change could only be initiated at the local level. When friends in the Dallas business community began urging him to run for mayor, he and his wife, Matrice, prayed about the decision and then announced his candidacy. The political commitment was not entered into lightly. Not only did Kirk have two preschool-aged daughters, but his wife also held a job. Mrs. Kirk was faced with resigning from a job she loved in order to further her husband's career, and this sacrifice was not lost on Kirk. "It's a lot to ask of someone," he stated in the *Dallas Morning News*. "Any two-career family can appreciate the difficulty with one [partner] sacrificing something they've given a lot of time, education, and passion to. It says more for her love and unselfishness that I'm in the position I am now."

Kirk was one of six candidates running for mayor of Dallas in the spring of 1995. Earning a broad base of support among the black community and the important backing of many influential black and white business people, he campaigned on a platform of stopping the "blame game" and ending the gridlock-producing bickering in City Hall. His more detailed plans for Dallas included targeting 400 city businesses for growth, a reduction in government regulations for small businesses, and a response team to help cut through government red tape.

Like his opponents, Kirk promised to be tough on crime, but he was the only candidate to suggest that Dallas's future prosperity as "the gateway to the largest free trade zone in the world" hinged on enhancing racial and ethnic harmony. "You don't become an international city until you become a city that understands diversity," Kirk told the *Washington Post*. "Historically, Dallas has been seen as a white power structure, but those days are over now.... We now live in a city [where] a candidate of color can now win with a coalition of blacks and browns and Anglos."

> "I became convinced some time ago that the most dynamic job in American politics was being the mayor of a big city."

Ron Kirk did just that. On May 6, 1995, he won the mayor's race with a phenomenal 62 percent of the vote. His closest opponent earned a meager 22 percent, and Kirk drew more white support than two other white candidates. Kirk's inaugural ceremony was the largest ever seen in Dallas and was attended by Ann Richards and other state dignitaries. At his request, a choir sang the civil rights anthem "We Shall Overcome." In his inaugural address, Kirk declared that his victory was all about vision, not color. He said he hoped the voters of Dallas had reacted to his positive, optimistic campaign and not to any history he would make as the first black mayor of any major Texas city. "I've always believed that if you have to choose between making history and making sense, you ought to make sense," he was quoted as concluding in the *Detroit Free Press*.

A "Big Picture Guy"

Many serious challenges await Kirk as mayor of Dallas. The city's tax base is 21 percent lower than it was in the 1970s--a result of suburban flight and a high crime rate. Although he is a Democrat and is seriously committed to social issues such as homelessness and the need for decent public housing, Kirk has placed a priority upon encouraging business expansion and new economic opportunities in Dallas. "We can't address any of the human-services issues we'd like to without a tax base," he explained in the *Christian Science Monitor*. Perhaps the most pressing issue facing Kirk is the need to build a new arena in order to keep the Dallas Mavericks basketball team and the Dallas Stars hockey team from pulling out of the city and relocating to the suburbs. Kirk told the *Dallas Morning News* that he hopes to provide a "legislative framework" that will expedite negotiations between the team owners and the city, as well as working to get financing for a new arena that will not put a new tax burden on the citizens of Dallas.

The city charter of Dallas provides the mayor, who serves primarily as head of the City Council, the small salary of $50 per council meeting. Kirk has therefore retained his partnership with the law firm of Gardere & Wynn, the office he joined in 1994. Kirk seems undaunted by the prospect of leading one of the nation's largest cities while still holding a private sector job. "Most people spend 10 minutes with me, and it's obvious I'm more a big-picture guy than a detail guy," he joked in the *Dallas Morning News*. "Now what I have to do is convince the city that what I said during the campaign wasn't gimmicky."

A dedicated family man whose chief vice is a fondness for fried foods, Kirk feels that his victory in Dallas is a harbinger of better times to come for a city that has known its share of racial discord. His greatest challenge, he told *Ebony*, "is to get people of different cultural and national backgrounds to work together peacefully and build a community that is economically viable and a wonderful place for families to live." As for himself, Kirk has declared supreme happiness at achieving his goals. "I became convinced some time ago that the most dynamic job in American politics was being the mayor of a big city," he said, "and I had decided a long time ago that if I ever did run, that there was only one job that I was interested in, and that was being mayor of Dallas."

Asked in the *Dallas Morning News* why he thought he had won so handily, Kirk replied: "I think people believe I will be fair. Everybody I've met in Dallas wants this city to be as vibrant and dynamic as it can be. Every person that is a parent wants their children to be as safe as they can be and go to the best schools there can be. Every person I know that's a homeowner wants their neighborhoods well maintained and adequately policed and proper code enforcement. Every business owner wants the city to be as much of a partner in a positive way than they do a hindrance in a negative way. And in that sense, as long as we keep articulating agendas that aren't defined by culture or race or demographics I think we have a chance to build a winning coalition for this city."

Sources

Christian Science Monitor, May 8, 1995, p. 4.

Dallas Morning News, January 25, 1995, p. 21A; April 30, 1995, p. 5J; May 8, 1995, p. 1A; May 14, 1995, p. 1J; June 4, 1995, pp. 1A, 1F.

Detroit Free Press, May 8, 1995, p. 4A.

Detroit News, May 7, 1995, p. 3A.

Ebony, September 1995, p. 32.

New York Times, May 5, 1995, p. 14A; May 8, 1995, p. 11A.

Philadelphia Daily News, June 6, 1995, p. 44.

USA Today, May 8, 1995, p. 3A.

Washington Post, May 7, 1995, p. 3A.

—Anne Janette Johnson

Suge Knight

1966—

Record company executive

Large and imposing--he's a menacing 6'4" and 315 pounds--Suge Knight, also known as "Sugar Bear," is a major force in rap music. As cofounder of Death Row Records, he has been able to sway established fan favorites to join his label while successfully signing new talents. Within three years of the company's founding in 1991, Knight's clients garnered three multiplatinum albums. Grammy Award-winning artist Dr. Dre's *The Chronic;* Snoop Doggy Dogg's *Doggy Style;* and the *Above the Rim* soundtrack have effectively placed Knight and the burgeoning, multimillion dollar Death Row enterprise on the very tip of the rap music mountain. The controversial 1995 release of *Dogg Food* by newcomers Tha Dogg Pound has helped keep Death Row at the peak.

Suge was born Marion Knight, Jr. in 1966; he was raised, along with his two older sisters, in a two-bedroom house in the rough Compton area of Los Angeles. His father, a truck driver originally from Mississippi, was a former college football tackle and R&B singer who inspired Suge's passion for music and sports. As a child, Knight was given the nickname "Suge" by his father because of his sweet, good-natured temperament. Knight's mother, Maxine, told *Spin* magazine's Chuck Philips, "My son is the type of person who still sends me roses all the time."

Success and Probation

When Knight was in high school, he devoted most of his energy to playing football and securing an athletic scholarship to college, which he hoped would lead to a National Football League (NFL) contract. Knight made the dean's list at the University of Nevada in Las Vegas, and in 1985 he won the Rookie of the Year title there on defense. His former coach told Philips, "He was Super Bowl material, the kind of guy you love having on your side." After college, Knight went to Japan with the Los Angeles Rams for a pre-season exhibition game. He quit football, though, in favor of concert promotion work when it became clear that he would not have a stellar career in the NFL.

Knight's promising future was almost derailed in 1987, when he was arrested for auto theft, carrying a concealed weapon, and attempted murder. He pleaded no contest and was placed on probation. Knight was arrested again in 1990, for battery with a deadly weapon, but this time the charges were dismissed. He told Philips, "Ain't nobody perfect in this world except God. We all make mistakes. Sometimes you end up in the wrong place at the wrong time."

After working as a bodyguard and making a name for himself on the concert circuit for a while, Knight formed a music publishing company in 1989 and assigned composition work to a small group of unknown songwrit-

At a Glance . . .

Born Marion Knight, Jr., April 19, 1966, in Los Angeles, CA; professionally known as "Suge"– short for "Sugar Bear"–Knight; son of Marion (a truck driver, former college football player, and R&B singer) and Maxine Knight; married Sheritha (a rap manager); children: one daughter. *Education:* Attended University of Nevada, Las Vegas.

Worked as a bodyguard and a concert promoter; formed a music publishing company, 1989; Death Row Records, cofounder and CEO, 1991; contracted Interscope Records as a distributor, c. 1992; Suge Knight Management, founder, 1994; adapted "Murder Was the Case" single from Snoop Doggy Dogg's *Doggy Style* album into a short film, 1994; Let Me Ride Hydraulics (car customization shop), cofounder, 1994; Club 662, Las Vegas, NV, owner, c. 1994; signed with Time Warner, 1995; Time Warner-Interscope relationship dissolved, 1995.

Awards: Multiplatinum Death Row recordings include Grammy Award-winning Dr. Dre's *The Chronic,* Snoop Doggy Dogg's *Doggy Style,* and the motion picture soundtrack *Above the Rim.*

Addresses: *Record company*–Death Row Records, 10900 Wilshire Blvd., Suite 1240, Los Angeles, CA 90024.

ers. Within a year, he made a significant amount of money from ownership rights to several songs on white rapper Vanilla Ice's successful debut album. Knight then expanded into the artist management realm of the music business, representing turntable maestro DJ Quik and solo artist the D.O.C. Through these musicians, Knight met Dr. Dre, who was then a member of the rap group N.W.A. [Niggers With Attitude]. Dre was popular for creating and producing the material on N.W.A.'s albums *Straight Outta Compton* and *Efil4zaggin,* the first number one hardcore rap album on the nation's pop chart.

Hood or Robin Hood?

According to Knight, Dre's contributions had garnered

more than six million units in sales for N.W.A.'s record label, Ruthless Records, yet Dre and fellow group member Ice Cube were short on cash. Ice Cube quit N.W.A. because he felt he was not being properly compensated for his work. Knight was able to verify Ice Cube's suspicions. Discovering that other Ruthless musicians were being paid less than the standard industry rate for their contributions, Knight bypassed Ruthless's management and negotiated a deal with their distributor, Priority Records, in 1990.

Knight was able to secure releases for Dre and two other Ruthless musicians which, in the long run, would benefit all of them handsomely. The manner in which Knight engineered the releases was a point of contention, however. Eric "Eazy-E" Wright, former N.W.A. member and then-president of the Ruthless label, claimed in court that he signed the release contracts under duress after Knight and two henchmen had threatened him--as well as his general manager--with pipes and baseball bats. DeVante Swing of the R&B group Jodeci was quick to come to Knight's defense when speaking with Philips: "I know Suge's got this reputation for being a guy who goes around strong-arming, but I think those rumors just come from jealous people. The thing is, he's a real sharp negotiator, and he won't let anybody walk over him or any of his artists--and a lot of people resent that."

Shining Knight

After Dre was released from his obligations at Ruthless, he and Knight founded Death Row Records, complete with a logo featuring a man strapped to an electric chair, his face hidden by a sack covering his head. "We called it Death Row," Knight told *Vibe's* Kevin Powell, "'cause most everybody had been involved with the law. A majority of our people was parolees or incarcerated...." For nearly one year, they searched for a major label willing to distribute their product, eventually landing a deal with Interscope Records.

In 1993 the label grossed more than $60 million and had released two of the most significant rap albums of the year: Dre's *The Chronic* and Snoop Doggy Dogg's *Doggy Style.* The following year, Death Row released the motion picture soundtrack *Above the Rim.* The album featured Dre's younger brother, Warren G. and sold more than two million copies to earn double-platinum status. The three albums set the stage for Knight's vision of Death Row as "the Motown of the '90s," referring to the formerly Detroit-based empire whose releases of the 1960s and 1970s once dominated the airwaves. Well on its way, *Vibe* has since described Death Row as "the most profitable, independently owned African American hip hop label of the 1990s."

Knight was able to convince R&B musicians Mary J. Blige, Jodeci, and DeVante Swing of MCA-owned Uptown Records to sign west coast management deals with him. In addition to doubling their royalty rates, Knight secured greater creative control for the musicians, landed them substantial back payments, and upgraded their contracts. Knight also tossed in a $250,000 white Lamborghini for one of the musicians to sweeten the deal. Snoop Doggy Dogg asserted in the interview with Philips, "Suge is the best businessman I could have ever hoped to hook up with.... He keeps the music real.... He's got an ear to the street."

Knight is not without his detractors, however. Besides Eazy E's shouts of foul play, the D.O.C. and rapper RBX left Death Row alleging nonpayment. But as top-selling rapper and actor Tupac Shakur assessed in an interview with *Vibe*'s Powell, "Suge's cool. A lot of cowards are trying to make like Suge's the scourge of the industry. All Suge's doing is ... making it so rappers can get what they deserve." Shakur was bailed out of prison by Knight in October of 1995; shortly thereafter, he signed with Death Row and Knight's management, adding yet another gold brick to the Death Row foundation. Shakur told Powell, "Death Row to me is like a machine. The biggest, strongest superpower in the hip hop world."

In 1995, shortly before Time Warner received serious criticisms for its links to "gangsta rap," the entertainment conglomerate signed Knight to a lucrative, long-term contract via Interscope Records. The short-lived relationship was dissolved later in the year, however, when Time Warner yielded to political pressure over the issue of reducing the prevalence of violence, misogyny, and pornographic reference in entertainment; Death Row's output was deemed a big offender.

The motivating factor in the headline grabbing break up was the debut effort by Tha Dogg Pound. *Dogg Food* almost immediately charted at no. 1 in the popular music category. Ironically, the album's success was at least partly spurred by the outcry of such anti-rap denizens as U.S. Senate Majority Leader Bob Dole, Republican conservative William Bennett, and National Political Congress of Black Women chairwoman C. Delores Tucker.

Knight actually met with Tucker and others in the summer of 1995 and was urged to make "rap songs more responsible to the black community," according to Bakari Kitwana of *The Source*. The clashes over what Knight and similar-minded considered censorship eventually led Death Row and Interscope to bring charges of racketeering and extortion against Tucker, who claimed, "Those who say that want to keep Suge and me from talking to each other." Meanwhile, Death Row was headed toward an estimated worth of more than $100 million, and Knight's artist roster, boosted by Shakur, continued to grow.

> "He's a real sharp negotiator, and he won't let anybody walk over him or any of his artists— and a lot of people resent that."

In keeping with Knight's goal to "establish an organization, not just no record company," as he stated in *Vibe,* Death Row has been branching out beyond record production. Knight worked on adapting "Murder Was the Case"--originally a popular cut from Snoop Doggy Dogg's *Doggy Style* album--into an 18-minute film, complemented by a new-and-improved soundtrack album. "Murder Was the Case" was such a hit that plans are in the works for Dr. Dre to direct future movies for a possible Death Row film company. On other fronts, both Snoop and Tha Dogg Pound have formed record labels backed by Death Row--Doggystyle Records and Gotta Get Somewhere Records, respectively--and Knight runs a night spot in Las Vegas known as Club 662. He has also toyed with the idea of publishing a magazine.

Despite those who accuse him of heavy-handedness in his business dealings, Knight is generous towards his community. His many plans for the future include the formation of a union for rap musicians and an organization for veteran soul musicians who need financial assistance. Knight already works in an anti-gang foundation in Compton and hopes to establish an organization that would put young unemployed people to work in the black community. One such venture is Let Me Ride Hydraulics, a car customization shop he formed with Dr. Dre in 1994. During that year's Christmas holiday, Death Row hosted a Mother's Day celebration in Beverly Hills, California, for 500 single mothers, sponsored toy giveaways at churches and hospitals, and doled out turkeys to the needy for Thanksgiving Day.

Regardless of how one feels about it, Suge Knight and Death Row have an undeniable presence in the popular culture of the 1990s. Knight's drive and skill is an almost unbeatable, unstoppable combination. As *Vibe*'s Kevin Powell has proclaimed: "Suge Knight has the muscle.

Dr. Dre has the skills. And with Snoop [Doggy Dog] and now Tupac, Death Row Records has the music industry all shook up."

Sources

Los Angeles Times, June 30, 1995, p. D4.
Newsweek, October 31, 1994, pp. 62-63.
The Source, January 1995; May 1995; November 1995, p. 12.
Spin, August 1994.
Time, July 31, 1995.
Vibe, September, 1995, p. 85; February 1996, pp. 44-50.
Wall Street Journal, August 16, 1995, p. B6.

—B. Kimberly Taylor and Lorna M. Mabunda

Gay J. McDougall

1947—

Attorney, civil rights activist

Gay McDougall made history in 1994 as the first African American to be appointed to the Washington, D.C.-based International Human Rights Law Group. Such landmark achievements have been typical for McDougall, however. A civil rights activist and international lawyer, she has perhaps been most noted for her role in loosening the grip of apartheid on South Africa. Recently, she has been at work on behalf of the oppressed peoples of other countries as well including Haiti, Nicaragua, Paraguay, and Bosnia.

McDougall was born in Atlanta in 1947, just as the civil right movement was beginning to grow. Her mother was a teacher and also active in the church. Additionally, Mcdougall had several aunts who were employed as social workers. It was these female role models who sowed the seeds of her desire to weave social concerns into her professional life. These women were not her only mentors, however. Growing up in Atlanta during the height of the civil rights era, she saw prominent figures of the movement such as Stokely Carmichael, Julian Bond, and Martin Luther King, Jr. working practically down the street.

McDougall enrolled in Agnes Scott College, a women's school in Decatur, Georgia in 1965. The only black student on campus, she was lonely, and so frustrated by the conservative and highly traditional attitudes and curriculum of the school that, in 1968, she transferred to Bennington College, in Bennington, Vermont. After

graduation from Bennington in 1969, she enrolled in Yale Law School and received her law degree in 1972. At both Bennington and Yale, she found a far freer atmosphere which nurtured her growing social conscience. She took an enthusiastic part in voter registration drives and civil rights projects, and developed a keen interest in the proliferating African independence movements as well as the United States' march towards true racial equality.

Began Professional Career

Upon graduation from Yale in 1972, McDougall put her civil rights activities on hold for a short time, while she worked for the New York City-based corporate law firm of Debevoise, Plimpton, Lyons & Gates. "I really was there to learn to be the best professional that I could be, because I thought that the issues that I cared about deserve that," she told the *Washington Post*. The training she wanted took her two years to achieve. After that, having saved a large proportion of her salary, she was able to follow her true wish and work as an unpaid employee for the not-for-profit National Conference on Black Lawyers (NCBL) in Washington, D.C.

The NCBL was formed in 1968, partly to help minorities and the poor with legal problems, racial issues and matters concerning voter's rights. The NCBL also addressed international civil rights concerns. Perfectly in

At a Glance . . .

Born August 13, 1947, in Atlanta, GA. Education: Agnes Scott College, 1965-67; Bennington College, 1967-1969; J.D. Yale Law School, 1972; London School of Economics (M.A. in public international law).

Career: Debevoise, Plimpton, Lyons & Gates; General Counsel, National Conference of Black Lawyers, NY City Board of Corrections, 1980; Director of the Southern Africa Project, Lawyers' Committee for Civil Rights under Law, 1980-1994; September, 1994— Executive director of the International Human Rights Law Group.

Member: National Conference of Black Lawyers; Black Forum on Foreign Policy; International Federation of Women Lawyers.

Awards: Candace Award, 1990, Presented by the National Coalition of 100 Black Women.

tune with the organization's mission, McDougall soon became the NCBL representative to the United Nations, and gained a unique opportunity to fuse her legal training and her civil rights interests by forming a task force to study the increasingly visible African liberation movements. Working for the NCBL was a stimulating experience that she enjoyed for two years.

After two years with the NCBL, McDougall took a job with the New York City Board of Corrections. The Board of Corrections was formed shortly after 43 inmates were killed in the Attica Prison riot of September 1971. An adjudicating body, the board dealt with the issues that had led to the uprising; inadequate medical attention, poor work wages, unresolved dietary concerns, and insufficient fresh air and exercise. McDougall tackled these issues with zest decided to return to the international human rights arena.

Had Interest in Africa

McDougall believed that further education would ease her transition into international law so, in 1977, she obtained her master's degree from the London School of Economics. Long favored as an educational institution by international humanitarian and liberation movements, the London School had trained Jomo Kenyatta of Kenya

as well as the contemporary leaders of the struggle for independence in Zimbabwe and South Africa whom she met when she arrived. "It was one of the best moves I've made in my life, in terms of the people I met, who inspired me and centered me and helped me find exactly what I think in many ways," McDougall told the *Washington Post*.

In 1980 McDougall returned to the United States to find a new challenge on her home turf. The challenge was offered by the Lawyers' Committee for Civil Rights Under Law, a civil rights group that was formed in the early 1960s to provide legal backing for racial equality issues. In 1967, however, with connections to human rights groups based in other parts of the world, the Lawyers' Committee responded to requests for help to counteract the South African government's increasingly sinister record of detentions, tortures and bannings.

As a result, the Lawyer's Committee formed the Southern Africa Project. The Project was charged with the responsibility of making contact with South African lawyers for the purpose of providing them legal assistance to aid South African victims of racism or torture. The Southern Africa Project also provided reports for both the U.S. government and the United Nations. The Project was formed too late to help Steve Biko, an anti-apartheid activist who was tortured and murdered in 1977 by the South African security police. The Project was quite effective in 1979, however, when it released a 72-page report that played a large part in then U.S.-President Jimmy Carter's decision against unilaterally lifting sanctions against Rhodesia.

Directed the Southern Africa Project

Highly qualified in the field of international public law, McDougall was asked to direct the Southern Africa Project, a post she kept until 1994. She took part in symposiums and accessed reports all which documented a horrifying record of tortures and murders, all aimed at keeping apartheid intact. However, as McDougall noted in a paper called "Proposals for a New United States Policy Towards South Africa," delivered during a 1988 human rights symposium, South Africa was not confining its policies to its own borders. The African country of Namibia, whose "independence" from South Africa had just been announced, was also under pressure by the South African government which was attempting to maneuver the upper hand in the upcoming Namibian elections.

Helped Seek Namibian Independence

McDougall saw to it that the aggression of the South African government towards Namibia was thwarted by the Southern Africa Project. She founded a new group called the Commission on Independence for Namibia, that consisted of 31 distinguished policymakers from the community. She supervised the Commission's monitoring of a United Nations-mandated system instituted to ensure ethical voting in the 1989 Namibian elections. Her efforts at securing a fair election were successful, as 96 percent of the people of Namibia cast their ball.

Focused on South Africa

The beginning of the 1990s found McDougall with even more challenging duties. Sanctions against South Africa, plus a rising red tide of anti-apartheid violence were now making majority rule in that country inevitable. With the prison release of South African political activist Nelson Mandela, McDougall began to spend long periods in South Africa, unraveling constitutional knots and helping to dismantle the hundreds of laws that had locked apartheid into place. Additionally, she was also asked to join 15 other experts on the Independent Electoral Commission, that was given the task of supervising the country's first multiracial election process. The Commission's duties varied widely. They dealt with the logistics of setting up more than 150,000 voting booths and other electoral equipment nationwide, plus printing and transporting more than 80 million voting ballots from England. Communications projects needed to e set up to persuade the country's estimated 22 million voters to come to the polls. Also, strategic methods to be designed to best ensure fairness in the election.

Not all South Africans were convinced the 1994 election would go smoothly. The primarily Zulu Inkatha Political Party, lead by Mangosuthu Gatsha Buthulezi, refused to take part in the elections until a scant five days before the polling began. Reasons for the boycott included a fear that, if the party lost the election to Nelson Mandela's African National Congress, the Zulu homelands would be abolished as prescribed by the new constitution, and Buthulezi's power would be removed. Despite the threatened boycott, and a wave of violence surrounding the political parties involved, McDougall remained confident. "We are committed to pulling off this election on April 26, 27 and 28," she said in *USA Today*. Her efforts paid off.

Conquered New Fields

After playing such a large role in setting South Africa firmly on its course towards majority rule, McDougall began to focus her attention on other tragic corners of the world. In September of 1994, she accepted a new position as executive director of the International Human Rights Law Group (IHRLG), a Washington-based international advocacy organization devoted to helping frontline advocates protect human rights around the world. Under McDougall's direction, one of the IHRLG's initiatives involved monitoring the repressive military regime of Haiti and its subsequent U.S.-led occupation.

> Influenced early in her life by family members, as well as major civil rights activists, McDougall developed quite a consciousness with regard to social issues.

McDougall's appointment to the position of executive director of the IHRLG was just one of the latest in a long list of accomplishments that have positively impacted the international human rights arena. Influenced early in her life by family members, as well as major civil rights activists, she developed quite a consciousness with regard to social issues. This sense of commitment has served her well during her career as advocate for those world citizens that have been forced to live under less than humane conditions.

Selected writings

Deaths in Detention and South Africa's Security Laws, Lawyers' Committee for Civil Rights Under Law, 1983.
South Africa's Death Squads, Lawyers' Committee for Civil Rights Under Law, 1990.

Sources

New Pittsburgh Courier, November 5, 1994, p. A2.
New York Amsterdam News, October 29, 1994, p. 22.
Southern Africa Project, Annual Report, 1979-80.
USA Today, March 31, 1994, p. 6A.
Washington Informer, November 9, 1994, p. 18.
Washington Post, December 7, 1989, p. B3.,

April 26, 1994, p. E1.

Additional information for this biography was obtained from *Annual Report,* Southern Africa Project, 1979-80.

—Gillian Wolf

Cynthia Ann McKinney

1955—

Congresswoman

The first black woman from the state of Georgia ever to fill a Congressional seat, Cynthia McKinney has proven a maverick presence on Capitol Hill. A liberal Democrat, McKinney represents Georgia's 11th district, which encompasses 22 counties and parts of suburban Atlanta, Augusta, and Savannah. McKinney's trademark gold running shoes and braided hair are symbols of her challenge to the mostly white, mostly male U.S. Congress. A divorced working mother who grew up during the civil rights era, she appreciates the needs of the poor, of blacks, and of women. In an *Atlanta Journal/Constitution* profile, McKinney reflected that her ability to win a seat in Congress is nothing less than a mandate from common Americans for more sensitive representation in the national government. "Now we have people in Congress who are like the rest of America," she said. "It's wonderful to have ordinary people making decisions about the lives of ordinary Americans. It brings a level of sensitivity that has not been there." Asked about the role black female legislators hope to play in Congress, McKinney declared in the *Washington Post:* "We're shaking up the place. If one of the godfathers says you can't do this, my next question is: `Why not? And, who are you to say we can't?'"

McKinney joined Congress in 1992 as a member of "an energetic and aggressive coterie of black female lawmakers," to quote *Washington Post* correspondent Kevin Merida. Since then she has proven to be an independent thinker who challenges conservative colleagues on such issues as abortion rights, welfare reform, and accepting gifts and services from lobbyists. In *Newsweek,* Bill Turque noted that from her first entree into the "kingdom ruled by an aging white patriarchy of Brooks Brothers pinstripes," McKinney "stood in bold relief: a divorced, black, single mother with gold canvas tennis shoes, flowing, brightly patterned skirts and hair braided in elaborate cornrows." The congresswoman from Georgia has never let anyone intimidate her, from President Clinton to the parking attendants in the House garage: she feels a powerful call to be an example not only to her own constituents but also to other black women. "My father cries every time he sees me on C-SPAN because people like me don't get this far," she told *The Hill.* "Especially black politicians like me." She paused and then added: "Especially black politicians from the South like me."

At a Glance . . .

Born March 17, 1955 in Atlanta, GA; daughter of Billy (a state legislator) and Leola (a retired nurse) McKinney; married Coy Grandison, c. 1983 (divorced); children: Coy Grandison, Jr. *Education:* University of Southern California, B.A., 1978; working on Ph.D. at Fletcher School of Law and Diplomacy, Tufts University. *Religion:* Catholic.

Spelman College, Atlanta, GA, diplomatic fellow, 1984; professor of political science at Clark Atlanta University and Agnes Scott College, c. 1986-88; Georgia State House of Representatives, Augusta, representative, 1988-92; congresswoman from Georgia's 11th district, 1992--. Member of Congressional Black Caucus, Progressive Caucus, and Women's Caucus (secretary, 1994-96). Former board member, HIV Health Services Planning Council of Metro Atlanta.

Member: National Council of Negro Women, National Association for the Advancement of Colored People (NAACP), Sierra Club.

Addresses: *Home*–Decatur, GA. *Office*–124 Cannon Bldg., Washington, DC 20515; 1 South DeKalb Center, Suite 9, 2853 Candler Rd., Decatur, GA 30034.

In Her Father's Footsteps

One of Cynthia McKinney's earliest memories is that of following her father to a sit-in at the segregated Sheraton Biltmore Hotel in Atlanta. Born in 1955, she was only four years old when the civil rights movement gained momentum, largely through the efforts of people like her father, Billy, a retired police officer and Georgia state legislator. Billy and his second wife Leola McKinney were determined to give their daughter opportunities that they had been denied as youngsters. Concerned about her education, they sent Cynthia to Catholic school, a decision that has had lasting ramifications in the congresswoman's life. At first the young McKinney was so taken with Catholic school that she announced her intention of becoming a nun. "The nuns wear the ring, and they say that they're married to God," she explained in the *Atlanta Journal/Constitution.* "I just thought that was what you wanted to be in life." Later she chose other career paths, but remained a member

of the Catholic church although her parents are Baptists.

McKinney attended parochial school until her high school graduation and then decided to leave her native Atlanta to study at the University of Southern California. She was not particularly happy there, but her parents encouraged her to stay, and she earned a bachelor's degree in 1978. The following year found her back on the civil rights path with her father. They travelled together to Alabama to protest the conviction of Tommy Lee Hines, a retarded black man accused of raping a white woman. For the first time since her earliest childhood, McKinney encountered the full force of racism at the protest. She was threatened by Ku Klux Klansmen in full regalia. Eventually the National Guard had to be called to the event, and four people were wounded by gunfire. "That was probably my day of awakening," McKinney recalled in the *Washington Post.* "That day, I experienced hatred for the first time. I learned that there really are people who hate me without even knowing me.... Prior to that day, everything was theory. On that day, I saw fact. That was when I knew that politics was going to be something I would do."

Entering graduate school to study international relations, McKinney began a pursuit of a doctorate at the Fletcher School of Law and Diplomacy of Tufts University. She is working on a thesis about the satellite states of the former Soviet Union. In 1984 she was a diplomatic fellow at Spelman College in Atlanta, and she has also taught political science at Clark Atlanta University and Agnes Scott College. Her short-lived marriage to a Jamaican politician, Coy Grandison, ended in the mid-1980s. McKinney says little in the press about her former husband, with whom she had one son. "Suffice it to say, he was no prince in shining armor," she commented in the *Washington Post.* "My radar just went down."

Trying the Political Waters

McKinney was still living in Jamaica in 1986 when, unbeknownst to her, her father put her name on the ballot for the Georgia state legislature. By that time Billy McKinney had become a respected state politician himself and was a leader among black lawmakers in the Georgia State House of Representatives. His daughter thought her inclusion on the ballot was just a joke--until she earned 20 percent of the vote in that district without any effort. She returned to Atlanta with her young son, sought a divorce, and entered state politics in earnest in 1987.

McKinney easily won her first election to the Georgia

State House of Representatives in 1988. She joined her father in the legislature--becoming the only father-daughter lawmaker team in the country--and immediately began to prove that she would set her own course. "[My father] thought he was going to have another vote, but once I got in there, we disagreed on everything and I ended up voting against him all the time," McKinney remembered in *Cosmopolitan*. "I was a chip off the old block, a maverick." Never was that more apparent than the day Cynthia McKinney stood in the Georgia legislature to condemn George Bush's decision to send troops to fight in the Persian Gulf. Declaring that President Bush "should be ashamed of himself," McKinney earned hisses from her colleagues, and quite a number of them walked out of the chamber. She was stunned by that reaction. "Those guys treated me like dirt. They were so nasty and mean," she said in the *Atlanta Journal/Constitution.* "Everything I did after that was suspect." Opponents, revelling in her troubles, took to calling her "Hanoi Cynthia."

In the late 1980s Cynthia McKinney joined a group of state legislators who were pressing Georgia's Justice Department to ensure proportional representation for blacks in the U.S. Congress. McKinney and her colleagues were successful in winning the right to draw three new congressional districts in such a way that they would have large populations of blacks. The 11th was one of the new districts. Its boundaries stretched 250 miles--roughly the same area as the whole state of New Jersey--through rural, suburban, and urban areas of 22 counties and three major Georgia cities. Predominantly Democratic, and 60 percent black, the district elected McKinney to Congress in an easy victory in 1992.

American voters elected 110 new members--or "freshmen"--to Congress in 1992. McKinney was among them and, very quickly, she established herself as a leader and innovator. She was named secretary of the Democratic freshman class, and she lobbied--unsuccessfully--for a place on the prestigious House Rules Committee. After new assignments had been made, McKinney found herself on the Agriculture Committee and the International Relations Committee. She also found that life in Washington would present its own set of problems. As Bill Turque put it, "Months after most freshmen were recognizable figures on Capitol Hill, McKinney still found herself treated like a wayward tourist. In February [1993], a House elevator operator tried to order her off a members-only car. In April, a Capitol garage attendant confronted her and two staff members and asked edgily: 'Who you folks supposed to be with?' She had assumed that over time such institutional slights would cease. But in early August, after a Capitol Hill police officer grabbed her by the arm at a metal detector that

members are allowed to bypass, McKinney complained to House Sergeant-at-Arms Werner Brandt. 'There's not that many people here who look like me,' she told him."

> "If the Congressional leadership thinks women will be satisfied with only the positions they tell us it's okay for us to have, we'll surprise them."

The "institutional slights" have declined since many members of Congress have come to recognize McKinney. The gold tennis shoes and cornrow braids have actually helped to establish her visibility and individuality on the House floor. According to the congresswoman in the *Atlanta Journal/Constitution,* the gold shoes were not meant to become a trademark item. "My feet were hurting, and I was complaining to my mother about these floors [in Washington]," she recalled. "My mom looks in a magazine, sees these gold tennis shoes, orders them and told me that I could wear those shoes. I wore them on the House floor, and the men loved it. They would come by and see if I had on my tennis shoes." The braids were a simple time-saving expedient that McKinney absolutely refused to change, even if they might cost her an election. "A lot of people judge me based on a stereotype," McKinney explained. "They look at me, they see a black woman, they say, She's got to be another Maxine Waters (a fiery liberal from Los Angeles). Well, heck, I don't mind being another Maxine Waters when it comes to the strength and force of advocacy. But to judge me in my entirety by what I look like is quite base."

A Seat Under Siege

An acknowledged liberal who will sometimes vote against liberal interests if they collide with those of her constituents, McKinney has established a vocal presence on Capitol Hill. She has supported President Clinton's legislative agenda on numerous occasions, but despite much presidential prodding, she voted against the controversial North American Free Trade Agreement in 1993. On behalf of her district, she has enlisted the Environmental Protection Agency to help clean up an Augusta neighborhood tainted with industrial pollution, and she has obtained federal money to pave some of the rural roads. At the same time, she has challenged the powerful kaolin companies in her district and has urged the Justice Department to investigate antitrust violations among the kaolin mines. She has also been a presence on the Congressional Black Caucus, the Progressive Caucus, and the Women's Caucus.

In the middle of her second term in Congress, McKinney faced a devastating blow in 1995 when the United States Supreme Court ruled that the boundaries of her 11th district were unconstitutional, as they had been drawn solely on the basis of race. Overnight McKinney became the symbol of a new sort of civil rights struggle, one she sees as imperative to black representation in national politics. "Cynthia McKinney's political future is uncertain," wrote Kim Masters in a 1995 *Washington Post* profile. "The [Supreme] court probably will order the state legislature to redraw the district and there could be a special election.... Or the matter might be deferred until 1996 or beyond." McKinney herself prefers not to feel victimized by the ruling, saying that the real losers are black voters and the other poor people of Georgia that she was trying to help. She declared in the *Atlanta Constitution* that she will absolutely remain in politics at some level and that hopefully she will retain her seat in Congress. "Anyone who is in public life has to look at all of the options that are available," she concluded.

Working in Washington, DC and trying to be a presence in a far-flung district has proven a challenge both for McKinney and for her young son, Coy. At first McKinney thought she might be able to cover all of her Capitol Hill business in just three days out of each week. That quickly proved impossible, and she soon found herself juggling a full congressional schedule, weekend visits to her state offices, and quality time with her son, who lives in Atlanta with his grandparents. The adjustment was difficult, but Coy has had the benefits of summer vacations in Washington and the opportunity to meet the president and numerous visiting dignitaries. McKinney reflected on the difficulties of single parenting in a 1994 *Ebony* profile. "While on the one hand, my commitment to the public good and public service is a part of what I stand for politically, I can't do that at the expense of raising my child," she said. "I've tried to expose my son to that public expectation and I think he rolls with the punches much better than I do." She added: "Even with its difficulties, the fact that I'm a member of Congress allows me to expose my son to all of the diversity of American life and to the world. It's been a positive experience for me and for him."

As long as she remains in Congress, McKinney says she will be fighting for the people who put her in office in the first place. "My constituents in Georgia were perceived by (former representatives) as I am perceived around here by security when I try to do just what I want to, and that is get around from place to place," she observed in *The Hill*. "I have the people nobody wanted, that everybody thinks is nobody." McKinney, treated as a "nobody" herself and beset by everyone from congressional conservatives to the Supreme Court, will not back down from her agenda--to be a voice for diversity in a government ruled too long by white male interests. Male members of Congress, she warned in *Cosmopolitan*, "had better keep an eye on us because there's no telling what we'll be up to. If the Congressional leadership thinks women will be satisfied with only the positions they tell us it's okay for us to have, we'll surprise them. We have ambitions for leadership ourselves."

Sources

Atlanta Constitution, November 4, 1992, p. 1A; November 27, 1992, p. 1A; July 1, 1995, p. 12A.

Atlanta Journal/Constitution, November 4, 1992, p. 8B; December 13, 1992, p. 10A; April 25, 1993, p. 2D; July 30, 1995, p. 3M.

Cosmopolitan, October 1994, pp. 220-21.

Ebony, September 1994, pp. 127-30.

Newsweek, November 30, 1993, pp. 32-38.

The Hill, March 8, 1995, p. 38.

Time, December 5, 1994, p. 59.

U.S. News and World Report, December 28, 1992, p. 86.

Washington Post, August 2, 1993, p. 1A; July 5, 1995, p. 1C.

—Anne Janette Johnson

James H. Meredith

1933—

Civil rights pioneer, lecturer

When James Meredith became the first African American to attend the University of Mississippi in 1962, he became one of the civil rights movement's most recognizable figures. His enrollment at the previously all-white school sparked riots and required the combined forces of the National Guard and the U.S. Army to enforce a court order. Since that time, Meredith frequently has shocked civil rights backers with his unusual and controversial views on race and politics. These views have led Meredith to forge some surprising alliances in later years, including well-publicized associations with conservative North Carolina Senator Jesse Helms and Louisiana politician David Duke, a former leader of the Ku Klux Klan. Along the way, Meredith repeatedly has proclaimed that he was selected by divine forces to save western civilization from its own self-destructive ways.

Meredith was born on June 25, 1933, in rural Kosciusko, Mississippi, the seventh of 13 children. His father, Moses "Cap" Meredith, owned an 80-acre farm, on which he grew cotton, corn, and a variety of other food crops. Cap Meredith was a strong-willed, fiercely independent patriarch, who refused to accept the second-class status thrust upon blacks by the white south. His way of combating white domination was to isolate his family from white society altogether. Cap's philosophy kept James--who went by his initials J. H.--from even entering the homes of white neighbors throughout his childhood. On a train trip home from Chicago at the age of 15, James and his brother were forced to move to a "colored car" as the train moved into southern territory. Meredith has often pointed to that event as the launching point of his personal battle against the racism that saturated every facet of southern life.

Used Air Force as Educational Opportunity

At 16, Meredith was sent to live with an aunt and uncle in St. Petersburg, Florida, where the public schools offered a much better education than was available in Kosciusko. He finished high school in St. Petersburg. Since there was no money for college, Meredith joined the Air Force, which was generally perceived as the least segregated of the U.S. armed services. Meredith served

At a Glance . . .

Born James Howard Meredith, June 25, 1933, in Kosciusko, MS; son of Moses "Cap" (a farmer) and Roxie (Smith) Meredith; married Mary June Wiggins (deceased), 1956-1979; children: John Howard, Joseph Howard, James Henry; married Judy Alsobrooks (television news reporter), 1981; children: Kip, Jessica Howard. *Education:* Attended Jackson (Mississippi) State College, 1960-62; University of Mississippi, B.A., 1963; University of Ibadan, Nigeria, certificate, 1964-65; Columbia University, J.D., 1968. *Politics:* conservative Republican. *Religion:* Christian.

United States Air Force, reaching the rank of sergeant, 1951-60; first black to enroll in University of Mississippi, 1962; civil rights activist, 1963-c.1968; Meredith Enterprises, independent businessman, 1968–; ran unsuccessfully for several political offices, 1972-79; University of Cincinnatti (Ohio), visiting professor of Afro-American Studies, 1984-85; domestic policy advisor to Senator Jesse Helms (Republican, North Carolina), 1989-91; Meredith Publishing, owner and operator, 1991–.

Addresses: *Office*--Meredith Publishing, P.O. Box 10951, Jackson, MS 39289.

in the Air Force from 1951 to 1960 where he began going by the name James rather than J. H.

During his Air Force years, Meredith was able to further his education. While stationed in Kansas, he took extension courses at the University of Kansas and at Washburn University in Topeka. Between 1954 and 1960, he also enrolled in the U.S. Armed Forces Institute, which offered courses to military personnel through colleges and universities all over the country. He also spent time in Japan, where he attended the Far Eastern Division of the University of Maryland. In 1955 Meredith met Mary June Wiggins at a USO dance. They were married the following year.

In 1960 Meredith returned to Mississippi. By this time, he had concluded that it was his mission in life not only to vanquish white supremacy in Mississippi, but also to return civilization itself to its proper, more humane course. Upon their arrival in Mississippi, both James and Mary June entered all-black Jackson State College (now University). By 1961, however, Meredith believed that the time was ripe for the color line to be broken at the state's premier academic institution, the University of Mississippi, known affectionately throughout the region as "Ole Miss."

Integrated Ole Miss

A number of factors contributed to Meredith's decision to begin his battle at that time. President John F. Kennedy had just been elected on a pro-civil rights platform, and it was widely believed that African Americans accounted for a significant share of Kennedy's slim victory margin. Meredith correctly presumed that Kennedy's administration would therefore be on his side if enrollment at Ole Miss boiled down to a power struggle between the federal and state governments. On January 31, 1961, Meredith submitted his application to the registrar at the university, along with a photograph of himself and the statement, "I am an American-Mississippi-Negro citizen." As expected, he was denied admission.

At this point, Meredith enlisted the help of Medgar Evers, Mississippi's field secretary for the National Association for the Advancement of Colored People (NAACP). Evers suggested that he contact Thurgood Marshall, director of the NAACP's Legal Defense Fund. With the NAACP working on Meredith's behalf, the matter became a legal battle, and the case was assigned to well-known civil rights attorney Constance Baker Motley. In May of 1961, Meredith filed a class-action suit in U.S. District Court claiming that the university's application process was discriminatory. The court ruled in favor of Ole Miss. In June of 1962, however, the U.S. Fifth Circuit Court of Appeals overturned the decision, and ordered that Meredith be admitted as a student.

Governor Ross Barnett of Mississippi had other ideas. Barnett refused to accept the court's decision, and when Meredith showed up to enroll, Barnett personally and physically blocked his entrance into the university. President Kennedy was enraged and ordered that federal marshals escort Meredith into the school. Barnett still refused to yield, invoking the concept of the state's right to control the affairs of its schools. Finally, the National Guard was brought in, and Meredith was able to enter the university by sheer force. Meanwhile, the campus around him was in turmoil. Violent riots left two men dead while scores more were injured and more than 200 were arrested amidst the tear gas fumes and debris. Not until approximately 33,000 Army troops joined the National Guardsmen already on the scene was some semblance of order restored to the campus.

Despite the ultimate success of Meredith's mission to

enter Ole Miss, his life there was anything but routine. Because of ongoing harassment and threats, federal marshals had to escort him to class every day. Students and professors who tried to befriend Meredith often were ostracized or tormented. He considered leaving school many times, but his supporters managed to convince him to stay. In August of 1963, Meredith graduated from the University of Mississippi with a bachelor's degree in political science.

Marched Against Fear

After graduating from Ole Miss, Meredith spent time in Nigeria, where he studied economics at the University of Ibadan. When he returned to the United States, Meredith settled in New York City and entered law school at Columbia University. In 1966 Meredith's autobiography, *Three Years in Mississippi,* was published. While at Columbia, he continued his work as a civil rights activist and organizer.

One such effort almost proved fatal. In June of 1966, Meredith organized a "March Against Fear" along Route 51 from Memphis, Tennessee, to Jackson, Mississippi. The purpose of the march was to encourage black voters to overcome the fear that too often kept them away from the polls. On the second day of the march, Meredith was wounded by scores of shotgun pellets fired by a would-be assassin named James Aubrey Norvell, who had waited in ambush along the march route. Many of the pellets have remained in Meredith's body since the attack, a proof and permanent reminder of his growing belief that nonviolent means of change are futile in a violent society.

By the late 1960s, Meredith was already at odds with a lot of the civil rights movement's most visible figures. He clashed with the NAACP, for example, over whose idea his enrollment at Ole Miss had been and about its policy of nonviolence. He also angered many Harlem residents by challenging the popular Adam Clayton Powell, Jr. for his congressional seat in 1967. Powell was being censured by the House of Representatives at the time, prompting many to believe Meredith was simply a pawn in the scheme to remove another powerful black man from his position of authority.

Meredith received his law degree from Columbia in 1968. He returned to Mississippi in 1971, settling in Jackson. Over the next several years, nightclubs, investment banking, cosmetics sales, farming, and television repair were among the businesses at which he tried his hand, mostly with little success. A healthy share of his income came from appearances as a guest lecturer, for which he was in fairly regular demand. Meredith also ran, unsuccessfully, for public office at least five times during the 1970s, including a run in the 1972 Republican senate primary in Mississippi. He also started his own church, the Reunification Under God Church, which sought, among other things, to teach African Americans to grow their own food.

The 1970s brought more changes. Meredith began to feel that the true enemies of blacks in America were not white supremacists, but white liberals. He believed the liberal-sponsored social welfare programs kept African Americans from becoming self-sufficient. Not surprisingly, these views alienated him even further from the civil rights mainstream.

> There is no doubt that James Meredith's unusual political meanderings and occasionally overzealous self-promotion have alienated him from many influential African American leaders. His position in history nevertheless remains secure.

Meredith began looking for college teaching positions in the 1980s. After failing to catch on at Ole Miss, his top choice, Meredith was offered a year-long job as a visiting professor in Afro-American Studies at the University of Cincinnati (Ohio). Controversy quickly surrounded Meredith at Cincinnati, as it had everywhere else he had made his home. He outraged university and city officials with claims of discrimination that were not supported by fact. He also provoked a confrontation with police by refusing to produce his identification at a health club--of which he was a paying member--so that he could then accuse both the club and the police of racism. Meredith made at least one friend in Cincinnati, however. In 1991, two years after the death of his wife, Mary June, he married a local television reporter, Judy Alsobrooks.

Hooked Up With Helms

In 1988 Meredith wrote a letter to every member of Congress and to the governor of every state. In the letter he proclaimed that he was destined to become the most important black leader in the world. He also wrote letters to newspapers outlining his belief that liberals were to blame for most of what was wrong with the United States. One of the two politicians who responded to Meredith's letter was Jesse Helms, the conservative Republican senator from North Carolina. Helms offered Meredith a $30,000 a year position as domestic policy advisor in 1989, an act of great irony given Helms's harsh criticism of Meredith in the 1960s.

As a member of Helms's staff, Meredith's odd and infuriating statements grew in number and shrank in credibility. In 1989 he told a *Washington Post* reporter that 60 percent of black leaders were involved in the drug culture and 80 percent were involved in corruption of one sort or another. He also turned the rhetoric up another notch about his role as the divinely appointed leader of the black race. In 1990 Meredith issued a press release on Helms stationery charging, among other things, that many NAACP officials and other black leaders were puppets of an elite group of white liberals. He did not offer any names or any evidence.

Meredith eventually found even Jesse Helms too liberal for his tastes, and the two parted company. In 1991 Meredith managed to shock those who had become accustomed to his flights of political fancy by throwing his support to the Louisiana gubernatorial campaign of David Duke, an acknowledged former Ku Klux Klan leader. Meredith asserted that Duke's current beliefs were actually fairly close to his own, since both felt that the restoration of family values and the elimination of affirmative action and other liberal social programs were among the keys to saving the country from ruin.

Throughout his life, but especially in the later years of his life, Meredith began devoting more of his time to writing, while still making an occasional lecture appearance. He formed Meredith Publishing in 1991 as an outlet for his own works. The bulk of his writings are contained in *Mississippi: A Volume of Eleven Books,* which covers topics ranging from his own experiences as a young man in Mississippi to his research on his ancestors, the Choctaw Indian Nation. The company has also published some small, Meredith-authored booklets that purport to educate black families on subjects like money, educa-

tion, and politics.

There is no doubt that James Meredith's unusual political meanderings and occasionally overzealous self-promotion have alienated him from many influential African American leaders. His position in history nevertheless remains secure. Despite the inevitable failure of his own messianic urges and predictions, Meredith remains an important icon in the struggle for racial justice in America.

Selected writings

Three Years in Mississippi, Indiana University Press, 1966, pp. 23-27.
Mississippi: A Volume of Eleven Books, Meredith Publishing, 1994.
"Big Changes are Coming," *Saturday Evening Post,* August 13, 1966.

Sources

Books

Flynn, James J., *Negroes of Achievement in Modern America,* Dodd, Mead & Co., 1970, pp. 159-167.
Lord, Walter, *The Past That Would Not Die,* Harper & Row, 1965.
Metcalf, George R., *Black Profiles,* McGraw-Hill, 1968, pp. 219-254.

Periodicals

Ebony, December 1984, pp. 38-40.
Esquire, December 1992, pp. 101-110.
Los Angeles Times, May 9, 1991, p. E1.
New York Times, July 21, 1990, p. 8.
People Weekly, October 16, 1989, p. 40.
Southern Sentinel (Blue Mountain, Mississippi), February 23, 1995.
Star-Herald (Kosciusko, Mississippi), February 16, 1995, p. 1A.
Washington Post, November 3, 1989, p. C1.

—Robert R. Jacobson

Gertrude Mongella

1945—

Educator, politician, diplomat, activist

Having risen to international prominence in 1992, when she was appointed as the United Nations (UN) Secretary-General of the Fourth World Conference on Women, Gertrude Mongella is one of the world's most influential people. The annual conference is one of the most important forums for women from all parts of the globe. Participants include dignitaries, members of nongovernmental organizations (NGOs), and anyone else interested in women's rights.

Mongella is a staunch advocate of equal rights for women around the world, particularly those from lesser developed countries, which she clearly emphasizes in her speeches and for good reason. "While African women are better organized than ever before, they remain poorer and no better represented in government," Colleen Lowe Morna relayed in *Africa Report*. In fact, results of a mid-1990s study conducted by the Economic Commission for Africa's Center for Women determined that political representation of women by women in African governments and political organizations had only increased from 7.65 percent to 7.77

percent in ten years

Thus, the significance of Mongella's stature--she's a black African woman--can not be understated. Even in the 1990s, women experience discrimination that can limit the scope of their careers and lives; the barriers for black women are even greater than for nonblacks. Furthermore, other than heads of state, few African politicians are well-known outside of their homelands; however, a 1995 *PARADE* article regarding Mongella's new international celebrity status announced that "her face is even featured on T-shirts."

Certainly Mongella's leadership extends beyond the boundaries of her ancestral home, but her efforts focus upon Africa. "The reality in most African countries," Lowe Morna has explained, "is that modern constitutions exist side by side with customary and religious laws which condemn women to minority status all their lives.... Few countries have had the courage to outlaw traditional practices ... such as bride price [dowry], female genital mutilation, and the denial of property rights." Mongella responded in *Africa Report* to accusations that the UN has not more blatantly condemned some of these practices by explaining, "Condemnation and attack are not the right approach when dealing with culture and tradition. You have to approach the issue through discussion and persuasion. You can legislate against traditional practices, but unless the reasons are understood, these laws will be ignored."

Broke Tradition

Mongella was born on September 13, 1945, coincidentally the same year the UN was founded. Along with two sisters and one brother, she grew up in her birthplace, a small Tanganyikan island called Ukerewe, in Lake Victoria. (Formerly a British colony, Tanganyika gained independence in 1961, and became known as the United Republic of Tanzania three years later). Her father, a carpenter, defied local customs by sending his children to school. In a society where leadership was, and still is, automatically accorded to males, Mongella and her sisters were encouraged early on to be the best they could. (One sister eventually became the attorney general of Lesotho, a small country in southern Africa.)

Like many other third world colonies at the time, Tanganyika had very few schools. Despite a population of approximately 7 million, not a single university and only a handful of secondary schools existed. Gaining entrance to these boarding schools was, and remains, very competitive. For young children, living far away from home could be very daunting, but at the age of 12, Mongella traveled hundreds of miles to Morogoro, where she had been accepted at Marianhill Secondary School, an institution run by the Maryknoll order of nuns. There she excelled in all subjects and particularly loved debating. Interviewed in *PARADE* nearly 50 years later, Mongella credited her colonial education for having "made her know everything."

After successfully completing her secondary education, Mongella enrolled at the newly formed Dar es Salaam University, located near the Indian Ocean in the eastern seaport city of Dar es Salaam, Tanzania. From 1967 to 1970 she worked towards and earned a degree in education. She began instructing others, first as a tutor and then as a curriculum developer. Meanwhile, her interest in politics was growing and shortly would divert her from teaching.

Mongella's political involvement began early on as she became one of the few female members of the only existing Tanzanian political party, and consequently, the ruling party--Chama Cha Mapinduzi, or Revolutionary Party. She quickly became highly respected, which eventually pushed her career in a different direction. In 1975, Mongella was appointed to serve as a member of the East African Legislative Assembly, throwing her into public service and giving her a taste of the limelight. Once in that position, she quickly rose to the supreme organ of Chama Che Mapinduzi through election by a 20-member Center Committee. Subsequently, Mongella was appointed to several ministerial posts, including Minister of State, during which time she was responsible for women's affairs, and then Minister of Lands, Natural Resources, and Tourism.

During the 1980s, Mongella represented Tanzania in various capacities at numerous global conferences and forums, particularly those emphasizing women's issues. For example, in the midst of that hectic ten year-period, she served as a vice chairperson of the World Conference to Review and Appraise the Achievement of the United Nations Decade for Women, held in Nairobi, Kenya. Pulling double duty, she also chaired the African delegation to that 1985 conference. Five years later she led a Tanzanian commission that presented a status report to the World Committee on the Elimination of Discrimination Against Women.

In 1991, Mongella was appointed Tanzania's High Commissioner to India. Her diplomatic obligations in India did not prevent Mongella from keeping apace with her other interests. She served as a member of the Board of Trustees of the UN's International Research and Training Institute for the Advancement of Women (INSTRAW) during the early 1990s. She was also able to appear at several functions, including the Global Assembly on Women and the Environment and the World Women's Congress for a Healthy Planet.

Prepared for Beijing

With such extensive qualifications, UN Secretary-General Boutros Boutros-Ghali made an unsurprising decision in 1992, when he designated Mongella as the Secretariat of the Fourth World Conference on Women to be held in Beijing, China. For the next 38 months, Mongella worked feverishly to organize what was to become "the largest and most important conference ever held on [women's] behalf in the history of the [UN]," according to the *New Pittsburgh Courier.* To carry off such an undertaking, Mongella met with NGOs; consulted senior government officials from all over the world, including heads of state; and attended several regional preparatory conferences around the world, including the Fifth Regional Conference on African Women.

The last in a series of conferences held before the Fourth World Conference, the Fifth Regional Conference on African Women "brought together a record 3,000 African women from around the continent," according to Lowe Morna, a Zimbabwean journalist who claimed that "for sheer energy, creativity, color, style, and rhythm, few gatherings could have matched the November 16 to 23 Dakar [Senegal] conference." Mongella was invigorated by the African caucus she met there. Through her own efforts and those of others similarly minded, Mongella felt that African women had made great strides in garnering higher status for themselves. Mongella enthused to Lowe Morna, "I have been overwhelmed by the energy of African women. These are not the same people who were being characterized as weak and vulnerable victims [of society] 10 years ago."

The conference ended on a hopeful note, as a *Platform for Action* was produced. *Africa Report* stated that the document "breaks new ground with a section ... which emphasizes the importance of gender equity starting at an early age, with girls given an equal opportunity to go to school; their work loads reduced; traditional practices harmful to health eliminated; and sex education made available to avoid teenage pregnancies." In an interview with Lowe Morna, Mongella emphasized the significance of reaching out to young people, reminding her that "they are the adults of tomorrow."

Fortified by the signs of progress she saw in Senegal, Mongella went to Beijing "conscious of the huge responsibility she carrie[d] ... and the great honor she ... brought to African women," Lowe Morna reported. 185 nations were represented at the September of 1995 function, whose agenda covered a wide range of topics such as the impact of Acquired Immune Deficiency Syndrome (AIDS), violence and abuse, and poverty on women. Literacy and education also rated high amongst the concerns addressed during the 12-day conference.

> "Women will change the world when they lead it."

The *New Pittsburgh Courier* quoted Mongella as saying that "a huge historical deficit remains among today's adult women, especially rural women, which denies them full-partnership in society." Confirmation came from a 1990 UN survey that had revealed 586.4 million of the world's women were illiterate--more than nine times the number of illiterate men, cited to be 64.4 million. Gearing up for a new millennium, Mongella suggested, "If women are to contribute effectively to national development into the 21st century, the fundamental question is whether they will be sufficiently equipped to participate fully by receiving a quality education that will prepare them to enter any field; expose them to sciences, technology, and communications; and stimulate their creativity."

Steadfastly Sought Sisterhood

Ironically, the need for actively seeking equality, development, and peace, was highlighted at the Fourth World Conference on Women by the very behavior of the host country. Food, rest rooms, and accommodations were poor; times and venues for workshops were frequently changed; Chinese security agents harassed participants and journalists; and as *Time* reporters Jaime A. Flor-Cruz and Mia Turner noted from Beijing, "even the heavens glowered, sending forth rain that churned up mud, mud *everywhere.*"

Time indicated that even before the first day of the conference, the Chinese government had denied "as many as 10,000 visas to prospective delegates." Those who were allowed to enter the country, but who came representing NGOs were inconveniently placed in living quarters more than 30 miles from the conference site, making it difficult for them to attend many of the goings-on. According to *Time,* "surly treatment of guests ... so dominated foreign news dispatches that conference leaders despaired of communicating their serious business."

Some issues, such as sex education/reproductive rights and gay rights remained unresolved at the end of the two weeks. Though conventions like bride burning, female infanticide, rape, and economic discrimination were condemned, the delegates were unable to come up with steps to eliminate the practices. Still, the conference was deemed by most to be a success. Attendees included Pakistan's Prime Minister Benazir Bhutto; First Lady Hilary Clinton and National Organization for Women (NOW) cofounder Betty Friedan from the United States; and Burmese political prisoner Aung San Suu Kyi, who was able to appear via a smuggled videotape.

As *Time* related, "for most of the women who had come from far corners of the earth to express their solidarity ... [the experience] proved exhilarating." *Newsweek* also disclosed that "the secret of China's controversy-ridden women's conference was that nearly everyone had a terrific time anyway. China's behavior was largely a temporary distraction from what the women had come to do." More than 5,000 delegates, headed by Mongella, were able to draft an official *Platform for Action.*

Hopes for Brighter African Future

Mongella, married and the mother of one daughter and three sons, has been described by *Africa Report* as "vivacious, motherly, [and] straight-talking," but she's also tough and determined. Her preoccupation with the treatment of women has been lifelong and continues to stoke her dreams. She shared one with *PARADE:* "In Africa, 75 percent of the food is produced by these so-called 'weak women' with simple tools. With science and technology, they would be great farmers."

Another of Mongella's major concerns is that political and economic gains for African women and children do not seem to be as high a priority in many nations as internal wars and military spending. The subject of high military expenditures leads Mongella to envisage something better: "Think what it would mean for rural women and children if some of the funds used could be reallocated to provide clean water, health care, schools, and housing. Think what it would mean to millions of refugees, the majority of whom are women and children, if they could return to their homes."

Mongella returned home herself as 1995 came to a frenzied end. In January of 1996, she sojourned back to Tanzania for a well-deserved respite from the international scene and to await her next official assignment. Meanwhile she continued to believe that equality between the sexes is the key to a better life for everyone. As she told *Maryknoll's* Janice McLaughlin, "Women will change the world when they lead it." Mongella's own role in global politics and the successes she's had should be ample evidence that women can indeed make a difference in humanity's state of affairs.

Sources

Books

Rake, Alan, *Who's Who in Africa: Leaders for the 1990s,* Scarecrow Press, 1992, p. 361

Periodicals

Africa Report, January-February 1995, pp. 55-60.
Maryknoll, July/August 1995, p. 34-37.
New Pittsburgh Courier, April 1, 1995, p. A2.
Newsweek, September 18, 1995, pp. 50-52.
The New York Beacon, May 17, 1995, p. 23.
PARADE, March 5, 1995.
Time, September 18, 1995, pp. 79-80.

Additional information for this profile was obtained from a biographical note provided from Mongella's United Nations office on January of 1996.

—Doris H. Mabunda

Rose Meta Morgan

1912 (?)—

Entrepreneur

Rose Meta Morgan began a beauty empire in Harlem, New York, during the 1940s and quickly became a powerhouse in the field and a doyenne of African American high society. *Ebony* magazine called her House of Beauty the Number One establishment of its kind in the world, and women flocked from across the country to patronize this fabulous salon. The poet Langston Hughes once said that Morgan was on a stairway to the stars.

Born around 1912 in Shelby, Mississippi, Rose Morgan always felt homely. But her father, Chaptle Morgan, was a great influence on young Rose, and he doted on her. She told *Essence's* Mike Moore, "He used to praise everything I did. And I'd work as hard as I could to please him. I believed I could do anything because he told me I could." An extremely successful sharecropper, Mr. Morgan moved his family of 13 to Chicago when Rose was six years old. Her father's prowess as a businessman fascinated her. She watched him keep his accounts for much of his life, knowing that one day she would have her own business. Her first foray in this area came with her father's help when Morgan was ten; she made artificial flowers and convinced neighborhood children to sell them door to door.

Morgan also worked in a laundry, shaking out sheets until her arms ached. She would get up at 5:30 in order to be at work by 7:00. Early one morning, when her father woke her for work, Morgan complained that her

arms hurt too much and that she needed more sleep. "You've made yourself a hard bed," her father said, as she recalled to Moore. "Now lie in it." Morgan went on to declare, "I was determined from that point it would not be a hard bed all my life."

Developed Styling Gift as a Teen

By 11 Morgan began to show an affinity for hairstyling and by 14 was earning money this way. Although some sources suggest she finished high school, Morgan seemed proud of her lack of a diploma when she extolled the merits of the beauty field to *Ebony,* saying, "I know [it's an important field] for I was a high school drop-out, and [the beauty industry] gave me an opportunity to prove that I could go as far as those who had been to college."

Her high school education notwithstanding, Morgan did attend Chicago's Morris School of Beauty, where her innate ability in styling, cutting, and grooming hair enhanced her progress. After school she rented a booth in a neighborhood salon and began taking on customers full-time. In 1938 a friend in the theater business introduced Morgan to singer/actress Ethel Waters. Morgan styled Waters's hair prior to a performance, and Waters was so impressed that she invited Morgan to accompany her back to New York City. When Waters's Chicago engagement ended, Morgan took her first vacation ever, traveling back with Waters in her car. "I

At a Glance . . .

Born c. 1912, in Shelby, MS; daughter of Chaptle Morgan (a sharecropper); married second husband, Joe Louis (a boxer), 1955 (marriage annulled, 1958); married Louis Saunders (a lawyer), early 1960s (separated). *Education:* Attended Morris School of Beauty.

Began styling hair professionally, c. 1926; rented booth in neighborhood salon, c. 1930s; styled Ethel Waters's hair, 1938; took job in salon, New York City, c. 1939; opened own salon, c. 1939; opened Rose Meta House of Beauty, Inc., Harlem, NY, c. 1943; opened Rose Morgan's House of Beauty, 1955; co-founded New Jersey savings and loan association, early 1960s; founded Freedom National Bank, 1965; retired, mid-1980s.

saw tall buildings for the first time," she told *Essence.* "I went on a boat ride and saw the most glamorous women, all dressed up. I wanted to stay."

Morgan would not stay, however, without her family's approval. When she returned to Chicago her father once again proved himself her biggest backer; he gave her his blessing and told her to go out and make something of herself. Accepting a job in New York, Morgan almost immediately became a very popular beautician. In just six months' time she had developed a large enough clientele to establish her own beauty shop. In the converted kitchen of a friend's apartment, Morgan's first business began to grow so rapidly that she was soon forced to hire and train five stylists to work under her. By then she also needed a bigger space. With her friend, Olivia Clark, she signed a ten-year lease on a rundown mansion that had been vacant for years— it was even referred to as the haunted house.

"All the men I knew thought I was out of my mind— doomed to failure," she told Moore. "They said I didn't know anything about renovation. But I'm in a business where a woman has to take care of herself. I've never been afraid to take the next step, to take on responsibilities." The renovation of the house cost $28,000 and the latest in hairdressing and health equipment was valued at $20,000. But within three years the Rose Meta House of Beauty was the biggest African American beauty parlor in the world, well in the black and earning handsome profits. Each co-owner was a specialist in a

different but related field, Morgan in hairdressing, Clarke in scientific body treatments.

Rejected Racist Conceptions of Beauty

Hairdressing had long been an important industry in the African American community. In order to dull the devastating effects of racism, blacks often yearned to look more like whites, with their more "accepted" conceit of what true beauty was. An early issue of *Ebony* reported, "Thousands of Negro men and women spend sizable sums annually on their hair, purchase enormous quantities of hair greases and pomades, and invest heavily in special dressing and curling treatments calculated to 'straighten' kinky hair. To some, de-kinking is synonymous with de-Negrofying and hence improvement."

Rose Morgan was one of the first people to begin quashing such racist notions. She spent her career pointing out the beauty inherent in everyone, insisting that there was no such thing as bad hair and that African American hair was equally beautiful to any other. "Miss Morgan contends," *Ebony* continued, "this belief [that African American hair is inferior] is a reflection of the extent to which white America has warped the values of certain Negroes who feel that the more Negroid a Negro the less attractive. 'Hair textures vary from race to race and type to type' she says, 'and it is very wrong to classify one kind as "better" than another. It's all in the way you care for the hair. All hair is bad if it isn't well-styled and groomed.'"

The House of Beauty's policy was to send the customer back into the world looking her best. This sometimes led to disagreements. "We don't always agree with what customers want and when we don't we say so frankly," Morgan told *Ebony.* "Thus, there are many women who want styles our experience and judgment tell us are unbecoming to them. In such cases we make suggestions on what we think is the suitable hairstyle for the person concerned." Sometimes Morgan actually refused to style a prospective customer's hair because she felt the look requested would be unattractive; she would rather do nothing at all than let a woman out on the street with an unflattering hairstyle.

This first incarnation of the House of Beauty drew an average of 1,000 customers a week. The staff of 29 included a registered nurse, 20 hairstylists, and three licensed masseurs, drawing a payroll of $40,000 in 1946. Morgan began selling her own line of cosmetics, in which she exhibited a progressive flair for marketing. By identifying her market, tailoring her cosmetics to it, and pricing them carefully, the cosmetics line sold extremely well. In time Morgan began staging fashion shows for which her employees and customers acted as designers and models.

Thousands of people turned out for these huge social events at the Renaissance Casino and the Rockland Plaza in Harlem. Models wearing exquisite dresses and luxurious furs were escorted by dashing men in tuxedos—all choreographed to the jazzy beat of swing. Great balls followed the shows. "The people had seen nothing like it," Morgan told*Essence*. "All the girls loved the shows because there was nowhere else they could show themselves off like high-fashion models." Customers came from coast to coast to the House of Beauty. Morgan sailed on the Queen Mary to Europe to spread her slogan: "To glorify the woman of color." When she went to Paris to demonstrate her technique, *Paris Match* referred to her as one of the richest businesswomen in New York.

By the mid-1950s Morgan had begun to look for a sleeker, more chic salon. She planned to invest $250,000 in refurbishing the new building she had purchased. For years she had been doing business with a certain bank, and during almost two decades she had deposited three million dollars there. She needed a $40,000 loan for her new venture, but asked the bank for only a modest $25,000. They said no. Ever resourceful, she tried another banker, one to whom she had given Harlem real estate advice in the past; he came through with the loan. Friends and family covered the rest. Ten thousand people came to the opening of Rose Morgan's House of Beauty on a rainy day in February of 1955. The mayor's wife cut a big pink ribbon inaugurating the new shop.

Anticipated Trends

One young woman quoted by *Ebony* attested of the salon, "This place is the end. Under one roof it has everything a woman needs to get re-styled, upholstered and reconditioned!" The new building included, in addition to the customary salon amenities, a dressmaking department, a reducing and body department, and a charm school. Cologne was infused regularly throughout the building to keep the House of Beauty smelling sweet. And in the late 1950s and early 1960s, when wearing wigs went from a fad to an entrenched trend, Morgan opened a deluxe wig salon, initiating a wig pickup and delivery service so woman could have their coiffures styled off the premises. Once again, Morgan had anticipated a major change in the industry and embraced it, greatly furthering her success. One area in which Morgan did not excel, however, was marriage.

Her husbands could not seem to compete with her career. Morgan's first marriage, which lasted only one year, occurred while she was still living in Chicago. But her second marriage would be by far her most famous match. On Christmas Day, 1955, Morgan married the heavyweight champion of the world, boxer Joe Louis, who had held the title for twelve years. Although he had earned five million dollars during his professional career, when he retired in 1949 Louis owed one million dollars in back taxes. He was a proud man who enjoyed the good life, but to maintain this style of living he took whatever work came his way. He tried hard to woo Morgan, whom he had met during several high society functions, though he had not met a woman who wouldn't jump when he said jump. The independent Morgan did finally fall for Louis, later accepting his spontaneous proposal of marriage. The small wedding was nonetheless a huge media event.

> "Hair textures vary from race to race and type to type, and it is very wrong to classify one kind as 'better' than another. It's all in the way you care for the hair. All hair is bad if it isn't well-styled and groomed."

Morgan was ever enterprising in her attempts to help Louis earn a living in pursuits that she considered more "dignified" than wrestling and other demonstrations. She got them on a quiz show, and during their run they won more than $60,000. She also tried a joint business venture with Louis, but this time her acumen was far too ahead of its time. The men's cologne—called My Man—that she developed, selling it with posters of Louis, was not a hit. Men, especially black men of the late 1950s, were not ready to wear cologne.

By then the marriage was in trouble, too. Each partner concluded that their lifestyles did not mesh. For one, he was a chronic night owl; she had to rise early to be at work. Neither was satisfied, but each had great respect for the other. In 1957 they separated; the marriage was annulled the following year. Morgan later married lawyer Louis Saunders. Together they founded a New Jersey savings and loan association. After two years the couple separated, though they never filed for divorce. Saunders later died.

In 1965 Morgan founded the Freedom National Bank, New York's only black commercial bank, in which she became a major shareholder. In 1972 she began franchising a new business, Trim-Away Figure Contouring. And then, after roughly 60 years in the beauty game, Morgan retired. Morgan's salon was among the first of its kind, providing full service for black women, including hair care, manicures, eyebrow shaping, massage, and cosmetics. She had employed and trained more than 3,000 people. In her eighties Morgan's skin was still flawless and she continued to exercise seven days a week. Reflecting on her life, she told *Essence,* "I have been happiest in knowing that I made women more beautiful, that people have leaned on my shoulder, that I have taught hundreds of hands to do what these two do." She concluded to another *Essence* reporter, "I don't need anyone to take care of me. I've made that possible myself."

Sources

Books

Contributions of Black Women to America, vol. 1, Kenday Press, 1982.

Ebony Success Library, vol. 1, Johnson Publishing, p. 228.

Notable Black American Woman, Gale, 1992, p. 769.

Periodicals

Black Enterprise, March 1971, p. 14.

Ebony, May 1946, pp. 25-29; March 1954, p. 26; June 1955, pp. 62-68; March 1956, pp. 45-49; November 1956, p. 112; August 1966, pp. 140-42; December 1966, p. 23.

Essence, January 1974, p. 20; June 1981, pp. 34-44; January 1995, p. 82.

Family Circle, November 1971, p. 35.

Pageant Press, 1962, p. 191.

—Joanna Rubiner

Robert Parris Moses

1935—

Educator, civil rights activist

A dedicated activist whose thoughtfulness and integrity match his courage and tenacity, Robert Parris Moses was one of the most important figures in the civil rights movement. Perhaps more than anyone else, he shifted the movement's emphasis from sit-ins and freedom rides to voter registration. Over a two-to-three year period with a handful of fellow volunteers, he led by example, helping to awaken black Mississippians to their moral and legal rights. "In Mississippi, Bob Moses was the equivalent of Martin Luther King," Pulitzer Prize-winning author Taylor Branch told the *New York Times*.

Moses's dedication and personal strength is epitomized in an anecdote from his years in Mississippi. Late at night on August 17, 1962, several carloads of angry white segregationists armed with chains and shotguns invaded and ransacked the Greenwood, Mississippi, office of the Student Nonviolent Coordinating Committee (SNCC). Three SNCC workers inside had to climb atop the roof to escape harm. When he heard of the attack, Moses immediately drove 40 miles to the scene to survey the damage. Despite the danger involved, Moses then made up a bed in a corner of the destroyed room and went to sleep.

This celebrated nap added to the young black New Yorker's growing mythic stature among black Mississippians and his fellow civil rights workers during this violent era. "I just didn't understand what kind of guy this Bob Moses is, that could walk into a place where a lynch mob had just left and make up a bed and prepare to go to sleep, as if the situation was normal," a new SNCC worker recalled in *Parting the Waters,* Taylor Branch's account of those years.

Activist in Training

Robert Moses's paternal grandfather, William Henry Moses was a well-educated and distinguished Baptist preacher who provided everything for his wife and children. Serious illness and the Great Depression, however, brought hard times that prevented Reverend Moses from supporting or educating his younger children. Robert's father, Gregory, a janitor at the 369th armory in Harlem, New York, retained a lifelong bitterness and frustration about his lack of education or

At a Glance . . .

Born January 23, 1935, in New York City, NY; son of Gregory (a janitor) and Louise Parris; married Dona Richards (an SNCC secretary; divorced 1966); married Janet Jemott (an SNCC field secretary) 1968; children: Maisha; three others. *Education:* Hamilton College, Clinton, New York, B.A., 1956; Harvard University, M.A., 1957, Ph.D. candidate 1977-1982.

Horace Mann High School, Riverdale, New York, Mathematics teacher, 1958-1961; Student Nonviolent Coordinating Committee (SNCC), Mississippi field secretary, 1961-1964; Council of Federated Organizations (COFO), voter registration program director, 1962-1964; Freedom Vote project, Mississippi, director, 1963; fled to Canada to avoid Vietnam War draft, working odd jobs, 1966-1968; Tanzania, Africa, mathematics teacher, 1969-1976; Algebra Project, Cambridge, Massachusetts, director, 1982--.

Awards:--MacArthur Foundation grant, 1982.

Addresses: *Office*--99 Bishop Richard Allen Drive; Cambridge, MA 02139.

professional accomplishment compared with his brother, a college professor.

This resentment was passed on to Robert. He was born in 1935, in New York City and raised in the Harlem River Houses. Together with his wife, Louise Parris, Robert's father encouraged his three sons to study hard and succeed. After scoring highly on competitive city-wide examinations, Robert Moses was admitted to Stuyvesant, a high school for gifted students. He enjoyed the school's liberal environment and was elected senior class president and captain of the baseball team before graduating in 1952.

Both parents wanted Moses to attend a small white liberal arts college instead of the more traditional black schools that they considered too social. They were thrilled when he won a scholarship to enter Hamilton College in upstate New York. As one of three black students among a school of upper-middle class whites, Moses gained a reputation for being quiet, thoughtful, and introspective. Excluded by race from the campus fraternity system, he gravitated toward a largely fundamentalist Christian study group, driving to New York

City on many weekends to preach in Times Square, a city landmark.

Moses became a philosophy major, reading Albert Camus in the original French, studying Eastern philosophers, and examining pacifist thinking. Encouraged by some of his professors, he attended Quaker workshops abroad, spent one summer working and living in France among pacifists who had survived Hitler's occupation, and lived in Japan to study with a Zen Buddhist monk. Graduating in 1956, Moses entered the philosophy doctoral program at Harvard University. He concentrated on analytic philosophy, a discipline that focuses on mathematical precision instead of the traditional questions of truth and being. Receiving his master's degree in 1957, he left school the following February after his mother's sudden death and his father's subsequent mental breakdown. To pay for his father's care, he became a mathematics teacher at Horace Mann, a prestigious private high school.

Moses was still teaching at Mann in 1960 when Southern blacks began sit-ins, demanding to be seated and served alongside whites at lunch counters. A racial awakening had begun. Watching on television and reading the newspapers, Moses recalled in *The Promised Land:* "Before, the Negro in the South had always looked on the defensive, cringing. This time they were taking the initiative. They were kids my age, and I knew this had something to do with my own life. It made me realize that for a long time I had been troubled by the problem of being a Negro and at the same time being an American."

Civil Rights Crusader

In June of 1960, Moses took a bus south to work for Dr. Martin Luther King's Southern Christian Leadership Conference (SCLC). Arriving at the SCLC's Atlanta office, the idealistic 25-year-old came face to face with the hard reality of the civil rights struggle. Expecting a room full of volunteers who would train, organize, and direct a nationwide movement, he found instead an understaffed and underfunded church office with constantly ringing telephones and three workers. One of these workers--Jane Stembridge, a fellow New Yorker--was a member of the recently-formed Student Nonviolent Coordinating Committee (SNCC). This new organization, more democratic in nature and less hierarchial and preacher-dominated than the SCLC, had been created to recruit and train students as nonviolent civil rights demonstrators.

In King's absence, nobody knew what to do with Moses. He and Stembridge prepared fund-raising packets for the SCLC and spent hours debating philosophy, nonviolence, and the best way to achieve equal rights for black America. In his spare time, he joined the picket lines outside Atlanta supermarkets that refused to hire black clerks. When Stembridge suggested he undertake a recruiting trip throughout the deep South as an SNCC field representative, he quickly volunteered.

Nothing in his background and experience had prepared him for the grinding poverty, racial animosity, and subhuman conditions under which rural Southern blacks lived. But in Cleveland, Mississippi, in the midst of this heart of darkness, Moses met Amzie Moore, a local activist and the head of the town's National Association for the Advancement of Colored People (NAACP) chapter. Through long talks, Moore convinced Moses that the key to achieving black empowerment and addressing the intolerable inequities of Southern life was not by the more popular and direct action of sit-ins or picketing, but by the quiet and steady, behind-the-scenes work of voter registration and the consequent power of the ballot box. Moore also believed that in Mississippi such a course of action would be safer in the short run than direct public confrontation even though it was ultimately more radical in its effect.

Working with Moore, Moses soon developed a plan to begin registering black Mississippians to vote. Both believed that outside help would be necessary to aid local blacks in overcoming the years of intimidation and enforced segregation. Under protection of the new civil rights laws, they recruited a workforce of SNCC student workers to spark awareness of, and education about, voter registration. Returning to New York City that September to complete his teaching contract at Horace Mann, Moses vowed to return and begin this campaign the following spring.

Mississippi Burning

That same spring of 1961, the Congress of Racial Equality (CORE) began its Freedom Rides in order to test the previous year's U.S. Supreme Court ruling in *Boynton v. Virginia* that required the desegregation of facilities used in interstate travel. Two buses with anti-segregation volunteers left Washington, D.C., only to encounter increasing antagonism and violence the further south they traveled. One of the buses was attacked and burned near Anniston, Alabama, while riders on the other were beaten in nearby Birmingham. In response, SNCC student activists joined the original riders as one bus continued to Jackson, Mississippi. Everyone aboard that bus was jailed.

This was the emotionally charged, racially tense atmo-

sphere that greeted Moses on his return to the "middle of the iceberg," as he later described Mississippi in a letter written during one of his jail stays. No other state so defiantly promulgated segregation nor used the burning cross, the lynch mob, the sheriff's badge, and the local court system to enforce it. "Mississippi set itself up to be our destiny," Moses later told the *New York Times*. "And so it attracted what it eventually got: us."

Because of the heightened tension, Moore was reluctant to begin registering voters in the towns around Cleveland in the state's Delta region. He suggested, instead, that Moses begin activity in McComb, a town in the state's southwestern corner. Newly appointed as SNCC's Mississippi field secretary, Moses spent his weekdays walking door-to-door to meet McComb's black citizens. He spent Sundays speaking in the churches about his voter registration project. He cultivated some local high school students to help him and began voter education classes to begin psychologically preparing the town's historically disenfranchised blacks to take the giant step-registering to vote.

On August 7, 1961, four blacks accompanied Moses to the county registrar's office and were registered. After a few days of similar successes, blacks in neighboring counties asked for his assistance as well. This was too much for the local segregationists, however. Moses was arrested, tried, and found guilty on vague charges. Instead of paying his fine, though, he called the U.S. Justice Department in Washington, D.C., alerting them to this violation of federal civil rights laws.

His ability to overcome such a misuse of local authority made Moses an immediate hero in the black community. After two days in jail, local NAACP officials paid his bail. Two weeks later he was badly beaten while escorting more blacks to the courthouse to register. Bleeding profusely from head wounds that later required eight stitches to close, he calmly continued to the registrar's office, only to be turned away.

By pressing charges against his assailant, despite a quick acquittal, Moses further demonstrated his policy of quiet perseverance. His determination encouraged local residents--particularly young people, many of whom became SNCC volunteers--to begin asserting their rights and attend his registration classes. White Mississippians countered violently, murdering several blacks and continually arresting others, including Moses.

Growing Legend

Throughout the winter of 1961 and into 1962, Moses

continued his work among the rural poor, rarely leaving Mississippi. Exhibiting almost mystical calm amidst the terrible violence and constant harassment, the soft-spoken Moses was becoming a legend. Besides his celebrated nap, he survived a vicious attack by a police dog outside the Greenwood City Hall and a highway ambush that riddled his car with machine-gun fire and wounded a fellow SNCC worker. Discussing this event years later in an interview for *Emerge* magazine, he said: "The issue was whether you were going to commit to the work and what that meant was that they would have to gun you down to [get you to] leave. Once you get that clear in your mind, then it isn't hard to go on. It becomes your whole life."

Despite his work and determined presence, by the spring of 1963, only 6,700 of the more than 60,000 black Mississippians who had made the attempt to vote had been registered. Moses began to realize that only the federal government confronting Mississippi and enforcing national voting rights laws would initiate greater progress. Nevertheless, the Council of Federated Organizations (COFO), a collection of civil rights organizations, appointed him its program director in charge of voter registration.

The murder of Medgar Evers, Mississippi's NAACP field secretary, in June of 1963 shocked the country, bringing national attention to the state. Many white northern liberals, including Allard Lowenstein, began seeking ways to correct the state's abysmal civil rights record. That fall, Lowenstein recruited liberal northern white students to work along with Moses and his fellow SNCC volunteers to organize nonregistered Mississippi blacks to vote in a "parallel" freedom election. At least 75,000 blacks, more voters than in the official Democratic state primary, participated in Freedom Vote, demonstrating their desire for ballot box equality.

Freedom Summer

Seeking to build on this success, Moses asked COFO and SNCC to build a coalition with northern white students in Mississippi. He realized the need for middle-class white students, not only to bolster the number of volunteers but also to focus national attention on the state and make the overall effort more safe for everyone involved. He hoped their presence would force the federal government into action. Again, with Lowenstein's help, more than 1,000 white volunteers headed south in June of 1964 for Freedom Summer. They worked alongside black volunteers; to register voters; staff Freedom Schools; and help to create community centers with libraries, arts, crafts, and literacy programs.

White Mississippians reacted in their usual manner. The most publicized of many incidents was the disappearance of three white civil rights workers and their subsequent discovery, dead and buried in an earthen dam. The final toll that summer was awesome: six killed, 80 beaten, 1,000 arrested, and 68 black churches and homes destroyed. The success of Freedom Summer, however, as Moses had hoped, was in exposing white supremacy in all its abhorrence, to a summer-long national media audience. The weight of popular opinion slowly forced the federal government into action.

Moses's final effort that summer was in the political arena. Denied the chance to register in the state's Democratic party, many black Mississippians enrolled in the newly formed Mississippi Freedom Democratic Party (MFDP). At the Democratic party's national presidential convention that August, Moses attempted to have the MFDP delegates seated in place of the state's all-white delegation, but the party's northern white liberals sided with the regular delegates to defeat the MFDP's appeal.

> "The issue was whether you were going to commit to the work and what that meant was that they would have to gun you down to leave. Once you get that clear in your mind, then it isn't hard to go on. It became your whole life."

Greatly disillusioned with the continuing violence and growing factionalism between black and white in the civil rights movement, Moses wearied from the struggle. "That summer, people who were talking to each other stopped [communicating with one another," he later told the *New York Times*. "People who had been working together left. The whole spectrum of race relations compressed, broke down and washed us away." Tired of being viewed as a leader, he announced in December of 1964 that he was dropping his surname and would use only his middle name, Parris. Shortly thereafter he resigned as head of COFO, took a leave of absence from SNCC, and began shifting his concern from civil rights to the Vietnam War.

With his divorce from Dona Richards, a fellow SNCC worker, Moses's personal life was coming undone, too.

Denied conscientious objector status, he received a draft notice in July of 1966 and fled to Canada at the end of the month. He spent two years there, working odd jobs, before marrying Janet Jemmott, a former SNCC field secretary. The couple moved to Africa in 1968 and settled in a small village in Tanzania the following year. For the next eight years Moses taught mathematics while his wife taught English.

The Algebra Project

Following President Carter's amnesty program, Moses and his wife returned to the United States in 1976. Moses resumed his doctoral studies in philosophy at Harvard and his wife entered medical school. Increasingly he grew concerned that the children of minorities were failing to achieve the mathematical skills necessary for college entrance and future job placement. Abandoning academia once again, he became a volunteer tutor in the school system.

In 1982, using funds from a five-year "genius" grant from the MacArthur Foundation, Moses established the Algebra Project, a math-science program for inner-city and minority school children centered in Cambridge, Massachusetts. "If the current technological revolution demands new standards of mathematics and science literacy," he was quoted in the *Utne Reader,* "will all citizens be given equal access to the new skills, or will some be left behind, denied participation in the unfolding economic and political era?" He applied many of the same principles used successfully in Mississippi: making families central to the work of organizing; empowering people at the grass roots and recruiting them for leadership; and organizing in the context of where you live and work. During the 1960s, Moses and his fellow civil rights volunteers used examples from poor black sharecroppers' experiences to teach them history and writing. In the 1990s, the Algebra Project students learned to think and speak mathematically through tackling problems that arose in their daily lives.

There is still insufficient data to assess the project's success, but in its first 12 years the program helped more than 10,000 students master fundamental algebraic skills in cities across the country. In 1992, Moses returned to Mississippi to start the Delta Algebra Project. "It's our version of Civil Rights 1992," Moses would later tell the *New York Times.* "But this time, we're organizing around literacy--not just reading and writing, but mathematical literacy.... The question we asked then was: What are the skills people have to master to open the doors to citizenship? Now math literacy holds the key."

Sources

Books

Branch, Taylor, *Parting the Waters: America in the King Years 1954-63,* Simon and Schuster, 1988.
Burner, Eric, *And Gently He Shall Lead Them: Robert Parris Moses and Civil Rights in Mississippi,* New York University Press, 1994.
Lemann, Nicholas, *The Promised Land: The Great Black Migration and How it Changed America,* Alfred A. Knopf, 1991.
Walter, Mildred Pitts, *Mississippi Challenge,* Bradbury Press, 1992.

Periodicals

Emerge, June 1994, pp. 24-29.
Essence, May 1994, p. 116.
New York Times Magazine, February 21, 1993, pp. 28-35, 50-51, 64, 72.
Utne Reader, March/April 1995, p. 142.

—James J. Podesta

Nichelle Nichols

1933—

Actress, singer, space travel advocate

As a starring member of the original *Star Trek* television series, Nichelle Nichols trod a pioneering path in network broadcasting. Her character, Lieutenant Commander Uhura, provided an unprecedented inspiration for a generation of young black viewers--an educated, dignified space traveler in a future world devoid of bigotry and sexism. Before Lieutenant Uhura took to the bridge on the starship *Enterprise* in the late 1960s, black women had assumed mostly subordinate--and unimportant--roles on television shows. Nichols changed that, serving as a role model not only for would-be black actresses but also as a symbol for young women who dreamed of becoming astronauts and scientists.

The Uhura role in television and movies is the crowning achievement of Nichols's long and productive career as an entertainer and advocate of space travel. The glamorous performer began working as a dancer in her native Chicago just after World War II, broke into television after years of traveling as a successful nightclub singer, and used her most visible role as a futuristic

space explorer to promote the reality of women and minorities in the real life U.S. space program. As testament to Nichols's success in her many roles, comedian Whoopi Goldberg once commented that when she was a young "kid from the projects," she saw in Nichols's Lieutenant Uhura "the only vision of Black people in the future," and a *Jet* magazine correspondent summed up Nichols's many contributions by calling her "the embodiment of Black beauty and intelligence."

Born Grace Nichols in the small Chicago suburb of Robbins, Illinois, Nichelle Nichols entered a fiercely independent and determined family. Her paternal grandfather was a white Southerner who defied the conventions of his time and alienated his wealthy parents by marrying a black woman. It was this grandfather who settled in Robbins, an integrated community, in the early part of the century. Nichols's father was a businessman who served as mayor of Robbins during the Prohibition era. Her mother had been a scholar who hoped to attend law school. Because both of her parents had children

At a Glance . . .

Born Grace Nichols c. 1933 in Robbins, IL; daughter of Samuel Earl (a factory worker and civic leader) and Lishia Mae (Parks) Nichols; married Foster Johnson (a dancer), 1951 (divorced); married Duke Mondy (a songwriter and arranger), ca. 1968 (divorced); children: (first marriage) Kyle. *Education:* Studied dance at Chicago Ballet Academy. *Avocational interests:* Oil painting, designing clothes, reading science fiction, writing, and sculpting.

Actress, dancer, and singer. Dancer in Chicago with "College Inn" revue, ca. 1947; toured United States and Canada as singer and dancer with Duke Ellington and Lionel Hampton, 1950-51; solo singer in club appearances, 1953–. Principal film appearances include *Porgy and Bess*, 1959; *Mister Buddwing*, 1966; *Truck Turner*, 1974; *Star Trek: The Motion Picture*, 1979; *Star Trek II: The Wrath of Khan*, 1982; *Star Trek III: The Search for Spock*, 1984; *Star Trek IV: The Voyage Home*, 1986; *The Supernaturals*, 1987; *Star Trek V: The Final Frontier*, 1989; *Star Trek VI: The Undiscovered Country*, 1991. Principal television appearances include *Star Trek*, NBC, 1966-69; *Star Trek* (animated), NBC, 1973-75; episodic appearances in *Tarzan, The Lieutenant, Head of the Class*. Narrator and star of *Space, What's in It for Me?*, Smithsonian Museum, 1978; star of one-woman show, *Reflections*, 1992–; host of *Inside Space*, USA Network, 1992.

Spokesperson for Kwanza Foundation; founder, Women in Motion (astronaut recruiting company); board member, National Space Institute; contributor to National Space Institute publications.

Address: *Agent*–The Artists Group, 1930 Century Park

from previous marriages, Nichelle was born into a large, close-knit family.

Started as a Dancer

In her autobiography *Beyond Uhura: Star Trek and Other Memories*, Nichols described herself as a precocious youngster who liked to sing Broadway show tunes

and entertain her siblings. At an early age she began dancing lessons and was captivated by classical ballet. She was so talented that as a young teen she earned an audition with the Chicago Ballet Academy. When she arrived at the audition with her father, she was informed by the instructor that blacks could not possibly hope to undertake a formal study of ballet--they just were not suited for it. Furious, her father insisted that she be allowed to audition. Equally furious at the humiliation, Nichols danced her very best and won the right to attend the academy. "It never occurred to either of my parents to feel inferior to anyone for any reason," Nichols recalled in her book. "My father taught us, 'You are not better than anyone else. But there is no one better than you.' Both my parents--and in my father's case his parents as well--had defied the odds and bucked the system. They saw no reason why we could not become whatever we wanted."

Nichols wanted to be a dancer. From the ages of 12 to 14 she studied classical ballet at the Chicago Ballet Academy and also pursued Afro-Cuban dancing under the tutelage of Carmencita Romero. The latter experience helped her to land her first professional engagement, at the tender age of 14, with a song and dance revue staged at the prestigious Sherman House Hotel. "Destiny had found me, and I embraced it," the actress wrote in her memoir.

Dancing Leads to Show Business

During her performance time at the Sherman House, Nichols met many of the prominent nightclub artists of the day, including the immortal Duke Ellington. Ellington was so impressed with her dancing that he later invited her to join his touring company, and she did so as a dancer with her first husband, Foster Johnson.

The birth of her only child, Kyle, in 1951 provided the only lull in Nichols's performing career. Separated from the child's father, she sought work in a downtown Chicago office in order to support her son. The work was not rewarding, however, and she longed to go back to the stage. She returned to Chicago nightclubs as a singer-dancer in the revue "Calypso Carnival," staged by Jimmy Payne. Then, in the mid-1950s, she went on tour as a solo act, singing and dancing in supper clubs all over America and Canada. She was paid so well for these engagements that she was eventually able to move her entire family to Los Angeles. The traveling lifestyle finally began to take its toll, however, and Nichols decided to try to find work in Hollywood. As she noted in her autobiography, "My decision to focus my sights on film or television wasn't an easy one. I knew that months, perhaps even years, of sacrifice and discipline lay ahead, but something inside me told me I could make it work."

> "I firmly believe in the power of vision, and Gene Roddenberry's Star Trek raised the prospect that space offered humankind the opportunity to start anew....He believed, as do I and many others, that this was not simply one possible version of the future, but the only viable one."

After serving as an opening act for comedian Redd Foxx, Nichols earned a part as a principal dancer in the film version of *Porgy and Bess.* That experience led to a lead in the Broadway play *Kicks and Company,* which ran only for a few weeks, and subsequent nightclub work in New York City. By 1963 she was back in Los Angeles, looking for work in television. On her very first television assignment, a guest role on the series *The Lieutenant,* she met an up-and-coming writer-producer named Gene Roddenberry.

A Pioneer on Star Trek

While working together on *The Lieutenant* in 1963, Roddenberry and Nichols began a romantic and business relationship that would develop into a long-lasting, close friendship. Roddenberry's brainchild, *Star Trek,* was meant to be an action-adventure series that would also make points about racial and political tolerance. Nichols's work on *The Lieutenant* convinced Roddenberry to add a role for her on *Star Trek.* She would play a high-ranking officer and communications specialist who would demonstrate the untapped potential of women in the field of space exploration. In *Beyond Uhura,* Nichols recalled: "It was only after I'd been brought on board, and Gene and I conceived and created her, that Uhura was born. Many times through the years I've referred to Uhura as my great-great-great-great-great-great-great-granddaughter of the twenty-third century. Gene and I agreed that she would be a citizen of the United States of America. And her name, Uhura, is derived from Uhuru, which is Swahili for 'freedom.'"

Star Trek had its premier in 1966. Nichols starred along with the actors who are now considered the "classic cast"--William Shatner, Leonard Nimoy, DeForest Kelley, George Takei, Jimmy Doohan, and Walter Koenig. Not only was Nichols the most important woman character on the show, she was also one of the most important black woman characters ever on network television. Fan mail poured in from across the country, but the actress was still dissatisfied with her treatment by the television studio and by the way in which her character's action was minimized. She was determined to leave the show after its first season until a chance meeting with civil rights leader Dr. Martin Luther King Jr. caused her to change her mind.

In her autobiography, Nichols noted that King was aghast when she said she might leave *Star Trek.* King told her that he understood her grievances, but that she had "created a character of dignity and grace and beauty and intelligence." Furthermore, he felt she was not a role model for African Americans only, but "more important for people who *don't* look like us. For the first time, the world sees us as we should be seen, as equals, as intelligent people--as we *should* be. There will always be role models for Black children; you are a role model for everyone."

Nichols stayed on *Star Trek* until it was cancelled in 1969. Among other challenges, her work on the show included the first televised interracial kiss--a moment the actress recalls with a great deal of amusement. After *Star Trek's* cancellation, Nichols experienced the inevitable letdown of a performer without a venue, but then a most extraordinary phenomenon occurred that has kept her busy--and provided her with many rewarding moments--ever since.

Celebrity Activist for Space Travel

In the wake of *Star Trek* Nichols began to serve as a catalyst for real women and minorities who wanted to be astronauts. In 1975 she established Women in Motion, Inc., a company that produced educational materials using music as a teaching tool. From its modest origins, Women in Motion expanded to become an astronaut recruitment project after Nichols won a grant from the National Aeronautics and Space Administration (NASA). Within four months in 1977, her company had helped to find almost 1,700 female applicants and 1,000 minority applicants to NASA's space program. Among these were Sally Ride, the first woman to go into space, as well as Judith Resnik, Ronald McNair, and Ellison Onizuka--all three of whom were killed in the U.S. space shuttle *Challenger* disaster of 1986. In October of

1984 Nichols was presented with NASA's Public Service Award for her many efforts toward an integrated U.S. space program.

The continued popularity of *Star Trek* also helped to pave the way for a series of *Star Trek* movies with the "classic cast," including Nichols. Between 1979 and 1991 Nichols appeared in six *Star Trek* feature films always enjoying the opportunity to re-unite with her associates from the original television show. She has also returned to the live stage in a one-woman show entitled *Reflections,* a musical tribute to such legendary black performers as Ma Rainey, Bessie Smith, Josephine Baker, Ella Fitzgerald, Katherine Dunham, and others. In 1992 she served as host of the USA Network series *Inside Space.*

While some of the "classic cast" *Star Trek* performers resent the popularity of the series and their characters, Nichelle Nichols has continued to be gracious to fans and loyal to the spirit of Uhura. Nichols found herself being invited to Star Trek conventions and being treated like royalty when she came. Even though the millions of "Trekkies," or *Star Trek* fans, might identify Nichols simply as the character she played on television, she stated in her autobiography that she was "proud of who [Uhura] was (or will be) and what she represented, not only in her time but in ours." She also commented, "I firmly believe in the power of vision, and Gene Roddenberry's *Star Trek* raised the prospect that space offered humankind the opportunity to start anew. The show's ethical premises certainly formed a new foundation upon which the classical elements of television drama could be redesigned. But to Gene, it all meant so much

more. He believed, as do I and many others, that this was not simply one possible version of the future, but the only viable one."

Selected writings

Beyond Uhura: Star Trek and Other Memories, G.P. Putnam's Sons, 1994.
Saturn's Child (science fiction novel), G.P. Putnam's Sons, 1995.

Sources

Books

Contemporary Theatre, Film, and Television, Volume 8, Gale, 1990, p. 311.
Nichols, Nichelle, *Beyond Uhura: Star Trek and Other Memories,* G.P. Putnam's Sons, 1994.

Periodicals

Atlanta Constitution, November 1, 1994, p. E1.
Chicago Tribune, December 7, 1986; January 1, 1987; March 10, 1989.
Ebony, August 1985, pp. 150-54.
Entertainment Weekly, October 21, 1994, p. 57.
Essence, January 1995, p. 50.
Jet, July 12, 1982, pp. 56-60; November 14, 1994, pp. 62-63.
Los Angeles Times, February 2, 1990, p. F10.
Publishers Weekly, August 22, 1994, pp. 48-49.
TV Guide, October 8, 1994, pp. 30-33.

—Anne Janette Johnson

Richard Dean Parsons

1948—

Corporate executive

Richard Parsons has become one of the most prominent figures in American business, without rising through the usual ranks required to reach a high-level corporate position. Named president of Dime Savings Bank of New York in 1988 even though he had had no previous experience in the banking industry, he masterminded a turnaround at the bank in just a few years. In the early 1990s he became president of Time Warner Inc., making him one of the most highly ranked African Americans in the corporate United States.

Hard work has been a crucial component of the Parsons success story, a value he claims to have learned from his father. As he told *Ebony,* "I have never missed a single day of work in my life. Never. Not one." Also fueling his rise were connections he has made with important people over the years. "A gregarious and thoughtful man, Mr. Parsons has risen by winning the affection and loyalty of influential mentors," wrote Laurence Zuckerman in the *New York Times.*

Born into a family of humble means in the Bedford-Stuyvesant section of Brooklyn, New York, and raised in

Queens, New York, Parsons revealed an inherent intelligence but had few aspirations as a youth. He graduated high school at the age of 16, then devoted much of his attention to sports as a student at the University of Hawaii. He played varsity basketball there, and was also the social chairman of his fraternity. His journey to future success was given some impetus by his girlfriend at the time, Laura Bush, who became his wife in 1968.

"Left to my own devices, I don't feel any compulsion to strive," he told the *New York Times* in 1990. "My wife became my focus and the person to whom I owed my best." His plans to become a fighter pilot were redirected to law school largely due to Bush's influence. According to *Ebony,* Parsons said that "the woman I was dating [Bush] told me, `You like to argue so much you ought to become a lawyer and get paid for it.'"

At Union University of the University of Albany Law School, Parsons helped pay his way through school by working part-time as a janitor and later as an aide in the State Assembly. He graduated number one in his class of more than 100 students at the age of 23, then received the highest marks among 3,600 lawyers who

At a Glance . . .

Born April 4, 1948, in Brooklyn, NY; son of Lorenzo Locklair (an airline technician) and Isabelle (a home-maker; maiden name, Judd) Parsons; married Laura Ann Bush, August 30, 1968; children: Gregory, Leslie, Rebecca. *Education:* Graduated from University of Hawaii, 1968; Union University, University of Albany Law School, J.D., 1971.

Served as assistant counsel to Governor Nelson Rockefeller, Albany, NY, 1971-74; called to the New York State Bar, 1972; appointed deputy counsel to the vice president, Washington, DC, 1975; general counsel and associate director of the White House Domestic Council, 1975-77; Patterson, Belknap, Webb & Tyler (law firm), New York, NY, attorney, 1977-88, became partner, 1979; Dime Savings Bank of New York (became Dime Bancorp, 1995), New York, NY, chief operating officer, 1988-90, chairman and chief executive officer, 1990-95; named head of mayor-elect transition council, New York, NY, 1993; served as chairman of New York City's Economic Development Corporation; Time Warner Inc., New York, NY, president, 1995-. Member of presidential Drug Task Force; chairman, Wildcat Service Organization. Member of the board of directors of Dime Savings Bank, Federal National Mortgage Association, Philip Morris Companies, Time Warner Inc., New York Zoological Society, and American Television & Communications Inc.; trustee of Rockefeller Brothers Fund, Howard University, and Metropolitan Museum of Art.

Addresses: *Office*–Time-Warner Inc., 75 Rockefeller Plaza, New York, NY

took the state bar examination in 1971.

Career Shaped by Rockefeller

Beginning his legal career as an aide on New York governor Nelson Rockefeller's legal staff, Parsons made a very favorable impression on the governor. Governor Rockefeller rewarded Parsons's solid performance by keeping him on his staff when he became vice president under President Gerald Ford in 1974. President Ford also used his services, first as a general council and then as associate director of the domestic council. In the latter post, Parsons focused on drug issues.

Rockefeller's influence on Parsons remained strong and prompted him to become a Republican whose views were liberal on social issues and conservative on economic ones. It also brought Parsons to the attention of high-ranking people who later sought his services. As Parsons said in the *New York Times* in 1994, "becoming a part of that Rockefeller entourage ... created for me a group of people who've looked out for me ever since." Parsons own concern for the underprivileged has been clearly shown by his work as chairman of the Wildcat Service Corporation, which has provided on-the-job instruction for people whose previous crimes, drug addiction, or poverty have made it difficult to find work.

By the mid-1970s Parsons was noted as a rising star among black professionals, and he was profiled in *Black Enterprise's* "Under 30 & Moving Up" series in 1975. When departing Deputy Attorney General Harold R. Tyler, Jr., became a partner at a well-established New York City law firm in 1977, he asked Parsons to come on board. Parsons became a partner in just two years at Patterson, Belknap, Webb & Tyler, a move that typically demanded seven years. In his 11 years with the firm, he made his mark in both corporate law and civil litigation. Among his clients were such high-profile figures as Happy Rockefeller and the cosmetics queen Estee Lauder.

Critical to the next chapter in the Parsons success story was his work with the Dimes Saving Bank of New York, which he provided with legal counsel for about six years while with Patterson, Belknap, Webb & Tyler. Just when he seemed poised to become the first black to head a major law firm, shock waves rippled through the New York corporate world in 1988 when Parsons was appointed chief operating officer of the Dime by chairman and CEO Harry Albright, Jr. Before being offered the position, Parsons had never even considered entering the banking business. As he later told *Black Enterprise*, "My wife talked me into it. She said I needed the change."

Parsons's appointment made him the first black to manage a lending company the size of Dime Savings Bank. "It's a statement by and to corporate America that there are no more areas where African Americans haven't succeeded," he told the *New York Times* in 1990. Some top officials at the bank questioned his appointment, both because of his lack of experience in the banking industry and his previous work in government that made him likely to leave the company for the political arena. Parsons answered these reservations by promising to devote his full attention to his new $525,000-a-year post. Over the years Parsons has, however, admitted the possibility of entering politics later in life. "It's a venue to which I could see myself returning at some point in time," he told the New York Times in 1994, referring to public service as the "highest calling, large and important work."

Parsons began working at Dime during a difficult period. The bank had suffered a series of losses due to the drastic devaluation of New York City real estate in the late 1980s, and during the previous year it had lost $92.3 million. Parsons also had to deal with an onslaught of unhappy regulators. Under his tutelage the bank staged a remarkable comeback, largely through his massive overhauling of the bank's management systems and work force. In just a few years he reduced the Dime's $1 billion in bad debts to $335 million.

During that time he also earned the respect of the staff for his fair treatment. "Colleagues say Parsons' management style helped smooth the painful layoffs that he had to make," wrote Fonda Marie Lloyd and Mark Lowery in Black Enterprise. "They credit him with keeping employees informed every step of the way, at one point even producing several videos that were distributed to employees." When Albright departed the Dime, Parsons became chairman and CEO. With the bank now on solid financial ground, he engineered a merger with Anchor Savings Bank to create Dime Bancorp in early 1995. The merger created the fourth largest thrift institution in the nation and the largest on the East Coast, with assets worth $20 billion.

Politics Differed From Most Blacks

In 1993 Parsons was criticized by other blacks for supporting Rudolph Giuliani in the New York City mayoral race, instead of the incumbent Democrat, black mayor David Dinkins. This political stance was consistent with his rejection of the Democrats' philosophy. According to an article in Black Enterprise, Parsons feels that the Democrats believe in taking from one group to give to another one, while the Rockefeller Republicans espouse a policy of equipping a group with skills so that they can achieve what they need on their own. "You can't give something to somebody to have," said Parsons in the same article. "Then, they don't value it. Value is associated with hard work."

After Giuliani was elected, he named Parsons to be head of his transition council. Peter J. Powers, New York

City's First Deputy Mayor at the time, complemented Parsons's leadership skills in the New York Times, noting that Parsons "really knows how to bring people together and find common ground." Mayor Giuliani later asked Parsons to become his Deputy mayor for Economic Development. Although Parsons refused that position, he consented to work as chairman of the city's Economic Development Corporation.

Admiration for Parsons's skills in the business world resulted in his being courted as a board member for a number of leading companies and institutions, including Time Warner Inc., Philip Morris, Tristar Pictures, Howard University, and the Metropolitan Museum of Art. His involvement with Time Warner resulted in his developing close ties with important company executives such as Robert W. Morgado, the chairman of the Warner Music Group, and Michael J. Fuchs, chairman of HBO. Parsons was asked to become the new president of Time Warner by its chairman, Gerald M. Levin, in the fall of 1994. In the Washington Post, Levin called Parsons "an exceptional business leader with the broad experience, financial acumen and the knowledge of our business that will strengthen and solidify our corporate management."

"Either you go for it, or it's gone forever."

Parsons accepted the presidency for a reported salary of several million dollars a year. The position placed him second in command over the entire Time Warner holdings in magazine and book publishing, music, film entertainment, theme parks, and cable television. Meanwhile, he answered complaints from colleagues at the Dime that he was deserting them. "This opportunity with Time Warner is a once in a lifetime one. It was either you go for it, or it's gone forever," claimed Parsons in Black Enterprise. "It's not a bad time for me to make a move. I know the bank is in good hands."

The Parsons appointment was not without controversy at Time Warner. He was again entering an industry that was new to him, and some doubted his qualifications. Parsons also inherited a number of problems when he assumed his new post in January of 1995. Time Warner's record division was experiencing difficulty, and company officials were suspicious about the designs of Edgar Bronfman of the Seagram Companies, which owned 15 percent of the company's stock. The conglomerate was also saddled with significant debt. Chief among his tasks since joining Time Warner have been the restructuring of the company's financial and administrative operations, as well as evaluating the responsibilities of artists regarding explicit displays of sex and violence.

Role of Race Downplayed

Some considered the Parsons appointment at Time Warner to be a significant achievement for black executives, one that helps pave the way for them to enter the highest positions in business. "There are a number of other black executives who have elevated positions in corporate America," said Parsons in *Black Enterprise.* "The process is rolling forward, even if it isn't moving as fast as some of us would like." Despite his distinction as a high-ranking black in business, Parsons downplays the racial aspects of his success. He has claimed that race was never a "defining character" in his life. "I don't do anything differently than I would otherwise because I have that responsibility to my family," he told the *New York Times* in 1994. "Whether I was an African-American, an Arab-American, a Jewish-American, or some other American, there are a lot of people who I cannot let down, so you have to live your life a certain way to be a role model to the people who are important to you."

Sources

Black Enterprise, October 1994, pp. 68-70, 72, 76, 77; January 1995, p. 15.
Business Week, November 14, 1994, pp. 38, 39.
Ebony, June 1988, pp. 156, 158.
Emerge!, February 1995, p. 69.
New York Times, May 8, 1990, p. D5; August 26, 1990, p. D5; July 7, 1994, p. D4; October 31, 1994, pp. D1, D6.
Wall Street Journal, May 8, 1990, p. B10; January 30, 1995, pp. B1, B3.
Washington Post, November 1, 1994, p. D5.

—Ed Decker

Walter Payton

1954—

Retired professional football player

One of the strongest and most talented men in football, Walter Payton could bench-press 390 pounds, leg-press more than 700 pounds, throw a football 60 yards, punt it 70 yards, kick 45-yard field goals, and walk the width of the field on his hands. It was this phenomenal combination of power and control that allowed Payton to play in every game except one during his 13 years of National Football League (NFL) competition.

Columbia, Mississippi, "a kid's paradise" in his own words. Woods extended from one side of his house to the Pearl River. Several factories were on the other side. Both settings provided numerous opportunities for mischief with his older brother and sister, Eddie and Pamela. Early on, Payton used his natural running ability to avoid being caught by security guards while playing hide and seek at the nearby factories.

Retiring after the 1987 season, Payton left behind 26 Chicago Bears team records and several NFL records. Ten years later, many of his records still stood, including most yards rushing in a career, most combined yards (rushing and receiving) in a career, most career touchdowns rushing, most 1,000-yard rushing seasons, most 100-yard rushing games in career, and most rushes in career. More than these individual achievements, however, his all-around team play--pass catching, blocking, personality, selflessness, and leadership--inspired his former coach Mike Ditka to call him, as quoted by Koslow, "the very best football player I've ever seen, period--at any position."

Walter Jerry Payton was born on July 25, 1954, in

Hyperactive, prankish, and strong-willed, young Walter was often punished by his Baptist parents, Peter and Alyne. Payton later assessed his parents as firm but fair disciplinarians who instilled strong religious faith in their children. "My parents spent a lot of time with us and made us feel loved and wanted. I didn't care much about what went on around me, as long as I was in solid at home," he later recalled to Koslow.

Peter Payton worked at a factory that manufactured packs and parachutes for the U.S. government. By 1962 he had saved enough money to move his family to a new home with separate rooms for each child. It was located just one block from John J. Jefferson High School, the segregated school that all black children attended from grades one through 12. Both parents instilled in their children an ideal of excellence, "never to settle for second best," as Payton later recalled.

Competed in High School

Taking his parents' principles to heart, Payton became a better-than-average student, though music took precedence over studies or sports. He was constantly drumming or tapping out a beat on anything in reach. Often he would dance or sing instead of doing his household chores, much to the dismay of his mother and siblings. "When you've got an angry brother and sister chasing you with a broom and a wet towel, well, you learn some good moves," he told a Football Hall of Fame audience at his 1993 induction.

In the ninth grade, Payton joined the track team as a long jumper and played drums in the school band. He

consciously avoided the football team where his brother, Eddie, was the star running back. Payton later claimed he did not want his mother having to worry about both of her sons being hurt. After Eddie Payton graduated, Jefferson High School's football coach asked Payton to try out for the team. Payton, then a sophomore, agreed only after being allowed to stay in the band as well. On his first high-school carry, he ran 65 yards for a touchdown. It was just a taste of things to come.

The next year, 1969, Jefferson merged with all-white Columbia High School, and Payton became the undisputed star of the newly integrated football team. Tommy Davis, Columbia's football coach, claimed that he could always count on Payton when the team needed to score. Payton's statistics proved that that was no exaggeration: he scored in every game during his junior and senior years. He was named to the all-conference team three years in a row. Payton also led the Little Dixie Conference in scoring his senior year and made the all-state team. In addition to excelling at football, Payton averaged 18 points a game for Columbia's basketball team, leaped three-quarters of an inch short of 23 feet in the long jump, played some baseball, and continued to drum in the school band.

Upon graduating, Payton followed his brother to nearby Jackson State College, soon starting alongside him in the team's backfield. Eddie Payton graduated after Payton's first year at college, however, and joined the NFL, allowing the younger Payton to become the lone star. Payton was the team's halfback, punter, and place kicker, and he even passed on occasional option plays. Playing against other predominantly black schools, he ended his sophomore season as the nation's second leading scorer including the highest single-game total (46 points) in college history. The following year, 1973, he ran for 1,139 yards, led the country in scoring with 160 points, was voted the most valuable player in the conference, and was named to the Black All-America team.

That summer, determined to become even better, Payton embarked on a new training program with his brother. The two Paytons sprinted up and down the sandbanks and steep levees alongside the Pearl River during the hottest part of the day. These workouts did more than just build up leg strength and endurance; the constantly shifting sand helped develop balance and the ability to better make a cut or abruptly change direction. Throughout the rest of his career, Payton would conduct similar workouts in comparable settings.

This grueling conditioning led to a successful senior year, capping his college career by becoming the National

Collegiate Athletic Association (NCAA) all-time leading scorer with 464 points. He was chosen to the Black All-America team again, made the NCAA Division II All-America team, and was named to the College All-Star team. About the only time he finished in second place was during a televised *Soul Train* dance contest. "He still swears that if he'd had a girl who could dance better, he could have won that contest," his coach Bob Hill told *Esquire* years later. Academically, Payton was an all-star as well, graduating in three-and-a-half years with his bachelor's degree in special education and beginning work on a master's degree. He studied so hard, he later wrote in his autobiography *Sweetness*, "to help dispel the myth that athletes in general and black athletes in particular don't have to work to get their diplomas and that they don't learn anything anyway."

Payton also picked up the nickname "Sweetness" during his college years; it would stick with him throughout his career. Some claimed it was because of his sweet moves on the football field. Others attributed it to his sincerity, humble disposition, soft high-pitched voice, and concern for others. Raised a devout Baptist, he always led the team in its pre-game prayer.

The Chicago Bears chose Payton in the first round of the 1975 NFL draft, making him the fourth player picked overall. His pride demanded a signing bonus larger than that received four years earlier by Archie Manning, quarterback from the University of Mississippi, a school formerly closed to blacks. The Bears offered him $126,000, the highest amount ever paid to anyone from Mississippi.

The Bears were one of the NFL's more storied teams, counting many legendary names among their former players--Red Grange, Bronko Nagurski, Sid Luckman, Gale Sayers, and Dick Butkus. But these stars and those glory days were long gone--the franchise had not had a winning season since 1967. Payton's first season, 1975, was no exception. The team lost six of its first seven games. Payton was slowed by an ankle injury, missed the only game in his NFL career, and played sporadically in others. After healing, though, he gave the Chicago fans an inkling of his talent by leading the league in kickoff returns and finishing the season with 679 yards rushing, the most for any Bears runner since 1969.

The following summer, Connie Norwood, his fiancee, graduated from Jackson State. The two were married, and she became a settling influence for his new life in Chicago. That season he became the focal point of the Bears' offense, carrying the ball 311 times, the most in the league, and gaining 1,390 yards. An injury in the season's final game cost him a chance at the league rushing title, though he led the National Football Conference (NFC) in yards gained. His performance helped the Bears finish with seven victories and seven losses, their best season in eight years.

Most Valuable Player

At training camp in 1977, reporters noticed a different Payton. No longer open and seemingly carefree, he was silent, moody, and irritable. Once the season started, the reason became clear--he had been preparing himself for one of the greatest individual seasons in NFL history. Payton gained 160 yards in the season opener. The first 200-yard game in his career came in the seventh week. He ran for 275 yards in the tenth game, to break O. J. Simpson's single-game rushing record. Many speculated he would break Simpson's season rushing record of 2,003 yards as well. He came close, but a freezing rain during the final game turned the field to ice, made footing a nightmare, and limited him to 47 yards.

Payton ended the season with 1,852 yards rushing, leading the NFL in yards gained and carries. The Bears finished 9-5 and qualified for the playoffs for the first time in 14 years. To nobody's surprise, Payton was voted the league's most valuable player, at 23-years old, he was the youngest player to win the honor. Further accolades came from United Press International (UPI) which designated him its Athlete of the Year.

As a national celebrity, fans from across the nation began to recognize Payton by his unique stutter step, running on his toes with short, stiff-legged strides. Though he could run 40 yards in 4.5 seconds, he was never a real breakaway threat, often getting caught from behind. Compact instead of graceful, he preferred running up the middle or off tackle, surprising would-be tacklers with frequent sudden cutbacks and punishing them with a forearm, shoulder, or helmet. No other halfback combined his speed, shiftiness, and brute power.

"I've never seen anybody who's more reluctant to get out of the way of a hit," his former coach Mike Ditka recalled in *Esquire*. "He really does look to punish the guy tackling him." No matter how hard he was tackled, Payton always would spring to his feet immediately and return to the huddle. He enjoyed blocking for other running backs or protecting his quarterback against blitzing linebackers seemingly as much as he loved running the ball. "That's what sets him head and shoulders above other running backs," Gale Sayers--also a running back--commented in *Esquire,* "the maximum effort he puts into the other phases of the game." After scoring a touchdown Payton would hand the football to one of the Bears offensive linemen who blocked for him, explaining in Koslow's biography, *Walter Payton,* that "they're the ones who do all the work."

Superstar

Before the 1978 season began, Payton signed contracts for the next three seasons reflecting his superstar status--$400,000 for 1978, $425,000 for 1979, and $450,000 plus incentive bonuses for 1980. Clearly the Bears were expecting big things from him and better days ahead for the team. But under new coach Neill Armstrong they slipped to 7-9 despite Payton's 1,395 yards, most in the NFC, and 50 pass receptions. Together with fullback Roland Harper's 992 yards, the two runners accounted for 72 percent of the Bears' offense.

The following year Payton played with a painful pinched nerve in his shoulder but still amassed 1,610 yards, again leading the NFC. The Bears finished 10-6 to make the playoffs, but they were eliminated in the first round. He gained 1,460 yards in 1980 for an unprecedented fifth consecutive NFC rushing title, but the Bears fell to 7-9. The team continued its mediocre play the next year, finishing 6-10, and Payton, injured most of the season with cracked ribs and a sore shoulder, slipped to 1,222 yards, failing to win the NFC rushing title or make the Pro Bowl. Even so, he became the first player in NFL history to run for 1,000 yards six years in a row.

The Bears realized his value, too, signing him to a three-year contract worth $2 million. They also hired Mike Ditka as the new head coach to shake things up. The 1982 season was crippled by a player strike, however, and the Bears finished 3-6. The next season, with Jim McMahon installed at quarterback, they finished 8-8. Payton ran for 1,421 yards and caught 53 passes for 607 yards, personally accounting for 36 percent of the Bears' total yardage. After the season he had arthroscopic surgery on both knees and renegotiated his contract to receive $240,000 a year for life, making him the highest-paid player in NFL history.

What Payton really wanted was to play for a Super Bowl champion. The 1984 Bears, much to Payton's liking, showed promise for becoming such a team. Their defense was strong and the offensive line was able to open big holes for Payton and the other running backs while effectively blocking for quarterback McMahon. Though the team finished 10-6, the big story was Payton breaking Jim Brown's 19-year NFL career rushing record of 12,312 yards on October 7. He finished the season with 1,684 yards and caught 45 passes to set a new Bears career receiving record.

In the divisional playoff game against the Washington Redskins, Payton ran for 104 yards, threw a 19-yard touchdown pass, and blocked with such ferocity that he knocked a defensive back out of the game. The Bears defeated Washington by a score of 23-19, but they were shut out by the San Francisco 49ers in the NFC title game the following week. Despite his 92 yards rushing and three pass receptions, Payton was despondent, calling it "the hardest thing I ever had to deal with."

Super Bowl Champion

Revenge would come the next year when no team could stand in the Bears' way. Running up a 15-1 record with a devastating defense and powerful offense, the Bears blasted through the regular season, strutting their superiority with an arrogant attitude and a music video entitled "The Super Bowl Shuffle." Payton, with 1,551 yards rushing, was his usual paragon.

> "My parents spent a lot of time with us and made us feel loved and wanted. I didn't care much about what went on around me, as long as I was in solid at home."

Chicago won its two playoff games at home to earn the right to play the New England Patriots in Super Bowl XX. Like most of the Bears' regular season games, the result was never in doubt. Chicago crushed New England by a score of 46-10. Payton had his Super Bowl ring, but he seemed unhappy and moody in the locker room. Reporters speculated that he was upset because he had not scored a touchdown. They underestimated his competitive nature. "It wasn't the touchdown," he told *Esquire* months later. "The game was dull."

The 1986 Bears showed every sign of repeating as champions. They finished 14-2, while Payton displayed his usual form with 1,333 yards rushing and 37 pass receptions. The team stumbled in the playoffs, however, losing to Washington by a score of 27-13. The next season was marred by another player strike. Though the Bears and Payton played well enough to win 11 of their 15 games, they again lost to Washington in the playoffs. Payton was 33-years old, and the Bears had started to split his playing time with talented newcomer Neal Anderson. After 13 years, he decided it was time to retire while still on top of his game, leaving behind 26 Chicago Bears team records and several NFL records: most rushes (3,838); most yards rushing (16,726); most combined (running and receiving) yards (21,736); most rushing touchdowns (110); most 1,000-yard seasons (10); and most 100-yard games (77) of any running back in history. Former teammate Dan Hampton accurately summed up Payton's career: "No one on this football team and no one in the NFL is actually in Walter Payton's league."

Never one to remain physically idle, he began racing cars and boats while turning his financial attention full time to Walter Payton Inc., his personal company holding investments in real estate, timberland, and restaurants. For many years, he has been working to become the first African American to own an NFL franchise. He also has devoted a great deal of time to various charities in the Chicago area and is on the Chicago Bears' board of directors. On July 31, 1993, he was inducted into the Football Hall of Fame. His son,

Jarrett, made the presentation, telling the assembled crowd: "Not only is my dad an exceptional athlete ... he's my biggest role model and best friend. We do a lot of things together ... I'm sure my sister will endorse this statement: we have a super dad."

Sources

Books

Koslow, Philip, *Walter Payton,* Chelsea House, 1995.
Payton, Walter, with Jenkins, Jerry B., *Sweetness,* Contemporary Books, 1978.

Periodicals

Chicago Tribune, September 2, 1979.
Esquire, October 1986, p. 91-97.
Jet, September 5, 1994, p. 48.
New York Times, January 4, 1985, p. 21.
Newsweek, December 5, 1977, p. 63.
Sport, December 1977 p. 57.
Sporting News, October 1, 1984, p. 2.
Sports Illustrated, August 16, 1982, p. 18.

—James J. Podesta

Calvin Peete

1943—

Professional golfer

Despite his deformed left arm and his not playing golf until he was in his mid-20s, Calvin Peete rose to a prominent position in professional golf ranks in the 1980s. He established a reputation for being able to hit the ball straighter than any other player on the PGA Tour, and he has been admired by peers and fans alike for his consistent, error-free play. Peete's golfing ability is entirely self-made; he has never received a single golf lesson.

Peete is also one of the few black golfers who never caddied before turning professional. "I've always been fascinated about being able to control the golf ball," Peete told *Esquire*. "I'm only going to hit the ball so far. I only have so much physical ability, and what I have to do is learn to play within that ability, and just play my game." Peete's "game" became extremely consistent during his peak years from 1982 through 1986, when he placed high on the earnings list and won 11 PGA tournaments.

Born in Detroit, Peete moved in with his grandmother in Missouri at age 11 after his parents were divorced. While living there he fell out of a tree and broke his left elbow in three places, giving him a permanently im-

paired left arm that had little mobility. He moved to Florida to rejoin his father's new family at age 13, becoming the oldest of his father's second crop of 10 children.

With money scarce, Peete was forced to quit school and help support the family by working in the cornfields with his father. While Dennis Peete picked ears of corn off stalks, son Calvin made crates for the corn for a penny apiece. Peete and his partner put together 6,000 to 7,000 crates a day. This heavy responsibility at an early age established a strong work ethic in Peete that would later serve him well as a golfer. As legendary golfer Jack Nicklaus once said, according to *Esquire,* "Calvin has a tremendous talent for hard work."

When the United States restricted Cuban imports following Fidel Castro's takeover of that country in 1960, numerous workers from Caribbean islands came to the United States to help cut sugarcane now being grown there. Peete was intrigued by the influx of men who would sell various products to these workers out of the backs of their station wagons, and figured that he could make good money doing the same. He secured a

At a Glance . . .

Born July 18, 1943, in Detroit, MI; son of Dennis (an automobile plant worker and farmer) and Irenia Bridgeford Peete; married Christine Peete, 1974 (divorced, 1988); remarried, 1992; children (first marriage): Charlotte, Calvin, Rickie, Dennis, Kalvanetta.

Worked as farm laborer, Florida, 1957-60; sold goods to migrant workers, East coast, 1961-71; played first game of golf at age 23, Rochester, NY; managed apartments, Fort Lauderdale, FL, late 1960s; became professional golfer, 1971; qualified for Professional Golfers Association (PGA) tour, 1975; became second black professional golfer to earn over $100,000 in one year, 1978; won first PGA tournament (Greater Milwaukee Open), 1979; won 12 tournaments on PGA tour during career, including the Anheuser-Busch Classic, 1982, Georgia-Pacific Atlantic Classic, 1983, Texas Open, 1984, Phoenix Open and Tournament Players Championship, both 1985, and MONY Tournament of Champions, 1986; finished third in PGA Tour earnings once and fourth twice, 1982-85; formed Calvin Peete Enterprises; founded Calvin Peete National Minority Golf Foundation, 1989; conducted golf clinics for children, early 1990s; joined PGA Seniors tour, 1993.

Awards: "Most Improved Player" Award, *Golf Digest*; led PGA in driving accuracy and greens in regulation strokes, 1982 and 1983; member, U.S. Ryder Cup team, 1983; honorary degree, Wayne State University, 1983; Ben Hogan Award, Golf Writers Association, 1983; Jackie Robinson Award, 1983; two-time winner of Vardon Trophy (for lowest scoring average per round); named to *Golf* magazine's All-American team; Black Achievement Award, *Ebony*.

Addresses: *Home*—North Fort Myers, Florida. *Office*—Calvin Peete Enterprises, 2050 Collier Avenue, Fort Myers, FL 33901.

peddler's license while still in his teens, then started buying products such as clothing and jewelry wholesale in Miami, and selling them to field hands at a profit.

For most of the 1960s, Peete followed the harvest as it traveled north, driving and selling as far away as upstate New York. While staying in Rochester, New York, in 1965, he was enticed into playing golf by friends who told him they were taking him to a clambake. He had always considered golf to be "a silly game," as he told *Esquire*, but his interest was sparked after he managed to par a hole during his first outing. That same day he found a driving range and drove hundreds of balls to try to improve his swing. "I knew at that time that it had to be some power shapin' my way, because I had the bug," he said in *Esquire*. He also became attracted by the financial lure of professional golf. "Just about that same time I saw a tournament on television and learned Jack Nicklaus was making around $200,000 a year chasing that ball," he was quoted as saying in *Ebony*. "I figured I could be happy making about one-third of that amount--so I decided to give it a try."

Major Asset in Controled Swing

Since his deformed left arm and smaller-than-average size--5'10", 165 pounds--prevented him from generating a lot of club speed, Peete compensated by perfecting his control. Typically he practiced alone, going to courses early or late in the day when other players were not there. He played as much as he could, and even took a new job as an apartment manager in Fort Lauderdale, Florida, so that he would have more time for golf. Right from the beginning, Peete felt that all it took to master the game was hard work. "I don't feel that there was any talent there," he told *Esquire*. "I feel that it's something any person could do."

Golf became Peete's obsession, compelling him to find ranges with floodlights so that he could practice after dark. Sometimes he got up in the middle of the night to go out and practice because he had suddenly thought of a problem with his stroke that needed work. Within six months after playing his first round, Peete broke 80 and set his sights on turning professional. While it would seem that his left arm's deformity, which prevented Peete from straightening it out, was a hindrance, some of Peete's fellow golfers maintained that it actually helped him hit a straighter shot because the arm could only be moved in certain ways.

After he became a pro golfer in 1971, it took Peete four more years to be accepted in the professional tour's qualifying school. He finally made the PGA tour at age 32, an incredibly late start for a professional career. For the first few years on the tour, Peete barely made ends meet. He also found it difficult to fraternize with the other pros, who tended to be much more educated than he was. Peete maintained a low profile on the tour, usually staying in his hotel room at night or socializing with the group of caddies.

Peete finished 94th on the Tour in 1976, earning $22,966, then slipped to 105th the next year. However, in 1978 he managed a fifth-place finish at the New Orleans Open. He also set a course record at the Greater Milwaukee Open, shooting a 19-under-par round. That year Peete earned more than $100,000, becoming only the second black golfer to pass that mark.

> "Jack Nicklaus was making around $200,000 a year chasing that ball....I figured I could be happy making about one-third of that amount—so I decided to give it a try."

In his first tournaments, Peete's perfectionist attitude sometimes got the better of him. He dropped out of tournaments after shooting especially bad rounds, angering tour officials. Helping him to maintain his cool was his wife, Christine, who often joined him on tour. When Peete needed to earn his high school equivalency degree in order to qualify for the U.S. Ryder Cup team in the early 1980s, his wife served as his tutor on the road.

Peaked After Age 40

After finishing 43rd on the PGA earnings list in 1981, Peete really found his stride in 1982, when he won the Greater Milwaukee Open. "After I'd won my first tournament, that's when I felt relaxed, and I felt that I belonged," he told *Esquire*. As he entered the 1980s, Peete became known for his steady on-target play. According to Chris Smith in *Golf* magazine, "throughout most of the 1980s, Peete was the most accurate player on Tour, hitting more fairways and greens than anyone." In the 1980s Peete started up Calvin Peete Enterprises and became active in a variety of business interests around the country. Despite his fame, he continued to shun the limelight and often didn't stay in hotels where the other pros did. He would remain his room when not playing, thinking about his next round and watching television, with the phone off the hook.

A chronically weak disk in Peete's back began to take its toll in the late 1980s, sending his career spiraling downward. After he was forced to quit playing after the first round of the PGA Championship in 1986, he took six months off. Although he finished 12th on the PGA earnings list that year, Peete's position plummeted to 140th in 1987 and 87th in 1988. He finished in the money in just seven of 24 tournaments in 1990, two of 11 in 1991, and none of the seven tournaments he entered in 1992. He was later diagnosed with a torn rotator cuff in his shoulder, which forced him to drop out of the 1992 Player's Championship.

National Minority Golf Foundation

Peete has always lamented the lack of black players on the PGA tour, and has maintained an active presence in trying to help minority groups get involved in golf. In 1989 he set up the Calvin Peete National Minority Golf Foundation and began holding 12 to 15 golf clinics a year for disadvantaged youths. However, lack of funding forced the Foundation to cease operation in 1992.

Despite the obvious physical problems hampering his game in the early 1990s, Peete felt at the time that his game had been hurt most by his mental framework. He began receiving guidance from John Newman, a minister in Jacksonville, Florida, to help gain more mental control over his body. Convinced that his game was getting back on track, Peete joined the Senior PGA Tour in 1993.

Although his high ranking on the PGA Tour was relatively short, Peete made the most of a career that started a decade later than those of most other pros. Peete had earned a significant $2,204,421 through 1992, and few professionals have matched his work ethic or the consistency he achieved during his peak years. As he told *Golf* magazine, "I've had a great life. I've had a successful career and I've been able to give of myself to the kids through my foundation."

Sources

Books

Ashe, Arthur, *A Hard Road to Glory: A History of the African-American Athlete Since 1946,* Volume 3, Amistad, 1988, pp. 138-141.

Periodicals

Black Enterprise, July 1983, pp. 13, 70; September 1994, pp. 68-81.

Ebony, January 1983, p. 44.

Esquire, February 1987, pp. 108-115.

Golf, July 1983, p. 58.

Jet, April 25, 1988, p. 49; August 21, 1989, p. 56; February 18, 1991, p. 48; September 14, 1992, p. 48.

New York Times, May 14, 1990, pp. C1. C5.

Sports Illustrated, February 18, 1991, p. 9.

—Ed Decker

Bill Pickett

1870–1932

Rodeo cowboy

Few entertainers have equalled the legendary Bill Pickett for bravery, showmanship, or physical prowess. A member of the National Cowboy Hall of Fame, Pickett spent most of his life touring in Wild West shows, "bull-dogging" steers and performing other rodeo stunts in front of huge audiences in the United States, Canada, and Europe. The height of his fame came at a time when few blacks performed in show business, but Pickett never disguised his race or played the buffoon. Instead he earned immense respect and a good degree of awe for his ability to pursue longhorn steers and wrestle them to the ground--sometimes without using his hands. In his book *Guts: Legendary Black Rodeo Cowboy Bill Pickett,* Cecil Johnson called Pickett "a genuine American hero, a man of courage and dignity, who did some incredible things that all Americans, white, black, and otherwise, should know about."

Some historians estimate that one in every four cowboys in the American West was of African origin. Black men were often given the job of driving cattle as plantation slaves. Indeed, some of the cattle ranching practices used in America had their origins in the ranching traditions of African peoples. After the Emancipation Proclamation, good black cowboys could always find work breaking horses, driving cattle to market, branding stock, and patrolling the huge ranches in Texas and Oklahoma. The work was extremely dangerous, rigorous, dirty, and sometimes lonely, but it provided a good living and was far less tedious and confining than a job in a factory or a cotton field.

Cowboys tended to train their sons to the profession, but Bill Pickett seems to have picked up cowboy ways in partnership with his brothers. He was born in Travis County, Texas, about 30 miles northwest of Austin, in 1870 and was the second oldest in a family of 13 children. His father, Thomas Jefferson Pickett, was a former slave, and his mother, Mary Pickett, was part Cherokee Indian. When Bill was still a baby, his family moved to Austin. There he attended public school through the fifth grade--an accomplishment in a time when schooling was poor, especially for blacks. Even as a youngster Pickett began to earn pocket change working odd jobs at the ranches surrounding Austin. By the time he was 18, and the family moved again to smaller Taylor, Texas, he was able to help support his siblings with his earnings as a ranch hand.

Invented "Bulldogging"

In the late 1880s, five of the Pickett brothers joined forces and opened their own stock business in Taylor. Their principal job was breaking wild horses, an extremely tricky occupation that required patience, strength, and a sophisticated knowledge of animal psychology. Some horses would fight for days before allowing a rider to stay on their backs, and the Pickett brothers were always in danger of being kicked, bitten, or bucked off. Nevertheless, the brothers became known for their abilities--and they had a reputation for not mistreating the animals.

Perhaps as a result of his bronco-busting activities--or perhaps from some infection he caught--Bill Pickett one day awoke to find himself completely blind. By that time he had married and was responsible for several young children. The ailment persisted for a year, proving very trying for the family, and then it disappeared as suddenly as it had come. The lasting effect of the blindness, for Pickett, was a fatalistic attitude he expressed as "What's gonna happen, gonna happen." What happened to Bill Pickett is the stuff of legend.

No one knows when Pickett bulldogged his first steer, but he is universally recognized as the originator of the sport. As a boy he spent much time on ranches observing the relationship between cattle and the bulldogs used to control them. Pickett noticed that dogs weighing less than fifty pounds could bring half-ton steers to their knees by biting the steers' lips and holding on. One day, in pursuit of a wayward cow, Pickett threw himself onto the animal's neck, grabbed it by the horns, twisted its face upwards, and took hold of its upper lip just as the dogs had. The ploy worked, and soon the cow was lying on its side in complete submission. Pickett called his maneuver "bulldogging."

At first Pickett put bulldogging to use only to control animals that were being herded or shipped in rail cars to the slaughterhouses. Another idea occurred to him when he saw how people stared at his accomplishment. Beginning around the turn of the century, he began to put on bulldogging exhibitions at county fairs and with small rodeo companies, and soon he made a name for himself not as a ranch hand or bronc buster but as an entertainer.

One of Pickett's first rodeo managers was a rancher named Lee Moore. Moore was the first to take Pickett's demonstration out of Texas into neighboring states such as Kansas and Oklahoma. Everywhere Pickett went he caused a sensation. In 1903 Pickett signed on with another manager, Doug McClure, who liked to give his performers nicknames. Thus, in McClure's promotional materials, Pickett became "The Dusky Demon," a tag that, according to Cecil Johnson, "suggested that Pickett possessed some kind of supernatural powers that enabled him to cast a spell on the steers. The demon characterization also may have served to explain to the spectators the apparent disproportion between Pickett's physical stature and the sizes of the animals he handled with such dexterity." Pickett was a mere five-foot-seven and weighed about 145 pounds. Many of the animals he bulldogged topped out at 1,000 to 1,200 pounds.

In 1905 Pickett's friend Will Rogers introduced the "Dusky Demon" to Zack Miller, co-owner of the magnificent 101 Ranch in Bliss, Oklahoma. Miller was looking for talent to fill the roster of a new Wild West show he was planning, and he had heard about Pickett from another Miller brother who had seen Pickett's bulldogging act. Miller persuaded Pickett to come to the 101 Ranch and join its show as a featured performer. The offer was sweetened by the promise of a full-time job on the ranch during the off-season.

Thus began one of the longest and most fruitful partnerships in the history of Wild West shows. Pickett, still known as the "Dusky Demon," became one of the featured acts in the Miller Brothers 101 Ranch Real Wild West Show. The show itself was a spectacular affair, at various times employing as many as 1,100 people and more than 600 animals--everything from the mundane to the exotic--as well as Sioux and Snake Indians, a troupe of Russian Imperial Cossacs, and rodeo riders and ropers. For the first few years with the 101 Ranch show, Pickett bulldogged longhorn steers with his teeth as he had in his early days. When various humane societies cited him for cruelty to animals, he modified his act into the sort of cattle wrestling seen in rodeos today--only the steers he wrestled were by some estimates twice the size.

Pickett's fame took a quantum leap on December 23, 1908 in Mexico City, Mexico. Having traveled south with the 101 Ranch show--and having performed his bulldogging for Mexican audiences--Pickett became the center of an avalanche of negative publicity. Mexicans who held their sport of bullfighting in high esteem were shocked to see a black man jump from his horse and wrestle steers to the ground using little more than his teeth. The Mexican press printed remarks by Zack Miller to the effect that no bullfighter was as tough as Pickett, that Pickett could probably ride one of the meanest Mexican bulls, or throw two steers in the time it would take the best bullfighter to throw just one.

A challenge was levelled: Mexico's leading bullfighters wagered 5,000 pesos that Pickett could not stay on the back of one of their fighting bulls for five minutes. Pickett accepted the challenge, and a crowd of more than 25,000 hostile Mexicans crowded into the city's new bullring to watch him. Pickett was used to hearing cheers and applause for his labors. This crowd wanted him to be killed and booed him lustily. His pride hurt, the cowboy proceeded to accomplish the feat at great peril to his own life and at the cost of having his favorite horse gored. In the end, Pickett stayed on the bull five minutes but was injured by bricks and bottles thrown by the crowd. He suffered several broken ribs and narrowly missed being trampled by the animal after his injuries led him to lose his grip on its horns. Nevertheless, his victory was apparent even to the hostile crowd, and in the United States the event made headlines everywhere.

New Horizons for the Show

Between 1910 and 1914 Pickett performed almost continuously with the 101 Ranch show, appearing in arenas such as Madison Square Garden in New York, Boston Garden, and the Chicago Coliseum. At various times he shared billing with the likes of Will Rogers and Tom Mix, both of whom would go on to fame in motion

pictures. As far as the Wild West show went, however, Pickett was the bigger star. Because the show was so large that it needed its own train, he rarely encountered the kind of racism that other black performers faced at the turn of the century: he had first-class accommodations on Miller's train and was admitted to hotels with the rest of the company. When racist members of audiences turned on him occasionally, he would quickly be surrounded by fellow cowboys of both races who called him a comrade.

Nowhere was Pickett treated better than in Europe. The 101 Ranch Real Wild West Show made a journey abroad in 1914, performing in England before some members of the royal family. Pickett's performance was so impressive that he found himself invited to white-tie dinners in some of the country's biggest mansions. The natives of Paris were equally enthralled. Unfortunately, the onset of World War I sent the show back to America prematurely, and all of its animals were requisitioned by the British government.

> "Many insist that [Pickett] was without debate the greatest all-around work and show business cowboy ever to straddle a horse."

The onset of vaudeville and motion pictures robbed the Wild West shows of bigger audiences, and after a brief appearance in Buffalo Bill's Wild West Show in 1917, Pickett restricted his cattle wrestling to rodeos. By the time Pickett switched from exhibition bulldogging to competition bulldogging, he had many younger imitators, such as Milt Hinkle, who often rode off with the prize money at the rodeos. As for Pickett, he made two short film documentaries, *The Bulldogger* in 1923 and *The Crimson Skull* in 1924. A copy of *The Bulldogger* has made the records at the Library of Congress, and it provides fine footage of Pickett performing his specialty as well as roping and riding.

Between 1920 and 1924 Pickett spent more time working on ranches than performing in rodeos and exhibitions. In 1924, at the age of 55, he was named to the cast of a revived Miller Brothers Wild West Show that was expensively mounted but failed to turn a profit. When the show folded, Pickett returned to his home near the 101 Ranch in Ponca City, Oklahoma, and resumed his duties as a ranch hand for the Miller

Brothers.

"What's Gonna Happen, Gonna Happen"

As Bill Pickett entered his sixties, he was remarkably spry and healthy, considering his long years as a bulldogger. He lived long enough to see his beloved 101 Ranch fall into foreclosure, and it was that event that hastened his own end. On the day that the ranch was put up for auction, Pickett was sent with a few other ranch hands to separate the few horses Zack Miller could keep from a larger herd that would be sold. In the process of completing this task, the 62-year-old Pickett was kicked in the head by a half-wild sorrel. He was rushed to the hospital in Ponca City, but he never regained consciousness. After lying in a coma for eight days, he died on April 2, 1932. He was buried just outside the boundaries of the 101 Ranch in a cemetery that also holds the remains of the great Ponca chief White Eagle.

Had Bill Pickett been a white man, he would have been inducted into the National Cowboy Hall of Fame early in its existence. Most rodeo historians agree that no single performer contributed more to the complicated series of rodeo events than did Pickett with his bulldogging techniques. As it was, Pickett was finally named to the Hall in 1971, almost 40 years after his death.

Another tribute in 1993 brought its own share of controversy. Pickett was chosen to grace a 29-cent postage stamp in the much-heralded "Legends of the West" issue. However, when the stamps were released, scholars noticed that the picture of Pickett was not *Bill* Pickett, but rather his brother Ben. The entire run of stamps was recalled, but not before a few had been sold. This caused an enormous controversy among stamp collectors, who clamored for the original issue. In the end, a limited number of sheets with the picture of Ben Pickett were sold to satisfy collectors. The rest, with the real Bill Pickett pictured, came on the market a few weeks later. If Bill Pickett had been all but forgotten as a turn-of-the-century cowboy, he became legendary once again as the featured face on an incorrect postage stamp.

Pickett's legacy has outlived any racist attempts to sabotage it, and today he is widely recognized as one of the finest cowboys in the history of the American West. As Johnson put it, "Many insist that [Pickett] was without debate the greatest all-around work and show business cowboy ever to straddle a horse.... He was the quintessence of the American cowboy."

Sources

Dunham, Phillip, and Everett L. Jones, *The Negro Cowboys,* Dodd, Mead, 1956.

Goss, Clay, *Bill Pickett: Black Bulldogger,* Hill & Wang, 1970.

Hanes, Colonel Bailey, *Bill Pickett: Bulldogger,* University of Oklahoma Press, 1977.

Johnson, Cecil, *Guts: Legendary Black Rodeo Cowboy Bill Pickett,* Summit Group, 1994.

Jordan, Terry G., *North American Cattle-Ranching Frontiers: Origins, Diffusion, and Differentiation,* University of New Mexico Press, 1993, pp. 119, 213.

Porter, Willard H., *Who's Who in Rodeo,* Powder River Book Co., pp. 96-97.

Weston, Jack L., The Real American Cowboy, New Amsterdam Books, 1985.

—Mark Kram

Sidney Poitier

1927-

Actor, director

At a 1992 banquet sponsored by the august American Film Institute (AFI), a bevy of actors, filmmakers, and others gathered to pay tribute to Sidney Poitier. Superstar Denzel Washington called the veteran actor and director "a source of pride for many African Americans," the *Los Angeles Times* reported, while acting luminary James Earl Jones ventured that his colleague had "played a great role in the life of our country." Poitier himself was typically humble in the face of such praise, but he has acknowledged that his presence on film screens in the 1950s and 1960s did much to open up larger and more nuanced roles for black performers. "I was selected almost by history itself," he averred to Susan Ellicott of the London *Times*.

After gracing dozens of films with his dignified, passionately intelligent presence, Poitier began to focus increasingly on directing; a constant in his life, however, has been his work on behalf of charitable causes. And he has continued to voice the need for film projects that, as he expressed it to *Los Angeles Times* writer Charles Champlin, "have a commonality with the universal human condition."

Born in Miami, Florida, but raised in the Bahamas, Poitier experienced severe poverty as a boy. His father, a tomato farmer, "was the poorest man in the village," the actor recalled in an interview with Frank Spotnitz for *American Film.* "My father was never a man of self-pity," he continued, adding that the elder Poitier "had a wonderful sense of himself. Every time I took a part, from the first part, from the first day, I always said to myself, `This must reflect well on his name.'" The family moved from the tiny village of Cat Island to Nassau, the Bahamian capital, when Poitier was 11 years old, and it was there that he first experienced the magic of cinema.

After watching rapt as a western drama transpired on the screen, Poitier recollected gleefully to Chris Dafoe of the *Los Angeles Times,* he ran to the back of the theater to watch the cowboys and their horses come out. After watching the feature a second time, he again went out to wait for the figures from the screen to emerge. "And when I told my friends what had happened, they laughed and they laughed and they said to me, `Everything you saw was on film.' And they explained to me what film was. And I said, `Go on.'"

Thrown Out of First Audition

Poitier made his way to New York at age 16, serving for a short time in the Army. He has often told the story of his earliest foray into acting, elaborating on different strands of the tale from one recitation to the next. He was a teenager, working as a dishwasher in a New York restaurant. "I didn't study in high school," he told *American Film*'s Spotnitz. "I never got that far. I had no intentions of becoming an actor." Seeing an ad for actors in the *Amsterdam News,* a Harlem-based newspaper, he went to an audition at the American Negro Theater. "I walked in and there was a man there—big strapping guy. He gave me a script."

The man was Frederick O'Neal, a cofounder of the theater; impatient with young Poitier's Caribbean accent and shaky reading skills, O'Neal lost his temper: "He came up on the stage, furious, and grabbed me by the scruff of my pants and my collar and marched me toward the door," the actor remembered to *Los Angeles Times* writer Champlin. "Just before he threw me out he said, 'Stop wasting people's time! Why don't you get yourself a job as a dishwasher.'" Stunned that O'Neal could perceive his lowly status, Poitier knew he had to prove his antagonist wrong. "I have, and had, a terrible fierce pride," Poitier told the audience at the American Film Institute fête, as reported by *Daily Variety.* "I determined right then I was going to be an actor."

Poitier continued in his dishwashing job; in his spare time he listened assiduously to radio broadcasts, he noted to Champlin, "trying to lighten the broad A that characterizes West Indian speech patterns." He had some help in one aspect of his informal education, however: *Daily Variety* quoted his speech at the AFI banquet, in which he thanked "an elderly Jewish waiter in New York who took the time to teach a young black dishwasher how to read, persisting over many months." Ultimately, Poitier returned to the American Negro Theater, persuading its directors to hire him as a janitor in exchange for acting lessons.

Poitier understudied for actor-singer Harry Belafonte in a play called *Days of Our Youth,* and an appearance one night led to a small role in a production of the Greek comedy *Lysistrata.* Poitier, uncontrollably nervous on the latter play's opening night, delivered the wrong lines and ran off the stage; yet his brief appearance so delighted critics, most of whom otherwise hated the production, that he ended up getting more work. "I set out after that to dimensionalize my understanding of my craft," he told Champlin.

Poitier made his film debut in the 1950 feature *No Way Out,* portraying a doctor tormented by the racist brother of a man whose life he couldn't save. Director Joseph Mankiewicz had identified Poitier's potential, and the film bore out the filmmaker's instincts. Poitier worked steadily throughout the 1950s, notably in the South African tale *Cry, the Beloved Country,* the classroom drama *The Blackboard Jungle,* and the taut *The Defiant Ones,* in which Poitier and Tony Curtis played prison escapees manacled together; their mutual struggle helps them look past racism and learn to respect each other. Poitier also appeared in the film version of George Gershwin's modern opera *Porgynd Bess.*

First Black Actor to Win Academy Award

It was in the 1960s, however—with the civil rights movement spearheaded by Dr. Martin Luther King, Jr., and others gathering momentum—that Poitier began to make his biggest mark on American popular culture. After appearing in the film adaptation of Lorraine Hansberry's play *A Raisin in the Sun,* in a role he'd developed on the stage, he took the part of an American serviceman in Germany in the 1963 production *Lilies of the Field.* This role earned him a best actor statuette at the Academy Awards, making him the first black actor to earn this honor.

"Most of my career unfolded in the 1960s, which was one of the periods in American history with certain attitudes toward minorities that stayed in vogue," Poitier reflected to Ellicott of the London *Times.* "I didn't understand the elements swirling around. I was a young actor with some talent, an enormous curiosity, a certain kind of appeal. You wrap all that together and you have a potent mix."

The mix was more potent than might have been anticipated, in fact; by 1967 Poitier was helping to break down filmic barriers that hitherto had seemed impenetrable. In *To Sir, With Love* Poitier played a charismatic schoolteacher, while In *the Heat of the Night* saw him portray Virgil Tibbs, a black detective from the North who helps solve a murder in a sleepy southern town and wins the grudging respect of the racist police chief there. Responding to the derisive labels flung at him, Poitier's character glowers, "They call me *Mister Tibbs.*" The film's volatile mixture of suspense and racial politics eventually spawned two sequels starring Poitier and a television series (Poitier did not appear in the small screen version).

Even more stunning, Poitier wooed a white woman in the comedy *Guess Who's Coming to Dinner*; his fiancée's parents were played by screen legends Spencer Tracy and Katherine Hepburn. The film was considered a watershed because it was Hollywood's first interracial love story that didn't end tragically. Poitier's compelling

presence—articulate, compassionate, soft-spoken, yet demanding respect from even the most hostile—helped make this possible. Reflecting on the anti-racist agenda of filmmakers during this period, Poitier remarked to Ellicott, "I suited their need. I was clearly intelligent. I was a pretty good actor. I believed in brotherhood, in a free society. I hated racism, segregation. And I was a symbol against those things."

Key Activist for Civil Rights

Of course, Poitier was more than a symbol. At the AFI banquet, reported David J. Fox in the *Los Angeles Times,* James Earl Jones praised his friend's work on behalf of the civil right struggle, declaring, "He marched on Montgomery [Alabama] and Memphis [Tennessee] with Dr. Martin Luther King, Jr., who said of Sidney: 'He's a man who never lost his concern for the least of God's children.'" Indeed, Rosa Parks, who in 1955 touched off a crucial battle for desegregation simply by refusing to sit in the "negro" section of a Montgomery bus, attended the tribute and lauded Poitier as "a great actor and role model."

> After watching rapt as a western drama transpired on the screen, he ran to the back of the theater to watch the cowboys and their horses come out.

In 1972 Poitier took a co-starring role with Belafonte in the revisionist western *Buck and the Preacher* for Columbia Pictures. After a falling out with the director of the picture, Poitier took over; though he and Belafonte urged Columbia to hire another director, a studio representative saw footage Poitier had shot and encouraged him to finish the film himself. "And that's how I became a director," he told *Los Angeles Times* contributor Champlin.

Poitier is best known for helming comedic features co-starring his friend comedian Bill Cosby; in addition to the trilogy of caper comedies of the 1970s—*Uptown Saturday Night, Let's Do It Again,* and *A Piece of the Action*—they collaborated on the ill-fated 1990 fantasy-comedy *Ghost Dad,* which was poorly received by both critics and moviegoers. Poitier also directed the hit 1980 comedy *Stir Crazy,* which starred Richard Pryor and Gene Wilder, as well as several other features.

Poitier took only a handful of film roles in the 1980s, but in 1991 he played Supreme Court justice Thurgood Marshall in the television film *Separate but Equal.* James Earl Jones described the performance as "a landmark actor portraying a landmark figure, in one of the landmark moments of our history." And in 1992 he returned to the big screen for the espionage comedy-drama *Sneakers,* which co-starred Robert Redford, River Phoenix, and Dan Aykroyd. "It was a wonderful, breezy opportunity to play nothing heavy," he noted to Bary Koltnow of the *Orange County Register.* "It was simple, and I didn't have to carry the weight. I haven't done that in a while, and it was refreshing."

That year also saw the gala AFI tribute to Poitier, during which the actor welcomed young filmmakers into the fold and enjoined them to "be true to yourselves and be useful to the journey," reported *Daily Variety.* "I fully expected to be wise by now," Poitier noted in his speech, "but I've come to this place in my life armed only with the knowledge of how little I know. I enter my golden years with nothing profound to say and no advice to leave, but I thank you for paying me this great honor while I still have hair, and my stomach still has not obscured my view of my shoetops."

Poitier observed to Champlin that during this "golden age" the demands of art had taken a back seat to domestic concerns to a large degree. "It's very important, but it's not the nerve center," he insisted. "There is the family, and there is music and there is literature" as well as political issues. Poitier noted that he and his wife, actress Joanna Shimkus, travel a great deal since they reside in California and have children in New York, and, as the actor put it, "I live in the world."

Poitier returned to the small screen for 1995's western drama *Children of the Dust.* As a presence, reported Chris Dafoe of the Los Angeles Times, "it's apparent that he's viewed with respect, even awe, by virtually everyone on the set." Costar Michael Moriarty observed that Poitier lived up to his legendary status: "You see a face that you've grown up with and admired, someone who was an icon of America, a symbol of strength and persistence and grace. And then you find out that in the everyday, workaday work of doing movies, he is everything he symbolizes on screen."

For Poitier, the challenge of doing meaningful work involves transcending the racial and social barriers he helped tumble with his early film appearances. He has insisted that large budgets are not necessary to make a mark and that violence too often seems the only way to resolve conflicts on the screen. "We suffer pain, we hang tight to hope, we nurture expectations, we are plagued occasionally by fears, we are haunted by defeats and unrealized hopes," he said of humans in general in his interview with Champlin, adding that "when you make drama of that condition, it's almost as if words are not necessary. It has its own language—spoken everywhere, understood everywhere."

Sources

American Film, September 1991, pp. 18-21, 49.
Daily Variety, March 16, 1992, p. 18.
Los Angeles Times, March 8, 1992 (Calendar), p. 8; March 14, 1992, pp. F1, F4; February 26, 1995 (Television Times), pp. 5-6.
Orange County Register, September 11, 1992, p. P6.
Times (London), November 8, 1992.

—Simon Glickman

James A. Porter

1905–1970

Painter, educator, and art historian

Just as many art historians prefer the dust of library stacks to the colorful mess of the studio, many artists choose to remain ignorant of the artistic past that has, without their knowledge, shaped their work. James A. Porter, however, relished the challenges and pleasures of both pursuits. As an instructor at Howard University for over 40 years, Porter's pioneering research into the work of early African American artists rescued a great deal of important art from obscurity. At the same time he worked with and inspired some of the 20th century's most successful black artists. Additionally, Porter was an acclaimed painter in his own right, remaining active as an artist throughout his distinguished academic career.

Porter was born on December 22, 1905 in Baltimore, Maryland. His father, the Reverend John Porter, was a leader in the African Methodist Episcopal church, and religion played a major role in Porter family life. The Reverend Porter wanted James, one of eight children, to become a minister. Instead, James fell in love with drawing and painting, and from an early age he knew he wanted to be an artist.

The Porter family moved to Washington, D.C., when James was in high school. Once settled in Washington, the Reverend introduced his son to James V. Herring, the head of Howard University's art department, in the hope that Herring would talk James out of pursuing his artistic dreams. The ploy backfired, and Herring, recog-

nizing the young Porter's talent, not only encouraged him to continue making art, but urged him to do it at Howard when he was done with high school.

Began Long Association with Howard

Porter graduated from high school at the top of his class and was offered a scholarship to Yale. Since the scholarship covered only tuition, and he could not afford living expenses, Porter had to decline the offer. Howard University, on the other hand, was close enough to allow Porter to live at home, so he accepted a scholarship, arranged by Herring, to attend that school.

Porter entered Howard in 1923. He performed so well as a student that, upon graduating in 1927, he was offered a teaching position. In preparation for his career as an art instructor, he spent the summer studying art education at Columbia University in New York. Porter continued to hone his painting skills at the same time, studying at the Art Students League with the well-known painting tutor Dimitri Romanovsky.

In the course of his studies, Porter became acutely aware of how poorly the art community in the United States had kept track of African American artists. He began to take an interest in unearthing information about gifted but forgotten black artists of the past. While conducting

At a Glance . . .

Born James Amos Porter, December 22, 1905, in Baltimore, MD; son of Reverend John Porter; married Dorothy Burnett (a research librarian), 1929; child: Constance. *Education:* Howard University, B.S., 1927; studied with Dimitri Romanovsky at the Art Students League; New York University, M.A., 1947; additional studies in Paris, Belgium, West Africa, Egypt, Cuba, and Haiti.

Professor, art historian, painter. Howard University, professor, 1927-1970; paintings and drawings in collections at Howard University, Lincoln University (MO), Harmon Foundation, IBM, Hampton Institute (VA), and National Archives; numerous exhibitions and one-person shows, 1928–; art department chairman and director of the Howard University Gallery of Art, 1953-1970; illustrator for *Playsongs of the Deep South* and *Talking Animals,* both published by Associated Publishers.

Awards: Harmon Foundation, honorable mention, 1929; Schomburg Portrait Prize, 1933; National Gallery of Art medal for distinguished service to art, 1966; Pyramid Club, Philadelphia, recognition for Achievement in Art; Association for the Study of Negro Life and History, awards for book reviews published in the *Journal of Negro History.*

Member: International Congress on African Art and Culture; American Federation of Arts; Arts Council of Washington, DC; Symposium on Art and Public Education.

research in this area at the Harlem branch library, he met Dorothy Burnett, a research librarian whose specialty was black American writing before 1835. Porter and Burnett found that their areas of interest overlapped quite a bit. The two fell in love, and were married in 1929.

Honored by Harmon Foundation

As his drawing and painting skills developed further, Porter began to gain recognition as an artist. In 1929 he won an honorable mention from the Harmon Foundation, an organization committed to honoring "distin-

guished achievements among Negroes." The Harmon Foundation honored Porter again in 1933, awarding him its Schomburg portrait prize for his painting *Woman Holding Jug.* By this time, Porter had brought Dorothy back with him to Howard where she joined the staff of the university's library. She eventually became director of the library, and earned a national reputation of her own for her work on early African American writers.

Porter's technical excellence at drawing was apparent from the start of his career. More than any other form, Porter's portraits and figural compositions most frequently gained attention. His early paintings, such as "Sarah"--for which he was first noticed by the Harmon Foundation--showed a great deal of emotion. Many of his best works were portraits of family, friends, and Howard University luminaries.

During the 1930s, Porter traveled widely and broadened his knowledge of artistic styles around the world and throughout history. In 1935 he received a fellowship from the Institute of International Education, which he used to study medieval archaeology at the Sorbonne in Paris. When his work in Paris was completed, Porter traveled throughout Europe studying European and African art with the aid of a grant from the Rockefeller Foundation. Returning to the United States, Porter earned his masters degree in art history from New York University in 1937. He then returned to Howard University to resume his teaching career.

Wrote Landmark *Modern Negro Art*

Porter continued his research on African American artists. The next several years of work in this area resulted in the 1943 publication of *Modern Negro Art,* a pioneering effort that has remained an important source of information on the topic ever since. *Modern Negro Art* was essentially a critical survey of African American artists through the time of its publication. The book brought many of the profiled artists back into the public eye after decades--sometimes more than a century--of obscurity.

Porter continued to travel in search of artistic insight over the next several years. During the 1945-46 academic year, he studied art in Cuba and Haiti, again with financial assistance from the Rockefeller Foundation. Much of the material he collected on this trip was used to develop a Latin-American art curriculum at Howard. Porter also spent a great deal of time during the 1940s studying the life and work of Robert S. Duncanson, a Civil War-era black artist from Cincinnati, Ohio. His research on Duncanson resulted in the 1951 publication of a monograph on the subject, as well as a major article in the journal *Art in America.*

After his trip to the Caribbean, Porter's paintings began to take on a more decorative quality. *On a Cuban Bus* and *Lydia,* for example, showed a warm, realistic style that attempted to interpret the lively side of the African American spirit. In the 1950s and early 1960s, Porter also dabbled in more modern approaches, such as cubism--for example, *Girl in a Shattered Mirror* (1955)--and fauvism--*Toromaquia* (1962).

When Herring retired from Howard in 1953, Porter inherited the positions of art department chairman and director of the Howard University Gallery of Art. Although the administrative tasks associated with these jobs ate into his time for painting and research, Porter adjusted by regularly working well into the night. Dorothy Porter's expertise in locating research references was also of great assistance. Porter made another trip to Europe in 1955, this time as a fellow of the Belgium-American Art Seminar. In Belgium, he followed up on his earlier research into Flemish and Dutch art of the 16th, 17th, and 18th centuries.

Developed African Themes in Painting

In 1963 the Washington, D.C., *Evening Star* newspaper awarded Porter a grant to travel to West Africa and Egypt, where he was to research the art and architecture of those regions for his next book. He was so inspired by what he saw that he set up a studio in Lagos, Nigeria, and quickly created at least 25 new paintings. "You can't help painting when you're in Africa--the skies, the red earth, the verdure and the dress of the people--all of them reinforce one's feeling for color," Porter was quoted in *Free Within Ourselves.*

In addition to being quite conscious of color, Porter's new paintings were in a style far more expressionistic than anything he had done before. Africa also had a profound effect on his thinking about art. He began to feel that African themes had been developing unconsciously in his painting for years, and he reexamined much of his past work with regard to that notion. Although he continued to work over the next several years on a book about the influence of African art in the West, it was never finished.

In 1966 Porter was one of 25 artists honored for outstanding achievement in the arts by President Lyndon B. Johnson as part of the National Gallery of Art's 25th anniversary celebration. The following year, Porter organized an exhibition as part of Howard's centennial festivities. Entitled "Ten Afro-American Artists of the Nineteenth Century," the exhibition included works by Edmonia Lewis, Henry Ossawa Tanner, Duncanson, and others whose artistic gifts had been ignored largely because of their race.

Toward the end of the 1960s, Porter was diagnosed as having cancer, and he became seriously ill. His illness did not stop him from traveling to Africa once more, this time to chair a conference in Rhodesia on Zimbabwean culture. His health continued to deteriorate, however, and he died on February 28, 1970, just a week after chairing a conference in the United States on African American artists.

> "You can't help painting when you're in Africa—the skies, the red earth, the verdure and the dress of the people—all of them reinforce one's feeling for color."

In 1992 the Howard University Gallery of Art mounted an exhibition of Porter's work. The retrospective, "James A. Porter, Artist and Art Historian: The Memory of the Legacy," emphasized Porter's unique ability to carry out the dual roles of artist and scholar, each with commitment and excellence. Porter's third role, that of teacher, has had perhaps the most lasting effect of all. Starmanda Bullock Featherstone, a Howard art professor and guest curator of the 1992 retrospective, was quoted as saying in a *Washington Post* review of the exhibition, that "all his students say that they studied under the master, James A. Porter."

Selected writings

Modern Negro Art, Dryden, 1943.
Robert S. Duncanson, Midwestern Romantic-Realist, Springfield, MA, 1951.

Sources

Books

Bearden, Romare and Harry Henderson, *A History of African-American Artists: From 1792 to the Present,* Pantheon, 1993, pp. 372-380.
Perry, Regenia A., *Free Within Ourselves: African-American Artists in the Collection of the National*

Museum of American Art, Pomegranate, 1992, pp. 150-153.

Periodicals

American Visions, December 1992/January 1993, pp. 26-30.
Negro History Bulletin, October 1954, pp. 5-6; April 1970, p. 99.
Washington Post, November 27, 1992, p. B2.

—Robert R. Jacobson

Bill "Bojangles" Robinson

1878–1949

Entertainer

One of the most famous black American entertainers in the first half of the twentieth century, Bill Robinson was a pioneering vaudeville performer and a star of stage and screen. Affectionately known as "Bojangles," Robinson forged his fame with his feet, tap dancing his way to superstardom in an era that imposed daunting obstacles to any black person's success. During the height of the Great Depression he earned in excess of two million dollars, working nonstop in travelling revues, Broadway shows, and motion pictures, and he was almost universally adored by fans of every race and creed.

Minister Adam Clayton Powell, Jr. eulogized Robinson at the dancer's funeral as "a legend because he was raceless." Powell added: "Bill wasn't a credit to his race, meaning the Negro race, Bill was a credit to the human race. He was not a great Negro dancer, he was the world's greatest dancer. Bill Robinson was Mr. Show Business himself. He stood out there at the end, as sort of a beacon light to all the little kids, the little hoofers, breaking their hearts out … living in their little rooms and starving themselves just for the chance to work now and then. He was Mr. Show Business. He was Broadway."

Unfortunately, in more recent decades, Robinson's "beacon light" has dimmed considerably. Some film and show business historians have labelled him an "Uncle Tom" who catered to white tastes and who ignored the racial injustices of his time in an effort to further his career. In the biography *Mr. Bojangles.* Jim Haskins and N. R. Mitgang challenge this view and characterize Robinson as a fierce and often temperamental defender of his race offstage who challenged and overrode stereotypes onstage as well.

According to his biographers, Robinson labored "under the pressure of knowing that if Bojangles ever tarnished his image as America's favorite colored performer, the consequences could trickle down to every other black person from Harlem to Hollywood. He may have thought of quitting [films] and shedding his subservient Hollywood rags for his top hat and tails. But he couldn't quit.… He couldn't quit because he knew he was breaking down doors. His rule for learning how to dance on stairs was the same rule he employed for living: small steps."

From Bootblack to Hoofer

Born Luther Robinson in Richmond, Virginia in 1878, Bojangles was orphaned at a very early age. Records documenting what happened to his parents do not exist,

At a Glance . . .

Born Luther Robinson, May 25, 1878, in Richmond, VA; died of heart failure, November 15, 1949, in New York, NY; son of Maxwell (a machinist) and Maria (a singer and choir director) Robinson; married Lena Chase, November 14, 1907 (divorced); married Fannie Clay, 1922 (divorced, 1943); married Elaine Plaines (a dancer), January 27, 1944.

Professional entertainer, 1892-1949; appeared in revue *The South before the War,* c. 1892; played cabarets and clubs in New York City, c. 1898-1902; joined with vaudevillian George W. Cooper in act, Cooper & Robinson, 1902-14; solo performer in vaudeville and revues, 1914-27, with European tour in 1926; performer in revues, Broadway plays, benefit performances, and motion pictures, 1927-49. Contract player for RKO Pictures, 1930-34, and Twentieth Century-Fox, 1934-38. *Military service:* U.S. Army, c. 1898-1900; entertained military troops, 1917-18.

Selected awards Named honorary "Mayor of Harlem," 1933; *Mirror*-Ted Friend Gold Medal, 1937; named honorary president, Negro Actors Guild, 1937; inspiration for "National Tap Dance Day," declared by Congress as May 25 in 1989. A statue of Robinson stands at corner of Adams and Leigh Streets in Richmond, VA.

but it is assumed they both died at the same time in some sort of accident. Robinson and his younger brother became wards of their paternal grandmother, Bedilia Robinson, a former slave who did not particularly want the responsibility of raising two small children. Bedilia Robinson was a strict Baptist who absolutely forbade dancing, gambling, and swearing in her presence. Thus young Luther, who early on appropriated his brother's name of Bill, began hanging out on street corners, picking up tap lessons from other local Richmond youths.

One of these youths, Lemmeul V. "Eggie" Eggleston, became a close friend and mentor to Robinson. Together Eggleston and Robinson worked as bootblacks to earn a few pennies, and if shoe shining did not pay them enough, they danced in public places and passed a hat. Bill's specialty was the "buck-and-wing," a type of tap that involved rapid foot patter and flailing arms, ac-

companied by scat-singing or just a rhythmic run of vocal sounds that would not be out of place in modern rap. It was during this period that Bill Robinson began to jokingly refer to himself as "Bojangles" and also to use a term he coined--"copasetic"--that eventually found its way into the Funk & Wagnalls dictionary.

At the age of 12, Robinson left Richmond in the company of Lemuel Gordon "Dots" Toney, an older youth who had ambitions either to play professional baseball or to become an entertainer. Toney had done some stage work in blackface--a common practice in those days when adult blacks were not welcome on stage--and he thought the juvenile Robinson might serve as a good sidekick. Black children who performed in those times were called "picks," short for pickaninnies, and were popular in minstrel shows. Robinson and Toney hopped a freight train to Washington, DC, where Robinson found work at a race track. Toney went on to Baltimore, where he found stage work under the name Eddie Leonard. In 1896 Toney helped Robinson to secure his first professional show business gig, in a musical revue called *The South Before the War*.

Robinson appeared as a "pick" in *The South Before the War*, but even then he was just a bit too large to pass as a child. When that show folded he could find no other work, so he returned to Richmond and enlisted in the service. After mustering out of the army in 1900, he traveled to New York City, determined to make his way as a performer.

A Vaudeville Pioneer

The task facing Robinson at the turn of the century was daunting. Although a whole new entertainment medium--soon to be known as vaudeville--was beginning, blacks were not welcome in its ranks. Instead, white performers blacked their faces and entertained as blacks, some of them becoming famous in the process. A few outstanding black performers were able to challenge vaudeville's segregation, however, and one of them was comedian George W. Cooper. In 1902 Cooper found himself in need of a new partner, and he persuaded Bill Robinson to join the act. "Working as Cooper's partner was a comedown for Bill in some ways," his biographers note. "With Cooper he played second fiddle. Cooper was the straight man; Robinson had to play the fool to his foil. While Cooper dressed in a suit and tie, Robinson had to put on a comical getup--not a small consideration for Bill, a natty dresser. To make matters worse, he was not allowed to dance."

Bojangles's reservations notwithstanding, the new team

of Cooper & Robinson proved a hit on the prestigious Keith Circuit in vaudeville. Between 1902 and 1914 the pair toured America almost constantly, performing their short routine as part of a vaudeville troupe in virtually every major American city north of the Mason-Dixon line. Throughout all of those years, Cooper continued as the straight man and Robinson as the clown, but Robinson eventually gained enough status that he was allowed to incorporate his dancing into the act. "Bill Robinson was a staunch professional," his biographers state. "He put the same effort into a performance for a scanty audience in Duluth as he did into a performance at the Palace in Chicago. But the counterpoint to his utter professionalism onstage was his complete lack of responsibility off it."

A free spender who gambled compulsively, doled out money to charitable causes, and dressed lavishly, Robinson perhaps allowed his vices a free reign because of the conditions imposed on black vaudevillians. He carried a concealed gun and befriended the local sheriff at each stop--in case he found himself beset by racist citizens. The posh hotels that housed other Keith Circuit performers were closed to him because of his race, and even the trains that transported him from city to city could impose ridiculous restrictions on him based on his color. Robinson could hardly respond to all of these frustrations in his act--he would quickly have lost his job. Instead he vented them offstage by spending his salary lavishly and--occasionally--brawling with racist troublemakers.

In 1914 Cooper and Robinson came to a parting of the ways. Cooper found another partner, but Robinson decided to become a solo act. It was an unprecedented move--no other black performed solo on the vaudeville circuit at the time. Robinson found the help he needed from a theatrical manager named Marty Forkins. Their partnership began with a handshake in 1914 and continued without pause until Robinson's death in 1949, making both of them wealthy and influential men.

As a solo performer Robinson started slowly, in the Chicago area where Forkins was based. The dancer was able to make a decent living from entertaining and giving tap-dancing lessons, and in 1917 he increased his exposure by performing for American troops bound for active duty in World War I. Around the same time Robinson began including the dance that would make his fame--a rapid tap up and down a staircase. Robinson made his stair dance debut in 1918 at the Palace Theater in New York and received a show-stopping standing ovation. On the strength of that performance he was hired again by the Keith Circuit, becoming the

first solo black performer in the highest vaudeville ranks. He continued primarily as a vaudevillian until 1927, undertaking a European tour in 1926.

Aimed for the Headlines

Despite the fact that his act was always well received, Robinson had great difficulty working his way into the role of show headliner. He and Forkins finally decided they needed an extra gimmick to drum up publicity for Robinson on the road. Having joined the well-known Orpheum Circuit in the early 1920s, Robinson began staging exhibitions of backward running in the cities where he played, often competing--and winning--against athletes running normally. This activity brought him extra attention from sports writers and ultimately achieved the desired effect of enhancing his popularity as an entertainer.

Vaudeville began to decline in the late 1920s, a result of the competition with motion pictures. Although Robinson liked traveling the circuit, he was willing to entertain offers for Broadway shows. The possibility of a Broadway play with a black cast would have been unthinkable before the 1920s, but the success of a revue called *Shuffle Along* opened new doors for black talent on Broadway. The even bigger success of *Show Boat,* which premiered in 1927, brought another surge of interest in casts including blacks. Robinson was offered a role in *Show Boat* but turned it down.

Robinson's Broadway debut occurred the following year in a revue entitled *Blackbirds of 1928* The show opened at the Liberty Theater in May of 1928, and it proved to be a star vehicle for Bill "Bojangles" Robinson. His biographers state: "Robinson did not appear until the second act, but from the moment he came on the stage he seemed to electrify it. His routine was similar to his vaudeville act: He sang and danced to a number titled 'Doin' the New Low Down' (later to become his radio theme song). He tapped up and down a flight of five steps. He flashed his infectious smile.... The audience for Broadway shows, often called the 'carriage trade,' was different from that for vaudeville, but it responded to Bill in the same way: They were enraptured." *Black-birds of 1928* ran for 518 performances with Robinson as one of its stars.

Robinson entered the Great Depression as one of the best-known and most beloved black performers in America. Legends of his generosity to fellow residents of Harlem during the hard years of the 1930s abound. As for the dancer himself, those years brought his greatest and most lasting success, as a partner to a curlyheaded movie phenomenon who was hardly old enough to attend school.

Controversial Film Career

If opportunities for blacks on stage were few, opportunities in film were almost nonexistent. Despite his vast popularity, Robinson only appeared in two full-length feature films between 1930 and 1935--*Dixiana* and *Harlem Is Heaven*. In 1934, however, producers at Twentieth Century-Fox decided they needed a new partner for their biggest star, Shirley Temple. Although only seven years old, Temple had been featured in dozens of short features and several full-length films. The choice to pair her with Robinson was inspired by a feeling that she appeared too precocious and invulnerable onscreen.

> "Bill Robinson was the one who treated me most as an equal....and I have always had great love for him. He is still important in my heart."

Whatever sparked the decision, it proved fortuitous for both Temple and Robinson. In their first film, *The Little Colonel,* they stair danced together and clearly exhibited an onscreen chemistry that was sometimes lacking between Temple and her other co-stars. Shirley Temple was the film industry's biggest box-office draw *every year* between 1935 and 1938. Not coincidentally, all of the films she made with Robinson were completed during this time.

In this day and age, watching Bill Robinson's performances in the Shirley Temple vehicles can be downright embarrassing. He always appears as a trusted family retainer, almost the quintessential Uncle Tom, ready to dance up the plantation staircase or shield his little mistress from harm. In the context of the time, however, Robinson's appearances with Temple were a giant step for blacks in Hollywood. The quiet dignity that Robinson exuded in his various roles was in stark contrast to the deplorable Hollywood caricatures of Stepin Fetchit and other black comedians.

Robinson and Temple were also film history's first interracial dancing couple--and few have followed in their footsteps even today. Temple has never been reticent about her feelings for her beloved "Uncle Billy," who patiently taught her the difficult stair routines that had made him famous. "None of the dancers I worked with were patronizing to me, or treated me as a child," she recalls in *Tap! The Greatest Tap Dance Stars and Their Stories.* "But Bill Robinson was the one who treated me most as an equal. Bill Robinson and I became very close personal friends throughout our lives, and I have always had great love for him. He is still important in my heart."

Robinson and Temple made four films together, and--other than a cameo role in the 1943 movie *Stormy Weather*--those motion pictures comprise the bulk of Robinson's film career. The energetic dancer was hardly idle, however. He became a headliner at the revived Manhattan Cotton Club, dancing there from 1935 through 1939. He was also accorded enthusiastic reviews for his performance in *The Hot Mikado* on Broadway. That show was so successful that it was featured at New York's 1939 World's Fair. Robinson also had a starring role in the short-lived Broadway revue *All in Fun* in 1940.

Never Stopped Dancing

At the dawn of World War II, Bill "Bojangles" Robinson was a man in his sixties who had achieved wealth and fame in a racist society. He might have settled into retirement, but instead he kept performing at the furious pace he had set himself many decades before. The war years found him on stage in live performances and on the radio with his own show. He was also one of the most active benefit entertainers, raising money for many causes, including the National Association for the Advancement of Colored People and the families of slain New York police officers or firefighters. In 1937 he was named honorary president of the fledgling Negro Actors Guild. His biographers write: "As the forties began, there were only a handful of black roles to be had either in Hollywood or on Broadway, and these were in otherwise white productions. The actors who got those parts counted themselves lucky. Bill Robinson was among them."

Just a month before his seventieth birthday, Robinson appeared in a major benefit for the American Heart Association, held at the Copacabana in New York City. He performed a standard routine in the show, adding some extra, more vigorous steps at the end when comedian Milton Berle tried to keep up with him. Backstage he suffered a massive heart attack. He lived another year and a half after that but was forced into retirement--a step that brought mental depression.

Robinson died of his heart ailment on November 15, 1949 and was given the biggest funeral Harlem had ever seen. Honorary pallbearers included Ed Sullivan and Irving Berlin. Ironically, although it is estimated that Robinson earned in excess of four million dollars during his more than fifty-year show business career, his estate was probated at less than $25,000. His biographers claim that a lifetime gambling addiction consumed most of the dancer's wealth, and a fondness for random acts of charity drained the rest.

Robinson's legacy suffered greatly through the years of the civil rights movement. When his name was mentioned, it was not as a great dancer or vaudeville pioneer, but rather as another shameless toady to white audiences and white prejudices. In recent years, however, his reputation has enjoyed a revival. His life did not serve as the inspiration for the popular song "Mr. Bojangles," but he has been named as the artistic inspiration for numerous other tap dancers, both white and black. In 1989, the U.S. Congress--led by Michigan representative John Conyers--designated May 25 "National Tap Dance Day." May 25 was Bojangles's birthday.

Robinson never used metal taps on his shoes. Instead he danced a lifetime in shoes with wooden soles, wearing out as many as 30 pairs per year. "They said Bill Robinson had the cleanest taps around," writes Rusty E. Frank in *Taps!* "They said that Bill Robinson could do the easiest routine in the world and get away with it because of his charm and charisma. They said that he could drive a dancer crazy with the complexity of a step that looked so easy. But when tap dancers talk about Bill Robinson, they talk about the greatest tap dancer of all time. There were others who could tap out a mean percussive piece. There were others who could flip and split. But, according to the best of them, nobody had Bill Robinson beat on sheer tap dancing ability."

Selected film appearances

Dixieana, RKO, 1930.
Harlem Is Heaven, Herald Pictures Inc., 1933.
King for a Day (two reels), Vitaphone, 1934.
The Little Colonel, Twentieth Century-Fox, 1935.
Hooray for Love, RKO, 1935.
The Big Broadcast of 1936, Paramount, 1935.
In Old Kentucky, Twentieth Century-Fox, 1935.
The Littlest Rebel, Twentieth Century-Fox, 1936.
One Mile From Heaven, Twentieth Century-Fox, 1937.
Rebeccah of Sunnybrook Farm, Twentieth Century-Fox, 1938.
Just Around the Corner, Twentieth Century-Fox, 1938.
Up the River, Twentieth Century-Fox, 1938.
By an Old Southern River, Panoram, 1941.
Let's Shuffle, Panorama, 1941.
Stormy Weather, Twentieth Century-Fox, 1943.

Sources

Books

Bogle, Donald, *Toms, Coons, Mulattoes, Mammies and Bucks,* Viking, 1973, p. 46.
Frank, Rusty E., *Tap!: The Greatest Tap Dance Stars and Their Stories,* Morrow, 1990, pp. 90-93, 180.
Haskins, Jim, *Black Theater in America,* Crowell, 1982, p. 22.
Haskins, Jim, *The Cotton Club,* New American Library, 1984, pp. 48-49, 67.
Haskins, Jim, and N. R. Mitgang, *Mr. Bojangles: The Biography of Bill Robinson,* Morrow, 1988.
Stearns, Marshall, and Jean Stearns, *Jazz Dance: The Story of American Vernacular Dance,* Macmillan, 1968, pp. 75, 180.

Periodicals

Jet, November 27, 1989.
Southern Living, May 1989.

—Anne Janette Johnson

Joseph Sanders

1954—

Exhibition designer

Joseph R. Sanders, the designer responsible for bringing together such prestigious New York City exhibitions as "The Black Male" at the Whitney Museum of Modern Art, "The Harlem Renaissance" at the Studio Museum and "The Cosmic Dancer: Shiva Nataraja" at the Asia Society, looks forward to the day he can design for himself, rather than clients. "You have more control that way," he explained in an interview with *Contemporary Black Biography (CBB)*.

was good with his hands. He would make things for us to play on: merry-go-rounds, seesaws. He made a go-kart, a lot of things other kids could never have. I believe it sort of led me into the art world." The value of working with his hands had a big impact on young Sanders and figured into his decision to study art at Benedictine College, a small school in Kansas. Art was "where I found myself, I liked doing it."

For now, however, Sanders enjoys being the man top New York curators entrust with arranging and dramatically displaying the hundreds of artistic masterpieces or historical treasures that make up any major exhibition. Sanders is also one of the few African American exhibition designers. Joseph Richard Sanders, Jr. was born on October 11, 1954 in Atchison, Kansas. His mother, Margaret May Robinson Sanders, was a housewife and his father, Joseph Sanders, Sr., was a postal worker whose first love was carpentry. Sander's father served as a strong catalyst for his son's future artistic career. "As a child, I used to follow my father around. He was constantly working on the house, working on cars," Sanders recalled during a *CBB* interview. "My father

Although his private Catholic school education shielded him from some of the worst racism of the twentieth century, Sanders still experienced the sting of discrimination. He was only about four or five years old when he walked into a store with his mother, called her attention to the lunch counter with its abundance of snacks, and was informed by her that they could not eat there, "I figured out what it was about," he told *CBB*. Sanders also experienced racism while he was in graduate school at Ft. Hays State College in western Kansas, pursuing a master's degree in art. Because the college had an extremely small African American population, Sanders was often the subject of unwelcome stares. "I really felt prejudice, more so by ignorance," he said. One night, while leaving a club with several Nigerian friends,

At a Glance . . .

Born Joseph Richard Sanders, Jr., October 11, 1954, in Atchison, KS; son of Joseph R., Sr. (a postal worker) and Margaret Mary (Robinson) Sanders (a homemaker). *Education:* Benedictine College, Atchison, KS, B.A., 1975; Ft. Hays State University, Hays, KS, M.A. , 1978; Pratt Institute, New York, MFA, 1980. The Studio Museum in Harlem, exhibit designer and art preparer, 1980-83; Brooklyn Museum, exhibits manager, 1983-86; Sanders Design Works, owner, New York, NY, 1985–.

Selected exhibits: "The Cosmic Dancer: Shiva Nataraja," The Asia Society, New York, 1992; "Hispanic Heritage Celebration," NYNEX, New York, 1993; "The African American Mosaic" and "Moving Back Barriers: The Legacy of Carter G. Woodson," the Library of Congress, both 1994; "Buddha of the Future," The Asia Society, New York, 1994; "Black Male:Representations of Masculinity in Contemporary Art," the Whitney Museum of American Art, 1994-95.

Addresses: *Office–*Sanders Design Works, 28 W. 38th St., New York, NY 10018.

Sanders and his group were attacked by a group of young whites. One youth approached him menacingly with a broken bottle but slipped and fell, which defused the situation.

Made It in the Big City

Sanders enrolled at New York City's Pratt Institute of Arts in 1978 and obtained his master of fine arts degree summa cum laude in 1980. Living in New York proved to be an eye-opening experience for Sanders, "I learned more from being in New York than going to school," he theorized to *CBB*. In his studies, Sanders explored abstract sculpture and worked with fiberglass and other materials. At Pratt, a course involving conceptual art particularly influenced him. "The whole idea was that instead of making beautiful objects we were to make something that communicated some beautiful idea," Sanders explained. "That meant changing your abstract artwork. Taking that course led me to analyze why I was doing this particular art." Simultaneously, he was ex-

ploring his interest in the history of religion, a natural extension of his religious upbringing. He told *CBB*, "I started trying to convey those kinds of ideas in a new form of art. The art I did, leaving Pratt, was very minimalist and tried to convey an idea. I wanted the viewer to look at the piece and be affected by it, to know what it was trying to communicate."

As a student, Sanders held several internships that entailed working at New York City art galleries and encountering firsthand the reality of trying to make a living as an artist. "My job was to tell artists coming in that we weren't accepting new artists. I realized how political it was and how artists have to manipulate their art and be commercial. I didn't want to do that."

Unsure of how to make a living and pursue his artistic ambitions, Sanders got a lucky break through the now-defunct federal program CETA Comprehensive Employment and Training Administration). "There's no telling where I'd be at if that hadn't been there," he said of the program to *CBB*. CETA helped Sanders land a much-coveted job as a preparer of artworks for installations at the renowned Studio Museum in Harlem. After two years he was promoted to designer and has been one ever since, rising through the ranks of his profession.

Working as a designer does have its disadvantages, though, according to Sanders. "You don't have as much freedom as an artist," he remarked during the *CBB* interview. "You're compromising all the time with your client. But you're still creating an artwork, putting together different elements, different ideas, the end result being that visual thing, the design. The designer's job is that you have to please the client, but you also create something that you feel good about in the end."

Sanders stayed at the Studio Museum until 1983. He also did exhibition design at the Harlem State Office Building. He soon landed a job at the Brooklyn Museum of Art, where he was one of two in-house designers. The job offered excellent learning opportunities, and Sanders was called upon to work on everything from architectural signage to calendars and brochures for the exhibitions themselves. He was also doing freelance work for the Studio Museum and the gallery of the Schomberg Center for Research in Black Culture.

Although the job at the Brooklyn Museum of Art allowed Sanders plenty of creativity, he was exhausted every day and desired more freedom. "Those two years at the Brooklyn Museum of Art were a big learning experience for me," he admitted to *CBB*. "But after three weeks of being there I wanted my own business." So, Sanders opened his own company, Sanders Design Works, in 1985. This company has given Sanders the opportunity to produce his most creative and prestigious work. Describing his work to *CBB*, Sanders explained, "My job is to work with the curator of the museum and sometimes the artists."

Worked for Himself

The curator gives Sanders a list of the objects to be displayed, which Sanders arranges in whatever order and design he deems appropriate for the exhibition's theme. Historical exhibitions are typically chronological; artistic exhibitions are far more creative and fun. As Sanders told *Upscale* magazine in 1994, "In designing a museum installation, the most important goal is that people walk away remembering the exhibit itself rather than the pieces in it. The lighting, the design of the display cases, the signage should all focus on making the exhibition experience the main event. Background should be background. The art should stand out."

Constraints do exist. "It depends on the budget; that's the bottom line," Sanders said in the *CBB* interview. Sanders typically brings to the job all the experts he'll need—people to fashion the lighting, display cases he designs, paint the walls, and hang the art. He has a computer graphic designer and interior designer who work for him regularly. Beyond that Sanders is in charge, free to come up with the floor plan he thinks will work, free to decide on the wall color he believes will work best.

"I tend to prefer doing sculpture exhibits, working with very old objects because, if the budget is right, I'm able to do something nice with architecture," Sanders told *CBB*. "There's a lot more design involved in three-dimensional objects than flat things you put on the wall." One of his favorite sculptural exhibits was "The Cosmic Dancer: Shiva Nataraja" at New York's Asia Society, in 1992. Nataraja or "Lord of the Dance" was the form of the great Hindu god Shiva that has most captured the Western imagination. The Asia Society responded to this interest with its exhibition celebrating Nataraja figures sculpted from bronze in south India during the Chola period (880-1279). It was Sander's job to echo the movement of the sculptures, with their legs raised for the dance, their multiple sets of arms flailing, their heads surrounded by a halo of flames.

Sander's solution was to use grandly curving display tables, dramatic lighting, and an exhibition logo contained within a lightbox fashioned to look like one of the rings of fire in the collection. Similarly, for a subsequent

Asia Society exhibit, "Buddha of the Future" in 1994, Sanders welcomed visitors to the event by having them walk through an archway framed by pillars made of styrofoam, closely mirroring the ancient temples of India. He also built pedestals to resemble the tops of temples. And he chose gray-green for the walls, echoing the color of the aging bronze.

> "I'm so involved in doing the work that I don't dwell upon those issues. And, if you do the work long enough, people see the work itself and know you're good."

For the "Hispanic Heritage Celebration," a 1993 corporate exhibit for the New York telephone company NYNEX, Sanders built a mini-roof over the walls of the galleries holding the photos and artifacts of the exhibit. The "roof" consisted of cardboard tubes painted to look like tiles. The color scheme he chose was warm "Southwestern" oranges and browns. For "The Decade Show," which paid homage to the 1980s with works of art displayed at three museums—The New Museum in New York City's Soho, the now-defunct Museum of Contemporary Hispanic Art and the Studio Museum in Harlem-Sanders needed a uniting device. He decided upon a diagonal wall built across the length of each gallery, piercing other walls. That way, visitors to all three galleries would have roughly the same architectural experience at each one, to pull the three-part exhibit together.

For the "Black Male—Representations of Masculinity in Contemporary Art" exhibition at the Whitney, from 1994 to 1995, including works of such renowned artists as Robert Mapplethorpe, and photographic images ranging from basketball star Michael Jordan to the criminal Willie Horton, Sanders built a "V"-shaped wall that visitors entering the gallery had to go around from either side. "One of the main problems was there were a lot of pieces and the difficult thing was to make people flow through the gallery space without it seeming crowded," Sanders said, "The curator didn't want a linear approach where you were forced to go one way. So I designed it to allow freedom of movement."

Sanders has designed many other exhibits through the years, including shows for the American Craft Museum, the New York City Transit Museum, the Schomberg

Center, and the Library of Congress. Sanders and his associates have also designed for trade shows, corporations. and private homes. For example, they were once hired by *New York Newsday* to redesign the home of a woman who had brought back artifacts from New Guinea. Their assignment included restoring the woman's home back to its original form.

Now in his early forties, Sanders enjoys his work but looks forward to designing for himself--items such as board games, books, and miscellaneous inventions. In a profession that is largely dominated by white males, Sanders says he feels little pressure as an African American. "I don't dwell upon not getting work because I'm black or upon discrimination," he said. "I'm so involved in doing the work that I don't dwell upon those issues. And, if you do the work long enough, people see the work itself and know you're good."

Sources

Additional information for this profile was obtained through museum exhibition catalogs for "The Cosmic Dancer: Shiva Nataraja," at the Asia Society; "Black Male" at the Whitney Museum of American Art; and "Blueprint for Change: The Life and Times of Lewis H. Latimer." and through a *CBB* interview with Sanders on March 16, 1995.

New York Newsday, September 15, 1991, Home Section, p. 22.
New York Times, April 5, 1992.
Upscale, June/July 1994, p. 76.

—Joan Oleck

Sister Souljah

1964—

Rapper, activist, author

"I'm inclined to remind people of the things they'd most like to forget," writes Sister Souljah in her 1995 memoir *No Disrespect*. The uncompromising views of this young "raptivist" began to make mainstream news when she was publicly criticized by then-candidate Bill Clinton during his 1992 presidential bid. Though she complained that the remarks Clinton attacked were taken out of context, Souljah has also underscored repeatedly that she has little concern for the views of white politicians or the mainstream media. And while she has been portrayed as a loose cannon and a demagogue, her considerable education and articulate manner have won her more sympathetic listeners than her critics might have imagined possible.

Sister Souljah was born Lisa Williamson in 1964 and raised along with her siblings in the Bronx, New York, by her mother. Her father's epilepsy had brought about the end of his job as a truck driver. "My mother and father were divorced real early," she explained in an extensive *Playboy* interview with Robert Scheer. "So I ended up in the projects with my mother. I've lived in a lot of places. The only thing that stays the same thematically in all the places I've lived is that I was always

either a welfare recipient or lived in [federally subsidized] housing. I was always connected to government programs." As she points out in her book, this connection was fraught with indignity; she claims that such "services were designed to make us feel inferior."

No Disrespect describes the projects as "an endless maze in which a wrong turn could result in a little bleeding, a `casual rape,' a critical beatdown, or even death." Living in this "war zone," surrounded by "tall brown buildings, unofficial garbage dumps, no parks, roaches, rats, and mice," she and other members of her community were forced to learn survival skills. A detour to Englewood, New Jersey, with a beau of her mother's exposed her to a cleaner environment that was nonetheless still poisoned by segregation and black self-hatred. Even so, young Lisa remained religious and focused, learning to cook, looking after her siblings, and doing her schoolwork. "I was articulate and prepared in math, science, reading, sport, and play," she writes. "After all, this is what I had promised God I would do."

Despite her studiousness, she notes that "what we were taught was ridiculous" insofar as it ignored the history and achievements of black people since antiquity. "No

At a Glance . . .

Born Lisa Williamson in 1964 in the Bronx, NY; daughter of a truck driver and a homemaker; married, 1994; children: a son. *Education:* Attended Rutgers University.

Anti-apartheid activist, early 1980s; co-founded and administered African Youth Survival Camp, Enfield, NC; performed and recorded with rap group Public Enemy, c. 1990-91; signed with Epic Records and released album *360 Degrees of Power,* 1992; published book *No Disrespect,* 1995.

Addresses: *Home*—New York, NY. *Publisher*—Times Books, New York, NY 10022.

teacher gave black children any reason to take pride in their color, in their origins, in their past," she points out. Redressing this wrong has been a major preoccupation of Lisa Williamson, both before and after she became Sister Souljah.

"I try to tell young people not to look for leaders but to try to identify the qualities in themselves—to develop the talents and skills that they have—so they don't become dependent on somebody else's talents and skills," she declared to *Playboy*'s Scheer. At the same time, she praised the work of numerous black leaders, particularly activist Malcolm X, politician Adam Clayton Powell, Jr., and especially nineteenth-century anti-slavery firebrand Harriet Tubman, whom she deemed "the strongest person in the history of African people in this country." Souljah also said of Tubman, "She was an activist. She took action. She was a soldier. She was a warrior." Tubman's unyielding efforts to free her people have clearly influenced Souljah's own self-conception.

During high school Williamson attended Cornell University's summer advanced placement program; she later traveled to Spain for a stint at the University of Salamanca. She pursued history and African studies at Rutgers University, forging her fierce rhetorical style in editorial pieces for the school's student newspaper and in speeches at political rallies. In particular, she lent her voice to the struggle against the racist apartheid system in South Africa. The acts of civil disobedience in which she participated led to periodic arrests. Yet such activism only brought home the necessity of addressing the

obstacles faced by blacks in America.

During an anti-apartheid march through Newark, New Jersey, Souljah told *Rolling Stone,* she had an epiphany: "I'm marching through with hundreds of other kids," she recalled, "and we're going: `Free South Africa! Free South Africa!' And it felt like about 5000 bricks dropped on my head. I said: `Oh, shit. These people can't free South Africa—they haven't even freed themselves!'" She left Rutgers before graduating, partly due to her increasing involvement in the administration of a North Carolina camp for homeless kids she'd helped establish with funds earned from rap benefit shows.

Worked With Public Enemy

It was as a lecturer that she captured the attention of rapper Chuck D., of the groundbreaking rap group Public Enemy. In 1991 Williamson appeared on a Public Enemy album, at which time she adopted her stage name, a combination of "soul" and the word for God in both Hebrew and Rastafarianism. Sounded out, it suggests "soldier." Souljah's own album, 360 Degrees_of Power, was released in 1992. "Rap music is powerful because it puts people in leadership who would not ordinarily be allowed to speak, rap, rhyme, sing or say anything," she insisted to Scheer in *Playboy.* "It puts an array of stories and experiences on the market—some funny and some painful." She added that the music had enraptured her since childhood: "It was going on at house parties and on street corners when I was a kid. Back then you had [hip-hop pioneers] the Sugarhill Gang, Grandmaster Flash, the Furious Five—and we controlled it."

Most of the commentary in mainstream periodicals about *360 Degrees* addressed it not as music but as a showcase of Souljah's viewpoint. "The album—a call for black unity and empowerment, stressing education and economic self-sufficiency—has its fair share of positive messages," opined *Rolling Stone*'s Kim Neely. "But [Souljah's] seeming inability to see whites as individuals and her tendency toward sweeping generalizations—the most patently ridiculous of these, found on a track called "Brainteasers and Doubtbusters," being that white feminists are lesbians—is a major chink in her generally on-the-mark commentary." Scheer, who expressed admiration for his subject's straightforwardness, admitted that he "found her album loud, intimidating and not completely comprehensible." *Newsweek*, meanwhile, attacked Souljah's "messianic rhetoric."

Target of Bill Clinton, but Not an Easy One

Of course, the reason such publications noticed Sister Souljah at all had less to do with curiosity about rap or black politics than with the fact that her words had been criticized by Bill Clinton, the Democratic Party's nominee for president. It was largely believed that Clinton—perhaps opportunistically—took issue with a remark made by Souljah at a meeting of the Reverend Jesse Jackson's Rainbow Coalition in order to appeal to white voters. Clinton complained that Souljah, a guest of the Coalition's Leadership Summit, had advocated violence against whites.

"She told the *Washington Post* ... 'If black people kill black people every day, why not take a week and kill white people?'" Clinton proclaimed in a speech excerpted in *Newsweek*. "If you took the words 'white' and 'black' and reversed them, you might think [former Ku Klux Klan member and ultraconservative Louisiana political hopeful] David Duke made that speech." If Clinton thought Souljah would be an easy target, however, he would soon find otherwise. "I do not advocate the murdering of anybody," Souljah told the *Los Angeles Times*. "Not white people. Not black people. That charge is absolutely ridiculous. Mr. Clinton took my comments completely out of context. In the quote he referred to I was speaking in the mindset of a gang member."

When pressed about his attack on her, Clinton insisted, as *Newsweek* reported, that he was simply calling "for an end to division." Ultimately, however, the mixed signals of an electoral season ensured that this bitter exchange would never be transformed into any kind of fruitful dialogue. Souljah went on to label Clinton—in keeping with the innuendo put forth by his Republican opposition—"a hypocritical, draft-dodging, pot-smoking womanizer," as the *Los Angeles Times* reported. She furthermore charged him with "using me as a political football, the Democratic version of Willie Horton," referring to Republican ads during the 1988 campaign that used a furloughed black felon as a symbol for liberal leniency.

During this blitz of publicity, Souljah was asked variations on the same question: did she hate whites? It was her refusal to let whites off the hook and espouse the "common ground" themes beloved by Jackson that allowed the mainstream press to paint her as a racist demagogue. Yet it was only in a few interviews—notably the one with Scheer—that she was allowed to express her opinions in any detail. "I don't think any white person who is not constructively fighting against injustice

should sleep easy on any given night," she insisted. "You should have fear and guilt and remorse about creating a world that's so destructive to people of color. And if you don't it means you don't value the lives of people who have not emerged from your culture." She also expressed pessimism about the possibility of peaceful co-existence and positive political change.

> "I don't think any white person who is not constructively fighting against injustice should sleep easy on any given night."

As her critics gleefully pointed out, Souljah's album dropped off the charts despite the rush of publicity from the Clinton affair. Indeed, the album failed to ignite the imagination of the record-buying public, no doubt partly due to its unflinching political content. "I'm an attractive young woman," Souljah mused to Scheer. "If I wanted to make money, I could just put on a miniskirt and a tube top, shake my ass, put out a video, and I'm straight. It's so easy to make money in America off sex, drugs, and violence." Noting that she "had these options," she declared, "My goal was to distribute a message that I thought was essential for African people—a message that would tell them what was going on, why it was going on and how they could, as individuals, form a powerful collective. That was my objective. Clearly, I'm satisfied." She further suggested that her record company was only lukewarm in its support.

Became a Mother and Author

Sister Souljah ultimately faded from the national spotlight; Clinton was elected president, and the march of hardcore "gansta" rap continued apace, despite heavy criticism from politicians. Yet Souljah was far from idle, continuing to travel and speak to youngsters. She married and had a child before writing her book; these experiences had a powerful effect on her worldview. "It has me more dedicated," she told *Jet*. "I already had a value for life and now I have an even deeper value for life. I think once a woman carries life in her womb she starts to really understand how precious the life of each person is." At the same time, she became even more critical of her own upbringing and of ghetto parenting in general. "Parents had a habit of trying to raise their children off of slogans, like 'do the right thing' or 'be a good boy,'" she asserted, insisting that "young girls need womanhood training and young men need manhood training."

No Disrespect met with decidedly mixed reviews. Many critics attacked what they saw as Souljah's constant sermonizing, and indeed, the book contains numerous episodes in which what seem like political manifestos spring fully formed from Souljah's lips. Considering that many of her quotes in interviews sound the same way, these may be accurate representations. Be that as it may, those reviewers who disliked the book found its protagonist strident and took exception to many of her views. Karu P. Daniels of the *Source,* however, may have spoken for much of the hip hop community when he lauded Souljah's "candid and provocative new memoir" for its honesty and clarity. "She's speaking the language of the ghetto, and with that, no one can walk away from this read feeling isolated and alienated."

It was apparently to combat feelings of isolation, in fact, that Souljah undertook her work, and her productivity as both an author and a mother seem to have dovetailed: "Mothers, to me, are the narrators of your life," she noted in *Jet.* "They either tell you a good story or a bad story or a balanced story." Telling the story of her experiences—regardless of anyone else's idea of balance—has certainly been a consistent theme in her life. "Remember," she urges at the conclusion of her book, "No one will save us but ourselves. Neither God nor white people will do so." The key, as she told *Jet,* is self-respect: "You just have to see yourself as a very powerful person, a very important human being."

Sources

Books

Souljah, Sister, *No Disrespect,* Times Books, 1995.

Periodicals

Jet, February 27, 1995, p. 27.
Los Angeles Times, June 17, 1992, pp. F1, F5.
Newsweek, June 29, 1992, pp. 47-48.
Playboy, October 1992, pp. 59-69.
Rolling Stone, August 6, 1992, pp. 15, 17, 72.

—Simon Glickman

Barbara Smith

1949(?)—

Restauranteur, author

Former model and actress Barbara Smith is the proprietor of B. Smith's, a hugely successful bistro with locations in New York City and Washington, D.C. Smith plans to open restaurants across the country. In 1995 her popularity resulted in *B. Smith's Entertaining and Cooking for Friends,* the first book of its kind by an African American and the first addressed to the African American community. High praise greeted the glossy guide, which encouraged the author to branch out into other areas of entertainment.

Smith was born on August 24, 1949 (according to most sources), outside of Pittsburgh, Pennsylvania. Her earliest role models were her parents and maternal grandmother. "My grandmother was an extremely strong woman, as matriarchs are," Smith told *Contemporary Black Biography (CBB),* "but at the same time she was a very loving and warm woman with a great sense of humor and laughter. My parents were exceptional because they were very talented as a couple and they had a great marriage. I was very influenced by what they did. They had beautiful vegetable gardens, beautiful flower gardens. They did all of their own restorations—they were the original Bob Villa [the famed remodeling king and television host] and Martha Stewart [guru of fine living]. It was a beautiful house that we lived in. They did a great job with their God-given talents."

Smith was also influenced by her hairdresser, a woman who traveled and worked throughout the small cities of western Pennsylvania. "As a young girl I saw her as a woman who was very independent," Smith told *CBB*. "She traveled, she made her own money, she had her own business." Being a stylist was Smith's first ambition. In fact, in the early 1950s this was one of the only areas in which an independent African American woman could thrive.

"You Should Be a Model"

From a very young age Smith worked hard in the kitchen and garden with her mother and grandmother and as a paper girl. Then, in high school, she became very involved in home economics, studying nutrition, cooking, sewing, and fashion. Moreover, she would take part in any event concerning fund-raising and also worked as a volunteer—a candy striper—at the local hospital. She was a tall, beautiful teenager, and people were always

At a Glance . . .

Born August 24, 1949 (according to most sources), near Pittsburgh, PA; daughter of William H. (a steel worker) and Florence (Claybrook; a part-time maid) Smith; married Donald Anderson, 1988 (divorced); married Dan Gasby (a television producer), 1992; children: Dana (stepdaughter). *Education:* Graduated from John Robert Powers Modeling School, c. 1967.

Model, beginning in Pittsburgh, c. 1967; participated in *Ebony* Fashion Fair, New York City, 1969; first African American woman to appear on the cover of *Mademoiselle,* 1976; actress, beginning in mid-1970s; retired from modeling, early 1980s; worked as hostess and floor manager at America restaurant, New York City, early 1980s; opened restaurant B. Smith's, New York City, 1986; opened second B. Smith's, Washington, DC, 1994; published *B. Smith's Cooking and Entertaining for Friends,* Artisan, 1995.

Member: Trustee of the Culinary Institute of America; member of the board of the Feminist Press and the New York Women's foundation; founding member of the Times Square Business Improvement District.

Addresses: *Office*—B. Smith's, 771 8th Ave., New York, NY, 10036.

but I kept going for interviews," she explained to the *New York Beacon.* "I didn't give up." Then TransWorld Airlines launched a national search for their first black ground hostess. Smith landed the coveted spot through the modeling agency representing her. She achieved other "firsts" while in Pittsburgh as well, among them being crowned the first black Miss Triad, Queen of the Three Rivers. She also went back to school to learn to teach modeling, which she did for some time. While in Pittsburgh, Smith applied repeatedly to the *Ebony* Fashion Fair, an annual fashion industry gathering. She was accepted on her third try, in 1969. She moved to New York City in order to participate in the fair and decided to stay.

Pictured on Mademoiselle

Smith signed with the prestigious Wilhelmina Modeling Agency and eventually appeared on five covers for *Essence* (she was only the second model to do so) and one for *Ebony.* Both publications cater to an African American audience. Smith's big break into the modeling mainstream came in July of 1976 when she appeared on the cover of *Mademoiselle;* she was the first black woman to grace the magazine's cover.

Smith loved modeling. She traveled throughout the world, living in Paris, France; Milan, Italy; and Vienna, Austria, as well as Los Angeles, California. She took a great many classes during her tenure as a model, including those in acting, singing, French, and German—anything that interested her. "There is no better education I think than being a student of the universe, so to speak," she told *CBB.* "Modeling is a fabulous business to be in because you are in some of the best locales in the world and there are opportunities to do many things. At the same time, it's extremely difficult, and I would suggest to any young person that they get their college degree so they always have something to fall back on because it's not a business that will sustain you forever."

Smith appeared in dozens of television commercials in the 1970s, but her acting career really took off in summer stock performances in the early 1980s. She also appeared in productions in and around New York City. Still, it was as challenging for a black woman to make her mark in acting as it was in modeling. "That situation has changed, but not entirely," she told *CBB.* "I probably would have left modeling entirely for acting, but I wasn't very pleased with the kind of roles available to African American women."

telling her that she should be a model. "And then you eventually want to be one," Smith told *CBB* with a laugh.

Smith enrolled in the John Robert Powers modeling school in Pittsburgh, attending classes on weekends throughout high school. She reveled in the curriculum, particularly the instruction in grace and poise. She graduated from Powers just before her high school commencement and today considers the experience a turning point in her life. She remembered to *CBB,* "It was great because I began to watch my weight and change my eating habits. I always was into clothes because my mother was a great dresser and my father was too, so style was always around; but modeling school took it to another level." An African American instructor at the Powers school was particularly encouraging, giving Smith the confidence she would need to excel in the white-dominated field of modeling.

Smith moved to Pittsburgh immediately after high school. "I was told I was too dark and that I would never get a job,

From nearly the beginning of her professional career,

Smith planned to open a restaurant. She liked dining out, she was fascinated by the business of restaurants, and she felt her personality was suited to such an occupation. "When you're a model," she told *Publishers Weekly*, "you go to wonderful places where you're introduced to wonderful food, and you're invited to marvelous parties. In the '70s, I cooked up a storm. I liked impressing New Yorkers with my cooking. That's the last thing people expect from a model." She also understood that her modeling career would be greatly limited as she got older. For years she had questioned people in the restaurant business, gleaning as much information as she could about the industry and discussing her plans with restauranteurs. She eventually connected with a company called Ark Restaurants. She liked their management style and asked if, when she was done with modeling, she could work for them and learn the business. They agreed.

Began Career in Restaurant Management

In the early 1980s Smith began honing her restaurant management skills. She first worked as a hostess at Ark's America, a popular Manhattan eatery, and then as a floor manager there. After a year she began scouting locations for her own restaurant. With help from a partnership with Ark, B. Smith's opened on November 22, 1986, in Manhattan's theater district. The second B. Smith's opened in October of 1994 in Washington, D.C.'s newly refurbished Union Station train terminal.

As Smith explained to *CBB*, "For me, a restaurant like B. Smith's is an extension of the fashion and style business. It's entertainment." Indeed, Smith has turned her bistro into a community center; she hosts a play reading series, showcases musical talent, and stages fund-raisers. B. Smith's also mounts weddings and memorials. "You name it," she says proudly, "I've done it in the restaurant."

To keep a restaurant flourishing in Manhattan—where rents are high and fashions change in the blink of an eye—is quite an accomplishment. But Smith wanted to do more. "A few years ago I wondered, 'Why isn't there a book on entertaining that speaks to African Americans?'" Smith told *Essence*. "I felt we needed ideas that address a new generation—one too busy and creative for staid staples such as expensive caterers or gold-leaf calligraphy." In 1995 she filled this void with *B. Smith's Entertaining and Cooking for Friends*. Smith ventured in *Publishers Weekly*, "Martha Stewart set the tone for so many of us. I think what makes my book so exciting is that there has never been one done by an African-American before."

Publishers Weekly contributor Robert Dahlin described B. Smith's thus: "More than 100 recipes, from appetizers to desserts, with 75 full-color photographs ... provide tempting glimpses into Smith's eclectic international and home cooking. There are also lush depictions of parties she has held, both small and large." The project actually began as an autobiography, but as the book developed, it focused more and more on Smith's cooking and entertaining. "You start with what you know best," she told Dahlin. "I've done a lot of parties at the restaurant. And being a model is dealing in fantasy. That's what you do in a restaurant, and that's what people do at home when entertaining guests."

> "The world doesn't know that African-Americans live like this. They forget that our grandmothers and great-great grandmothers ran the houses of white people—in incredible style."

In *Essence* Smith said, "My book isn't so much a how-to as it's a why not? Why not entertain? Just do it with style and conviction!" Noting how the African American community has grown as a market, Smith remarked in *Publishers Weekly,* "A lot of black television shows are on the air now. Things have changed. For years we would go to restaurants and not see anyone else black. That's different now. We're out there spending and buying. My book reinforces that idea." In a similar vein, she commented to the *Chicago Tribune*, "The world doesn't know that African-Americans live like this. They forget that our grandmothers and great-great grandmothers ran the houses of white people—in incredible style."

Over the years Smith has continued to make television appearances and accepts three or four commercial jobs a year. She has been seen on "The Cosby Show" and "The Cosby Mysteries." In the mid-1990s she became a spokesperson for Oil of Olay moisturizers. Having established herself in the restaurant and home entertaining fields, Smith hopes to produce shows for children and women. She also has plans to develop a television show for herself and is at work creating a magazine.

When asked how these myriad projects would affect her

restaurant business, Smith responded that the more she's in the limelight, the better it is for her restaurants. She expects the business to continue its growth, with more restaurants opening nationwide. Smith's leisure time is devoted to her second husband, Dan Gasby, a television producer, and his daughter, Dana. Their summers are spent at Sag Harbor, New York, where entertaining is a casual affair. "When we throw parties, we personally prefer to do most of our socializing on the sand," Smith confided in *Essence.*

Sources

Chicago Tribune, July 26, 1995, sec. 7, p. 11.
Essence, May 1987, p. 97; August 1989, pp. 83-88; June 1995, p. 52.
Gourmet, August 1989, p.126.
New York, March 16, 1992, p. 66.
New York Beacon, March 17, 1995, p. 13.
Publishers Weekly, February 27, 1995, pp. 38-39.
Washington Post, July 5, 1995, p. E1.

Addtional information for this profile was obtained through a *CBB* interview with Barbara Smith on January 4, 1996.

—Joanna Rubiner

Roderick K. von Lipsey

1959—

Fighter pilot, U.S. Marine Corps

"I was glad to have the opportunity to serve my country," is how Lieutenant-Colonel Roderick von Lipsey acknowledges the Distinguished Flying Cross he was awarded after a daring Desert Storm air strike into Iraq. "We worked as a team," he says, about the Defense Meritorious Service Medal he received as an outstanding aide-de-camp to former Chairman of the Joint Chiefs of Staff General Colin Powell. "A great learning experience," is his assessment of the year he spent as a special assistant to White House Chief of Staff Thomas F. McLarty III.

Von Lipsey has always regarded patriotism, teamwork, and the promise of new experience as the three essential ingredients for job satisfaction. He has never had trouble finding them in the U.S. Marine Corps, for whom he has traveled the world in the roles of fighter pilot, tactics and weapons instructor, and researcher on security issues. In addition to constantly-expanding ways to use his talents for leadership and organization, his enthusiasm for his work has brought him several military honors as well as a place on *Time* magazine's 1993 list of promising young professional people: "Fifty for the Future."

Roderick von Lipsey's road to the U.S. Marine Corps began in a Philadelphia household headed by Police Officer Karl von Lipsey and his wife Mary-Elizabeth, a teacher. Theirs was a disciplined family, with steadfast values about integrity, responsibility, and the need to select goals with care. These maxims were constantly underscored with another parental adage: a good education is a key to future success, and well-worth whatever personal sacrifice it takes to achieve it.

Education Was the Key

To ensure their son this vital start in life, Roderick von Lipsey's parents sent him to private schools where smaller classes meant closer attention from the teachers. As expected, these benefits came with hefty price tags, but were worth every hour of overtime it took to meet the bills. First at the Norwood Academy and later at La Salle College High School, Roderick received an excellent education, augmented during his high school years with a wide range of sports and cultural activities.

At a Glance . . .

Born January 13 1959, in Philadelphia, PA; son of Karl (a police officer) and Mary-Elizabeth (a teacher); married Kori N. Schake.*Education:* Norwood Academy (Elementary: 3rd grade on); La Salle College High U.S. Naval Academy, Annapolis, MD, 1976-80; Catholic University, Master of Arts, 1989: Amphibious Warfare School, Quantico, VA; Private Pilot's License, June, 1980.

US Marine Corps Training in leadership, Aviation and Air Combat aircraft, 1980-83; Phantom squadron maintenance department, Fort Beaufort, South Carolina, 1983-88; Promoted to Captain, 1984; Logistics Department Head, 1986; NATO exercises in Europe, 1986; Marine Fighter Attack Squadron, at MCAS Kaneohe Bay, HI, 1989-91; Aide-de-Camp to Chairman of the Joint Chiefs of Staff, 1991-93; White House Fellow, 1993-94; Council on Foreign Relations International Affairs Fellow, 1994-95; MCAS El Toro, Santa Ana, CA, 1995.

Member: Council on Foreign Relations (New York); International Institute for Strategic Studies (London).

Awards: Distinguished Flying Cross (with Combat V); Defense Meritorious Serivce Medal; Single Mission Air Medal (with Combat V); Strike/Flight Air Medal (with Numeral 4); Joint Service Commendation Medal; 2 Navy Commendation Medals; First Lt.Col. Robert Johnson award, for leadership and contribution to aviation studies while participating in the Aviation Occupational Field Expansion Course; Roy S. Geiger Award on completion of the course.

A latchkey kid with eclectic interests, he plunged into ice-hockey and ballet, enjoying the rough-and-tumble competitiveness of the sport as much as the precise, studied movements he learned in dance classes. "Each taught me something about coordination that improved my performance of the other," he later recalled, though he acknowledged that ballet had added a little something extra. "It gave me a love of music, which remains one of my greatest pleasures." Drama was also a particular favorite, involving frequent rehearsals that gave him plenty of time to socialize with other student-actors and their teachers.

Even as a teenager, Roderick von Lipsey was obviously an excellent team player. Yet sixteen years later he looked back on his high school self as a "fairly unremarkable student," with the usual adolescent uncertainty about his future. However, all ambivalence was neatly banished one day when a young midshipman visited La Salle College High School on a recruitment mission for the United States Navy. The young naval officer was typical of the poised, patriotic graduates that the U.S. Naval Academy had been grooming for leadership since its 1845 establishment. Crisp and self-confident, he was a perfect role model for a high school senior on the edge of adulthood. By the end of his visit, Roderick von Lipsey had no further doubts about his prospective career. He had made up his mind that the road ahead began in Annapolis, Maryland.

Entered Annapolis

Whether conducted by university personnel or, as in the case of Annapolis, by the prospective recruit's congressman or senator, an interview for nomination is always a make-it or break-it process. Von Lipsey's was no exception. Any hopeful candidate without a carefully-considered answer could well have been discouraged by the piercing question--What do you think is America's main problem today? But even at the age of seventeen, Roderick von Lipsey had definite ideas of what that problem was, and how he wanted to help to resolve it. "We lack spirit," he said. "We need national pride."

In 1976, he entered Annapolis as a freshman and started on the leadership training, thermodynamics, and physics courses which are vital to naval officers serving in space-age submarines and ships. Once these requirements had been filled, he majored in English literature. During his final year as an undergraduate the English Department asked him to participate in a special program, by teaching a course, Introduction to Rhetoric and Literature, to academy freshmen.

Teaching was a pleasant sideline, but von Lipsey did not let it distract him from planning for the future. Like his classmates, he had been aware since his freshman days that his final career track would have to be mapped out before he graduated, so he had thought long and hard about different possibilities. In the end, the matter was settled in favor of the U.S. Marine Corps. His reasons were clearcut: "I saw there was an incredible degree of professionalism in the Marines, a deep spirit and strong caring for subordinates, and a long heritage."

U.S. Marine Corps: Semper Fidelis

Though the U.S. Marine Corps has been a separate fighting force within the U.S. Navy since 1834, its beginnings date back to 1775, when anti-British feeling had just raised the curtain on the Revolutionary War. Historians tell us that the Corps won their first battle in the Bahamas in March 1776, and that their victorious exchange of unpleasantries with a British warship they encountered on their jubilant voyage home earned them a congratulatory visit from Commander-in-Chief George Washington. A masterstroke on Washington's part, this gesture gave the newly-established Marines pride in their achievements and an appetite for service to their country that are still symbolized by the motto "Semper Fidelis"—Always Faithful.

In May 1980 "Semper Fidelis" became a watchword for Roderick von Lipsey, who was commissioned a Second Lieutenant in the Marine Corps. Still a long way from the streamlined executive ability that stamps the well-trained officer, he began to learn the marksmanship, leadership, and infantry skills every Marine must master. Then, in January 1981 he went to Pensacola, Florida, then on to Kingsville, Texas, to learn to fly Trojan, Buckeye, and Skyhawk aircraft. This training earned him the designation "Naval Aviator," but did not mark him as "combat ready." To earn this qualification he spent the six months between September 1982 and March 1983 stationed at the Marine Corps base at Yuma, Arizona, where he learned to fly the F-4 Phantom.

Equipped with Experience and Leadership

Now a fully-fledged fighter pilot, von Lipsey spent the next four years gaining the background experience he would need to command pilots and maintenance crews under conditions of actual warfare. He passed several months learning the intricacies of aircraft maintenance and maintenance quality assurance. Then, shortly before a 1984 promotion to the rank of captain, he became the officer in charge of this service for top-flight Phantom aircraft maintenance.

A year later, his operational flying duties began to focus on the Hornet, a fighter plane whose designation "F/A" shows it can be used for either air-to-air or air-to-ground combat. Then, in 1986 came a deployment to NATO exercises in Europe and the Mediterranean. With six years of experience under his belt, Captain von Lipsey was tasked with both his normal flying assignments plus the formidable responsibility of logistics—moving supplies, troops, and weapons and vehicles from place to place. Attracted by the chance to expand his horizons, he organized the myriad logistics details with enough flair to merit a Navy Commendation medal.

TOPGUN

In January 1987, von Lipsey was sent to the Navy Fighter Weapons School at Naval Station Miramar in California. Known informally as TOPGUN since a 1986 movie about it was released, the facility had been in existence since the Vietnam War years, when a dismayed Congress discovered that seasoned American pilots not only lacked the accuracy of their Vietcong adversaries, but were flying supposedly state-of-the-art aircraft that seemed inferior to the Communist-built MIGs. Tracing both deficiencies to defense-spending cuts during the Kennedy years, Congress established the Weapons School in 1969, and set its goal at all-round excellence for America's fighter pilots.

About twenty years later, the TOPGUN mission had not changed. The facility still existed primarily in order to hone the technique of experienced fighter pilots to the highest degree of accuracy that they could achieve, so that they could return to their own squadrons and pass their expertise on to others. Von Lipsey fully appreciated this ceaseless search for perfection, summing up his grueling six weeks of lectures, flight simulations, and air "battles" against remorseless instructors as "absolutely the most thrilling and exciting training program, which taught me a lot about how to instruct others."

Waited: Operation Desert Shield

On August 2, 1990, headlines all over the world blared the news: Iraq had sent hundreds of tanks trundling across its border to invade Kuwait. Meeting no resistance to his unwarranted stranglehold on one-fifth of the world's known oil reserves, Saddam Hussein then closed all Kuwait's ports and airports and began to shut down its communications with the outside world. Within the week, he was confident enough to announce that Kuwait had ceased to exist as a separate country and was now the nineteenth province of Iraq.

President George Bush reacted quickly. Ordering an American trade embargo, he urged all other countries to do the same. Warships began to steam towards the Persian Gulf. Huge transport planes brought American troops to neighboring Saudi Arabia; military personnel from other countries came to join the buildup. On August 7, 1990, the world unveiled a plan for a united stand against Saddam Hussein. Operation Desert Shield was born.

Captain von Lipsey left for the Middle East to join Marine Fighter/Attack Squadron 235. An accomplished instructor as well as a fighter pilot with the best training

America could offer, he now had two new additions to his own extensive air combat schedule. First, he had to rehearse his pilots to keep them at the pinnacle of combat readiness. Then, he had to follow up his instruction with relentless testing, so that each squadron member could match any challenge the highly-trained Iraqi Air Force possessed.

It Began: Operation Desert Storm

United Nations Resolution 678 had given Saddam Hussein until January 15, 1991, to withdraw from Kuwait. He chose to stay, his soldiers chalking up a record of stealing and vandalism that left 50,000 cars wrecked, Kuwaiti museums and libraries empty, and even lamp posts and street lights uprooted and on their way to Baghdad. Tensely the world waited as the United Nations gave Iraq another few hours of grace. Then, before dawn on January 17th, a Tomahawk cruise missile left the USS San Jacinto stationed far out in the Persian Gulf, skimmed out over the water and soared more than 500 miles into downtown Baghdad. The first of 100 Tomahawks fired that day, it was step one in the liberation of Kuwait.

On the night of January 20, 1991, 35 aircraft from the Third Marine Aircraft Wing thundered down a runway off the coast of Saudi Arabia, took off into a swirling fog and began a 600-mile journey into Eastern Iraq. Led by Captain Roderick von Lipsey, the planes headed for a secret Iraqi air base, where they used cluster munitions and laser-guided bombs to demolish both the base's maintenance and repair hangars and the web of railroad tracks which constituted its supply lines. It was a difficult double-duty and neither the mist nor heavy Iraqi anti-aircraft fire made it any easier. But von Lipsey had studied the weather conditions earlier, and had decided that the fog could be counteracted to a certain extent by flying at an altitude low enough to show their targets without recklessly endangering the American aircraft. He was right. The Iraqi ground-to-air destroyed no Marine planes, and, as he himself said later: "The performance of the individual crews in locating and engaging the targets was superlative."

Though Captain von Lipsey led other combat missions and flew more than 40 sorties during Operation Desert Storm, this particular operation went down in military annals as a special success. An announcement from the Secretary of the Navy tells us why: "Captain von Lipsey precisely planned, weaponeered, and led a strike package on a 600-mile night, inclement weather strike into Eastern Iraq." Subsequent allied air attacks were not required on the targets.

Aided General Colin Powell

The reward for this remarkable feat was the Distin-

guished Flying Cross—a medal Roderick von Lipsey shared with such previous legends of American aviation as Charles Lindbergh and Amelia Earhart. But prized as the award was, it was not the only accolade awaiting his return from the Middle East. Though he had not yet received his expected promotion to the rank of major, in 1991 he was chosen as one of two aides-de-camp to then-Chairman of the Joint Chiefs of Staff, General Colin Powell.

> "I saw there was an incredible degree of professionalism in the Marines, a deep spirit and strong caring for subordinates, and a long heritage."

Because this appointment usually went to an officer of far higher rank, this new post was a spectacular tribute to von Lipsey's competence. Yet the implied praise was not the most significant memory the incident left behind. Instead, his reminiscences dwelled on his preliminary impression of the General: "He's a very big man--very commanding. A very serious man, a talented leader who inspires loyalty." Powell also inspired an energetic work force. A key player in strategic humanitarian operations involving starvation-wracked Somalia, Bosnia's war zones, and refugee camps for fleeing boat people in Guantanamo Bay, Cuba, the general marched smartly through a dizzying schedule involving travel, press conferences, and contacts with embassies, which his aides-de-camp had to orchestrate into a seemingly-effortless whole. Initially as junior aide and later as the senior, Major von Lipsey planned itineraries, organized the General's media communications, and handled the financial and security arrangements for 35 trips to Poland, Czechoslovakia, Hungary, Belgium, Somalia, and even Powell's ancestral homeland, Jamaica. It all added up to a huge workload, but it brought von Lipsey priceless opportunities for travel, and it gave him membership in a team playing a small but indispensable role in America's history. Yet, even this was not sufficiently fulfilling. Somehow he also found the time to earn a master's degree in international affairs from Catholic University.

Worked at the White House

Von Lipsey's two-year term of duty with General Powell was almost up when the prospect of a White House

Fellowship arose. A program initiated during the Lyndon Johnson administration, this Fellowship offers up to 17 young Americans a chance to work with influential Washington policy-makers. It is a once-in-a-lifetime opportunity to see the inside workings of the Federal Government, but it did not tempt von Lipsey when a group of White House Fellows urged him to apply. However, he changed his mind when he received a note asking "Are you interested in this?" from Powell, a former Fellow himself. Easily clearing the entry hurdles of strong leadership skills and extensive community service, von Lipsey captured a coveted 1994 slot as a special assistant to White House Chief of Staff Thomas McLarty III.

One similarity between this new post and his previous position as a member of General Colin Powell's staff was that both involved a great deal of travel. But this time von Lipsey's role usually had little to do with itineraries or financial arrangements. Instead he often traveled on Air Force One with President Clinton's entourage, providing national security updates and background information for McLarty at the United Nations General Assembly, the NATO summit in Brussels, and meetings with political leaders in Russia, the Ukraine, and Belarus.

The Council on Foreign Relations

From here, in 1994 it was a natural progression to a second fellowship, this time with the Council on Foreign Relations. One top priority issue at this time was international security, and the strategy under discussion was the prospect of expanding NATO'S 16-nation roster to offer membership and limited military participation to Eastern European governments. Von Lipsey was asked to join a task force co-chaired by the legendary Dr. Henry Kissinger, which had been formed to study this complicated question and its far-reaching implications. Although Von Lipsey was strongly in disagreement with the preference for rapid expansion that Kissinger favored, he forcefully presented his own compelling argument, thereby earning the respect of his co-members.

In mid-1995 the fellowship ended, and Major von Lipsey received new orders posting him to California. Once again, his duty to his country placed him in the cockpit of an F/A-18 Hornet, after, as he puts it "flying a desk for four years." Soon after his return to active participation in America's defense arena, von Lipsey received notification that another promotion was on the way—this time, to the rank of Lieutenant-Colonel.

Sources

Books

Brenner, Eliot et al, *Desert Storm: The Weapons of War,* New York, Orion, 1991.

David, Peter, *Triumph in the Desert: The Challenge: The Fighting: The Legacy,* New York, Random House, 1991.

Dorr, Robert F., *Desert Shield: The Build-Up: The Complete Story,* Osceola, Wisconsin, Motorbooks International, 1991.

Kinzey, Bert, *The Fury of Desert Storm: The Air Campaign,* Blue Ridge Summit, PA., Tab Books, 1991, pp. 44, 121-128.

Lawliss, Chuck, *The Marine Book: A Portrait of America's Military Elite,* New York, Thames and Hudson, 1988.

Mostyn, Trevor, "Major Political Events in Iran, Iraq and the Arabian Peninsula: 1945-1990" *Facts on File,* New York, 1991, pp. 265-267.

Scholarships, Fellowships, Grants, and Loans: College Blue Book, 25th ed. New York, Macmillan Library Reference USA, 1995, p. 169.

Wilcox, Robert K., *Scream of Eagles,* New York, Wiley, 1991, pp.96-99.

Periodicals

U.S. Department of State Dispatch, June 27, 1994, pp. 431-434. Supplement, July 1994, p. 28, December 26, 1994, p. 351.

U.S. News & World Report, January 28, 1991, pp. 24-32.

Interviews with Major Roderick von Lipsey, U.S. Marine Corps, 3rd Marine Aircraft Wing, MCAS, El Toro, California. Assistance: U.S. Marine Corps, Joint Public Affairs Office: 3rd Marine Aircraft Wing/MCAS El Toro.

—Gillian Wolf

Lenny Wilkens

1937—

Professional basketball coach

On January 6, 1995, Lenny Wilkens became the National Basketball Association's (NBA) all-time leader in coaching victories. Wilkens's milestone--a phenomenal 939 wins in 22 seasons as an NBA coach--places him at the top of a list that includes such basketball luminaries as Red Auerbach, Dick Motta, and Jack Ramsay. What is most remarkable about Wilkens, however, is the fact that he has achieved in such spectacular fashion while never quite becoming a national superstar. As *Newsday* reporter Shaun Powell put it, Wilkens "is not larger than life; he is grounded to earth.... He wins quietly. He loses quietly. Whenever he moved from one team to another, he tip-toed.... There is very little about Wilkens that screams. Not his tone. Not his gestures. Not even his neckties."

Indeed, Wilkens has only one NBA championship to his credit, having spent his career coaching such second-tier teams as the Cleveland Cavaliers, Seattle SuperSonics, and Atlanta Hawks. Few underestimate his abilities, though, especially since he has crafted playoff-caliber teams from franchises that were expected to crash and burn. "I used to kid that I was the NBA's best-kept secret," Wilkens told *Newsweek*. "But I'm in control. I

know what the hell I want to do."

A Rough Beginning

"Dignified" is the word most often associated with Wilkens. In a league that too often values flash over substance, the impeccably attired coach who drills his players incessantly on their assignments is "a genuine role model," remarked Mark Starr in *Newsweek*. This ability to maintain a professional demeanor in a volatile sport is part of the secret to Wilkens's longevity as a coach. His other major strength is empathy--he himself was a professional basketball player who made the Hall of Fame at the end of his 15-year playing career. "I relate to people," Wilkens told *Newsday*. "I know what young players are going through. I understand their backgrounds. I didn't come from anything either, so I've been there."

Leonard Randolph Wilkens was born October 28, 1937, in the Bedford-Stuyvesant section of Brooklyn, New York. Almost from birth he faced extreme difficulties, the kind of character tests that force children to grow up quickly. Wilkens's father was black; his mother was white. He often faced the taunts of other children and-

At a Glance . . .

Born Leonard Randolph Wilkens, October 28, 1937, in Brooklyn, NY; son of a chauffeur and a candy factory worker; married Marilyn; children: Leesha, Randy, Jamee. *Education:* Providence College, B.A., 1960. *Military service:* U.S. Army, 1961-62, became second lieutenant.

Athlete, coach. St. Louis Hawks, basketball player, 1960-68; Seattle SuperSonics, player-coach, 1968-72, head coach, 1978-85, general manager, 1985-86; Cleveland Cavaliers, basketball player, 1972-74, head coach, 1986-93; Portland Trail Blazers, player-coach, 1974-76. U.S. Olympic basketball team, assistant coach, 1992, head coach, 1996; Atlanta Hawks, head coach, 1993–.

Selected awards Inducted into Naismith Memorial Basketball Hall of Fame, 1990; named 1994 coach of the year by *Basketball Weekly, The Sporting News, Basketball Digest,* and National Basketball Association (NBA). Participated in nine NBA All-Star games as player, four as coach.

Addresses: *Office*--Atlanta Hawks, One CNN Center, Suite 405, South Tower, Atlanta, GA 30503.

-even more disturbing--the rude stares and insolent remarks of racist adults. Wilkens was still a preschooler when his father, a chauffeur, died suddenly. Leonard, as the oldest of four children, was called upon at the tender age of five to be the "man of the family."

The Wilkens children grew up in a Brooklyn tenement, supported only by the wages their mother earned by working in a candy factory. Whatever emotions the young Leonard felt, he kept them to himself while working hard in school and staying out of trouble. "I couldn't have sympathy," Wilkens told *Sports Illustrated.* "I couldn't trust. I couldn't get involved with people because then I'd have to feel. What scared me so much was seeing no one going out of their way to help my mother and family after my father died. Seeing people look down their noses at us. You realize that no one really cares. So how do you get through? You start building the wall. You never let anyone know what's inside. It sounds awful now to say I'd *never* cry."

Quiet Success as a Player

Wilkens took his first job, delivering groceries, at the age of seven. In his spare time he played basketball with various youth leagues in the Brooklyn area. Once Wilkens learned the mechanics of the game, he became a star player. A priest named Tom Mannion, a longtime family friend, persuaded Wilkens to play for the Boys High School team as a senior. There Wilkens made enough of a mark to win an athletic scholarship to Providence College, a Catholic university in Rhode Island.

One of six blacks in a school with 1,200 students, Wilkens often felt the slights of racism. He learned to get even by perfecting his basketball game, honing his skills until he became an effective point guard and a brilliant defender. "There were people looking at me like I was some kind of insect," Wilkens recalled of his college years. "People who assumed that because I was from Bed-Stuy, I was carrying a knife or gun. One drop of black blood in this country ... and you're tainted. If I let that hurt me, who has the anxiety? *Me.* I was not going to let anyone hurt me or make me feel anxious. I'd learned something by then. If I could control myself, I could make *them* feel anxious." Majoring in economics, Wilkens earned his bachelor's degree in 1960. In his senior season at Providence, his basketball team reached the National Invitational Tournament (NIT) finals, and he was named tournament Most Valuable Player. Even so, he was passed over for the U.S. Olympic basketball team.

Wilkens received several offers after graduation, including more than one to play professional basketball. He chose to join the NBA after the St. Louis Hawks picked him sixth in the first round of the 1960 draft. Though being drafted that highly in the 1990s guaranteed multimillion dollar contracts, the Hawks' won his services with a salary of $8,000 and a signing bonus of $1,500.

Wilkens became a starter as a rookie and threw his energy into his basketball game. Off the court he was considered aloof by teammates and fans alike. His natural reticence was heightened by the abundant racism he and his new wife, Marilyn, encountered in the suburb of St. Louis to which they had moved shortly after he joined the team. Asked about those days by *Sports Illustrated,* Wilkens said: "I was learning to watch people, to read eyes and body language. I never let anyone know what I was thinking or feeling. I *worked* at that. I really didn't care if people misread me. If *I* read them and *they* misread me, it's to my advantage."

Became a Coach

Within two years Wilkens had established himself as a perennial all-star, one whose considerable reputation rested upon his ability as a team player rather than a star in his own right. In ten years between 1963 and 1973 he was voted to nine All-Star teams, and in 1968 he finished second in the NBA's Most Valuable Player voting to Wilt Chamberlain. That same year the Hawks moved to Atlanta. When the new team owner could not negotiate a satisfactory contract with Wilkens, the enigmatic player was traded to the Seattle SuperSonics, a second-year expansion team with little chance of becoming a playoff contender. What seemed like an outright banishment became a golden opportunity for Wilkens. As the 1969-70 season began, Wilkens was asked to be player-coach for the struggling SuperSonics.

Wilkens had never coached a game before, but he began to implement the fundamentals that had made his own playing career so successful--emphasis on defense, passing, and executing assignments correctly. Under his guidance, the SuperSonics turned in a 47-35 record in the 1971-72 season, their first-ever winning year. The following season found Wilkens with the Cleveland Cavaliers as a player only, but in 1974 he moved to the Portland Trail Blazers, again as a player-coach. He was released in 1976, and for some time contemplated finding another line of work altogether. Instead, he returned to Seattle as head coach midway through the 1977-78 season.

The SuperSonics were 5-17 when Wilkens took over in 1977. By season's end the team had compiled a 47-35 record and made it all the way to the NBA championship finals where they lost to the Washington Bullets in seven games. Despite leading the team through its dramatic turnaround, Wilkens was overlooked in Coach of the Year balloting. The following season, the SuperSonics not only reached the NBA finals, but also won the championship by beating the Bullets in only five games. Again, for reasons that more than one observer considered racist, Wilkens was not honored with the Coach of the Year award. *Sports Illustrated* contributor Gary Smith wrote of Wilkens: "He's a man fated to exist in the NBA's outback.... And some will wonder if it's Lenny who's drawn to obscurity, or obscurity to Lenny."

The dedicated coach was not quite as unfamiliar as all that. After coaching the SuperSonics for eight years and serving as general manager for another season, he joined the Cleveland Cavaliers as head coach in June of 1986. He spent seven seasons with Cleveland, transforming the franchise from one that won only 29 games

in 1985-86 to a playoff qualifier with more than 50 victories in five of his last six seasons. Wilkens's misfortune in Cleveland can be summed up with one name: superstar player Michael Jordan. The Cavaliers met Jordan and his Chicago Bulls four times in the Eastern Conference playoffs and were eliminated each time.

> "I relate to people. I know what young players are going through. I understand their backgrounds. I didn't come from anything either, so I've been there."

In 1993 Wilkens decided to retire from the Cavaliers even though he had another year remaining on his contract. He was not idle long. The Atlanta Hawks signed him to a five-year, $6.5 million contract as head coach, thus extending his career into a third decade. In Atlanta he continued his largely-unheralded winning ways, taking a franchise that was expected to have a mediocre year at best and transforming it into a playoff contender with a 57-25 record and the Central Division championship. Finally, as the 1993-94 season came to an end, Wilkens gained the honor that had eluded him for so long--he was named Coach of the Year.

Long-Deserved Recognition

Another major milestone occurred early in 1995 when the Hawks brought Wilkens his 939th career victory, surpassing by one game the legendary Red Auerbach, who led the Boston Celtics in the late 1950s and early 1960s. Wilkens now holds records for having participated in more games as a player and/or head coach than anyone else in league history as well as contributing to more victories than anyone in NBA history. The coach says he wants to win 1,000 games before he quits. At the end of the 1995 season, he was only 32 games away from that goal with several years remaining on his contract. "The satisfaction is that only one person can be number one at a time," Wilkens told the *Washington Post* after breaking Auerbach's record. "It's a great thing to win a championship, and I hope to do that again. But it's great to be on top of an individual thing. I may not be there very long, but I got there."

Other honors have helped to elevate Wilkens's visibility as well. In 1990 he was inducted into the Naismith

Basketball Hall of Fame for his exploits as a player. In 1992 he travelled to Barcelona, Spain as assistant coach for the U.S. Olympic men's basketball team. The "Dream Team," as it was popularly known, marched unscathed to the gold medal.

Shortly after the Olympics Wilkens had a brush with serious illness. Wilkens ripped an Achilles tendon during a pickup basketball game in Barcelona. As the injury healed, blood clots from his leg found their way into his lungs, forcing him into the hospital and seriously jeopardizing his life. "I think that was the first time I realized my own mortality," Wilkens told the *Akron Beacon Journal.* "I was always healthy. Now I see how fragile it is. I felt vulnerable."

Since his recovery Wilkens has tried to relax more and has taken an immense enjoyment in his career and the achievements of his various teams. The most recent team under his direction will be the 1996 U.S. Olympic team that will play in the games in Atlanta. Wilkens was named Olympic head coach at the end of the 1995 NBA season. His longevity as a coach is all the more remarkable considering the obstacles presented by his race. Wilkens was only the second black man hired to coach an NBA team, he has outlasted numerous competitors, both black and white. Wilkens finds it amusing that some

of the players he coaches are not even familiar with his career as a player. For Wilkens, however, recognition has never been as important as winning. According to Mark Starr in *Newsweek,* the winningest NBA coach in history "has earned the respect of two decades' worth of NBA players by being patient, by being demanding and by asking no more of his players than he asked of himself.... Nothing can detract from Wilkens's historic accomplishment. He has proved himself a man for all seasons, not just any one."

Sources

Akron Beacon Journal, February 17, 1993, p. 1C.
Black Enterprise, April 1995, p. 20.
Chicago Tribune, December 2, 1994, p. 3.
Detroit Free Press, January 7, 1995, p. 4B.
Jet, May 15, 1995, p. 47.
Los Angeles Times, January 7, 1995, p. 6C.
Newsday, October 30, 1994, p. 28.
Newsweek, November 21, 1994, p. 103.
Sports Illustrated, December 5, 1994, p. 68-78.
Upscale, June/July, 1995, p. 94.
Washington Post, May 17, 1993, p. 6C; January 21, 1994, p. 8C; January 7, 1995, p. 1H.

—*Mark Kram*

Gregory Williams

1943—

Educator, administrator

Dean of Law at The Ohio State University College of Law, Gregory Williams has had a successful career in academia, having earned a doctorate from George Washington University in 1982. His true claim to fame, however, is a unique life episode that not only shaped who he is but also has contributed an interesting sidelight to the experience of race relations in the United States. Initially raised as white, Williams discovered that at least part of his immediate roots were black; in a racially divided society where even "one drop" of black blood defined one as being African American, the implications were immense. As he emphasized in the *Detroit Free Press,* "Looking white only goes so far. The issue in America has never been color. It's always been race. Once racial heritage is discovered, that's all that's required. I don't look black, but that didn't make any difference to the people in Indiana in 1954."

Born on November 12, 1943, in Muncie, Indiana, where most of his maternal family resided, Williams spent the earliest years of his life in Virginia. His father James "Tony" Williams owned a bar and restaurant in Gum Springs, Virginia between Alexandria and Fort

Belvoir; the establishment was often frequented by Korean War-bound U.S. soldiers stationed at the fort. U.S. Highway 1, where the Williams tavern was located, was the dividing line in the county between the white populace and the black community. Gum Springs itself was a predominately black neighborhood and had been since the time of the first U.S. president, George Washington. To the east of Route 1 was the white neighborhood.

Knew Himself to be White

The Williams's tavern had both a "front area," where whites were served and a "back area," for blacks. Although it was illegal in Virginia to operate an establishment with a liquor license that served both races, Tony Williams was allowed to do so because his saloon was the nearest one to Fort Belvoir and served the needs of those about to risk their lives for the rest of the country as well as those who had returned from having done so. "I saw segregation of the races as the natural order of life," Gregory Williams expressed in his memoir *Life on the Color Line: The True Story of a White Boy Who Discovered He Was Black.*

Born Gregory Howard Williams on November 12, 1943, in Muncie, Indiana; son of James Anthony (a businessman) and Mary (a homemaker) Williams; married Sara Catherine Whitney, August 29, 1969; children: Natalia Dora, Zachary Benjamin, Anthony Bladimir, Carlos Gregory. *Education:* Ball State University, B.A., 1966; University of Maryland, M.A., 1969; George Washington University, J.D., 1971, M.Ph, 1977, Ph.D. 1982.

Delaware County, IN, deputy sheriff, 1963-66; Falls Church, (VA) Public Schools, teacher, 1966-70; U.S. Senate, legislative assistant, 1971-73; George Washington University, director of experimental programs, 1973-77; University of Iowa College of Law, professor, 1977-93; University of Iowa, associate vice president of academic affairs, 1991-93; The Ohio State University College of Law, dean and professor of law, 1993–.

Member: Foreign Lawyer Training Program, Washington, DC (consultant, 1975-77); U.S. Civil Rights Commission (Iowa Advisory Commission member, 1978-88); Iowa Law Enforcement Academy Council (member, 1979-85).

Selected awards Certificate of Appreciation, University of Iowa Black Law Students Association, 1984; Distinguished Alumni Award, George Washington University National Law Center, 1994.

Addresses: *Office*—Ohio State University College of Law, 55 West 12th Ave., Columbus, Ohio, 43210-1338

The nature of segregation became clear to Williams early in life. In his autobiography he recalled an powerful event that occurred while at his father's tavern: a black military figure entered the premises, sat at one of the front booths, and ordered a meal. The waitress recited the law against serving "coloreds" in the white area. "The soldier yelled, `Whaddya mean I can't be served? I gave a leg for this f___ing country!' Angrily the soldier jerked his khaki trousers to his calf and knocked on a brown artificial limb to emphasize his point. I struggled to reconcile the contradiction of what the country required of the soldier and what the state permitted him to

do." Tony Williams told the veteran he would be proud to serve him, took the man back into the family quarters, and gave him a free steak dinner.

Despite writing of such colorful incidents, Williams noted that his family life deteriorated as his childhood advanced. His father drank much of the time and gambled extensively. His parents fought on a regular basis, and his father would beat his mother when drunk. Gregory's mother left part of the family when he was nine years old; she took the two youngest children, leaving behind Gregory and his younger brother Mike. From that point life was rough for Gregory. Eventually Tony Williams's businesses failed due to his drinking and gambling. He packed up the kids and headed to Muncie, Indiana by Greyhound bus. En route Gregory received the news that would change his world forever.

Before the bus reached Muncie, Tony Williams revealed a startling secret to his sons. As Gregory Williams related in the *Detroit Free Press:* "My father said ... that we were going to be staying with his family, a family I knew absolutely nothing about. And he said `Do you remember Miss Sallie?' I remembered a Miss Sallie, a tall thin black woman who would come into and out of our lives, identified as a maid, a cook. She was around, but we just didn't know who she was. He said, `Well that's my mother, and that's your grandmother. That means you boys are part colored, and I'm colored. And in Indiana, you're going to be colored boys. In Virginia you were white boys. Now, you're not any different today than you were yesterday, but in Indiana people are going to treat you differently.'"

Transition

Not surprisingly, Williams was shocked by the information his father had disclosed. He knew from Virginia that life would indeed be different; at first he denied what his dad was told him. He remembered swimming in "whites only" pools, drinking from "whites only" fountains, and going to "whites only" movies in his former life. Having had only heard his dad referred to as Italian, but never as "colored," young Gregory soon came to understand that his father was a "high-yellow mulatto," or a very light skinned black of mixed parenting.

Williams and his brother were re-classified in school once their racial heritage was discovered. According to *Ebony,* Williams's official transcript contained a warning to teachers not to be "fooled" by his appearance. Initially Gregory and his brother stayed with their aunt and uncle; later, the brothers were taken in by their grandmother Sallie, who lived in a tar paper-covered, 3-room shack at the edge of the town junkyard. Sallie drank as much as their father did and entertained a variety of men when she did.

After a few months Sallie could no longer care for the boys, so they went to live with a 52-year-old widow of one of their father's gambling and drinking buddies. Ms. Dora Terry-Weekly was a poor woman who supported the boys on her monthly $25 social security check in addition to a housekeeping job she heldd. A very religious woman, "Miss Dora" introduced the Williams's brothers to the Pentecostal Church. Miss Dora proved to be one of the few stable people in Williams's life. She provided the loving home that Gregory and his brother needed until they reached adulthood. "She basically saved my life," Williams told *Ebony*. "She took us in when no one else would or could. She provided help when we were getting hit with all this stuff ... [including] the racial intolerance...."

Williams was able to learn more about his family background while staying with and later visiting his grandmother. He learned that he came from a mixed racial ancestry going back several generations. His great-grandfather was a Cherokee Indian, Gregory's grandfather was a rich white Kentuckian who never acknowledged paternity, and of course Gregory's own mother was white. Williams had relatives that were all colors from "honey to brown to chocolate" he specified in *Life on the Color Line.*

Of all of Williams's mother's extensive family--several aunts and uncles as well as his maternal grandparents--only one of his mother's sisters ever allowed him into her house. His maternal grandmother visited once, nearly one year after they arrived in Muncie. Pulling up to the house where Williams's was staying, she honked her car horn until he came out, refusing to enter the home of a Negro. Once in the car all his grandmother would say was that she had seen his mother. Williams stated in his autobiography that his grandmother would not forward messages from him to his mother because she said "I don't carry messages for niggers."

The prejudice Williams faced ran both ways; in *Life on the Color Line,* he noted that though he was often attacked by white youths because they knew he was a "nigger," he also fought black youths who thought he was a "cracker," or white. Williams used these difficulties to focus only upon school-- studying hard and receiving excellent grades--but his work went largely unrecognized by adults because most academic commendations were reserved for white students. The only time he was able to see the guidance counselor was in the ninth grade, he remembered in *Ebony*. He had been seen talking to white girls and was told by the school

official that "this interracial dating thing is something that just isn't done in Muncie...." Summarily reprimanded, he was threatened with suspension. Williams also excelled in athletics during high school: he was the starting quarterback on the football team and a forward on the basketball team.

Self-defined as Black

After graduating from high school Williams attended Ball State University in Muncie, where, in 1966, he acquired his B.A. in criminal justice. He worked as a janitor and as the deputy sheriff of Delaware County to pay his way through college. After completing his undergraduate education, Williams moved to the Washington, DC area to pursue a law degree, enrolling at the University of Maryland. He taught in a public school system, while earning his graduate degree.

> "The issue in America has never been color. It's always been race. I don't look black, but that didn't make any difference to the people in Indiana in 1954."

While in the Washington area, Williams tried to re-establish contact with his mother, whom he had only seen once in the 12 years since she had left him. Williams related in *Life on the Color Line* that his attempts were unsuccessful. She made it clear to Williams that the only way for him to re-enter her life would be for him to reject the life he had lived for the past 10 years--i.e. the "black" life. A hurt Williams assessed in *Ebony* that "there was no acknowledgment that she might have messed up or that she was sorry she turned her back on her children and hadn't sent us a card or letter or anything in 12 years." He has not had much contact with her since.

In 1969, the same year he obtained a master's degree in government and politics, Williams married his high school sweetheart, Sara Whitney. She was one of the white girls he had been warned about talking to while in Muncie. Whitney had also encountered racism in Indiana. Neighbors would telephone her parents home and call her "nigger lover," Williams acknowledged in *Life on the Color Line.* After her parents moved out of town, Whitney stayed with her grandmother. Williams and

Whitney managed to keep their relationship fairly quiet to avoid harassment, until they attended a wedding together one day. Folks called Whitney's grandmother to tell that they had witnessed the couple together. When she found out that Williams was black, Whitney's grandmother responded by throwing all her granddaughter's belongings into the street. The ensuing turmoil caused an initial breakup between the two adolescents, shortly after high school ended, but having kept in touch, the two grew close again.

Meanwhile, Williams still had his sights set on being involved in the legal profession. To that end, he applied for and was accepted at George Washington University, earning a J.D. there in 1971. That year Williams put his training to the test as a legislative assistant in the U.S. Senate. A couple years later, George Washington University offered him a position as head of experimental programs. At the end of his four years in that post, he had also earned a master's of philosophy from the school. Williams and family relocated to Iowa in 1977, where he took an academic post at the University of Iowa College of Law. For nearly 20 years, Williams served the institution as a professor of law; then in 1991, the University of Iowa gave him the additional title of associate vice president of academic affairs. Two years later the Williams moved to Ohio.

Williams has made a comfortable life for himself. After marrying, he and his wife had two children by birth and two children through adoption, thus continuing the tradition of opening one's home to those that need love, as Miss Dora had. They live in an upper-middle-class neighborhood in Columbus; since 1993, Williams has been administrative head the College of Law at Ohio State University. Obviously a driven man, Williams still managed to find the time to record his life story. In speaking about his 1995 book *Life on the Color Line,* Williams told *Ebony,* "I'm sure I'll write other books in my life. But I hope this one is the one that endures, the one that tells America it cannot be so consumed by race that it discards people, the one that tells little kids who faced or are facing what I did that life can be different, better. Because if it happened for me, it can happen for them."

Selected writings

The Law and Politics of Police Discretion, Greenwood, 1984.

(Contributor with University of Iowa Continuing Legal Education Staff) *Iowa Guide to Search and Seizure,* University of Iowa Law, 1986.

Life on the Color Line: The True Story of a White Boy Who Discovered He Was Black, NAL-Dutton, 1995.

Sources

Books

Williams, Gregory Howard, *Life on the Color Line: The Story of a White Boy Who Discovered He Was Black,* Viking, 1995.

Periodicals

Detroit Free Press, March 3, 1995, pp. 1J, 4J.
Ebony, October 1992, pp. 88-96.

—Stephen Stratton

Patricia J. Williams

1951—

Attorney, author, essayist, legal educator

In her writings and teachings Patricia J. Williams always begins with the notion that experience counts. Society should not let case law--law established by judicial decisions--commercial interests like Hollywood, or powerful political figures manipulate reality and obscure the real motivations and fate of human beings. "The law becomes a battleground of wills," she stated in *The Alchemy of Race and Rights: Diary of a Law Professor.* "But the extent to which technical legalisms are used to obfuscate [obscure] the human motivations that generate our justice system is the real extent to which we as human beings are disenfranchised. Cultural needs and ideals change.... The need to redefine our laws in keeping with the spirit of cultural flux is what keeps a society alive and humane," she added.

For example, in a 1994 *The Nation* essay Williams theorized: "The continuing struggle for racial justice is tied up with the degree to which segregation and the outright denial of black humanity have been naturalized in our civilization." To some, such views are unorthodox, but Williams does not shy away from commenting on what she sees as social maladies. For instance, in a

Newsday opinion/editorial column, she linked the tragic fate of Nicole Brown Simpson--the slain ex-wife of former football superstar O. J. Simpson--to "the invisibility of black and poorer white women who die at the hands of their spouses." (Following a lengthy criminal trial in 1995, a jury found Simpson not guilty of murdering his former wife.) Such outspokenness has led Williams to be regarded as the proverbial fly in the ointment--the bearer of bad news about society, which refuses, Henry Louis Gates, Jr. wrote in *The Nation,* "to play by the rules of relevance, to stay behind those velvet ropes." Perhaps the question is less what she is than how she got there.

Learned to Live in a Racist Society

Patricia Joyce Williams was born on August 28, 1951, in Boston, one of two daughters of Isaiah Williams, a technical editor, and Ruth Williams, a teacher. Her community, the Roxbury section of Boston, was a white working-class neighborhood when Patricia was quite young. Her mother's black family was apparently ac-

was 'the colored kid' in school." Things would get worse. About the time Patricia entered seventh grade, classmates began whispering about how "The colored are coming," she told *CBB.* Parents were going door-to-door talking about declining property values—a vicious rumor fostered by realtors. "It was classic block-busting," Williams said. Her parents fought back by instilling in their daughters a sense of their worth and history.

The encouragement by Williams's parents to work hard at achieving her educational goals paid off when she was admitted to a leading institution, Wellesley College, in Wellesley, Massachusetts. She graduated one year early in 1972. Williams then went on to Harvard Law School to become one of "the first crop of affirmative action babies," Williams mused to *CBB.* It was there that she encountered racial backlash head-on. The *Regents of University of California v. Allan Bakke* case that challenged admission quotas at a California medical school was being debated and would eventually reach the U.S. Supreme Court. Bakke, a white student was denied admission to the University of California because although he had received higher admissions test scores than some of the students who were admitted, the school's policy was to limit the number of white students to allow for more minorities. Bakke sued the school and later won the right to be admitted. "I spent a lot of time dealing with people who'd come up and ask your LSAT [law school admissions test] scores; it was very confrontational," Williams recalled, during her *CBB* interview.

After graduating from Harvard in 1975, Williams took a job as deputy city attorney with the Office of the City Attorney in Los Angeles, a locale that "was as far from Boston as I could go without jumping into the ocean," she told *CBB.* The job gave her both civil and criminal trial experience, mostly in consumer protection. "People don't think of consumer protection as criminal, but there were cases, for example, where people were saying 'This is a cancer cure' and it was actually volcanic ash," Williams revealed to *CBB.* She prosecuted cases revolving around issues like sterilization and phony doctors.

In 1978, Williams moved on to a position as staff attorney with the Western Center on Law and Poverty, also in Los Angeles. It was there

that she began to focus on her future legal specialty of commercial and contract law. At the Western Center, she also worked on cases concerning credit card scams and questionable banking practices. Her appetite for this line of work soured after a couple of years. Teaching seemed a viable alternative, and Williams also wanted to explore creative writing, an interest that is rarely consid-

cepted because of its long tenure in the area. Still, Williams said in an interview with *Contemporary Black Biography, (CBB),* "There was always the sense that I

ered an asset in the dry, just-the-facts practice of law.

Williams's next stop, accordingly, was as associate professor of law at Golden Gate University School of Law for four years beginning in 1980. Then in 1984, an excellent opportunity arrived that afforded her the chance to return to New York, where she had family, and to join in a new public interest law school at City University of New York. Williams was attracted to the idea of a law school that emphasized legal practice and a commitment to the needs of the underserved, particularly the poor. "It was an enormously exciting time," Williams enthused during her *CBB* interview. "I still think of it as the height of my teaching career." However, the political patron for the law school committed suicide, and the still-not-yet-accredited and left-leaning school ran into political problems with the surrounding conservative community. Then came the first wave of faculty firings. So in 1988 she decided to depart of her own volition. As she told *CBB*, "The idea of being fired from an unaccredited school because of politics was not the way I wanted my career to go down."

Nomadic Years and Creative Writing

Williams received a tenured-teaching offer at the University of Wisconsin. In addition, she had already committed herself to a visiting associate professorship at Stanford University School of Law in California, teamed with a visiting scholar role at Stanford's Institute for Research on Gender and Women. All told, Williams was with Wisconsin from 1988 to 1993. During that period Williams also accepted a visiting scholar-in-residence spot at Duke University in North Carolina for the fall of 1990. This was followed two years later by a visiting professor of women's studies job at Harvard University's Women's Studies Program in the spring of 1992. She began a professorship at Columbia University School of Law in New York City the same year.

Two very different interests began consuming Williams. One was motherhood; at age 40 and still single, she adopted her son, Peter. The second interest was writing. Williams was never one for the world of endless legal citations and starchy formalism. Indeed, her law review articles sported such colorful titles as "Fetal Fictions: An Exploration of Property Archetypes in Racial and Gendered Contexts" in *University of Florida Law Review 81,* 1990, and "Spirit-Murdering the Messenger: The Discourse of Fingerpointing as the Law's Response to Racism" in *University of Miami Law Review 127,* 1987. During the next few years she branched out to the consumer media by writing for publications associated with protest and leftist politics such as *Ms., The Village Voice,* and *The Nation* magazines, as well as main-

stream periodicals like *The New York Times Book Review* and *The Christian Science Monitor.*

At times, Williams's creative flair clashed with occupational expectations. She was told by the editors of one law review that since she had a very poetic way of writing, she should consider writing short stories. Williams wrote in *Alchemy* that these editors deemed her style "far too personal for any legal publication," and they added, "if you don't mind our saying so, its publication anywhere will risk your being perceived as quite unstable in the public eye."

Provoked Thought

Published in 1991 by Harvard University Press, *The Alchemy of Race and Rights: Diary of a Law Professor* is a collection of Williams's legal writings and essays on a range of subjects. The book's subtitle, "Diary of a Law Professor," was not her idea, nor was it her idea to publish the work as a consumer rather than academic book. This categorization "resulted in people reading it as my real diary, and in my mind, it's more calculated than that, a mimicry of various styles," she mentioned to *CBB.* In her opening chapter, for example, she introduces herself as a bathrobe-clad woman pondering whether she's losing her mind—a takeoff on a similar self-description by the seventeenth-century philosopher René Descartes.

> "The need to redefine our laws in keeping with the spirit of cultural flux is what keeps a society alive and humane."

For *CBB* Williams described *Alchemy* as "a story of my struggle to expand what in the law has been called `the reasonable man category'—a sense of the tension between myself, historically, and the unreasonable man, to enter into a political, legal, and social debate that challenges the normality that's made a cult of the standard of the reasonable man. To what extent can you expand it to include the `reasonable woman,' `reasonable people?' The experience of people who originally weren't considered citizens, human." In her book, Williams also provided commentary on a number of controversial and well-publicized court cases.

Writing about the "Baby M" case, for instance, where surrogate mother Mary Beth Whitehead sued to retain the baby she had borne for a married man and his wife, Williams worries about "the market ethic that says there is nothing that can't be sold." The most troublesome historical example of this of course is slavery, but now Williams sees its legacies, "when you have markets in bodies and babies ... I'm concerned about how 'Baby M' puts children in a market context".

Williams commented on the 1987 Tawana Brawley case in which a 15-year-old black female in upstate New York was found wandering, apparently dazed, with cigarette burns and feces on her body. She implicated three white men but her story was attacked by the press. Prior to admitting that she fabricated the story, Brawley was defended by such well-known figures as the black social activist Al Sharpton. Williams saw a scenario where "a cast of extraordinarily self-interested men did all her [Brawley's] speaking for her," and the press barely considered what Brawley herself said, much less felt. Williams saw the Howard Beach case, where three black men with car problems were severely beaten, one fatally, by whites in a white neighborhood for just being there as "a story of how boundaries are drawn, how little sub-nation-states get drawn in the name of neighborhood values and also the tension between property values and human rights."

Critics were generally enthusiastic about *Alchemy.* Henry Louis Gates, Jr. writing for *The Nation* magazine called it "one of the most invitingly personal, even vulnerable books I've read," while the *New York Times* admired its "valuable insights" but criticized its academic language, which at times "shuts you out." *Alchemy* also received a number of book awards including one from *Ms.* magazine who called the work one of "the feminist classics of the last 20 years [that] literally changes women's lives." In October of 1995 Williams's *The Rooster's Egg: On the Persistence of Prejudice* was published. Like *Alchemy,* this book was in keeping with Williams's concern about social issues.

Clearly, Williams is disturbed about her society and cares deeply about change. She seldom hesitates to bring to light those injustices that impact the human condition. Issues such as welfare reform, affirmative action, and congressional attacks upon what she considers the weak and defenseless members of society are all potential subjects for her legal mind and her writer's heart.

Sources

Washington Post, August 16, 1991, p. D-5.
The New York Times Book Review, May 26, 1991, p. 10.
The Nation, June 10, 1991, p. 766.

Additional information for this profile was obtained through a *CBB* interview with Williams on April 6, 1995.

—Joan Oleck

Robert F. Williams

1925—

Civil rights and political activist

Almost ten years before the formation of the Black Panther Party (a militant group formed during the "Black Power" movement), National Association for the Advancement of Colored People (NAACP) branch president Robert F. Williams's 1959 press statement advocating "meeting [racist] violence with violence" sent a wave of reaction through white and conservative black circles. As an ex-serviceman disillusioned by legalist and pacifist civil rights tactics, Williams launched a local campaign of armed self-defense in his hometown of Monroe, North Carolina. Beginning in 1961, he lived in exile in Cuba and the People's Republic of China for eight years because of his alleged kidnapping of a white Monroe couple. Meanwhile, he established--through radio, newsletters, and correspondence--a revolutionary black liberation front in the United States.

Robert Franklin Williams was born on February 26, 1925, in Monroe--a once thriving antebellum railroad town located 14 miles from the border of South Carolina. The son of a railroad boilermaker's helper, Williams grew up in a seven-room, two-story home on Boyte Street. He attended Winchester School and took inter-

est in history, geography, and writing. Though his school books portrayed slavery as socially beneficial, he was awakened to the brutal aspects of racism at age ten, when a policeman dragged a black woman down Monroe's main street. Williams was haunted by the laughter of white onlookers and the victim's screams. He recalled in his autobiography *Negroes With Guns* how "the cop was grinning as he pulled her by the heels, her dress up over her hips and her back being scraped by the concrete pavement."

World War II

In 1942, at age 17 Williams left high school to receive vocational training as a machinist with the National Youth Administration (NYA). After his education at an NYA camp near Rocky Mount, North Carolina, he continued his studies at Elizabeth City State Teachers College (now Elizabeth City State University), an all-black, teachers college in Elizabeth City, North Carolina. One year later, he arrived in Detroit to gain employment in the city's thriving war industry. Living with his oldest brother, Edward, he worked at Ford Motor

At a Glance . . .

Born Robert Franklin Williams, February 26, 1925, in Monroe, NC; son of John Lemuel (a boilermaker's helper) and Emma (Carter) Williams; married Mabel R. Williams, 1947; children: Robert F. (deceased), John Chalmers. *Education:* Attended Elizabeth City State Teachers College (now Elizabeth City State University), Elizabeth City, NC, c. 1942; West Virginia State College, 1949; North Carolina State College, 1951; Johnson C. Smith University, 1953.

National Youth Administration, machinist-in-training, 1942; Ford Motor Company, Detroit, MI, machinist, 1943; Mare Island Navy Yard, San Francisco, CA, 1944; *Daily Worker,* contributor, 1947-48; worked as a field laborer in upstate New York, 1952; National Association for the Advancement of Colored People (NAACP), Monroe, NC, branch president, 1955; launched local civil rights and self defense campaign, 1955-61; *Crusader* magazine, founder and publisher, 1959-c.1965, 1966; exiled in Cuba, 1961-66, People's Republic of China, 1966-68; Radio Free Dixie (radio show), creator, 1962-65; Republic of New Africa (RNA), Detroit, president in exile, 1968; returned to the United States, 1968; resigned as president of RNA, 1969; American Program Bureau, lecturer, 1969-73; University of Michigan, Ann Arbor, consultant, 1970-71; People's Association for Human Rights, Inc., organizer, legal advisor, 1974--. Author, *Negros With Guns,* Marzani & Munsell, 1962, Third World Press, 1973. *Military Service:* U.S. Army, c.1943-46; U.S. Marine Corps, 1954-55.

Selected awards Malcolm X Black Manhood Award, Malcolm X Society, 1989; JB Gold Medal Award, John Brown Society, 1991; Outstanding Contributions, Association of Black Social Workers, 1987; Black Image Award, Lake/Newaygo NAACP, 1992.

Member: National Rifle Association (NRA), 1950--.

Addresses: *Home*--P.O. Box 611, Baldwin, MI 49304.

program of racial equality.

After 18 months of profitable employment in Detroit, Williams faced the destructiveness of racial tensions again--the outbreak of the 1943 race riot. In the days that followed, rioting spread across the city, resulting in 34 deaths. Shortly thereafter, Williams took a six-month job at the Mare Island Navy Yard near San Francisco. Unable to tolerate the outbreaks of racial violence that occurred in the employee dormitories there, he quit and returned home to Monroe.

Drafted into the army, Williams was sent to Fort Bragg, North Carolina. After earning high scores on a radio aptitude test, he was transferred to a Signal Corps battalion at Camp Crowder, Missouri, to be trained as a radio operator. To his disappointment, however, he was assigned to a school for telephone linesmen. Before completing his telephone line training, he became ill and was re-assigned as a clerical typist. In the months following World War II, Williams experienced the effects of low morale that spread among Camp Crowder's segregated black troops. Defiant of the harsh treatment by white officers, Williams was confined in the camp stockade for insubordination. As Robert Carl Cohen pointed out in *Black Crusader,* "Williams was proud of being in the stockade because he felt he was there for resisting an unjust system--not for committing a crime." In 1946, after a six-month stay at Fort Lewis Washington, Williams received an honorable discharge without a good conduct medal.

Proletarian Poet

Back in Monroe, Williams earned his high school diploma and wrote poetry and prose--works that appeared in *Hearth Strings Journal* and *Westminster Magazine*-- as well as a weekly column in the *Monroe Enquirer.* Some months later, during another brief stint as an auto worker in Detroit, his short story, "Some Day I Am Going Back South," was published in the *Daily Worker.* After leaving Detroit for Monroe, he attended college under the educational benefits of the G.I. Bill, which allowed members of U.S. armed forces to pay for their college education. He took courses in psychology and creative writing at West Virginia State College. During his year there, he joined the staff of the college newspaper, *The Quill.* He subsequently transferred to North Carolina College in Durham, where he studied literary classics and read the works of Karl Marx and Vladimir Lenin introduced to him by a group of college communists. In the fall of 1950, he continued his study of literature at Johnson C. Smith College in Charlotte.

Company as a mill operator. Williams also attended Communist Party meetings and read the organization's publication, *Daily Worker.* Though he did not become a party member, Williams was drawn to the party's

When his G.I. benefits expired in 1952, Williams went to New York City to look for employment. Living with an aunt in Harlem, he took a job at the Curtis-Wright aircraft plant across the river in New Jersey. In New York he befriended a group of white left-wing intellectuals, some of whom were active in the American Labor Party. With the fall of war production, Williams lost his job and returned to Monroe. Desperate to support his family, he found employment as a laborer on a farm in upstate New York. In the *Black Crusader,* Robert Cohen wrote, "Sharing the lot with those migrant farm workers proved to Williams that exploitation isn't limited to the cotton fields of Dixie or to blacks."

Nearly destitute and only 29-years old, Williams raised bus fare and traveled to Los Angeles to work as a machinist in the city's aircraft plants. By the time of his arrival, however, the post-Korean War recession had left few employment opportunities. Unable to find a job, he joined the U.S. Marine Corps in 1954 to be trained as an information specialist. Instead of receiving training in communications, he underwent special combat training at Camp Pendleton, learning the use of rifles, machine guns, grenades, rocket launchers, and various infantry weapons. After refusing to salute the flag at a parade ceremony, he was sentenced to 180 days in the brig. After being released, he underwent special mountain warfare training in Nevada. Prior to embarking for a tour of duty in Korea, Williams was discharged.

Not long after his return to Monroe in October of 1955, Williams, joined the predominately white local Unitarian Fellowship and the Human Relations Group--a coalition of Unitarians, Catholics, and Protestants. Williams's increasing civil rights activity prompted him to join the Monroe NAACP as well. One year later, the organization's dwindling membership fell to six. Rather than dissolve the branch and risk the appearance of submitting to local racist pressure, members held an election and voted Williams in as president and Dr. Albert Perry as vice president. To build up the strength of the branch, Williams recruited members among black domestics, laborers in pool halls, and from the ranks of the unemployed. As opposed to the NAACP's traditional membership of middle and upper-class professionals and intellectuals, Williams provided Monroe's branch with a distinct working-class composition. Members ranged from white pacifists to African American war veterans who, as Williams described in *Negroes With Guns,* "were very militant and did not scare easy."

A Call to Arms

Following the 1954 U.S. Supreme Court decision *Brown*

v. Board of Education of Topeka, which called for an end to the "separate but equal" doctrine, Williams sought to desegregate Monroe's Union County Library. Though he expected harsh opposition, the board chairman agreed, without protest, to desegregate the library. After Williams's first victory, he moved to desegregate Monroe's municipal swimming pool. Outraged over the deaths of several black children in backwoods swimming holes and the use of their tax dollars that went to support a segregated public facility, a large number of Monroe's blacks supported the campaign. When city government officials ignored requests for obtaining equal swimming facilities, Williams suggested blacks could use the pool on a one-day-a-week basis. City officials argued that such an arrangement would prove too costly since the water would have to be drained each time black people used the facility. Determined to desegregate the pool, Williams led groups of black youths on sit-ins, organized protests by refusing to leave segregated establishments.

In retaliation against Williams's civil rights activity, the Ku Klux Klan, a white supremacist organization, held rallies. As the regional headquarters of the Klan, Monroe's rallies attracted several thousand members from neighboring counties and South Carolina. After their evening gatherings, Klansmen rode by car cavalcade through Monroe's black neighborhood of Newtown, honking horns, shouting obscenities, and firing pistols. Stepping up its campaign to quell the activities of Monroe's NAACP, the Klan launched a petition campaign to drive Williams and Perry out of Union County.

Because the Monroe police department refused to intervene against the Klan, Williams urged Monroe's black community to undertake a program of armed self-defense. Within a year of obtaining a gun club charter from the National Rifle Association (NRA), he recruited 60 members who armed themselves with military surplus weapons and mail-order firearms. As quoted in *White Violence Black Response,* Williams recalled how his self-defense unit "spent the summer in foxholes behind sandbags. We had steel helmets. We had gas masks. And we had a better communication system than they have now."

As a result of death threats against Perry, Williams posted a 24-hour vigil outside the doctor's home. On October 5, 1959, while the Klan made a routine night ride through Newtown, they unexpectedly met the fire of Williams's defense guard. In *Making of Black Revolutionaries,* writer Julian Mayfield described the scene: "It was just another good time for the Klan.... Near Dr. Perry's home their revelry was suddenly shattered by the sustained fire of scores of men who had been instructed not to kill anyone if it were not necessary. The firing was blistering, disciplined, and frightening. The motorcade, of about 80 cars, which had begun in a spirit of good fellowship, disintegrated into chaos, with panicky, robed men fleeing in every direction. Some abandoned their automobiles and had to continue on foot."

The Double Standard

Following the incarceration of Dr. Perry on charges of performing an illegal abortion, Williams became increasingly involved in the defense of blacks wrongly accused of crimes. In October of 1958, two black Monroe youngsters, James Hanover Thompson age seven, and David "Fuzzy" Simpson age nine, were arrested on a charge of rape for kissing a white girl on the cheek. Though Williams contacted U.S. president Dwight Eisenhower and the national NAACP in regard to the matter, both parties failed to come the boys' defense. Williams then brought in New York defense lawyer Conrad Lynn whose involvement in the case, along with photographs of the convicted youths in the *New York Post* and the *London News Chronicle,* prompted the NAACP to intervene. The boys were released on February 13, 1959. Despite the victory, Williams was disappointed with the national NAACP office. During the case, as Robert Shapiro pointed out in *White Violence and Black Response,* "Williams and the NAACP leadership saw each other as opponents rather than collaborators in a common cause."

In the spring of 1959, a local white man was charged with the attempted rape of a pregnant young black woman, Mrs. Ruth Reed. In keeping with the old South's double racial standard concerning attacks upon women, the white man was acquitted. Embittered by the court's decision, Williams turned to the crowd of black men and women on the steps of the courthouse, and, as he was quoted in *The Making of Black Revolutionaries,* delivered his legendary statement: "Since the federal government will not bring a halt to lynching in the South, and since the so-called courts lynch our people legally, if it's necessary to stop lynching with lynching, then we must be willing to resort to that method. We must meet violence with violence."

Early the next day, NAACP executive director Roy Wilkins called Williams to confirm the statement. Williams informed Wilkins that he had not spoken on behalf of the NAACP and refused to retract the statement. A few hours later the national office suspended Williams for six months. "I first heard that I was suspended," related Williams in *Negroes With Guns,* "when Southern radio stations announced and kept repeating every 30 minutes that the NAACP suspended me for advocat-

ing violence." Though he appealed his suspension to the NAACP Committee on Branches and before the NAACP's 50th anniversary convention in New York City, his suspension was upheld both times.

From Protest to Exile

In the weeks before appearing at the NAACP convention in New York City, Williams launched his newsletter, *The Crusader.* As Williams later explained in *Negroes With Guns,* "Through my newsletter ... I started appealing to readers everywhere to protest the U.S. government, to protest the Justice Department; to protest the fact that the 14th Amendment [providing all U.S. citizens with equal protection under the law] did not exist in Monroe." Williams gained reelection as president of Monroe's NAACP chapter in 1960, the same year that lunch counter sit-ins occurred throughout the South, including Monroe. At this time Williams chose to reinstate picket lines at the town's municipal swimming pool, a decision that nearly resulted in his death when an unidentified automobile ran his car off the road. Williams was not daunted, however. He retaliated by setting up an integrated picket line around Monroe's courthouse.

In August of 1959 several Freedom Riders--members of the civil rights movement who rode buses to effect the desegregation of public transportation facilities--arrived in Monroe to assist in the Williams-led protest. Among them were Martin Luther King, Jr.'s representative Reverend Paul Brooks and James Forman. In his work *The Making of Black Revolutionaries,* Forman described Williams as a "determined man" who "wanted the world to know that law and order had broken down here, and that he was going to protect his home and family by any means necessary." Under the supervision of Williams, Brooks and Forman drafted a ten-point petition and presented it to Monroe's City Aldermen. The document even included demands for equal employment opportunities for Monroe's black citizens. The petition, like Williams's appeal to the U.S. Justice Department, proved unsuccessful.

As black and white Freedom Riders picketed outside the courthouse, local whites began to attack the demonstrators. The Klan sent out a call inviting whites to Monroe to help counter the Freedom Riders' campaign. In late August, with threats on his life and the expectation of a Klan invasion of Newtown, Williams posted guards around his Boyte Street home. Around six o'clock in the evening, a white couple, the Steagalls, drove into Newtown. Entering Boyte Street, the Steagalls encountered several hundred blacks. Drawn outside his home from the sounds of shouting voices, Williams came upon the Steagalls surrounded by a crowd of blacks who sent up a cry of "Kill them, kill them!" Fearing for their lives, Williams led the Steagalls into his house. On the way to the front door, Mrs. Steagall repeatedly shouted, "We have been kidnapped!" Williams attempted to calm the couple, assuring them his motive was to protect them from the angry crowd. Alerted that the police had blockaded both ends of Boyte Street, Williams decided to flee rather than face arrest by state troopers.

Around nine o'clock that evening, Williams left Monroe with his wife and two sons and traveled to Harlem in New York City, where he learned of his indictment for kidnapping by the Union County Grand Jury. Though his indictment came after he crossed the North Carolina state line, Williams remained a fugitive wanted by the Federal Bureau of Investigation (FBI). From Harlem he fled to the Canadian cities of Toronto and Montreal. Aware that Canadian authorities were also seeking his arrest, Williams sought refuge in Cuba--a country he had twice visited in 1960. In *Negroes With Guns,* Williams explained that he "could think of no other place in the Western Hemisphere than Cuba where a Negro would be treated as a human being; where the race problem would be understood." From Vancouver, British Columbia, he crossed into the state of Washington, headed south into Mexico, and entered Cuba.

Expatriate Revolutionary

Through his Havana-based revolutionary radio program, Radio Free Dixie, and his Cuban edition of the *Crusader,* Williams called for blacks to take up arms against their white oppressors. In the pages of the *Crusader* he told how to launch a guerilla self-defense campaign with the use of Molotov cocktails and other homemade weapons. In a 1964 issue, reprinted in *Black Protest Thought in the Twentieth Century,* he wrote: "The hour is fast approaching when our people must make a decision to meekly submit to fascist forces of terror and extermination or surge forth to the battle to liberate ourselves, save America and liquidate its domestic enemies."

In 1966 Williams left Cuba and sought refuge in the People's Republic of China. He resumed publication of the *Crusader* and in 1968 published the pamphlet, "Listen Brother!," which informed African American combat troops in Vietnam to stop fighting against their Asiatic "dark-skinned brothers." In March of 1968, a group of African Americans gathered at the Shrine of the Black Madonna in Detroit to found the Republic of New Africa (RNA)--a revolutionary Marxist-Leninist organization dedicated to establishing a separate black

nation within five of the southern states in the United States. The RNA elected Williams as its president in exile.

Between 1968 and 1969, Williams twice visited Tanzania in east Africa. In the cosmopolitan Tanzanian city of Dar es Salaam, he met revolutionaries from Mozambique, Angola, Rhodesia, and South Africa. Not long before his return to the United States, Williams was quoted in *The New Racism,* "I am not guilty of the crime. I am not a criminal, and I refuse to be intimidated on the grounds that I am. Those white people who are trying to frighten and oppress us cannot be allowed to get away with this.... I am going home to do whatever my people want me to and with the intention of leading." While in Dar es Salaam, the U.S. embassy granted Williams a passport to re-enter the United States. In mid-September of 1969, he left London on a near-empty Trans World Airlines (TWA) jet and arrived in Detroit. After being taken to the federal building in downtown Detroit for a seven-minute hearing before Judge W. Kaess, Williams was released on $11,000 bond.

> "Through my newsletter...I started appealing to readers everywhere to protest the U.S. government, to protest the Justice Department; to protest the fact that the 14th Amendment did not exist in Monroe [South Carolina]."

To celebrate Williams's return, Black Panther leader Huey P. Newton, as quoted in *The Black Panthers Speak,* wrote, "Greetings to the Republic of New Africa and President Robert Williams. I am very happy to welcome you back home. I must add that it is perfect timing. And we need you very much, the people need you very much." Despite the optimism of Newton and other leaders, Williams was disillusioned about the RNA due to the organization's prevalent internal struggles. He resigned as its president in early December of 1969.

Since his resignation from RNA, Williams has been interviewed in scholarly publications and newspapers and appeared as a guest speaker before student groups, especially in Michigan, where he still lives. His work toward bettering the lives of African Americans continued with the formation of the People's Association for

Human Rights, yet another effort that garnered praise and gratitude. And even though his relationship with the NAACP has not always been a positive one, Williams has worked for the organization as a member and vice president of the Lake/Newaygo (Michigan) branch. This work earned him the chapter's Black Image Award in 1992.

Sources

Black Protest Thought in the Twentieth Century, edited by August Meier, Elliot Rudwick, and Francis L. Broderick, Bobbs-Merrill, 1971.

Cohen, Robert Carl, *Black Crusader: A Biography of Robert Franklin Williams,* Stuart, 1972.

Foner, Phillip S., *The Black Panthers Speak,* Da Capo, 1995.

Forman, James, *The Making of Black Revolutionaries,* Open Hand, 1985.

Geschwender, James A., *The Black Revolt: The Civil Rights Movement, Ghetto Uprisings, and Separatism,* Prentice Hall, 1971.

Lokos, Lionel, *The New Racism: Reverse Discrimination in America,* Arlington House, 1971.

Shapiro, Herbert, *White Violence and Black Response,* University of Massachusetts, 1988.

Williams, Robert F., *Negroes With Guns,* Marzani & Munsell, 1962 (reprinted by Third World Press, 1973).

—John Cohassey

William T. Williams

1942—

Abstract, expressionist painter

The fact that he is an African American excelling in his profession is of little concern to William T. Williams, an abstract expressionist painter. As the soft-spoken, mustachioed artist told *Contemporary Black Biography (CBB),* "My job is to make as much art as I can as well as I can." Still, Williams's own emphasis does not stop others from focusing on the fact that he is the first black artist included in H. W. Janson's widely used textbook, *History of Art.* His works hang in such prestigious New York City galleries as the Museum of Modern Art (MOMA), the Whitney Museum, and Harlem's Studio Museum. A Guggenheim Fellowship recipient, Williams has been awarded a trio of grants from the National Endowment for the Arts (NEA), and he has exhibited and lectured all over the world.

William's ethnic heritage is part of the cumulative experience of his life that is reflected in his large, heavily encrusted, acrylic canvasses. Abstract yet in many instances autobiographical, Williams's works reveal much of his personal history and his interest in his ancestry. For example, the diamond shapes and earth tones of his earlier geometric works are reminiscent of the tribal art of the Kuba Kingdom in what is now Zaire, Africa. More recent lyrical works suggest a tonal interplay evocative of the flicker of sunlight off the tree leaves of Williams's rural North Carolina childhood. Summarizing the source of his motivation, Williams told *CBB,* "When you're living an aesthetic as opposed to experiencing an external idea, some things become part and parcel of you. It's impossible for me," he added by way of example, "to take quilts out of my consciousness."

The quilts were made by his grandmother and aunts in Cross Creek, North Carolina, where William Thomas Williams was born July 17, 1942, the second son of William Thomas and Hazel Davis Williams. His father was a federal employee who worked at nearby Fort Bragg; his mother was a domestic worker and telephone operator. Home was a tight-knit group of small tobacco and cotton farms operated by relatives. Life there was poor--the homes had no electricity or running water--but it was also loving and insulated from the worst of Southern racism.

Seeing family members construct and craft everything from furniture to household goods like quilts was an early artistic influence on Williams. All the patterns and textures stayed in young William's consciousness--the diamond shapes his grandmother included in her quilts, a motif passed down from her ancestral African roots, continue to appear in Williams's work. The clay bank where he and his friends fashioned childish pottery and the farmyard where his grandmother encouraged him to draw in the dust remain strong influences as well.

Williams's rural upbringing quickly became urban, however. He was four years old when his father moved the family to New York City to find better employment. Growing up in Queens and a housing project in Far Rockaway, Williams showed artistic talent which his teachers encouraged. The beginnings of a lifelong love affair with color compelled Williams to draw endlessly and pick up the paper scraps tossed out by a printing firm near his home in order to experiment with form.

Committed Himself to Art

At age 14 Williams was admitted to New York's High School of Industrial Arts (now the High School of Art and Design). Despite the two-hour commute, he relished the daily trip into the city. "The advantage of it was it was three-and-a-half blocks from the Museum of Modern Art, so MOMA became an extension of the classroom," he explained to *CBB*. The Metropolitan Museum was another alternate classroom, and expressionists Jackson Pollock, Mark Rothko and Willem DeKooning became his heroes. Although steered toward a commercial art career as were most minority students in those days, Williams soaked up all the art history and technique he could. An African American role model was Jacob Lawrence, who helped guide the teenage artist.

Graduating in 1960, Williams attended New York City Community College for two years on a scholarship, then took his first and last commercial art job, as a production assistant on a trade magazine. He worked there for only two-and-a-half months. The fine arts kept calling him, and Williams responded, first enrolling in the Skowhegan School of Painting and Sculpture where he finally found his true niche. "That was the turning point where I decided I wanted to be a painter, he informed *CBB*. The following year he gained admittance to the prestigious Pratt Institute; there he joyfully immersed himself in the classical art program, trying out different media.

Committed now, Williams attended Yale for his Masters in Fine Arts, then returned to New York City in 1968. With money from his parents, he purchased the Soho loft that remained his home and studio in the mid-1990s. Around that time he married Patricia DeWeese, now manager of his studio; the couple had two children, Aaron and Nila. By 1970, Williams found financial security in the form of a teaching career. First he earned a place on staff at Pratt's School of Visual Arts, then a long-term position as professor of art at Brooklyn College, beginning in 1971. These developments allowed Williams to pursue his art without hindrance. Not long afterward, Williams's years of preparation paid off in a big way.

Shimmering Canvasses

In 1971 Williams had his first show, at the Reese Paley Gallery where, remarkably, he sold out his entire stock. The art world sat up and took notice. As writer Valerie Mercer indicated in a catalogue accompanying a show at the Montclair Art Museum, Williams's work during the 1960s related to his "interest in the prevailing minimal formalist aesthetic, with its mechanistic sensibility and insistence that painting avoid reference to an object or event beyond the painting itself."

Williams avoided rigid adherence to minimalism, though. "By allowing color to do more than emphasize flat surfaces, through an almost violent emission of light produced by the clashing of juxtaposed planes of contrasting high-key color, [Williams] imbued the work with a tension that was indicative of a need to refer to the drama of urban life outside his New York studio," Mercer noted. Williams's huge canvasses--generally 5' x 7'--depicted large geometric forms in fuchsias, chartreuses, and other bold colors. What resulted were his "shimmering paintings" such as *Equinox* and *Redfern,* in which a pearlescent base added to his paint allowed his geometric forms to shimmer when touched by light.

During Williams's interview with *CBB,* he described his mid-1970s works: "It was a drastic break from the prevailing aesthetic. On one hand it seemed to be an allegiance to minimalism, but the surface is implying a physicality and implied illusion that is drastically different." In short, Williams was displaying his trademark fascination with the tactile. Using only paint and brush in *Equinox,* he built borders around his geometric shapes, creating almost a satiny, collage effect. Though his geometric shapes echoed his grandmother's diamonds and the African art in which he was immersed intellectually, Williams yearned in his art to get closer still to personal experience.

As always, Williams turned his back on the commercial. "In 1972 curators wouldn't look at paintings with tactile surfaces," Williams told the Raleigh, N.C., *News and Observer.* Nonetheless, he pushed on in his own direction. What resulted was a series of paintings in the 1980s that were far more lyrical than his previous works. Speaking of his painting *Strange Fruit* (1982), Williams described "a landscape-sense, a horizon, a division between parts," seemingly between earth and a sky. "It's a lot more lyrical," Williams said, than his shimmering minimalist works. "There's a sense of tonal relationships." The difference, Williams explained, "is a trip to Africa."

Williams was invited to be a member of the American delegation to a world gathering, in Lagos, Nigeria, of people of African descent from the international fine arts and performing arts communities. While there, he was struck by the uniting connections he found in Africa. "It was a turning point not so much in terms of what my art had been about, but an attitude in how to make it," Williams said. He was seeing "the relationship between what I had experienced as a child and the way things were made."

> "What I try to do is be the very focused on my own history, my own experience. I don't consciously try to make 'ethnic art.' What I'm assuming is the sum total of my experience will come to bear on my art."

Williams began dividing his paintings into sections, favoring raw colors such as those in *Savannah* in 1979 and *Roseville* in 1982. Reminiscences of rural North Carolina and African textile patterns emerged. Because layers can be built quickly with acrylics, Williams incorporated the cracks in the surface of his paintings into his art. A painstaking process, some paintings have taken as long as two or three years to complete. "That encrustation has a great deal to do with embedding a life into the painting," Williams explained to *CBB.* "It's a result of time involvement rather than just producing an image."

En route, Williams does with a brush what a musician does with a favorite instrument. "The thing that has been a hallmark," the artist said of his work during his *CBB* interview, is "a sense of musicality and a sense of structure underneath." Historian William Janson has likened this to jazz improvisation, and Williams agreed. Even his earlier paintings showed this influence: "Though geometric abstraction, it was never based upon formalism. It was all done on the spot, intuitively and with a great deal of improvising."

Reflected His Heritage

"Williams marries the language of the abstract expressionist tradition with the collective beliefs and response of his Southern heritage," Mercer concluded. Early in his career Williams painted works in homage to his grandparents, Elbert and Sophie Jackson. In the 1980s the artist began another autobiographical series, *111-and-a-half*, the Harlem address of a favorite aunt and uncle of his. A deep blue in these works recalls the light in the apartment hallway.

One painting--still in his living room, unfinished--features panels of blue superimposed with symbols--hearts and birds, for Charlie "Bird" Parker, a musician beloved by the family. Titles such as *Carolina Shout* and *Harlem Sunday* reflect Williams's origins. A work called *Winter Roses* includes a collage of actual quilt batting. When asked by *CBB* to comment on how the observer can recognize this reflection of his African American heritage, Williams demurred: "It's kind of like 'how do we recognize the difference between [bandleaders] Louis Armstrong and Benny Goodman?' They're both playing jazz, but there's a difference between the two and the difference is the sum total of their experiences."

For Williams, the experiences of the artist determine what can be created in the work of art. "What I try to do is be very focused on my own history, my own experience. I don't consciously try to make 'ethnic art.' What I'm assuming is the sum total of my experience will come to bear on my art." This focus on the individual artist's life does not prevent art from communicating across social boundaries such as race or upbringing, however, because, as he emphasized in his *CBB* interview, "anything that hits a resonant note for other people means they have had the same cumulative experience that I have had."

As a teacher, Williams told *CBB* he tells his students that "every time you walk into the studio, you have to start with your first experiences all over again, to relearn every time you go to that painting." For himself, he said that creating one's own experience incorporates all experience. "My experience is the American experi-ence and you can't talk about America without talking about both black and white. To linger on that is to misunderstand the accomplishments of all of its artists." Williams continued along those lines in summing up the value of learning about others' experiences: "If you're going to [write my biography and educate], then what one has to focus on are the accomplishments as opposed to the discipline. That's the issue, not my reaction to racism. The issues are my accomplishments in spite of that."

Sources

Books

History of Art, Fourth Edition, edited by H.W. Janson, Harry N. Abrams Inc., p. 746.

Periodicals

American Visions, April 1991, pp. 15-19.
Detroit Free Press, July 3, 1994, p. 3G.
Metro Times (Detroit, MI), July 8-12, 1994, p. 18.
New York Times, November 17, 1991, p. 20; Aug. 28, 1992.
Raleigh News and Observer, July 18, 1993.

Others

Mercer, Valerie, *William T. Williams* (catalogue essay for the Montclair Art Museum exhibition), 1991.

Additional information for this profile was obtained by a personal interview with Williams on March 10, 1994.

—Joan Oleck

Stevie Wonder

1950—

Singer, songwriter, multi-instrumentalist

In the course of following Stevie Wonder on his relentless travels, journalists come to realize just how beloved an entertainer he is. "It dawned on me," wrote Giles Smith in the *New Yorker,* "that a substantial part of Stevie Wonder's public life consists of the voices of complete strangers telling him they love him." *Rolling Stone's* David Ritz had a similar epiphany. "Following Stevie Wonder around New York is exhilarating work," he wrote. "I get the feeling that he loves being Stevie Wonder. He loves the attention, the adulation, the chance to perform." What's more, Ritz remarked, Wonder's "optimism is infectious." Such optimism may spring from a deep spiritual wellspring, but it is also sustained by decades spent creating indelible, meaningful pop music.

It is estimated that Wonder—born Stevland Judkins Morris in Saginaw, Michigan—was blinded by a surfeit of oxygen in his incubator shortly after his premature birth. "I vaguely remember light and what my mother looks like," he ventured in a 1986 *Life* interview, "but I could be dreaming." His father left the family early on, and he and his five siblings were raised by their mother; she moved the clan to Detroit, where they struggled mightily

to survive. Though he has groused good-naturedly in adulthood at the limitations his sightlessness has placed on him, Wonder told Ritz that as a child he soothed his mother's tears by telling her that he "wasn't sad." He recalled, "I believed God had something for me to do." Along with his siblings, he paid musical tribute to the Almighty in the Whitestone Baptist Church Choir, along with his vocal prowess demonstrating a gift for piano, harmonica, and drums by age 11.

"This Boy Can Give Us Hits"

Thanks to the intercession of a friend, Stevland was brought to the attention of Berry Gordy, president of Detroit-based Motown Records, and Gordy's producer Brian Holland. Gordy placed the exceptional youngster's career in the hands of his associate Clarence Paul, whom he designated as Stevie's mentor. Paul told *Rolling Stone's* Ritz that Gordy had instructed him, "Your job is to bring out his genius. This boy can give us hits." Handed the show business moniker "Little Stevie Wonder," the prodigious adolescent—signed to the

At a Glance . . .

Born Stevland Judkins Morris, May 13, 1950, in Saginaw, MI; son of Lulu Mae Morris; married Syreeta Wright (a singer), 1971 (divorced, 1972); children (with women other than Wright): Aisha, Keita, Mumtaz, and Kwame.

Signed to Motown Records, 1963; billed as "Little Stevie Wonder"; founded Black Bull Music publishing company, 1971; sponsored Stevie Wonder Home for Blind and Retarded Children, 1976; founded Wondirection Records, 1982; contributed songs to *The Woman in Red* film soundtrack, 1984; appeared on AIDS benefit single "That's What Friends Are For," 1986; contributed songs to *Jungle Fever* film soundtrack, 1991; activist for and contributor to various political and social causes, including Mothers Against Drunk Driving, the establishment of a national holiday honoring Martin Luther King, Jr., the anti-apartheid movement, AIDS awareness, and Charge Against Hunger program.

Selected awards: 15 Grammy awards, including those for best male vocalist in both pop and R&B categories, best pop song, and best album; Distinguished Service Award, President's Committee on Employment of Handicapped People, 1969; Academy Award for best song, 1985, for "I Just Called to Say I Love You"; inducted into Rock and Roll Hall of Fame, 1989; Whitney M. Young Award, Los Angeles Urban League, 1990; Carousel of Hope Award, Children's Diabetes Foundation, 1990; Honorary Global Founder's Award, Mothers Against Drunk Driving, 1990; *Essence* magazine award, 1995.

Addresses: *Record company*—Motown Records, 1350 Avenue of the Americas, 20th Floor, New York, NY 10019; 5750 Wilshire Blvd., Los Angeles, CA 90036.

Motown offshoot label Tamla—did indeed yield hits.

Wonder's fourth single, "Fingertips, Pt. 2," appeared in 1963 and became the first live performance of a song to reach the top of the U.S. pop chart. Also that year, Wonder became the first recording artist to reach the Number One position on the *Billboard* Hot 100, R&B singles, and album charts simultaneously. Unable to attend a regular Detroit school while becoming a pop

sensation, Wonder was sent to the Michigan School for the Blind at Motown's expense.

"Motown meant discipline to me," Wonder recalled to Ritz. "The attitude was 'Do it over. Do it differently. Do it until it can't be done any better.'" Under such demanding circumstances the young performer grew up fast. In 1964 he put aside the "Little" label and let fans focus on the Wonder; over the next few years he churned out pop-soul smashes like "Uptight," "Nothing's Too Good for My Baby," "I Was Made to Love Her," and "For Once in My Life." By 1968 his label had amassed enough chart-toppers to fill his first *Greatest Hits* album.

In 1969 Wonder met President Richard Nixon at the White House, where he received a Distinguished Service Award from the President's Committee on Employment of Handicapped People. Meanwhile, he continued to pile up hits as "My Cherie Amour" sold over a million copies and "Signed Sealed Delivered (I'm Yours)" vaulted up the charts. 1970 saw Wonder marry Syreeta Wright, a Motown employee and aspiring singer; the two wrote together, and Wonder produced several successful records for her. The marriage was short-lived, however; they divorced in 1972. By all accounts, they remain friends.

Wright has said that Wonder's music was her chief rival. "He would wake up and go straight to the keyboard," she recalled to Smith of the *New Yorker*. "I knew and understood that his passion was music. That was really his No. 1 wife." Wonder fathered children by three other women over the next couple of decades, though he did not remarry. "I was at the birth of two of my children," he confided in *Life*. "I felt them being born— it was amazing." In a 1995 *Rolling Stone* interview, the 44-year-old artist did express a yearning for matrimony, calling it "the space where we're most relaxed and able to give and receive maximum love. I'm not there yet— but soon. It's one of my goals."

When Wonder turned 21 in 1971 he was due the money he had earned as a minor (this arrangement had been stipulated in a previous agreement). But Motown only paid him one million of the $30 million he'd earned during that time. After considerable legal wrangling he managed to attain a unique degree of artistic and financial autonomy. "At 21, Stevie was interested in being treated well and in controlling his life and in presenting his music, and all those things were extraordinary things for a young man to ask at that point," explained Johanan Vigoda, Wonder's longtime attorney, to Smith of the *New Yorker*. "It wasn't the freedom to be dissolute or undisciplined. He wanted to be free so that he could bring the best of himself to the table."

What Wonder brought to the table—with the establishment of his own music publishing company and near-total creative freedom—was an increasingly sophisticated body of work that managed to fuse the high spirits of classic soul, the down-and-dirty syncopations of funk, exquisite melodies, and his own introspective and increasingly politicized lyrical sensibility. From a sonic standpoint, too, he was a trailblazer, demonstrating the versatility of the synthesizer when it was still something of a novelty instrument in the R&B world.

Accident Redoubled Commitment

Wonder's momentum was almost stopped permanently by a 1973 automobile accident that nearly claimed his life and left him with deep facial scars. If anything, however, this event provoked him to redouble his efforts. Virtually all of Wonder's work during the early

to mid-1970s is essential pop, most notably his albums *Talking Book, Innervisions, Fulfillingness' First Finale,* and the epic *Songs in the Key of Life.* His songs from this period, including the percolating funk-rock workouts "Superstition" and "Higher Ground," the effervescent "Boogie on Reggae Woman," the jubilant paean to classic jazz "Sir Duke," the grittily nostalgic "I Wish," and the breezy chartbuster "You Are the Sunshine of My Life," left most of Wonder's competition in the dust both artistically and commercially. "What artist in his right mind," mused singer-songwriter and soul icon Marvin Gaye in the presence of *Rolling Stone*'s Ritz, "wouldn't be intimidated by Stevie Wonder?"

1979 saw the release of Wonder's musically beguiling *Journey Through the Secret Life of Plants,* the theme of which many listeners found a little eccentric, to say the least. "It was a consideration of the physical and spiritual relationships between human beings and plants," Wonder explained to Ritz, quipping that "some called it shrubbish." Though he increasingly failed to match his

Stevie posing for Motown.

creative and sales peaks of the preceding decades, Wonder was still a giant presence in the world of pop. His *Hotter Than July,* with its reggae-driven hit "Master Blaster (Jammin')," indicated his continuing creative restlessness. And "That Girl," the unstoppable love song "I Just Called to Say I Love You"—which won an Academy Award for best song and stands as Motown's top-selling single internationally—and his duet with ex-Beatle Paul McCartney on the anti-racism anthem "Ebony and Ivory" all burned up the charts.

> "I was in the Hard Rock Cafe in Tokyo last week, and they started playing my records, and I started crying, crying like a little kid, thinking how God has blessed me with all these songs."

Over the years Wonder also became progressively more involved in politics, lobbying for gun control, against drunk driving and the apartheid system enforced by South Africa's white minority, and on behalf of a national holiday in recognition of civil rights martyr Martin Luther King, Jr. He played a number of benefits and made public service announcements, often winning honors for his advocacy. The slogan underneath his picture on a poster for Mothers Against Drunk Driving read: "Before I ride with a drunk, I'll drive myself." He also contributed his labor to the Charge Against Hunger campaign organized by American Express.

By the late 1980s, Wonder had become less prolific than he had been in the past, but he was still phenomenally successful. He snagged a Grammy for 1986's *In Square Circle* and in 1989 was inducted into the Rock and Roll Hall of Fame. He won plaudits for his work on the soundtrack to Spike Lee's 1991 film *Jungle Fever,* allegedly composing the material for it in the space of three weeks. "Movies are always a good challenge," he told Neil Strauss of the *New York Times,* "because it's taking what's happening visually and, even though I'm not able to see it, getting a sense of the movie and finding a new way to work with it." His work for *Jungle Fever* had preempted a collection of songs he'd been crafting while living in the African nation of Ghana; the resulting disc would not hit stores for several years.

Lifetime Pact with Motown

In 1992—by which time multimillion-dollar deals had become commonplace—Wonder signed a unique lifetime pact with Motown. "This is a guy you don't ever want to see recording for anyone else," company president Jheryl Busby told the *New Yorker's* Smith in 1995. "I worked hard to make Stevie see that we had his interests at heart. Stevie is what I call the crown jewel, the epitome. I wasn't looking at Stevie as an aging superstar but as an icon who could pull us into the future." Wonder himself seemed to share this sense of his eternal newness: "I'm going to be 45," he reflected to Ritz in *Rolling Stone,* "but I'm still feeling new and amazed by the world I live in. I was in the Hard Rock Cafe in Tokyo last week, and they started playing my records, and I started crying, crying like a little kid, thinking how God has blessed me with all these songs."

When *Conversation Peace*—the album on which Wonder had been working for nearly eight years—was released in 1995, it garnered a range of reactions. *Vibe* deemed it "a decidedly mixed bag, leapfrogging back and forth between divine inspiration and inoffensive professionalism"; reviewer Tom Sinclair took particular exception to the "cloying sentimentality" of some of the songs, as did other critics. *Entertainment Weekly* praised the album's sound, but noted that "the song selection here, while frisky, is thin, making this comeback small Wonder." *Time's* Christopher John Farley, however, while allowing that the recording "isn't a slam dunk," called it "another winner for Wonder." Regardless of their respective verdicts, most reviewers concurred that Wonder's versatility, passion, and chops remained intact.

Wonder proved the validity of these observations during his 1995 concert tour. "Running 2 1/4 hours, it was an outstanding show—full of pure, old-fashioned R&B," declared *Los Angeles Times* writer Dennis Hunt of Wonder's performance at the Universal Amphitheatre. Pondering the performer's endurance and the disappearance of most of his contemporaries from the scene, Hunt observed, "Some may point to exquisite taste as the key to Wonder's success, but the real secret is his ability to stay current, to be fluent in the R&B style of the moment." Not surprisingly, critics were virtually unanimous about Wonder's 1995 live double CD, *Natural Wonder,* which *Rolling Stone* called "an important and revelatory statement."

Wonder expressed the desire to do an album of "all praise"—that is, gospel—in his interview with Ritz. But regardless of the genre he pursues, his music will undoubtedly always reflect his undeniably compassionate spirituality. While he has inspired a new generation of artists—including rockers the Red Hot Chili Peppers, who made their bid for mainstream popularity with a version of "Higher Ground," Lenny Kravitz, Michael Franti of Spearhead, and virtually every aspiring young soul artist—he nonetheless expressed his determination to keep growing. "You're influenced all the time," he asserted to *New York Times* writer Strauss, "and the day that you cannot be influenced by anything good is the day that you really have let your art die."

Selected discography

On Motown, unless otherwise noted

Little Stevie Wonder: The Twelve-Year-Old Genius, 1963.
Recorded Live (includes "Fingertips, Pt.2 "), 1963.
Uptight (includes "Uptight"), 1966.
Down to Earth, 1967.
I Was Made to Love Her (includes "I Was Made to Love Her"), 1967.
Stevie Wonder's Greatest Hits, 1968.
For Once in My Life (includes "For Once in My Life"), 1969.
My Cherie Amour (includes "My Cherie Amour"), 1969.
Stevie Wonder Live, 1970.
Signed Sealed and Delivered (includes "Signed Sealed Delivered [I'm Yours]"), 1970.
Where I'm Coming From, 1971.
Greatest Hits, Vol. 2, 1972.
Music of My Mind, 1972.
Talking Book (includes "You Are the Sunshine of My Life" and "Superstition"), 1972.
Innervisions (includes "Higher Ground"), 1973.
Fulfillingness' First Finale (includes "Boogie on Reggae Woman"), 1974.
Songs in the Key of Life (includes "Sir Duke" and "I Wish"), 1976.
Journey Through the Secret Life of Plants, 1979.
Hotter Than July (includes "Master Blaster [Jammin']"), 1980.
Stevie Wonder's Original Musiquarium (includes "That Girl"), 1982.
In *Square Circle,* 1985.
Characters, 1987.
Jungle Fever (soundtrack), 1992.

Conversation Peace, 1995.
Natural Wonder, 1995.

With others

Paul McCartney, "Ebony and Ivory," *Tug of War,* Columbia, 1982.
Chaka Khan, "I Feel for You," *I Feel for You,* Warner Bros., 1984.
The Woman in Red (soundtrack; includes "I Just Called to Say I Love You"), 1984.
Dionne Warwick, "That's What Friends Are For," 1986.
(With Lenny Kravitz) "Deuce," *Kiss My Ass,* 1995.
"Stubborn Kind of Fellow," *Inner City Blues: The Music of Marvin Gaye,* Motown, 1995.
Quincy Jones, *Q's Jook Joint,* Qwest/Warner Bros., 1 995.

Also contributed songs to albums by Rufus, Minnie Riperton, and other artists.

Sources

Books

Rees, Dafydd, and Luke Crampton, *Rock Movers & Shakers,* Billboard, 1991.

Periodicals

Entertainment Weekly, March 31, 1995, p. 61.
Jet, May 8, 1995, pp. 56-58; May 22, 1995.
Life, October 1986, pp. 67-74.
Los Angeles Times, January 16, 1995, p. F1.
New Yorker, March 13, 1995, pp. 78-87.
New York Times, January 25, 1995, p. C15.
Rolling Stone, July 13, 1995, pp. 82-85, 126; January 25, 1996, p. 72.
Time, September 4, 1995, p. 76; April 10, 1995, p. 88.
Vibe, March 1995, pp. 97-98.

Additional information for this profile was obtained from Motown Records publicity materials, 1995.

—Simon Glickman

Malik Yoba

1967—

Actor, singer, musician, youth activist

Malik Yoba was an accomplished talent and community activist before being cast in the Fox network television drama *New York Undercover* in 1994, a show with the noteworthy distinction of being the first prime-time network television drama to feature two actors of color. Set in Yoba's hometown of New York City, its plots usually engage his character, the New York City Police Department detective J. C. Williams, in crime-solving activities with his partner Eddie Torres, played by Michael DeLorenzo, along the rough streets of their Harlem beat. Secondary storylines in the hip, jazzy drama feature Williams working toward establishing a good bond with his school-age son and the vagaries of romance with his upwardly-mobile fiancee, all the while worrying about keeping his son from meeting the same fate as he sees other boys in the city encounter on a daily basis.

Yoba's success on *New York Undercover* is in part due to his screen presence and the believability of his character, two factors whose roots lie in the actor's assured sense of self. "With his sculpted physique, the six-foot three-inch Bronx-born actor could have easily been a successful model," noted Deborah Gregory in *Essence* during the first successful season of *New York Undercover*. "Instead he spent the last six years being a real-life role model to black teens."

Since 1986, Yoba has been involved full-time with several different community organizations that target underprivileged youth in the New York City area and has served for many years as vice president of CityKids Foundation. He is also a singer and songwriter with a record contract and a style he terms "urban folk," as well as the head of a company called Nature Boy Enterprises, which offers keynote addresses and motivational workshops headed by the challenging title "Why Are You on This Planet?"

Loved Make Believe

Ironically, Yoba grew up in a home without a television set by decree of a strict Muslim father. Born in 1967, the actor was one of six children raised in a single-parent household; his father also created the surname Yoba for his family so that they might take pride in their own heritage. Yoba spoke of his childhood to *Vibe* magazine

At a Glance . . .

Full name, Abdul-Malik Kashie Yoba; born September 17, 1967, in Bronx, NY; son of Abdullah Yoba and Mahmoudah Lanier.

Actor, singer, musician, and youth activist. CityKids Foundation, New York, NY vice-president, 1986-93; ABC-TV, co-musical director of Henson Productions' *CityKids*, 1992. Nature Boy Enterprises, New York, NY president and chief executive officer, 1994--. "Why Are You on This Planet?" (youth self-esteem program), founder, 1994. Film appearances include *Cool Runnings*, 1992; *Smoke*, 1995; and *Blue in the Face*, 1995. Television appearances include guest spots on *Law and Order* and *Where I Live* and lead role in *New York Undercover*, Fox, 1994--. Signed to Chaos/Columbia Records, 1995.

Member: Reach, New York, NY, (board member, 1992--); CityKids Foundation (advisor, 1993--); Hale House (committee member, 1995--); Children's Peace Memorial. Also a member of several semi-professional entertainment groups.

Awards: Named "one of 30 young artists under the age of 30 who will change American culture in the next 30 years," *New York Times Magazine*, 1994.

Addresses: *Office*--Nature Boy Enterprises, Inc., 163 Third Ave., New York, NY 10003.

reporter Scott Poulson-Bryant, recalling how he and his siblings would script and perform plays for friends and family. "We didn't have a lot of toys ... so we wrote songs and performed those."

Yoba's growing performing experience led him to seek a larger audience. His first stage role was in a production of *Alice in Wonderland* that ran off-off Broadway. "The magic of the theater, the lights, and the music, and the fact that it was a fairy tale come to life probably set it off for me," Yoba told *Ethnic NewsWatch* writer Heather Keets. Despite his stage ambitions, Yoba led the life of a rather typical New York City kid until a gunshot wound at the age of 15 changed his perspective enormously.

Surviving the trauma "inspired me to challenge the climate of violence that almost took my life, and I began working as a volunteer with youth organizations in my community," Yoba explained in an introductory letter for the motivational seminar "Why Are You on This Planet?" Working for many years as a youth activist in New York City, he came into contact with young people from all walks of life and from around the world.

"What I've found with most kids is, no matter how rich or poor they are, or which cultural or ethnic backgrounds they represent, most don't have a clue what their purpose in life is," Yoba clarified in the missive. "I believe that we all have a mission in life and kids especially need to know this. They need to know that they do have a voice, that they can find that voice and use it to affect positive changes in their own lives, their communities, and in the world."

In his capacity as a youth activist, Yoba took a guitar and his ideas of empowerment to junior-high and high school students. His prominence in the community eventually led to invitations to appear on television talk shows like *Oprah* and *The Arsenio Hall Show*. Over the years he had balanced his career with some experience in semi-professional entertainment ensembles and on a whim decided to audition for a role in a Disney movie based on a true story about a Jamaican bobsled team that competed in the 1988 Winter Olympics in Calgary. "I didn't have an agent ... or even a head shot. I went to an open casting call, and they chose me," Yoba said in some press material about how he landed his role in *Cool Runnings*. "I guess it was that I had perfected my Jamaican accent hanging out with the Jamaicans in Washington Square Park."

Arrested Audiences

The success of the movie led to other roles for Yoba, including guest appearances on the television shows *Law and Order* and *Where I Live*. His presence so impressed Wolf Productions, looking to cast one of the two leads for a new show about young, hipster police detectives in New York City, that he was invited to read for the role and won the part. *New York Undercover* debuted in the fall of 1994 to laudatory praise by critics and soon developed a cult audience.

The storylines engage the detectives played by Yoba and DeLorenzo in a plethora of urban drama, ranging from the shooting of a graffiti artist by a vigilante to a biker gang enmeshed in black-market computer fraud. The show is also popular for its cutting-edge soundtrack that features noted African American musical artists.

Many, like Teddy Pendergrass and Boyz II Men, appear in special guest-star spots as performers in a nightclub frequented by the characters.

John J. O'Connor, television critic for the *New York Times,* favorably described the look of *New York Undercover.* "Wandering around the city, the two detectives' slip-slide against each other easily, goofing through routines that often leave older colleagues mystified," O'Connor wrote. "The beat and the look are unmistakably urban, taking clear aim" at the network's trendy, youthful target audience. "But the strength of this show is in the characters of Williams and Torres."

New York magazine writer John Leonard, also pointed out the uniqueness of the show's Harlem setting, "which doesn't mean entirely desolate," the critic asserted. "If there's a sense of subject peoples in occupied territory, of sullen tenements, night-shriek car alarms, and ghostly transactions on the crack exchange, there's an expansiveness too (broad boulevards, theater marquees, hospital spaces), and a vitality (street markets, churches, basketball), and a civility (genteel stoops, jazz liquidities, the occasional brother from another planet)."

New York Undercover catapulted Yoba to certain fame and made him one of the hottest new actors of the 1994-95 television season. The *New York Times Magazine* named him one of 30 artists under the age of 30 predicted to shape American culture over the next three decades, and female viewers swooned over Yoba's drop-dead handsome looks coupled with impassioned, intelligent persona. When asked by *Essence* special reporter Garcelle Beauvais whether he considers himself a sex symbol, Yoba replied: "I think that we're all sex symbols…. Because our parents had sex, we're symbolic of that sexual consummation."

The irony of Yoba's role as a member of the "establishment" is not lost on the street-savvy actor. "*Undercover* gets real, not just because the show is really filmed mostly on the Uptown streets of New York City, but also because the characters and the actors who portray them are from the same place," wrote Keets in *Ethnic NewsWatch* after interviewing Yoba on the show's set. "He's philosophical, almost poetic, about growing up and the irony of playing a cop on TV when blacks and Latinos, perhaps rightly so, have less than favorable things to say about police activity in their neighborhoods. Keets recounted.

Yoba sees his starring role in the much-lauded prime-time drama as "a continuation of the work I've been doing with young people for many years. It's in large part why I was cast," the actor noted in a press biogra-phy, recalling that the woman who helped make that casting decision averred "'when you get Malik Yoba you will also get his spirit.' That's my whole trip."

Yoba's new high profile led to other roles in feature films, including the Miramax art-house dramas *Smoke* and *Blue in the Face,* both released in 1995. As the second season of *New York Undercover* got underway Yoba had landed a recording contract with Chaos/Columbia Records and was working on an album of original music. "Music can be a conduit," Yoba proclaimed in his press release. "You can reach people through music."

Motivates Youth

The sound of contemporary African American youth, rap music, is an especially significant force, Yoba went on to remark. The genre "is a new entry point into success for young minority kids. You don't have to sing or even play an instrument. You just play your vocals." In the interview with *Essence* reporter Beauvais, Yoba cited the late Jamaican reggae star Bob Marley as an influence. "Bob wrote about the suffering of everyday people and oppressed people. I don't think that half of the stuff that's on the radio now really needs to be heard. I mean, how much more can you hear about sex, violence, and guns?"

"I believe that we all have a mission in life and kids especially need to know this. They need to know that they do have a voice, that they can find that voice and use it to affect positive changes in their own lives, their communities, and in the world."

Despite the vagaries of a career in entertainment, with the mercurial nature of its success, future accomplishment seems assured no matter what avenue Yoba decides to pursue. In the *Essence* article the actor told Gregory that he feels grateful to have been made aware early on what his own goal in life should be—"to help young people." Yoba plans to continue with his motivational message as CEO of Nature Boy Enterprises, giving the inspirational "Why Are You on This Planet?"

workshops to youth groups and other organizations—but on an international scale this time.

Yoba seems very certain about why he was put on earth. "Very few people have a sense of mission in life," Yoba noted in a press release. "If you have it you can affect the lives of other people simply by being who you are. However, if you are a role model, you have an obligation to keep your personal life in order. But that's what I would do anyway!"

Sources

Essence, October 1994, p. 64; July 1995, p. 76.
Ethnic NewsWatch, March 31, 1995, p. 31.
New York, September 5, 1994, p. 48.
New York Times, September 21, 1994, p. C18.
Vibe, April 1995, p. 95.

Additional information for this profile was provided by Nature Boy Enterprises and The Lippin Group.

—Carol Brennan

Cumulative Indexes

Cumulative Nationality Index

Volume numbers appear in **bold.**

Cumulative Occupation Index

Volume numbers appear in **bold.**

Art and design
Bailey, Xenobia **11**
Barboza, Anthony **10**
Basquiat, Jean-Michel **5**
Bearden, Romare **2**
Brandon, Barbara **3**
Burroughs, Margaret Taylor **9**
Catlett, Elizabeth **2**
Douglas, Aaron **7**
Driskell, David C. **7**
Feelings, Tom **11**
Gantt, Harvey **1**
Golden, Thelma **10**
Guyton, Tyree **9**
Harrington, Oliver W. **9**
Hope, John **8**
Hunt, Richard **6**
Johnson, William Henry **3**
Lawrence, Jacob **4**
Lee-Smith, Hughie **5**
Lewis, Edmonia **10**
McGee, Charles **10**
Mitchell, Corinne **8**
Moutoussamy-Ashe, Jeanne **7**
Pippin, Horace **9**
Porter, James A. **11**
Ringgold, Faith **4**
Sanders, Joseph R., Jr. **11**
Serrano, Andres **3**
Shabazz, Attallah **6**
Simpson, Lorna **4**
Sleet, Moneta, Jr. **5**
Tanner, Henry Ossawa **1**
Tolliver, William **9**
VanDerZee, James **6**
Wells, James Lesesne **10**
Williams, Billy Dee **8**
Williams, Paul R. **9**
Williams, William T. **11**
Woodruff, Hale **9**

Business
Abdul-Jabbar, Kareem **8**
Ailey, Alvin **8**
Al-Amin, Jamil Abdullah **6**
Amos, Wally **9**
Baker, Dusty **8**
Baker, Ella **5**
Baker, Gwendolyn Calvert **9**
Banks, William **11**
Barden, Don H. **9**
Bennett, Lerone, Jr. **5**

Bing, Dave **3**
Borders, James **9**
Boyd, T. B. III **6**
Brimmer, Andrew F. **2**
Brown, Les **5**
Brunson, Dorothy **1**
Burroughs, Margaret Taylor **9**
Busby, Jheryl **3**
CasSelle, Malcolm **11**
Chenault, Kenneth I. **4**
Clay, William Lacy **8**
Clayton, Xernona **3**
Cobbs, Price M. **9**
Cornelius, Don **4**
Cosby, Bill **7**
Cottrell, Comer **11**
Divine, Father **7**
Driver, David E. **11**
Elder, Lee **6**
Ellington, E. David **11**
Evers, Myrlie **8**
Farmer, Forest J. **1**
Fauntroy, Walter E. **11**
Franklin, Hardy R. **9**
Fudge, Ann **11**
Gaston, Arthur G. **4**
Gibson, Kenneth Allen **6**
Gordy, Berry, Jr. **1**
Graves, Earl G. **1**
Griffith, Mark Winston **8**
Hale, Lorraine **8**
Hamer, Fannie Lou **6**
Handy, W. C. **8**
Hannah, Marc **10**
Harrell, Andre **9**
Harris, Alice **7**
Henderson, Gordon **5**
Henry, Lenny **9**
Holland, Robert, Jr. **11**
Houston, Whitney **7**
Hudlin, Reginald **9**
Hudlin, Warrington **9**
Ice Cube **8**
Johnson, Eddie Bernice **8**
Johnson, John H. **3**
Johnson, Robert L. **3**
Jones, Carl **7**
Jones, Quincy **8**
Jordan, Michael **6**
Julian, Percy Lavon **6**
Kelly, Patrick **3**
Kimbro, Dennis **10**

King, Dexter **10**
Knight, Suge **11**
Lane, Vincent **5**
Lawless, Theodore K. **8**
Lawson, Jennifer **1**
Leary, Kathryn D. **10**
Lewis, Delano **7**
Lewis, Reginald F. **6**
Lott, Ronnie **9**
Louis, Errol T. **8**
Lucas, John **7**
Madhubuti, Haki R. **7**
Maynard, Robert C. **7**
McCabe, Jewell Jackson **10**
McCoy, Elijah **8**
McDonald, Erroll **1**
Micheaux, Oscar **7**
Morgan, Garrett **1**
Morgan, Joe Leonard **9**
Morgan, Rose **11**
Nichols, Nichelle **11**
Parks, Gordon **1**
Parsons, Richard Dean **11**
Payton, Walter **11**
Perez, Anna **1**
Pleasant, Mary Ellen **9**
Powell, Maxine **8**
Price, Hugh B. **9**
Rand, A. Barry **6**
Rhone, Sylvia **2**
Rice, Linda Johnson **9**
Rice, Norm **8**
Robinson, Jackie **6**
Robinson, Randall **7**
Rodgers, Johnathan **6**
Rogers, John W., Jr. **5**
Ross, Diana **8**
Russell, Bill **8**
Sanders, Dori **8**
Simmons, Russell **1**
Smith, Barbara **11**
Smith, Joshua **10**
Smith, Willi **8**
Spaulding, Charles Clinton **9**
Sullivan, Leon H. **3**
Taylor, Kristin Clark **8**
Taylor, Susan L. **10**
Thomas, Franklin A. **5**
Thomas, Isiah **7**
Tribble, Israel, Jr. **8**
Trotter, Monroe **9**
Van Peebles, Melvin **7**

VanDerZee, James **6**
Walker, Madame C. J. **7**
Walker, T. J. **7**
Wattleton, Faye **9**
Wells-Barnett, Ida B. **8**
Wharton, Clifton R., Jr. **7**
White, Walter F. **4**
Wiley, Ralph **8**
Williams, Paul R. **9**
Williams, Walter E. **4**
Wilson, Phill **9**
Wilson, Sunnie **7**
Winfrey, Oprah **2**
Woodson, Robert L. **10**
Yoba, Malik **11**

Dance

Ailey, Alvin **8**
Baker, Josephine **3**
Byrd, Donald **10**
Dove, Ulysses **5**
Dunham, Katherine **4**
Guy, Jasmine **2**
Hines, Gregory **1**
Horne, Lena **5**
Jamison, Judith **7**
Johnson, Virginia **9**
Jones, Bill T. **1**
McQueen, Butterfly **6**
Miller, Bebe **3**
Mitchell, Arthur **2**
Nichols, Nichelle **11**
Powell, Maxine **8**
Primus, Pearl **6**
Robinson **11**
Vereen, Ben **4**
Washington, Fredi **10**

Education

Achebe, Chinua **6**
Archer, Dennis **7**
Aristide, Jean-Bertrand **6**
Asante, Molefi Kete **3**
Baker, Gwendolyn Calvert **9**
Baker, Houston A., Jr. **6**
Bambara, Toni Cade **10**
Baraka, Amiri **1**
Barboza, Anthony **10**
Bell, Derrick **6**
Berry, Bertice **8**
Berry, Mary Frances **7**
Bethune, Mary McLeod **4**
Bosley, Freeman, Jr. **7**
Boyd, T. B. III **6**
Brooks, Avery **9**
Brown, Sterling **10**
Burroughs, Margaret Taylor **9**
Burton, LeVar **8**
Callender, Clive O. **3**
Campbell, Bebe Moore **6**
Cannon, Katie **10**
Carver, George Washington **4**
Cary, Lorene **3**
Catlett, Elizabeth **2**
Clark, Joe **1**
Clark, Kenneth B. **5**
Clark, Septima **7**
Clayton, Constance **1**
Clements, George **2**

Cobbs, Price M. **9**
Cole, Johnnetta B. **5**
Collins, Marva **3**
Comer, James P. **6**
Cone, James H. **3**
Cooper, Edward S. **6**
Cosby, Bill **7**
Cottrell, Comer **11**
Crouch, Stanley **11**
Cullen, Countee **8**
Davis, Angela **5**
Days, Drew S., III **10**
Delany, Samuel R., Jr. **9**
Diop, Cheikh Anta **4**
Dodson, Howard, Jr. **7**
Douglas, Aaron **7**
Dove, Rita **6**
Dove, Ulysses **5**
Driskell, David C. **7**
Dyson, Michael Eric **11**
Edelman, Marian Wright **5**
Edley, Christopher **2**
Edwards, Harry **2**
Elders, Joycelyn **6**
Ellison, Ralph **7**
Fauset, Jessie **7**
Franklin, John Hope **5**
Frazier, E. Franklin **10**
Freeman, Al, Jr. **11**
Gaines, Ernest J. **7**
Gates, Henry Louis, Jr. **3**
Giddings, Paula **11**
Giovanni, Nikki **9**
Greenfield, Eloise **9**
Guinier, Lani **7**
Hale, Lorraine **8**
Handy, W. C. **8**
Hansberry, William Leo **11**
Harris, Alice **7**
Harris, Patricia Roberts **2**
Haynes, George Edmund **8**
Hill, Anita **5**
Hinton, William Augustus **8**
Holland, Endesha Ida Mae **3**
hooks, bell **5**
Hope, John **8**
Houston, Charles Hamilton **4**
Hunt, Richard **6**
Jeffries, Leonard **8**
Jenifer, Franklyn G. **2**
Johnson, James Weldon **5**
Joplin, Scott **6**
Jordan, Barbara **4**
Jordan, June **7**
Josey, E. J. **10**
Just, Ernest Everett **3**
Karenga, Maulana **10**
Kimbro, Dennis **10**
Komunyakaa, Yusef **9**
Kunjufu, Jawanza **3**
Lawrence, Jacob **4**
Leffall, LaSalle, Jr. **3**
Lawrence-Lightfoot, Sara **10**
Lester, Julius **9**
Lewis, David Levering **9**
Locke, Alain **10**
Lorde, Audre **6**
Madhubuti, Haki R. **7**
Major, Clarence **9**

Marable, Manning **10**
Marshall, Paule **7**
Massey, Walter E. **5**
Maynard, Robert C. **7**
Mays, Benjamin E. **7**
Meek, Carrie **6**
Meredith, James H. **11**
Mitchell, Corinne **8**
Mongella, Gertrude **11**
Moses, Robert Parris **11**
Norton, Eleanor Holmes **7**
Owens, Major **6**
Page, Alan **7**
Patterson, Orlando **4**
Porter, James A. **11**
Poussaint, Alvin F. **5**
Primus, Pearl **6**
Reagon, Bernice Johnson **7**
Ringgold, Faith **4**
Satcher, David **7**
Schomburg, Arthur Alfonso **9**
Shabazz, Betty **7**
Shange, Ntozake **8**
Smith, Anna Deavere **6**
Soyinka, Wole **4**
Stone, Chuck **9**
Sudarkasa, Niara **4**
Sullivan, Louis **8**
Terrell, Mary Church **9**
Thurman, Howard **3**
Tribble, Israel, Jr. **8**
Tutu, Desmond **6**
Walcott, Derek **5**
Wallace, Phyllis A. **9**
Washington, Booker T. **4**
Wattleton, Faye **9**
Wells, James Lesesne **10**
Wells-Barnett, Ida B. **8**
Welsing, Frances Cress **5**
West, Cornel **5**
Wharton, Clifton R., Jr. **7**
Wilkins, Roger **2**
Williams, Gregory **11**
Williams, Patricia J. **11**
Williams, Walter E. **4**
Woodruff, Hale **9**
Woodson, Carter G. **2**

Fashion

Banks, Tyra **11**
Beckford, Tyson **11**
Berry, Halle **4**
Bailey, Xenobia **11**
Barboza, Anthony **10**
Campbell, Naomi **1**
Davidson, Jaye **5**
Henderson, Gordon **5**
Iman **4**
Johnson, Beverly **2**
Jones, Carl **7**
Kani, Karl **10**
Kelly, Patrick **3**
Powell, Maxine **8**
Smith, Barbara **11**
Smith, Willi **8**
Walker, T. J. **7**
Webb, Veronica **10**

Cumulative Subject Index

Volume numbers appear in **bold.**

AA
See Alcoholics Anonymous

AAAS
See American Association for the
Advancement of Science

ABC
See American Broadcasting
Company

Academy awards
Freeman, Morgan **2**
Goldberg, Whoopi **4**
Gossett, Louis, Jr. **7**
McDaniel, Hattie **5**
Poitier, Sidney **11**
Washington, Denzel **1**
Wonder, Stevie **11**

A cappella
Reagon, Bernice Johnson **7**

ACDL
See Association for Constitutional
Democracy in Liberia

ACLU
See American Civil Liberties
Union

**Acquired Immune Deficiency
Syndrome (AIDS)**
Ashe, Arthur **1**
Gayle, Helene D. **3**
Hale, Lorraine **8**
Johnson, Earvin "Magic" **3**
Mboup, Souleymane **10**
Moutoussamy-Ashe, Jeanne **7**
Norman, Pat **10**
Riggs, Marlon **5**
Satcher, David **7**
Wilson, Phill **9**

Acting
Ailey, Alvin **8**
Amos, John **8**
Angelou, Maya **1**
Baker, Josephine **3**
Banks, Tyra **11**
Bassett, Angela **6**

Berry, Halle **4**
Borders, James **9**
Brooks, Avery **9**
Brown, Jim **11**
Campbell, Naomi **1**
Campbell, Tisha **8**
Carroll, Diahann **9**
Cosby, Bill **7**
Dandridge, Dorothy **3**
Davidson, Jaye **5**
Davis, Ossie **5**
Dee, Ruby **8**
Duke, Bill **3**
Dutton, Charles S. **4**
Esposito, Giancarlo **9**
Fishburne, Larry **4**
Foxx, Redd **2**
Freeman, Al, Jr. **11**
Freeman, Morgan **2**
Givens, Robin **4**
Glover, Danny **1**
Goldberg, Whoopi **4**
Gossett, Louis, Jr. **7**
Grier, Pam **9**
Guillaume, Robert **3**
Gunn, Moses **10**
Guy, Jasmine **2**
Harris, Robin **7**
Henry, Lenny **9**
Hines, Gregory **1**
Horne, Lena **5**
Houston, Whitney **7**
Ice Cube **8**
Iman **4**
Ingram, Rex **5**
Jackson, Janet **6**
Jackson, Samuel L. **8**
Jones, James Earl **3**
Kotto, Yaphet **7**
Lane, Charles **3**
Lawrence, Martin **6**
Lee, Canada **8**
Lee, Joie **1**
Lee, Spike **5**
Lincoln, Abbey **3**
McDaniel, Hattie **5**
McQueen, Butterfly **6**
Murphy, Eddie **4**
Nichols, Nichelle **11**
Pinkett, Jada **10**
Poitier, Sidney **11**

Pryor, Richard **3**
Reese, Della **6**
Richards, Lloyd **2**
Robeson, Paul **2**
Rock, Chris **3**
Ross, Diana **8**
Smith, Barbara **11**
St. Jacques, Raymond **8**
Sinbad **1**
Smith, Anna Deavere **6**
Smith, Will **8**
Snipes, Wesley **3**
Taylor, Meshach **4**
Taylor, Regina **9**
Townsend, Robert **4**
Turner, Tina **6**
Tyson, Cicely **7**
Underwood, Blair **7**
Van Peebles, Mario **2**
Van Peebles, Melvin **7**
Vereen, Ben **4**
Warfield, Marsha **2**
Washington, Denzel **1**
Washington, Fredi **10**
Waters, Ethel **7**
Wayans, Damon **8**
Weathers, Carl **10**
Webb, Veronica **10**
Whitaker, Forest **2**
Williams, Billy Dee **8**
Williams, Vanessa **4**
Winfield, Paul **2**
Winfrey, Oprah **2**
Woodard, Alfre **9**
Yoba, Malik **11**

**Active Ministers Engaged in
Nurturance (AMEN)**
King, Bernice **4**

ACT UP
See AIDS Coalition to Unleash
Power

Acustar, Inc.
Farmer, Forest **1**

ADC
See Agricultural Development
Council

Cumulative Name Index

Volume numbers appear in **bold.**

11

Fauset, Jessie (Redmon) 1882-1961 **7**
Feelings, Thomas 1933– **11**
Fela 1938– **1**
Fielder, Cecil (Grant) 1963– **2**
Fishburne, Larry 1962– **4**
Fishburne, Laurence III
　See Fishburne, Larry
Fitzgerald, Ella 1918– **8**
Flipper, Henry O(ssian) 1856-1940 **3**
Flood, Curt(is) 1963– **10**
Folks, Byron
　See Allen, Byron
Foreman, George 1949– **1**
Forman, James 1928– **7**
Fortune, T(imothy) Thomas 1856-1928 **–6**
Foxx, Redd 1922-1991 **2**
Franklin, Aretha 1942– **11**
Franklin, Carl 1949– **11**
Franklin, Hardy R. 1929– **9**
Franklin, John Hope 1915– **5**
Franks, Gary 1954(?)– **2**
Frazier, Edward Franklin 1894-1962 **10**
Freeman, Al(bert Cornelius), Jr. 1934– **11**
Freeman, Morgan 1937– **2**
Fresh Prince, The
　See Smith, Will
Fudge, Ann (Marie) 1951(?)– **11**
Fuhr, Grant 1962– **1**
Fulani, Lenora (Branch) 1950– **11**
Fuller, Charles (Henry) 1939– **8**
Gaines, Ernest J(ames) 1933– **7**
Gantt, Harvey (Bernard) 1943– **1**
Garrison, Zina 1963– **2**
Garvey, Marcus 1887-1940 **1**
Gaston, Arthur G(eorge) 1892– **4**
Gates, Henry Louis, Jr. 1950– **3**
Gay, Marvin Pentz, Jr.
　See Gaye, Marvin
Gaye, Marvin 1939-1984 **2**
Gayle, Helene D(oris) 1955– **3**
Gibson, Althea 1927– **8**
Gibson, Kenneth Allen 1932– **6**
Gibson, William F(rank) 1933– **6**
Giddings, Paula (Jane) 1947– **11**
Gillespie, Dizzy 1917-1993 **1**
Gillespie, John Birks
　See Gillespie, Dizzy
Gist, Carole 1970(?)– **1**
Giovanni, Nikki 1943– **9**
Giovanni, Yolande Cornelia, Jr.
　See Giovanni, Nikki
Givens, Robin 1965– **4**
Glover, Danny 1948– **1**
Goldberg, Whoopi 1955– **4**
Golden, Thelma 1965– **10**
Gomez-Preston, Cheryl 1954– **9**
Goode, W(oodrow) Wilson 1938– **4**
Gordon, Ed(ward Lansing, III) 1960– **10**
Gordy, Berry, Jr. 1929– **1**
Goreed, Joseph
　See Williams, Joe

Gossett, Louis, Jr. 1936– **7**
Gourdine, Simon (Peter) 1940– **11**
Gravely, Samuel L(ee), Jr. 1922– **5**
Graves, Earl G(ilbert) 1935– **1**
Gray, Frizzell
　See Mfume, Kweisi
Gray, William H. III 1941– **3**
Green, Dennis 1949– **5**
Greene, Joe 1946– **10**
Greenfield, Eloise 1929– **9**
Grier, Pam(ala Suzette) 1949– **9**
Griffith, Mark Winston 1963– **8**
Gregory, Dick 1932– **1**
Gregory, Frederick D(rew) 1941– **8**
Grimké, Archibald H(enry) 1849-1930– **9**
Guarionex
　See Schomburg, Arthur Alfonso
Guillaume, Robert 1927– **3**
Guinier, (Carol) Lani 1950– **7**
Gumbel, Greg 1946– **8**
Gunn, Moses 1929-1993 **10**
Guy, Jasmine 1964(?)– **2**
Guy, Rosa 1925(?)– **5**
Guyton, Tyree 1955– **9**
Habré, Hissène 1942– **6**
Habyarimana, Juvenal 1937-1994 **8**
Haile Selassie 1892-1975 **7**
Hale, Lorraine 1926(?)– **8**
Haley, Alex (Palmer) 1921-1992 **4**
Hall, Lloyd A(ugustus) 1894-1971 **8**
Hamblin, Ken 1940– **10**
Hamer, Fannie Lou (Townsend) 1917-1977 **6**
Hamilton, Virginia 1936– **10**
Hampton, Henry (Eugene, Jr.) 1940– **6**
Handy, W(illiam) C(hristopher) 1873-1937 **8**
Hani, Chris 1942-1993 **6**
Hani, Martin Thembisile
　See Hani, Chris
Hannah, Marc (Regis) 1956– **10**
Hansberry, Lorraine (Vivian) 1930-1965 **6**
Hansberry, William Leo 1894-1965 **11**
Harper, Frances Ellen Watkins 1825-1911 **11**
Harrell, Andre (O'Neal) 1962(?)– **9**
Harrington, Oliver W(endell) 1912– **9**
Harris, Alice 1934– **7**
Harris, Leslie 1961– **6**
Harris, Patricia Roberts 1924-1985 **2**
Harris, Robin 1953-1990 **7**
Harris, "Sweet" Alice
　See Harris, Alice
Harvard, Beverly (Joyce Bailey) 1950– **11**
Hastie, William H(enry) 1904-1976 **8**
Hawkins, Adrienne Lita
　See Kennedy, Adrienne
Hawkins, Coleman 1904-1969 **9**

Hayes, James C. 1946– **10**
Hayes, Roland 1887-1977 **4**
Haynes, George Edmund 1880-1960– **8**
Height, Dorothy I(rene) 1912– **2**
Hemphill, Essex 1957– **10**
Henderson, Gordon 1957– **5**
Henderson, Natalie Leota
　See Hinderas, Natalie
Hendricks, Barbara 1948– **3**
Hendrix, James Marshall
　See Hendrix, Jimi
Hendrix, Jimi 1942-1970 **10**
Hendrix, Johnny Allen
　See Hendrix, Jimi
Henry, Lenny 1958– **9**
Henson, Matthew (Alexander) 1866-1955 **–2**
Hickman, Fred(erick Douglass) 1951– **11**
Hill, Anita (Faye) 1956– **5**
Hilliard, David 1942– **7**
Himes, Chester 1909-1984 **8**
Hinderas, Natalie 1927-1987 **5**
Hines, Gregory (Oliver) 1946– **1**
Hinton, William Augustus 1883-1959– **8**
Holder, Eric H., Jr. 1951(?)– **9**
Holiday, Billie 1915-1959 **1**
Holland, Bob 1940– **11**
Holland, Endesha Ida Mae 1944– **3**
Holyfield, Evander 1962– **6**
hooks, bell 1952– **5**
Hooks, Benjamin L(awson) 1925– **2**
Hope, John 1868-1936 **8**
Horne, Lena (Mary Calhoun) 1917– **5**
Houphouët, Dia
　See Houphouët-Boigny, Félix
Houphouët-Boigny, Félix 1905– **4**
House, Eddie James, Jr.
　See House, Son
House, Eugene
　See House, Son
House, Son 1902-1988 **8**
Houston, Charles Hamilton 1895-1950 **–4**
Houston, Whitney 1963– **7**
Howard, Corinne
　See Mitchell, Corinne
Howlin' Wolf 1910-1976 **9**
Hudlin, Reginald 1962(?)– **9**
Hudlin, Warrington, Jr. 1953(?)– **9**
Hughes, Albert 1972– **7**
Hughes, Allen 1972– **7**
Hughes, (James Mercer) Langston 1902-1967– **4**
Hunt, Richard (Howard) 1935– **6**
Hunter, Charlayne
　See Hunter-Gault, Charlayne
Hunter-Gault, Charlayne 1942– **6**
Hurston, Zora Neale 1891-1960 **3**
Ice Cube 1969(?)– **8**
Ice-T 1958(?)– **6**
Iceberg Slim 1918 -1992 **11**
Iman 1955– **4**
Ingram, Rex 1895-1969 **5**
Innis, Roy (Emile Alfredo) 1934– **5**